Communications
in Computer and Information Science   **531**

Commenced Publication in 2007
Founding and Former Series Editors:
Alfredo Cuzzocrea, Dominik Ślęzak, and Xiaokang Yang

More information about this series at http://www.springer.com/series/7899

Jerzy Mikulski (Ed.)

Tools of Transport Telematics

15th International Conference
on Transport Systems Telematics, TST 2015
Wrocław, Poland, April 15–17, 2015
Selected Papers

 Springer

Editor
Jerzy Mikulski
Polish Association of Transport Telematics
Katowice
Poland

ISSN 1865-0929   ISSN 1865-0937 (electronic)
Communications in Computer and Information Science
ISBN 978-3-319-24576-8   ISBN 978-3-319-24577-5 (eBook)
DOI 10.1007/978-3-319-24577-5

Library of Congress Control Number: 2015949407

Springer Cham Heidelberg New York Dordrecht London

Printed on acid-free paper

Springer International Publishing AG Switzerland is part of Springer Science+Business Media
(www.springer.com)

Preface

It is a pleasure to welcome you to the selected papers of the 15th International Conference on Transport Systems Telematics. The 15th event in the series was held at the Wroclaw University of Technology Congress Center, during which the latest achievements and applications of telematics systems in practice were presented. The conference was organized by the Polish Association of Transport Telematics, together with the Polish Chamber of Commerce for High Technology.

Intelligent cities are becoming a reality in Europe today. Advanced technologies are transforming towns into smart cities. We can observe a dynamic increase in the importance of ITS applications. During the previous 14 editions of our meetings, we had the opportunity to observe and participate in the development of these solutions. The range of topics and the number of participants have grown significantly since then. To keep up with the pace of development in telematics applications, in the TST 2015 conference the topics of road, rail, air and ship transport were extended to include city telematics.

Not by accident, the first conference in a new form was held in Wroclaw. In recent years, the city has become a training ground for development and implementation of modern intelligent transport systems. We had the possibility to gain understanding of this type of system covering 150 road intersections of the fourth largest city in Poland, through which important European, national, and provincial roads pass.

The aim of the conference was to present the newest trends in transport improvement, arising in connection with the present worldwide telematics achievements and to share experience and exchange opinions between transport-related practitioners and scientists. Participation in the conference was an excellent opportunity to present current achievements and outline the direction of developments in transport telematics.

This year the conference was a part of the forum "Mobile City – Challenge of the Future." The forum was held under the patronage of the Union of Polish Metropolises, the Association of Polish Cities, and the Ministry of Infrastructure and Development. The key topic of the forum were conditions of development and modernizing of urban transport systems, including the functioning of support instruments of the projects undertaken in this respect. Urban mobility is on the most important factors impacting the quality of life of a city's inhabitants and its economic efficiency, and it is also one of the most difficult problems that Polish and European cities face today. During the sessions and exhibitions accompanying the forum, the most advanced technological solutions improving urban mobility and facilitating traffic management were presented. Therefore, the event was a perfect opportunity to share experience and discuss improvements in urban transport systems and mobility. The papers published in this volume were reviewed (double-blind review) by independent reviewers in accordance with the Scientific Committee's criteria for high quality.

April 2015   Jerzy Mikulski

Organization

Organizers

- Polish Association of Transport Telematics
- Polish Chamber of Commerce for High Technology

Co-organizers

- Transport Committee of the Polish Academy of Sciences
- Polish Federation of Engineering Associations
- Mayor of Wroclaw

Co-operating Universities

- University of Economics in Katowice
- University of Technology and Humanities in Radom
- Silesian University of Technology
- Warsaw University of Technology
- Wroclaw University of Technology
- University of Bielsko-Biała
- Gdynia Maritime University
- Maritime University of Szczecin
- WSB Schools of Banking in Wrocław
- Katowice School of Technology
- Silesian School of Management in Katowice

Program Committee

Chair

Jerzy Mikulski   Chair of the Polish Association of Transport Telematics

Co-chairs

Janusz Dyduch   Chair of the Transport Committee of the Polish Academy of Sciences

Ryszard Pregiel   Chair of the Polish Chamber of Commerce for High Technology

Wojciech Wajda   Deputy Chair of the Board of Polish Chamber of Commerce for High Technology

Grażyna Wojewódzka   Deputy Director of the Roads and Wroclaw City Maintenance Authority

Scientific Program Committee

J. Mikulski	Polish Association of Transport Telematics, Poland
A. Bujak	WSB Schools of Banking in Wroclaw, Poland
M. Bukljaš-Skočibušić	University of Zagreb, Croatia
W. Choromański	Warsaw University of Technology, Poland
T. Čorejová	University of Zilina, Republic of Slovakia
A. Dewalska-Opitek	Silesian School of Management, Poland
M. Franeková	University of Zilina, Republic of Slovakia
J. Gnap	University of Zilina, Republic of Slovakia
S. Iwan	Maritime University of Szczecin, Poland
M. Jacyna	Warsaw University of Technology, Poland
A. Janota	University of Zilina, Republic of Slovakia
J. Januszewski	Gdynia Maritime University, Poland
A. Kalašová	University of Zilina, Republic of Slovakia
J. Klamka	Polish Academy of Sciences, Poland
B. Kos	University of Economics in Katowice, Poland
A. Križanová	University of Zilina, Republic of Slovakia
M. Luft	University of Technology and Humanities in Radom, Poland
B. Łazarz	Politechnika Śląska, Poland
Z. Łukasik	University of Technology and Humanities in Radom, Poland
A. Maczyński	University of Bielsko-Biala, Poland
M. Michałowska	University of Economics in Katowice, Poland
G. Nowacki	Military University of Technology, Poland
T. Nowakowski	Wrocław University of Technology, Poland
D. Peraković	University of Zagreb, Croatia
Z. Pietrzykowski	Maritime University of Szczecin, Poland
K. Rástočný	University of Zilina, Republic of Slovakia
M. Siergiejczyk	Warsaw University of Technology, Poland
J. Skorupski	Warsaw University of Technology, Poland
E. Szychta	University of Technology and Humanities in Radom, Poland
A. Szydło	Wrocław University of Technology, Poland
R. Tomanek	University of Economics in Katowice, Poland
R. Wawruch	Gdynia Maritime University, Poland
W. Wawrzyński	Warsaw University of Technology, Poland
A. Weintrit	Gdynia Maritime University, Poland
M. Wierzbik-Strońska	Katowice School of Technology, Poland
E. Załoga	University of Szczecin, Poland

Contents

Data Flows in Urban Freight Transport Management System

Stanisław Iwan[1(✉)] and Krzysztof Małecki[2]

[1] Maritime University of Szczecin, Pobożnego 11, 70-507 Szczecin, Poland
s.iwan@am.szczecin.pl
[2] West Pomeranian University of Technology, Żołnierska 52,
71-210 Szczecin, Poland
kmalecki@wi.zut.edu.pl

Abstract. The fast growth of cities and the rising number of their users leads to an increase in demand for freight transport, thus contributing to an increase in logistic flow streams within a limited area. Currently, freight transport is usually done in an uncoordinated and chaotic manner. Specifying the information needs in the field of urban freight transport (UFT) will make it possible to take control over the increasing disorder in this area and enable its development in accordance with the principles of sustainable growth. This paper is focused on the analysis realized under the project "Analysis of information needs of heterogeneous environment in sustainable urban freight transport system". The aim of the project is to determine the structures of data relevant for the management of sustainable UFT, establish the sources of data acquisition, the scope and degree of integration, and also indicate the methods of knowledge extraction from the acquired data and information, necessary for improving freight transport efficiency in cities.

Keywords: Urban freight transport · Data collection process · Freight transport management · Sustainable development · Efficiency of city logistics · Efficiency of transport systems

1 Introduction

One of the key factors necessary for taking control over the increasing disorder inurban freight transport (UFT) and its sustainable development are effective data flows between the various parties involved in its functioning in a greater or lesser extent. Lack of knowledge about freight flows, their direction and structure contributes to the difficulty in controlling and guiding them in a way that minimizes the negative impact on the urban organism, in particular, on the environment and residents [1]. In addition, in the area of the development of information society and digitalization of all spheres of life, an increasingly important aspect becomes studying the structures and data flows directions occurring between objects of different systems operating in the economy and their impact, both at the micro, as well as the regional, national, or even global level. This is particularly important taking to the account the increasing demand for data, resulting from the constant increase of the importance of multimedia techniques in

© Springer International Publishing Switzerland 2015
J. Mikulski (Ed.): TST 2015, CCIS 531, pp. 1–10, 2015.
DOI: 10.1007/978-3-319-24577-5_1

management processes [2]. The necessity to take control over the data resources inUFT is therefore absolutely essential for its proper functioning, especially in the context of many different devices and functions utilize in transport management systems [3]. This is the most important for local authorities, taking to the account their impact on the quality of life of cities inhabitants and leading role in the implementation of city logistics projects [4]. This becomes even more important provided the fact that the vast majority of solutions supporting management of these systems are now directly or indirectly dependent on the smooth functioning of telematics technology [5].

In light of the above assumptions, the question is: what is the real need for data reported by the stakeholders of the above mentioned urban transport processes? Moreover, what should be the source of certain data, what should be their structure and scope and what would be the cost of its acquisition? Finally, as a consequence, what can be the impact of the demand for data on the efficiency of UFT?

Identifying the information needs in UFT, as well as relations between it and the other elements of the urban transport system, allows to have control over increasing disorder in this area and allows for the effective management and its development in accordance with the principles of sustainable development.

2 Difficulties in Data Acquisition in UFT

Effective transport system depends largely on the proper data and information flow and knowledge acquisition allowing for effective management of processes occurring in this system. The complexity of relationships occurring in this system and its considerable heterogeneity implies the need to carry out research on the demand for specific data and data aggregates reported by the individual entities involved in the functioning of the transport system (transport market participants, local governments, administrations, etc.). It should be added that the analysis of data flows in UFT is a much more difficult task than for the transport of persons. Attempts are being made to formulate the theoretical basis for determining the data streams and their scope, however, there is currently no universal model based on the direct study of the needs of different stakeholders in UFT.

In recent years, the use of intelligent transport systems to support freight management is becoming increasingly important both in terms of theoretical as well as practical examples [6]. The need to support the transport and distribution of goods in urban areas with telematics solutions results mainly from the complexity of these processes and different expectations of the stakeholders in UFT. In addition, these solutions allow to limit the negative impact of the transport system on the urban environment [7]. However, in order for these systems to operate effectively, it is necessary to provide adequate data resources on the transport, which would form the basis for their control, optimization and management of various processes in UFT.

However, providing these data resources faces considerable difficulties. Next to the diversity of needs and expectations of stakeholders, significant fragmentation of transport and high functional complexity of the system itself, a major obstacle to its effective management and implementation of intelligent transport systems is the difficulty in data acquisition. It results from barriers to access data sources, in particular [8]:

- technical barriers, when entity generating information is unable to access the information source, instruments for its overview, measurement tools, means of communication to contact the respondent, etc. due to technical reasons,
- legal barriers resulting from the applicable rules of the political and legal system and the provisions of statutory law and practice of business and government authorities,
- organizational barriers associated with a lack of organizational structures necessary for the perception of real objects or their attributes and generation of information acquired in this way,
- economic barriers resulting from the lack of economic resources, especially financial resources needed to access data sources and to generate information,
- psychological barriers that occur when sources of information are the people or organizational units represented by the people,
- meta-information barriers resulting from the lack of information about the sources of information, their content, quality and methods of access to information.

The principal effectors of the difficulties in obtaining data within the urban freight system include the following facts [9]:

- urban deliveries involve mainly private companies, which usually do not want to share data on their transactions, supplies and transported goods with their competitors and the public sector (it is, of course, observed not only in the case of transport within cities, but also in interurban, national, or international transport),
- there are no standardized research methods in the field of urban freight deliveries.

Issue that is especially problematic is the first aspect. The fact that private companies realizing the vast majority of transport within the city do not want to share data on the type of delivery, the degree of load capacity utilization, routes, etc. results primarily from their concerns about maintaining a competitive position in the market. A certain solution, which does not address all of the difficulties in this respect, is the use of telematics technologies based on motion detection and classification of vehicles. These systems allow for making measurements, which are non-invasive, undetectable for drivers and independent of freight companies. The fundamental difficulty resulting from the specificity of delivering goods in the city is, however, the need to deploy a large number of detectors, allowing for acquiring data in a wide area. The solution to this problem could be the use of mobile sensors (e.g. a radar traffic detection deviceSR4 by Sierzega - Fig. 1 or pneumatic vehicle classifier system MetroCount 5600 - Fig. 2).

It should be noted, however, that such devices have limited capacity to simultaneously control lanes (both of these devices can control only 2 lanes). On the other hand, they allow for flexibility in terms of the measurement points and adaptation of areas of analysis to current needs.

Fig. 1. Radar traffic detection device SR4 by Sierzega [10]

Fig. 2. Pneumatic vehicle classifier system MetroCount 5600 [11]

3   Categories of Data in Urban Freight Transport

In the area of UFT, data can be classified according to three basic criteria [12]:

- variability:
    - static (fixed),
    - dynamic (variable);
- reliability:
    - deterministic (certain),
    - probabilistic (random),
    - diffused (ambiguous)

- sources from:
  - public sector (road and area administrators),
  - private sector (carriers or customers).

Table 1 shows examples of the types of data divided by the above categories.

Table 1. Features of selected data in UFT [own study based on [13]]

Data	Variability	Reliability	Source
Features of the system			
The geometry of the transport network and regulations	Static	deterministic	public sector
Forms of land use	Static	deterministic	public sector
System requirements: • back data on traffic volume • other data on vehicles	Static	deterministic	public sector/ private sector
Use of the system			
Travel time – back data	Static	probabilistic	public sector/ private sector
Travel time – current data	Dynamic	probabilistic	public sector/ private sector
Data on road accidents and incidents	Dynamic	deterministic	public sector

Identification of data sources should also take into account the following criteria [13]:

- the availability of data:
  - the ability to collect - not all of the necessary data are collected,
  - availability - not all of the data that are collected are available; this particularly applies to data held by private companies,
  - universality - there is often a lack of information about data that have already been collected,
  - the way of utilization - available data are not always used in the right way,
  - interpretation - data can be interpreted in the wrong way, usually there are problems with their accuracy and comparability,
- data quality:
  - accuracy – it is of particular importance in the case of small differences in the results or when the analysis covers value changes over time; it must be able to properly reflect the trends,
  - comparability - differences may occur in the process of defining, grouping and presenting data,
  - complexity - data do not have to reflect all aspects of the analysed system; it is necessary to collect a wide range of data associated closely with the analysed part of the system, specified as a key factor for its effectiveness,
  - timeliness – data should be up to date to reflect current changes.

4   Study on the Needs for Data in the Urban Freight Transport System

Data needs in UFT are the subject of the project called "Analysis of information needs of heterogeneous environment in a sustainable urban freight" conducted by the Faculty of Economics and Engineering of Transport at the Maritime University of Szczecin. The aim of the project is to define data structures essential for the operation of sustainable UFT, identify the sources of their acquisition and the degree of integration, as well as to indicate methods for extracting knowledge from acquired data and information resources necessary to improve the efficiency of freight transport in cities.

As part of the task called "Specifying the demand for data, information and knowledge in the selected systems", there has been prepared survey to study the needs of stakeholders for data and the ability to provide data for the management of UFT-Table 2. Each category of data includes two options of nonexclusive answers: Need and Provide. Each respondent could select one, both or no answer.

Table 2. Survey questions regarding data categories [own study]

Area of impact	Indicator	Data on...
Economy	Transport needs	the volume of freight brought into the urban area
	The efficiency of urban logistics processes	the number of recipients of the goods
		logistics costs
		the delivery transport cost in the overall cost of the supply chain
		wages in urban freight transport
		load capacity utilization
	The efficiency of deliveries (operators) within the city	total deliveries
		days and hours of deliveries
		regularity of trips
		the places, where the trip starts
		the places, where the trip ends
		number of stops per trip, day
		length of trips
		the distance between network nodes
		travel times
		travel times to and through the city centre
	The efficiency of deliveries (receivers) within the city	deliveries in enclosed areas (within the enterprises)
		time spent within the city area
		loading and unloading time
	The impact on the labour market (in %)	the number of jobs in urban freight transport

(Continued)

Table 2. (*Continued*)

Area of impact	Indicator	Data on...
		the number of companies involved in urban freight transport
		the number of jobs in sectors related to the functioning of the urban freight transport
Social area	City population	population density and distribution of the population within urban areas
		household size
	Commercial vehicles in the city	the number of vehicles by DMC and age
		the share of trucks in total vehicular traffic
		vehicle ownership
		vehicles used within the city
	Accidents and casualties in urban freight transport	the number of accidents
		the number of deaths
		share of freight vehicles in accidents
		the weekly schedule of accidents involving trucks
	Types of road users	the number of cyclists
		the number of pedestrians
		total number of car drivers
		the number of drivers of commercial vehicles and trucks
Environment	Energy consumption	typical fuel consumption of by vehicle category
		energy consumption in urban freight transport
		consumption of non-renewable fuels
	Exhaust emissions	pollutant emissions by vehicle type
		share of urban freight transport in exhaust emissions
	Noise	the noise level generated by the commercial vehicle
		the noise level when loading / unloading commercial vehicles
Mobility	Urban traffic flow	the number of vehicles entering the city
		traffic / congestion level
		the average speed of vehicles
	Measures of use	the number of kilometres travelled by commercial vehicle
		the degree of load capacity utilization
	Home deliveries	home delivery services provided by stores
		the number of kilometres per capita

The project involves the identification of the needs for information in the following areas of impact: economy, social aspects, environment and mobility. Each area is defined in detail by the indicators and characteristic data.

5 Preliminary Results

Pilot studies were carried out in the period from November 2014 to January 2015 and included units and entities representing different groups of stakeholders of UFT, including representatives of municipal authorities, insurance companies, fire department, police, rescue services, driver training centres, as well as private transport and freight forwarding companies.

The greatest demand (over 69 % of respondents) was reported on data on the traffic and congestion level. Only representatives of insurance companies were not interested in this category of data. Other categories that respondents were most frequently interested in included:

- the volume of freight brought into the urban area– 58 %,
- days and hours of deliveries – 53 %,
- length of trips – 53 %,
- the average speed of vehicles – 46 %,
- total volume of deliveries – 46 %,
- trips (routes) and places, where the trip ends – 42 %.

The lowest interest was showed in data on such aspects as:

- the delivery transport cost in the overall cost of the supply chain,
- the number of jobs in urban freight transport,
- the number of companies involved in urban freight transport,
- the number of jobs in sectors related to the functioning of the urban freight transport,
- population density and distribution of the population within urban areas,
- household size,
- the weekly schedule of accidents involving trucks,
- typical fuel consumption of by vehicle category,
- home delivery services provided by stores.

In terms of availability of resources, the majority of entities declared to have data on:

- days and hours of deliveries – 38 %,
- the distance between network nodes – 38 %,
- travel times – 38 %,
- the places, where the trip starts – 35 %,
- length of trips – 35 %,
- number of stops per trip, day – 35 %,
- travel times to and through the city centre– 35 %,
- the number of deaths – 35 %,
- regularity of trips – 31 %,
- the number of accidents – 31 %.

The study showed that the most problematic aspect for the management of urban freight transport is to obtain data on home delivery services provided by the stores and the number of kilometres per capita as none of the entities participating in the study declared to have these categories of data.

The largest demand for data was reported by municipal authorities. At the same time research has shown that these entities usually have relatively limited resources. They could provide data on the impact of freight transport on the labour market (the number of jobs in the urban freight transport and companies involved in urban freight transport, as well as the number of jobs in sectors related to the functioning of the urban freight transport) and data on social aspects such as population density and the distribution of the population within the urban areas, the size of the households or the number of commercial vehicles by DMC and age. An important part of data resources required by municipal authorities were data on environment. Beside municipal authorities, the demand for this type of data was also reported by training companies. Transport and shipping companies reported the greatest interest in data on:

– the average vehicle speed - over 70 % of respondents in this group,
– traffic/congestion level - more than 80 % of respondents in this group,
– real-time information about the situation on the road - 90 % of respondents in this group.

This group declared the greatest ability to provide economic data related to urban freight transport, in particular related to:

– efficiency of deliveries within the city,
– transport needs.

Representatives of the municipal authorities and the police have reported willingness to provide data on social aspects and mobility, with particular emphasis on urban traffic flow. In the case of data on accidents and deaths in UFT, the greatest demand was reported by representatives of insurance companies.

6   Conclusion

Currently, sustainable development becomes one of the key challenges for the increasingly diverse and complex economic systems. The development of appropriate guidelines for the implementation of these concepts becomes the key to success and to minimize the costs associated with both the implementation process, as well as the subsequent use of solutions. Due to its great importance for the functioning of cities, and thus for the whole economy, UFT is a very important area of research in the implementation of the concept of sustainable development. However, it is particularly difficult area due to its heterogeneous nature and the presence of many relationships, which are diverse in terms of their functionality. The basis for the efficient management of UFT is the effective information flow and the ability to extract knowledge from dynamically growing data resources. While these aspects have been fairly well studied for a variety of other sectors of the economy (particularly for the enterprises), whereas UFT still lacks uniform and sufficiently detailed models, which contributes to the insufficient degree of process integration. General data flow models are also the basis for determining the degree of impact of data and information resources on the efficiency of the transport system, its operating costs, and above all, limitation of the negative impact on the urban environment. The research will help to correct these deficiencies by carrying out an in-depth analysis of still unexplored areas of the urban transport management.

The results presented are the effect of the first stage of the pilot study. Completion of ongoing activities will help to build a generalized model of data flows in UFT. It will also indicate the most critical elements of the system and the major deficiencies regarding the availability of data.

Acknowledgements. This paper was financed under the project "Analysis of information needs of heterogeneous environment in sustainable urban freight" by the Polish National Science Centre, decision number DEC-2012/05/B/HS4/03818.

References

1. Mikulski, J., Kwaśny, A.: Role of telematics in reducing the negative environmental impact of transport. In: Mikulski, J. (ed.) TST 2010. CCIS, vol. 104, pp. 11–29. Springer, Heidelberg (2010)
2. Kiełtyka, L.: Komunikacja w zarządzaniu. Techniki, narzędzia i formy przekazu informacji. Agencja Wydawnicza Placet, Warszawa (2002)
3. Kot, S., Marczyk, B., Ślusarczyk, B.: Identification of information systems application in road transport companies in silesia region. In: Mikulski, J. (ed.) TST 2014. CCIS, vol. 471, pp. 273–283. Springer, Heidelberg (2014)
4. Kiba-Janiak, M., Cheba, K.: How local authorities are engaged in implementation of projects related to passenger and freight transport in order to reduce environmental degradation in the city. Procedia Soc. Behav. Sci. **151**, 127–141 (2014)
5. Iwan, S.: Wdrażanie dobrych praktyk w obszarze transportu dostawczego w miastach. Wydawnictwo Naukowe Akademii Morskiej w Szczecinie, Szczecin (2013)
6. Gattuso, D., Pellicanò, D.S.: Advanced methodological researches concerning ITS in freight transport. Procedia Soc. Behav. Sci. **111**, 994–1003 (2014)
7. Małecki, K., Iwan, S., Kijewska, K.: Influence of intelligent transportation systems on reduction of the environmental negative impact of urban freight transport based on Szczecin example. Procedia Soc. Behav. Sci. **151**, 215–229 (2014)
8. Oleński, J.: Elementy ekonomiki informacji. Katedra Informatyki Gospodarczej i Analiz Ekonomicznych, Warszawa (2000)
9. Taniguchi, E., Thompson, R.G., Yamada, T.: Data collection for modelling, evaluating and benchmarking city logistics schemes. In: Taniguchi, E., Thompson, R.G. (eds.) Recent Advances in City Logistics. Elsevier, Melbourne (2006)
10. www.sierzega.com. Accessed on 10 February 2015
11. metrocount.com. Accessed on 10 February 2015
12. Taniguchi, E., Thompson, R.G., Yamada, T., van Duin, R.: City Logistics: Network Modelling and Intelligent Transport Systems. Pergamon, Oxford (2001)
13. Kaszubowski, D.: Zastosowanie benchmarkingu w logistyce miejskiej, Logistyka 5/2011. ILiM, Poznań (2011)

Multicriteria Decision Support in Designing Transport Systems

Marianna Jacyna[⊠] and Mariusz Wasiak

Faculty of Transport, Department of Logistics and Transport Systems,
Warsaw University of Technology, Koszykowa 75, 00-662 Warsaw, Poland
{maja,mwa}@wt.pw.edu.pl

Abstract. Paper presents selected aspects of multicriteria decision making in transport. One of the significant problems of modern transport systems is proper assessment of selection of transport system equipment to performed tasks. This assessment is difficult due to the complexity of issues. On the one hand it results from technical limitations, financial and ecological constraints, and public interest, but on the other hand various points of view of individual participants of transportation process trying to maximize their individual advantage must be taken into account. As a result the examination and evaluation of transport systems requires multi-criteria decision-making models. These models allow taking into account a number of contradictory points of view and lead to the identification of a "best compromise". Assessment of transport organization alternatives was performed by Super Choose application. The application implements ranking method and MAJA method to support decision-making.

Keywords: Decision support · Vector criteria function · Multi-faceted issue

1 Introduction

The primary objective of transport and logistics is movement of goods resulting from the type, number and characteristics of moved objects, as well as transport relations and quality parameters like safety, velocity, comfort, etc. Implementation of this objective means transformation of input streams into output streams with the right system equipment. In general, the input to transport and logistics systems is a stream of necessary technical and organizational resources like materials, energy, machinery and equipment, manpower, financial resources, etc., and most of all the work-tasks reported by the environment [10–12].

Searching for optimal solutions according to selected evaluation criteria can be done through analytical, experimental or simulation methods of system research [9, 10]. Gaining experimental results by experiments is usually very time-consuming and extremely expensive. Even for relatively simple issues getting closer to the optimal solutions needs a lot of experimental work. In this case the mathematical methods are very helpful [9].

Applying mathematical methods in searching for optimal solutions usually chase up obtaining the results and allows for significant time and cost savings. The analytical methods can be used only if there is a mathematical description of the studied

© Springer International Publishing Switzerland 2015
J. Mikulski (Ed.): TST 2015, CCIS 531, pp. 11–23, 2015.
DOI: 10.1007/978-3-319-24577-5_2

phenomena. Lack of the formal mathematical model enforces carrying out experimental studies. In cases where only partial mathematical description of the phenomena exists, the mathematical methods of search for solutions are only auxiliary tools for experimental investigations.

The way of description of reality by a model depends on disposed describing tool and needs. Tools of description are determined by programming language and mathematical formalisms which can be effectively used by modeler. The needs result from the research goals and accepted method of achieving those goals.

One of the issues of modern transport systems is correct assessment of the adjustment of service potential of transport companies to handled demand for transport. This assessment is difficult due to the complexity of issues. On the one hand it results from technical limitations, financial and ecological constraints, and public interest, but on the other hand various points of view of individual participants of transportation process trying to maximize their individual advantage must be taken into account. Hence the need to develop a multi-criteria decision support methods for the modernization and expansion of the transport network appears.

Multi-criteria decision problem needs the parameters of the task to be set, scope of the actions to be determined, boundary conditions to be set and range of acceptable potential changes. Therefore decision problem arises when decision maker is faced with many permitted variations and only one can be choose. With the decision comes the responsibility of decision maker. By taking the right decision policymaker sets both priorities – the order of solving problems, as well as define the availability of resources – formulates limitations. This is a problem of choosing the right actions on the base of observation of reality by the decision maker.

The selection of suitable optimization methods adequate to the analysed decision-making problem is complex and depends on many factors [9]. The issue of choosing the best solution gets complicated when the problem itself is complex and difficult to clear choose the best solution. Then many assessment criteria should be considered. Evaluation of the results under several criteria is complicated when apparent criteria can't be straightly compared (especially when results are expressed in different units of measure). It would be also difficult to assemble a group of experts who would choose the best solution due to narrow specializations. The solution becomes possible with the use of analytical methods of multi-criteria assessment. When decision-maker preferences are known before solving the problem then weighted objective function methods can be used, or for countable set of variations, a scoring method is permitted. If the decision maker is unable to determine the exact preferences, one of the dialog methods can be used.

In addition to the choice of method, the ability to ensure comparability of ratings of analysed options (when the goals are divergent and are expressed in different units) is a significant aspect [10, 21, 23]. Failure to comply this condition leads to incorrectness of any inference arising from used methods. To avoid this, it is necessary to carry out the normalization of the evaluation of the options.

2   The Tools Used in Multi-criteria Decision Problems in Transport

2.1   General Remarks

Decision-making in real decision situations needs analysing them by the vector objective function [9, 10, 15, 22]. Therefore different, potentially opposite sub-criteria must be set. The key question of theory and practice of decision-making under a multiplicity of objectives is establishing principles for optimality solutions.

Multicriteria decision problem is composed of decision-maker, set of solutions, a set of characteristics of alternatives, and a set of decision-making strategies. The literature [10, 11, 17, 20] generally describes four main categories of multi-criteria decision problems concerning:

- description of the data analysed during the decision-making process,
- ordering variants and creating rankings,
- choosing one variant or subset of variants,
- sorting involving the allocation of variants to predefined classes of decision.

In general methods of multi-criteria decision support are divided into [22]:

(1) methods for multi-attribute utility theory called synthesis methods to a single criterion, bypassing incomparability of criteria,
(2) methods based on outranking relationship, called excess synthesis methods taking into account the non-comparability,
(3) the interactive method called dialogue of local assessment methods based on trials and errors in each iteration.

The first group of methods is based on aggregating different criteria to a single utility function which is optimized. In this approach, a number of criteria will be reduced to a single global criterion. Multi-attribute utility theory assumes that all options are comparable to resolve the issue.

The second group of methods models decision maker preferences by so-called outranking relationship allowing occurrence of non-comparable variants, when decision-maker is not able to identify the better of the two variants. The methods of this group interweave computational phase and the decision phase being a dialogue with the decision-maker. In the first phase the decision maker obtains a sample of compromise solutions. In the second phase, the sample is subjected to the assessment by introducing additional preferential information. Most of these methods are used within a multi-criteria mathematical programming. Dialog-based methods gained in recent years a great popularity. This is due to the fact that decision-maker has greater confidence in the final result by his involvement in solving process, and also has better awareness of the undertaken problem.

Important classes of multi-criteria decision support methods are based on equilibrium point and non-dominated solution [21]. Multicriteria methods based on the concept non-dominated solutions are classified as:

- methods of weighted objective function (parametric scalarization, construction of utility function)
- lexicography (sequential) method,
- unordered lexicography method
- method of limited criteria (ancillary restrictions).

Multi-criteria methods based on the point of balance (point of reference), include method of minimum distance from the optimal solution, Nash method, whether the target programming method.

2.2   The Issue of Decision-Making in the Literature

As mentioned in point 1 and 2.1 the analysis of complex multi-faceted decision problems in transport requires compromise solutions which take into account the interests of various participants of the transport process. These problems apply multi-criteria methods.

Overall, multi-criteria optimization task is described as follows [5, 10]:

While complying with constraints:

$$\mathbf{X} \in D \tag{1}$$

one must set vector of decision variables $\mathbf{X} = \bar{\mathbf{X}}$, for which:

$$f(\bar{\mathbf{X}}) = extr\langle f_g(\mathbf{X}) : g = 1, \ldots, M \rangle \tag{2}$$

Multi-criteria decision-making problems are based on two fundamental postulates:

- Postulate of dominance – if there are proposed two acceptable solutions and it is recognized that one of them has at least one criterion more favourable than the other, and in all other respects it is not worse, the first of them should be considered as better;
- transitive postulate – if as a result of comparisons the Option α is considered as better than β, and β as better than η, then consistently we should recognize that Option α is better than η.

This means that once adapted evaluation system must be respected during whole multi-criteria optimization.

The literature review [12, 14, 18] reveals that different optimization methods used to solve transport-related problems and their selection depends on the purpose of research and given assumptions. These methods can be broadly divided into classical heuristics and metaheuristics.

The main difference between above methods is that the quality of solution obtained by metaheuristic algorithms is higher than the obtained by classic heuristics algorithms, but searching time is longer. The classical heuristics can be divided into: routes construction heuristics [8] and routes improving heuristics [16]. Among the metaheuristic algorithms a taboo-search algorithms [2, 7], genetic algorithms [19], simulated annealing algorithm [3] and ant colony [6] can be distinguished.

Multi-criteria approach to classical transportation problem is presented in [23]. The concept of non-dominated solutions was used to set rational solution. In general classic technics of linear programming are used to determine non-dominated solutions [2, 4].

Many authors use the approach of setting compromise solutions to solve multi-criteria optimization problems [5]. In that case the solution closest to the ideal is achieved [2]. The issue of multi-criteria optimization of transport systems can be varied and involve many issues, depending on:

- objective, like minimum costs and maximum profit or minimum time and cost of transport,
- type of constrains imposed on the transport network,
- technical and economic constraints imposed on the transport network infrastructure.

Multi-criteria decision support in transport [1, 10–13] aims to equip decision-makers with the tools to solve complex decision problems which include many (often opposing) points of view. When solving such problems the optimality in the classic sense is of little use, because it is impossible to obtain optimal solutions simultaneously from all points of view.

It should be noted that development of methods of multi-criteria decision support [5, 11, 12, 17, 18, 23] is primarily due to their practical usefulness. They lead to the "optimal compromise". These methods allow choosing the best solution according to different evaluation criteria and with regard to both qualitative and quantitative factors usually expressed in different units of measure. In such cases the criterion of comparability of ratings is provided through standardization of assessments. Multi-criteria analysis methods include weight system related to the individual evaluation criteria, so that the criteria can be divided into more and less important. The results obtained by multi-criteria assessment methods are dependent on the parameters, such as criteria weights, which must be previously defined by a group of experts.

2.3 Standardization of the Variants Ratings in Multi-criteria Decision Support Methods

The complexity of the problem of choosing the best solution stems from the fact that a number of criteria, which are often expressed in different units, must be taken into account. It is necessary then to ensure a comparability of variants ratings.

Assuming that one dispose a:

- Set V, $V = \{v : v = 1, \ldots, N\}$ of variants of design solutions, where v is a single design solution, and N is a number of variants, where $N \geq 2$, and
- Set F, $F = \{f : f = 1, \ldots, M\}$ of evaluation criteria, where f is a partial evaluation criteria, and M is a number of partial criteria to evaluate variants evaluations of all variants according to the particular criteria are stored in the matrix X of variants ratings:

$$\mathbf{X} = \left[x_{vf} \in \mathbf{R}^+ \right]_{N \times M} \tag{3}$$

where x_{vf} is an evaluation of v-th variant in relations to f-th criterion ($v \in \mathbf{V}, f \in \mathbf{F}$). Partial evaluation criteria often are referred as diagnostic variables, being:

– stimulants – their increase in value implies an increase in the value of variant assessment,
– destimulants – their increase in value implies a decline in the value of variant assessment,
– nominants – variables containing the specified limits, called the nominal values.

The values of diagnostic variables may be expressed in various measures of (like money and distance measures). To compare the normalization of assessment values must be done. Only in that case the assessments for all criteria will include a certain range of values, and therefore will be comparable. Normalization of the variants ratings are most often carried out by two methods: unitarisation or normalization by the extreme value.

Unitarisation causes such normalization of design variants assessments for which values are in the range [0, 1], but the normalized ratingsvalues have different standard deviation from a fixed reference point which is the range of diagnostic variable. This group of methods embraces zero-unitarisation method that allows scaling of variables taking negative, positive or zero values. In case of zero-unitarisation method, for each type of diagnostic variables (stimulant, destimulants and nominants) standardization takes place in a different way. When the value of v-th variantrating according to f-th criterion after normalization is described as w_{vf}, normalization by zero-unitarisation method can be formally written as follows:

– for stimulants:

$$w_{vf} = \frac{x_{vf} - \min\limits_{v' \in V}\{x_{v'f}\}}{\max\limits_{v' \in V}\{x_{v'f}\} - \min\limits_{v' \in V}\{x_{v'f}\}} \tag{4}$$

– for destimulants:

$$w_{vf} = \frac{\max\limits_{v' \in V}\{x_{v'f}\} - x_{vf}}{\max\limits_{v' \in V}\{x_{v'f}\} - \min\limits_{v' \in V}\{x_{v'f}\}} \tag{5}$$

- for nominants, with single nominal value cn_f:

$$w_{vf} = \begin{cases} \dfrac{x_{vf}-\min\limits_{v' \in V}\{x_{v'f}\}}{cn_f-\min\limits_{v' \in V}\{x_{v'f}\}} & \text{gdy } x_{vf} < cn_f \\ 1 & \text{gdy } x_{vf} = cn_f \\ \dfrac{x_{vf}-\max\limits_{v' \in V}\{x_{v'f}\}}{cn_f-\max\limits_{v' \in V}\{x_{v'f}\}} & \text{gdy } x_{vf} > cn_f \end{cases} \tag{6}$$

- for nominants, with nominal value range of $\{cn1_f, cn2_f\}$:

$$w_{vf} = \begin{cases} \dfrac{x_{vf}-\min\limits_{v' \in V}\{x_{v'f}\}}{cn1_f-\min\limits_{v' \in V}\{x_{v'f}\}} & \text{gdy } x_{vf} < cn1_f \\ 1 & \text{gdy } cn1_f \leq x_{vf} \leq cn2_f \\ \dfrac{x_{vf}-\max\limits_{v' \in V}\{x_{v'f}\}}{cn2_f-\max\limits_{v' \in V}\{x_{v'f}\}} & \text{gdy } x_{vf} > cn2_f \end{cases} \tag{7}$$

Methods for standardization by the extreme value are used to regulate variants ratings with positive values. Applying this approach results in normalizing design solutions assessments to a values of the range [0,1]. This normalization preserves ratios between primary values (before normalization) and normalized values. Normalization by the extreme value is carried out as follows [15, 21]:

- for stimulants:

$$w_{vf} = \frac{x_{vf}}{\max\limits_{v' \in V}\{x_{v'f}\}} \tag{8}$$

- for destimulants:

$$w_{vf} = \frac{\min\limits_{v' \in V}\{x_{v'f}\}}{x_{vf}} \tag{9}$$

2.4   Methods of Variants Ranking in Multicriteria Decision Support

The paper describes two methods used for multi-criteria comparison of variants: the point-method and the method MAJA. Both methods were used to solve exemplary decision-making problem in the following part.

The essence of each multi-criteria assessment method is to set proper weight to each criterion. If there are different targets or scenarios, they should be also described by proper weights. The sum of set weights may not exceed 1 or 100 % if the criteria importance is expressed as a percentage.

The procedure of point method of variants evaluation can be summarized as follows:

- defining a set V of variants of design solutions and set of evaluation criteria F,
- determining the importance of particular partial criteria c_f, where the weight of each criterion c_f belongs to the range [0, 1] and the sum of weights for all criteria is equal to 1:

$$\forall f \in F \ c_f \geq 0 \ \wedge \ c_f \leq 1, \text{ where } \sum_{f \in F} c_f = 1 \tag{10}$$

- determining values of individual assessments of design options in terms of involved partial criteria – elements of matrix $\mathbf{X}$.
- standardization of assessments of individual design variant in terms of involved partial criteria – setting values w_{vf}'
- determining aggregate values of assessment indicators W_v for individual v-th variants of design solutions by the formula:

$$W_v = \sum_{f \in F} c_f \cdot w_{vf} \tag{11}$$

- ordering the variants of the decreasing value of W_v and selection of variant v^*:

$$v^* : W_{v^*} = \max_{v \in V}\{W_v\} \tag{12}$$

Variant v^* with the highest evaluation index is most preferred.

Choosing the best option by MAJA method is carried out using detailed assessments of design variants and indexes of relative importance of criteria, as well as thresholds of compliance or non-compliance of the variants assessments. The first stage of the MAJA method (as in point method), is to define alternative design solutions as a set V and the set F of partial evaluation criteria. Similarly, in the next three stages the importance of partial assessment criteria (c_f) is determined, the variants ratings according to criteria (x_{vf}) are identified, and they are normalized (w_{vf}).

The next step is constructing compliance matrix $\mathbf{Z}$. The elements of the matrix are determined as compliance rates $z_{vv'}$ and are obtained by comparing pairs of every two variants (v, v') identifying criteria $f \in F$, for which the design variant v has a better assessment than the variant v':

$$z_{vv'} = \frac{1}{\sum\limits_{f \in F} c_f} \sum\limits_{f \in F : w_{vf} > w_{v'f}} c_f \tag{13}$$

where $z_{vv'} \in [0, 1]$. It takes the maximum value when the evaluation of variant v by all criteria f is higher than the ratings of variant v'

Similarly, the next step is to compare to what extent assessment of variant v is worse than the assessment of the variant v'. For this purpose the rate $n_{vv'}$ of evaluation non-compliance (element of non-compliance matrix $\mathbf{N}$) is expressed by the formula:

$$n_{vv'} = \frac{1}{d} \max\limits_{(v,f) \in V \times F : w_{v'f} > w_{vf}} \{w_{v'f} - w_{vf}\} \tag{14}$$

where d is the difference between the components of matrix with the largest and smallest values of ratings after normalization calculated by the following formula:

$$d = \max\limits_{(v,f) \in V \times F} \{w_{vf}\} - \min\limits_{(v,f) \in V \times F} \{w_{vf}\} \tag{15}$$

The rate of discordance $n_{vv'} \in [0, 1]$. It takes the highest value when ratings of the variant v'f or all criteria are higher than ratings of the variant v.

The next step is the appointment of compliance threshold pz and non-compliance threshold pn necessary to choose the best variant from a set V. They take values in the range $[0, 1]$ and are used for selecting design variants that meet the criteria specified by both thresholds. The thresholds of compliance and non-compliance can be reduced and increased if necessary, but the compliance threshold pz should stay within the range $[0; 1]$, and non-compliance threshold pn should stay within the range $[0; 1]$.

An important step in MAJA method is determining binary matrix of domination $\mathbf{A}$:

$$\mathbf{A} = [a_{vv'}]_{N \times N} \tag{16}$$

However, if $a_{vv'} = 1$, then the variant v dominates (is better) on a variant of v' – in the sense of compliance and non-compliance of criteria assessments. This can be defined using the graph $\mathbf{Gf}$ of domination:

$$\mathbf{Gf} = \langle \mathbf{Wf}, \mathbf{Lf} \rangle \tag{17}$$

for which $\mathbf{Wf}$ is a set of nodes mapping the set of analyzed variants V, and $\mathbf{Lf}$ is a set of edges (v, v'). If $a_{vv'} = 1$ for pairs of nodes, then there is edge from node v to node v', but if $a_{vv'} = 0$ then edge connecting v with v' does not exist. The graph $\mathbf{Gf}$ is a base for final selection of preferred design variant. Dominant variant (the best one) is a variant from which most edges come out.

3   An Example of the Practical Use of Multi-criteria Decision Support

3.1   General Characteristics of SuperChoose Application

Application SuperChoose is a tool supporting multi-criteria decision-making about servicing potential of selected transport company. The application is an implementation of MAJA ranking method. Application operating scheme is shown in Fig. 1.

3.2   Selection of a Variant of Servicing Potential of a Company

One analysed servicing potential of selected transport company performing domestic and international transport services. Taking into account forecasted demand for company's services five organizational variants of company's transport potential were considered:

- variant 1 – trucks with Euro 5 emission standard and drivers not organized in crews,
- variant 2 – tractor-trailers with Euro 3 emission standard and drivers not organized in crews,
- variant 3 – tractor-trailers with Euro 3 emission standard and drivers organized in double-driver crews,
- variant 4 – tractor-trailers with Euro 6 emission standard and drivers not organized in crews,
- variant 5 – tractor-trailers with Euro 6 emission standard and drivers organized in double-driver crews,

Variants were compared in terms of total annual costs of transport, expenditures for the purchase of vehicles, reserve of transport potential and total annual emissions of CO and NO_x. The values of evaluation criteria for different variants are summarized in Table 1.

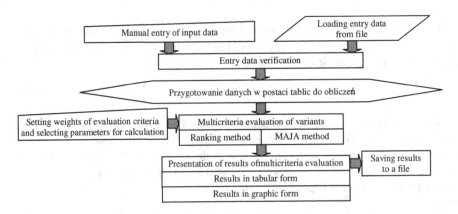

Fig. 1. The general scheme of SuperChoose application [own study]

Table 1. The values of evaluation criteria for variants [own study]

Criterion	Unit of measure	Criterion value				
		Variant 1	Variant 2	Variant 3	Variant 4	Variant 5
Total cost of transport	thous. PLN/year	3 941,8	3 345,0	3 527,7	3 261,8	3 380,3
Expenditures for vehicles purchase	thous. PLN	2 400,0	2 240,0	1 600,0	3 150,0	2 250,0
Reserve of transport potential	%	7,41 %	0,79 %	3,85 %	0,79 %	3,85 %
CO emission	t/year	1,018	1,224	1,224	0,821	0,821
NO_x emission	t/year	3,800	8,165	8,165	0,767	0,767

The i of the individual evaluation criteria was adopted as follows: 0.45; 0.15; 0.20; 0.10 and 0.10.

SuperChoose application was used for multi-criteria evaluation of alternatives by the ranking and MAJA methods. The results are shown in Tables 2 and 3.

The ranking method points variant 5 as the best one, while MAJA method under adopted thresholds of compliance 0,4 and non-compliance 0,6, pointed variant 4 as non-dominated and consequently recommended.

Table 2. Results gained from ranking method (SuperChoose application) [own study]

Variant	Evaluation according to criteria					
	Criterion 1	Criterion 2	Criterion 3	Criterion 4	Criterion 5	Total
1	0,372	0,100	0,200	0,081	0,020	0,773
2	0,439	0,107	0,021	0,067	0,009	0,644
3	0,416	0,150	0,104	0,067	0,009	0,746
4	0,450	0,076	0,021	0,100	0,100	0,748
5	0,434	0,107	0,104	0,100	0,100	**0,845**

Table 3. Results gained from MAJA method – domination matrix (SuperChoose application) [own study]

Variant	Variant 1	Variant 2	Variant 3	Variant 4	Variant 5
1	0,000	1,000	1,000	0,000	0,000
2	0,000	0,000	1,000	0,000	0,000
3	1,000	0,000	0,000	0,000	0,000
4	0,000	1,000	1,000	0,000	1,000
5	1,000	1,000	1,000	0,000	0,000

4 Conclusion

Making informed investment decisions by businesses is a key element of their operation. Often the decision-making process is complex and requires consideration of different criteria. A multitude of options and criteria can lead to confusion and, consequently, to financial losses. It is therefore necessary to use tools to support decision-making processes. Multi-criteria decision support methods used to evaluate and create a ranking of investment options are to assist and allow only to set certain conditions of decision making.

The development of multi-criteria decision support models results mainly from their practical usefulness. These models allow taking into consideration many – often contradictory – points of view and lead to establishing "optimal compromise". They are designed to equip decision-makers with tools to solve complex decision problems.

Tools like SuperChoose application may be useful in the analysis of complex investment projects. They allow for quick comparative analysis of many variants from different points of view (different criteria for analysis of individual participants in the decision-making process).

References

1. Ambroziak, T., Jacyna, M., Wasiak, M.: The logistic services in a hierarchical distribution system. In: Goulias, K. (ed.) Transport Science and Technology, Chap. 30, pp. 383–393. Elsevier (2006)
2. Ameljańczyk, A.: Optymalizacja wielokryterialna. Wydawnictwo Wojskowej Akademii Technicznej, Warsaw (1986)
3. Chiang, W.C., Russell, R.A.: Simulated annealing metaheuristics for the vehicle routing problem with time windows. Eur. J. Oper. Res. **63**, 3–27 (1996)
4. Elmaghraby, S.E., Kamburowski, J.: The analysis of activity networks under generalized precedence relations. Manag. Sci. **38**(9), 1245–1263 (1992)
5. Galas, Z., Nykowski, I., Żółkiewski, Z.: Programowanie wielokryterialne. Polskie Wydawnictwo Ekonomiczne, Warsaw (1985)
6. Gambardella, L.M.E., Taillard, G.: A multiple ant colony system for vehicle routing problems with time windows. In: Corne, D., Dorigo, M.F. (eds.) New Ideas in Optimization. McGraw-Hill, London (1999)
7. Garcia, B.L., Potvin, J.Y., Rousseau, J.M.: A parallel implementation of the tabu search heuristic for vehicle routing problems with time window constraints. Comput. Opera. Res. **21**, 1025–1033 (1994)
8. Gaskell, T.J.: Basis for vehicle fleet scheduling. Oper. Res. Int. J. **18**, 281–295 (1967)
9. Gutenbaum, J.: Modelowanie matematyczne systemów. PWN, Warsaw-Lodz (1978)
10. Jacyna, M.: Modelowanie i ocena systemów transportowych. Oficyna Wydawnicza Politechniki Warszawskiej, Warsaw (2009)
11. Jacyna, M.: Multicriteria Evaluation of Traffic Flow Distribution in a Transport Corridor. Railway Engineering, London (2001)
12. Jacyna, M.: Some aspects of multicriteria evaluation of traffic flow distribution in a multimodal transport corridor. Arch. Transp. **10**(1–2), 37–52 (1998)

13. Jacyna, M.: The modeling of the external cost influence on the modal split in the transport network. In: IEEE Computer Society Order Number P3331 BMS Part Number CFP08369-PRT (1989)
14. Jacyna, M., Wasiak, M.: The some aspects of multiobjective evaluation to choose the option of transport infrastructure modernization. In: Proceedings of 10th International Conference on Applications of Advanced Technologies in Transportation 2008, pp. 7533–7543. Curran Associates Inc., Red Hook (2010)
15. Jacyna, M., Wasiak, M.: Zastosowanie wielokryterialnej oceny do wyboru wariantu modernizacji elementów infrastruktury kolejowej. Problemy Kolejnictwa **146**, 27–35 (2008)
16. Pyza, D.: Optimization of transport in distribution systems with restrictions on delivery times. Arch. Transp. **21**(3–4), 125–147 (2009). Polish Academy of Sciences Committee of Transport
17. Roy, B.: Decision-aid and decision making. Eur. J. Oper. Res. **45**, 324–331 (1990)
18. Steuer, R.: An interactive multiple objective linear programming procedure. TIMS stud. Manag. Sci. **6**, 225–239 (1977)
19. Thangiah, S.R.: Vehicle routing with time windows, rusing genetic algorithms. In: Chambers, L. (ed.) Application Handbook of Genetic Algorithms, vol. 2. CRC Press, BocaRaton (1995)
20. Trzaskalik, T.: Wielokryterialne wspomaganie decyzji. Metody i zastosowania, Polskie Wydawnictwo Ekonomiczne, Warsaw (2014)
21. Wasiak, M.: Wybrane aspekty optymalizacji wielokryterialnej. In: Kacprzyk, J., Budziński, R. (eds.) Badania operacyjne i systemowe 2006. Metody i techniki, Akademicka Oficyna Wydawnicza EXIT, pp. 109–116, Warsaw (2006)
22. Vincke, P.: Multicriteria decision-aid. John Wiley & Sons, Chichester (1992)
23. Zeleny, M.: Multiple Criteria Decision Making. McGraw-Hill, New York (1982)

Impact of Road Conditions on the Normal Reaction Forces on the Wheels of a Motor Vehicle Performing a Straightforward Braking Maneuver

Jarosław Zalewski[✉]

Warsaw University of Technology, Pl. Politechniki 1, 00-661 Warsaw, Poland
j.zalewski@ans.pw.edu.pl

Abstract. In the paper analysis is presented, which concerns the impact of both the road surface condition and the change in a vehicle model center of mass location on the course of the normal reaction forces, acting on the wheels versus the distance travelled during the braking maneuver. The road was flat in one case, and randomly uneven in the other.

Research was based on the simulation of a motor vehicle model in MSC Adams/Car, for two different road conditions, with braking starting from the speed of 100 km/h. Such attempt enabled analysis of the influence of both mass – inertia and road condition on the wheel normal forces. The results may as well serve as a cognitive element, showing the specifics and the range of changes in the derived parameters.

Keywords: Normal reaction forces · Brake maneuver · Road conditions

1 Introduction

The aspect of motor vehicle safety seem to be an important issue in research on dynamics of the means of transport, particularly considering the motion in difficult road conditions. From the point of view of different types of road users the motor vehicle safety seems to be a key element in terms of traffic disturbances.

One of the issues often analysed is the problem of the contact between the wheels and a road surface. In the papers devoted to it the following aspects, among others, were distinguished:

- the problem of radial elasticity of tires rolling on flat and uneven surfaces (e.g. [1, 10, 12]);
- normal (perpendicular to the road surface) reaction forces of the road surface on the wheels (e.g. [6, 7, 9]);
- forces occurring in the contact plane between the wheel and the road (e.g. [2, 5, 8]), causing e.g. the lateral drift or slip.

In this paper attention was paid to the issue of changes in the values of the normal reaction forces on the wheels of a sports vehicle model, which rode along a straight line, realising the braking maneuver. In relation to that, analysis was conducted on the

© Springer International Publishing Switzerland 2015
J. Mikulski (Ed.): TST 2015, CCIS 531, pp. 24–33, 2015.
DOI: 10.1007/978-3-319-24577-5_3

influence of road conditions and load of the selected motor vehicle model on the course of the normal reaction forces on the wheels as a function of distance traveled during the completion of the braking maneuver along a straight line. Such research can be carried out on real objects, however it generates additional logistical problems, simultaneously extending time and increasing costs.

In further parts of the paper, by mentioning the normal reaction forces, the author means the resultant forces in the area of contact between road and tire, perpendicular to the road surface.

2 The Assumptions for the Simulation

In order to determine the changes in the road surface normal reaction forces on the wheels of a braking vehicle a simulation was conducted in the MSC Adams/Car environment. The following assumptions were taken:

(a) the vehicle model has nonlinear characteristics of spring - damping suspension elements, as in [12], and its body is treated as a quasi-rigid solid;
(b) vehicle model starts braking at the speed of 100 km/h on the fifth gear;
(c) the motion during braking is rectilinear;
(d) the brake value was set at 10, which is relevant to the vertical pressure on the brake pedal, and the time of reaching that value was set at 1 s;
(e) the weight distribution in the vehicle body is illustrated in Figs. 1 and 2.

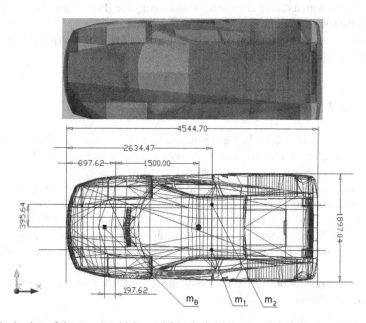

Fig. 1. Projection of the sports vehicle model body from the top along with the dimensions and location of the driver, passenger and baggage [own study]

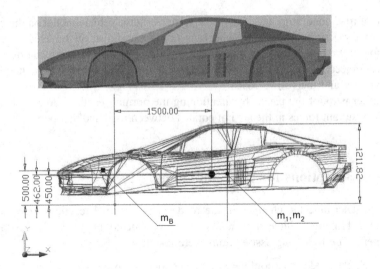

Fig. 2. Projection of the sports vehicle model body from the left side [own study]

The simulation was prepared for four configurations:

– unladen vehicle on a dry, flat road surface with a coefficient of friction between wheels and road μ = 0.8;
– unladen vehicle on a dry and uneven road surface (μ = 0.8), where the surface irregularities occur randomly;
– vehicle laden with a driver, a passenger and a baggage (Figs. 1 and 2) on a dry, flat road surface with a coefficient of friction μ = 0.8;
– vehicle laden as above, moving on a dry and uneven road surface (μ = 0.8) also with randomly occurring inequalities;

3   Selected Model of the Motor Vehicle

The motor vehicle model used in the simulation was previously described e.g. in [12]. It is a model of a two-seater sports vehicle with the drive unit located above the rear axle. The model is available in the database of the MSC Adams/Car software. The load consisted of three masses representing the driver (m1), the passenger (m2) and the baggage (mB), distributed in the vehicle as shown in Figs. 1 and 2. The mass-inertia disturbances were derived according to the so-called "origo" [12], which represents the origin of a coordinate system associated with the road, but moving along with the vehicle during motion. The coordinates of the center of mass is also relative to the point "origo".

Selected parameters of the vehicle body and the vehicle as a whole before adding the load are as follows:

– total mass of the vehicle body $m_{VB} = 995kg$ and of the whole vehicle $m_V = 1528kg$;

- coordinates of the center of mass of the vehicle body relative to the point "origo":
  $x_c = 1,5\,m$, $y_c = 0$, $z_c = 0,45m$;
- coordinates of the center of mass of the vehicle relative to the point "origo":
  $x_c = 1,75\,m$, $y_c = -0,001m$, $z_c = 0,43m$;
- moments of inertia of the vehicle body relative to the axes passing through the
  "origo": $I_{xx} = 401\,kg \cdot m^2$, $I_{yy} = 2940\,kg \cdot m^2$, $I_{zz} = 2838\,kg \cdot m^2$;
- moments of inertia of the vehicle relative to the axes passing through the "origo":
  $I_{xx} = 583\,kg \cdot m^2$, $I_{yy} = 6129\,kg \cdot m^2$, $I_{zz} = 6022\,kg \cdot m^2$;
- moments of deviation of the vehicle body relative to the axes passing through the
  "origo": $I_{xy} = 0$, $I_{zx} = 671\,kg \cdot m^2$, $I_{yz} = 0$;
- moments of deviation of the vehicle relative to the axes passing through the "origo":
  $I_{xy} = -1,9kg \cdot m^2$, $I_{zx} = 1160\,kg \cdot m^2$, $I_{yz} = -1,3kg \cdot m^2$.

The following configuration of the vehicle body load was adopted. It was assumed
that the body is loaded with the masses representing the driver ($m_1 = 70kg$), the
passenger ($m_2 = 70kg$) and the baggage ($m_B = 50kg$). Selected parameters of the
vehicle body after loading were as follows:

- total mass of the vehicle body $m'_{VB} = 1185kg$ and of the vehicle $m'_V = 1718kg$;
- coordinates of the center of mass of the vehicle body relative to the point "origo":
  $x'_c = 1,456\,m$, $y'_c = 0$, $z'_c = 0,454m$;
- coordinates of the center of mass of the vehicle relative to the point of "origo":
  $x'_c = 1,69\,m$, $y'_c = 0$, $z'_c = 0,43m$;
- moments of inertia of the vehicle body relative to the axes passing through the
  "origo": $I'_{xx} = 444\,kg \cdot m^2$, $I'_{yy} = 3256\,kg \cdot m^2$, $I'_{zz} = 3112kg \cdot m^2$;
- moments of inertia of the vehicle relative to the axes passing through the "origo":
  $I'_{xx} = 626\,kg \cdot m^2$, $I'_{yy} = 6445\,kg \cdot m^2$, $I'_{zz} = 6295\,kg \cdot m^2$;
- moments of deviation of the vehicle body relative to the axes passing through the
  "origo": $I'_{xy} = 0$, $I'_{zx} = 783kg \cdot m^2$, $I'_{yz} = 0$;
- moments of deviation of the vehicle relative to the axes passing through the "origo":
  $I'_{xy} = -1,9kg \cdot m^2$, $I'_{zx} = 1272\,kg \cdot m^2$, $I'_{yz} = -1,3kg \cdot m^2$.

4 Disturbances Coming from the Road Surface

Braking examination of a vehicle model from a speed of 100 km/h was carried out for
the road with both a flat and dry, and an uneven (the irregularities occurred randomly)
and dry surface. Disturbances coming from the road were realised using the "2d_
stochastic_uneven.rdf" file, which describes the random surface irregularities using the
function described in Adams/Car as ARC 901 [11].

Randomly occurring road irregularities are obtained as follows. First, white noise
signals are generated on the basis of random variables with almost uniform distribution.
Two of those variables are assigned to the road at a distance of every 10 mm. The
obtained values are integrated over the road length, using the time-discrete filter, whose
independent variable is the road. The result of this operation is the obtaining of two

approximated realisations of the white noise velocity. Signals of such properties make the road profiles having the waviness equal to 2 (waviness for the measured wave spectral density of the roads is in the range between 1.8 and 2.2 [4]).

Then the two realisations $z_1(s)$, $z_2(s)$ are correlated in order to obtain a profile of the road for the left and right wheels $z_l(s)$, $z_r(s)$ (1). The correlation coefficient is 0 for two different profiles, and 1 for the same. In the file defining the road profile with random irregularities the value of the correlation coefficient was assumed equal to 1.

$$z_l(s) = z_1(s) + \frac{corr_{rl}}{2}(z_2(s) - z_1(s))$$
$$z_r(s) = z_2(s) + \frac{corr_{rl}}{2}(z_2(s) - z_1(s)),$$
(1)

where: $corr_{rl}$ - correlation coefficient between the road profiles for the realisation of the signals $z_1(s)$, $z_2(s)$.

As it can be seen, random irregularities of the road are described as realisations of the white noise velocity, which is a stochastic process. In order to be used in the simulation of motion, where the expected result is a trajectory, those realisations must be a stochastic process with the properties: stationary in a broader sense and globally ergodic. Both of these characteristics are satisfied here, because each of the realisations is a signal representing the road profile for the left and right wheels. In addition, these signals have a length of the road as a specificity domain, which made it necessary to take the stochastic process into account as a component describing unevenness of the roads [3].

In the described vehicle model, the default model of tires, PAC89, was removed, because it was unable to cooperate with the road surface, for which the wavelength of the irregularities is smaller than the radius of the rolling wheel [11]. Instead the FTIRE model (flexible structure tire model), consisting of panels connected to each other with the deformable spring elements, was used. The panels may deform in three mutually perpendicular direction (Fig. 3).

5   Simulation of the Brake Maneuver

Simulation of the brake maneuver was carried out at an initial speed of 100 km/h for each configuration described in p. 2. For each configuration four trajectories were obtained, which are presented in Figs. 4, 5, 6 and 7. The MSC Adams/Car 2005r2 software was used, however without the built-in solvers to solve the sets of equations of motion for the presented vehicle model and its components. Instead, an external solver assigned to Adams, but not embedded in the package was used, making it possible to perform calculations in the ordinary command window, rather than directly in the Adams/Car interface, which reduced the use of the operative memory. Of course, in this case it is necessary to generate certain executable files that enable calculation somewhat outside of the program. These files are obviously generated in the Adams/Car environment.

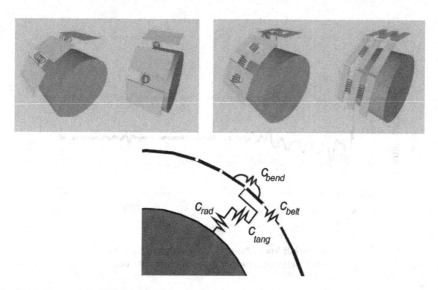

Fig. 3. Scheme of the FTIRE model for the deformation in radial, transverse and circumferential direction [13]

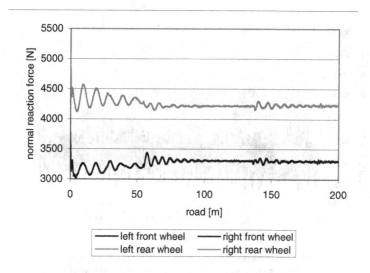

Fig. 4. The normal reaction forces on wheels of the unladen vehicle model as a function of distance traveled during braking on a flat, dry road surface [own study]

In all configurations the vehicle model has traveled for about 200 m during the simulation, which lasted 10 s. The road length resulted from the low pressure on the brake pedal of the vehicle model. In this case more important was to track changes in the normal reaction forces for each wheel than the braking effectiveness. Another important issue was the time of increasing the pressure on the brake pedal to its

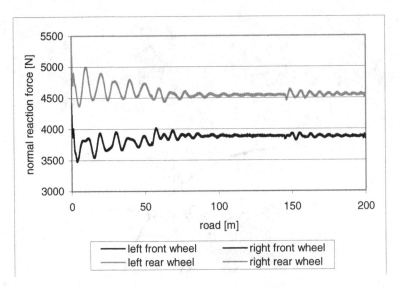

Fig. 5. The normal reaction forces on wheels of the laden vehicle model as a function of distance traveled during braking on a flat, dry road surface [own study]

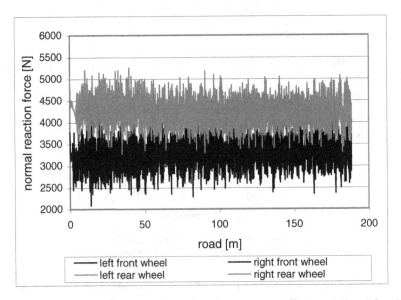

Fig. 6. The normal reaction forces on wheels of the unladen vehicle model as a function of distance traveled during braking on an uneven, dry road surface. [own study]

maximum value, which lasted 1 s. In the simulation of the laden vehicle, with random disturbances coming from the uneven road, braking distance was shorter by about 10 m due to an error in calculations for low speed motion at the end of the maneuver, when the laden vehicle model travelled at low speed.

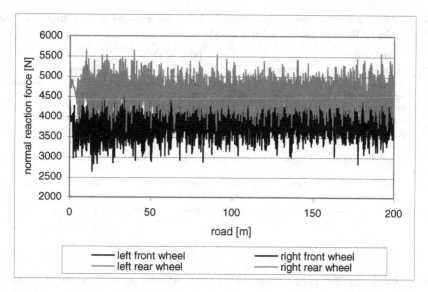

Fig. 7. The normal reaction forces on wheels of the laden vehicle model as a function of distance traveled during braking on an uneven, dry road surface [own study]

6   Analysis of the Obtained Results

By analysing the results a qualitative assessment of the received trajectories has been made. It shows that during braking on a flat road the normal reaction force values stabilize after driving a particular part of the road, and the deflection of the mean value in the second half of the braking distance is negligible. Regarding the impact of random road surface irregularities the amplitudes of normal reaction force search the peak values over the entire length of the braking road. Note, however, that for uniform loading of the vehicle the course of road surface reaction as a functions of the distance covered is moderately uniform.

A quantitative assessment of the values of the road surface normal reaction forces on the wheels was also prepared. In tab. 1 the mean values of reaction forces for each wheel are shown, as well as the maximum amplitude of these values for each wheel in the presented road conditions and for the laden and unladen vehicle model.

From the values presented in Table 1 it can be seen that when braking the unladen vehicle with the drive unit in the rear, both on the flat and uneven road the rear axle was burdened. That is also confirmed by the fact of the occurrence of the normal reaction force amplitudes acting on the wheels, which, especially in case of motion on uneven roads, are about 1000 N higher than the average. In case of motion of the laden vehicle model the rear axle is also more burdened. However, the differences between the maximum amplitude and the mean value of the normal reaction forces do not seem to be as great as for the unladen vehicle, especially for the front wheels.

As it can be observed from the prepared analysis, the disturbance of the center of mass location in connection with the poor condition of the road may affect both the

Table 1. Mean values of the normal reaction forces for each wheel and their maximal amplitudes during the brake maneuve [own study]

Wheel	unladen vehicle				laden vehicle			
	Flat road		Uneven road		Flat road		Uneven road	
	normal reaction force mean value [N]	amplitude [N]	normal reaction force mean value [N]	amplitude [N]	normal reaction force mean value [N]	amplitude [N]	normal reaction force mean value [N]	amplitude [N]
Left front	3280	3780	3280	4300	3870	4420	3870	4900
Right front	3270	3770	3270	4270	3850	4400	3850	4870
Left rear	4230	5060	4240	5190	4580	5430	4580	5640
Right rear	4220	5040	4220	5250	4560	5410	4560	5640

average values of the normal reactions on the wheels, as well as the maximum amplitudes of these reactions, particularly on a certain road section, on which a specified maneuver takes place. Such approach seems important both for reconstruction of accidents and as a part of infrastructure improvement connected with road vehicle dynamics.

7   Conclusion

Based on the simulation of motion of the unladen and laden vehicle model in Adams/Car software the courses of the normal reaction forces on wheels for two different road conditions were obtained. Taking into account the results, the following conclusions can be reached.

The mean values of reaction forces differ in each case by 10 to 20 N, which, considering that these are mean values, and the vehicle is braking, do not seem of great importance. The changes may occur due to the momentary roll of the vehicle body on the suspension and temporary, minor burden or relief on either left or the right pair of wheels. It is true that the motion was straightforward, but in such case as vehicle ride, minor movements in other directions than longitudinal should be expected.

When laden vehicle motion is considered, the differences in normal reaction forces on the wheels of the same axle were also between 10 and 20 N. The existence of larger forces and amplitudes in case of the laden vehicle can be explained by the better contact between the wheels and the road surface (coefficient of friction remains the same, but the area of contact between the wheel and the road may be greater). It is understood that the wheels rolling along the uneven surface may temporarily lose contact with the road, or their burden could be even momentarily relieved. Additional masses (driver, passenger and baggage) can compensate vibrations occurring in the suspension. If the oscillating system increase sits mass, than at the same driven force the expected response may be of the lesser value than for the smaller mass.

The simulation results can be used to determine the location of the center of mass on the basis of normal reaction forces with which the road affects the wheels. Also the nature and dynamics of these changes can be presented on the basis of the instantaneous normal reaction forces and investigate their influence on motion of the vehicle as a mechanical system.

Further research will provide analysis of the impact of non-uniform load on the normal and contact forces within the area of contact between the road and wheels, basing on computer simulations.

References

1. Cebon, D.: Handbook of Vehicle-Road Interaction. Taylor & Francis, London (2000)
2. Guiggiani, M.: The Science of Vehicle Dynamics, Handling, Braking and Ride of Road and Race Cars. Springer Science+Business Media, Dordrecht (2014)
3. Kisilowski, J.; Zalewski, J., On a certain possibility of practical application of stochastic technical stability, Maintenance and Reliability, 1(37)/2008
4. Kisilowski, J., Zalewski, J.: Wybrane problemy bezpieczeństwa w ruchu drogowym, Logistyka, 3/2014. (in Polish)
5. Pacejka, H.B.: Tyre Models for Vehicle Dynamics Analysis. Taylor & Francis, London (1993)
6. Prochowski, L.: Mechanika ruchu, Warszawa 2005, WKŁ (2005) (in Polish)
7. Rajamani, R.: Vehicle Dynamics and Control, 2nd edn. Springer, Newyork (2012)
8. Reński, A., Sar, H.: Wyznaczanie dynamicznych charakterystyk bocznego znoszenia opon na podstawie badań drogowych, Zeszyty Naukowe Instytutu Pojazdów, SIMR, PW, 4(67)/ 2007. (in Polish)
9. Rill, G.: Road Vehicle Dynamics: Fundamentals and Modeling. CRC Press, Boca Raton (2011)
10. Siłka, W.: Teoria Ruchu Samochodu. WNT, Warszawa (2002). (in Polish)
11. Using Adams, MSC Software Corporation
12. Zalewski, J.: Influence of road conditions on the stability of a laden vehicle mathematical model, realising a single lane change maneuver. In: Mikulski, J. (ed.) TST 2014. CCIS, vol. 471, pp. 174–184. Springer, Heidelberg (2014)
13. www.cosin.eu. (Accessed on 22 May 2015)

Video Processing for Detection and Tracking of Pedestrians and Vehicles at Zebra Crossings

Witold Czajewski[1(✉)], Paweł Mrówka[2], and Piotr Olszewski[3]

[1] Faculty of Electrical Engineering, Warsaw University of Technology,
pl. Politechniki 1, 00-661 Warsaw, Poland
w.czajewski@isep.pw.edu.pl
[2] Neurosoft Sp. z o.o., ul. Robotnicza 72, 53-608 Wrocław, Poland
pawel.mrowka@neurosoft.pl
[3] Faculty of Civil Engineering, Warsaw University of Technology,
al. Armii Ludowej 16, 00-637 Warsaw, Poland
p.olszewski@il.pw.edu.pl

Abstract. This paper describes results of experiments with camera setup, calibration and image processing algorithms for automatic detection and tracking of pedestrians and vehicles. The aim of the MOBIS project was to develop a method of assessing safety of unsignalised pedestrian crossings. Correct detection and tracking proved to be more difficult in the case of pedestrians than vehicles due to variability in people's appearance, movement in groups and poor visibility in bad weather. Application of cameras with built-in pedestrian tracking programs was successful only in very good visibility conditions, so a computationally efficient PC algorithm providing a high pedestrian detection rate was used instead. The paper presents comparison of results obtained using different image processing methods as well as selected problems of pedestrian tracking. Statistical analysis of pedestrian behaviour with and without vehicles present is also shown. The proposed approach seems to be accurate enough for the purpose of assessing pedestrian safety.

Keywords: Pedestrian detection and tracking · Image analysis · Pedestrian safety · Conflict technique

1 Introduction

The pedestrian fatality rate of 30 deaths per year per million population in Poland is the second highest among the EU countries. During the 6 yrs 2007–2012 on Polish roads 9101 pedestrians were killed and 71328 injured. About 30 % of such accidents occurred at marked pedestrian crossings where pedestrians should theoretically be safe. Improvement of pedestrian safety is one of the priority goals of the Polish National Road Traffic Safety Programme [1].

One of the main reasons for taking up the MOBIS project described in this paper was shortening the pedestrian crossing safety assessment procedure [2]. It is currently

© Springer International Publishing Switzerland 2015
J. Mikulski (Ed.): TST 2015, CCIS 531, pp. 34–44, 2015.
DOI: 10.1007/978-3-319-24577-5_4

based on long-term accident reports and additional safety measures are introduced only after a series of injuries or deaths. Instead, it is proposed to use automatic video analysis that can give concluding results after days and not years of observations.

The method is based on detection of traffic conflicts, or near-accidents. Such situations are not reported in any way, although they are several times more likely to happen than accidents. Therefore, it is hoped that the proposed solution will make it possible to conduct safety assessments based on relatively short observation periods and will provide an objective evaluation of measures used to improve pedestrian safety.

The aim of the paper is to give an overview of selected technical aspects of the project with focus on detection and tracking of pedestrians and vehicles. Moreover, statistical analysis of pedestrian behaviour with and without vehicles present is also shown.

2   Automatic Pedestrian Detection and Tracking

There is a growing interest in infrastructure-based pedestrian detection systems at pedestrian crossings that communicate with vehicles or crossing signalization to improve safety [3–6]. Five most commonly used types of pedestrian detection technologies include: piezometric, ultrasonic, passive infrared (PIR), microwave/Doppler radar and video analysis.

The first three methods can be used primarily for pedestrian detection at kerbside, but are inadequate for tracking people across the street. Microwave radar technology, successfully used for car tracking, shows reduced ability to detect and track multiple moving targets, especially in presence of frequent occlusions unless a multiple sensor network is used [7], which can result in 100 percent detection rate (tracking accuracy is not reported) [8]. Other sources [9], however, quote slightly lower detection rates for several representative studies, especially for real life applications.

2.1   Video Analysis

Although it may not be as accurate as a network of microwave radars, video-based detection and tracking technology has attracted attention of many researchers mainly due to its versatility, low cost and content-rich data [10–14]. Another undisputable advantage of such systems is their capability of acquiring and storing raw data in a way that humans can easily understand and verify. This is particularly important in conflict analysis, where video recordings can be readily used by human operators to assess the severity of captured incidents before a fully automated and highly accurate method is developed.

At the current state of the art it is not yet possible to have a real-time system capable of tracking individual persons of variable pose, colour of clothes, size and shape in cluttered and dynamic urban scenes, where occlusions and changing lighting and weather conditions occur. It should be noted, however, that in the present project such a high performance is not required. For the purpose of conflict detection and safety assessment, it is not necessary to track individuals in the crowd. Large groups of pedestrians are very unlikely to be a part of a conflict, so they can be represented as a single object or even disregarded. What is important is the correct tracking of single pedestrians, who are most often exposed to danger. Such a limited but real-time algorithm is used in this project not only to track pedestrians, but also to trigger an active signage system.

3 Test Sites

The experiments were conducted at two pedestrian crossing in Warsaw and two in Wrocław. The test sites were selected based on: high pedestrian traffic volume, considerable number of pedestrian-vehicle accidents in the near past and availability of facilities for equipment installation in the vicinity of the crossing.

For each crossing a dedicated video recording and processing system was installed and recordings were conducted for a period of two to three months. Finally, a batch of approximately 25 days for each crossing was selected for further processing.

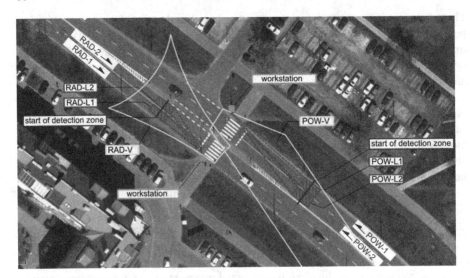

Fig. 1. Warsaw test site with marked video recording and processing *workstations* and approximate viewing areas of the overview (*RAD-V, POW-V*) and directional cameras (*RAD-L1, RAD-L2* and *POW-L1, POW-L2*) [own study]

The crossing at the intersection of Wrocławska and Blatona streets in Warsaw, where 6 pedestrian-vehicle accidents were reported from 2006 to 2011, was selected as one of the test sites. It is a four-lane undivided road with a refuge island as shown in Fig. 1. All 4 lanes were monitored in the direction of the incoming traffic.

The second test site was selected in Wrocław at the intersection of Mickiewicza and Godebskiego streets. According to the Police records, there were 5 pedestrian-vehicle accidents from 2006 to 2011. This test site is a two-lane undivided road with two zebra crossings in the vicinity of the intersection. Each pedestrian crossing was fully covered by the vision system, but due to technical reasons the vehicle traffic was monitored from only one direction for each zebra as marked by arrows in Fig. 2.

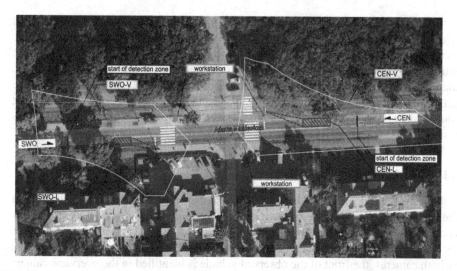

Fig. 2. Wrocław test site with marked video recording and processing *workstations* and approximate viewing areas of the overview (*SWO-V, CEN-V*) and directional cameras (*SWO-L, CEN-L*) [own study]

4 Video Processing Methodology

The video recording and processing system that was installed on a lamp post at each crossing consisted of the following components:

- one or two (depending on the number of lanes) directional cameras covering road sections approximately 3.5 m wide and 6 m long as marked by dashed areas in Figs. 1 and 2,
- a fish-eye overview camera covering the area of the pedestrian crossing and its road approach section[1],
- a workstation used for recording and preliminary analysis of the captured video for the purpose of pedestrian detection and dynamic signage control.

The directional cameras need no lens calibration as image distortions are minimal. In order to use them not only as a trigger for vehicle tracking, but also for vehicles' speed estimation, their intrinsic and extrinsic parameters must be established during calibration. This procedure is based on the observation of thousands of licence plates of passing vehicles captured by the cameras. An assumption is made that a significant number of vehicles travel at constant speed. An optimization routine selects these vehicles and finds an estimate of cameras' parameters by using the well-defined licence plates as calibration patterns. Final adjustments are made manually by comparing the overlapping images from the directional and the overview cameras.

---

[1] The length of road approaches covered by camera varied from approximately 30 to 80 meters as measured on the ground level, but the effective vehicle tracking range was usually shorter, as marked in Figs. 1 and 2.

The fish-eye lens of the overview cameras that were used to cover the entire area of interest (i.e. the crossing and the road approach) introduced significant distortions. These were successfully removed by using the equidistant mapping, parameters of which were estimated by optimizing the reprojection error of selected straight lines such as curbs, tram rails or road markings. Image rectification was followed by establishing the inverse perspective projection by fitting selected image and geodetic road points with the least squares method. A typical image from one of the overview fish-eye cameras after lens distortion removal is shown in Fig. 3.

4.1   Vehicle Detection and Tracking

Vehicles are initially detected by the directional cameras that observe a small patch of the road and identify licence plates. Once a licence plate has been detected in a few consecutive frames, instantaneous position and speed of that vehicle is calculated and the overview camera takes over the tracking process. Based on the previous calibration of both cameras, the front of the observed vehicle is identified in the overview camera image and normalized to a constant size. This specific template is approximated with a 2D discrete cosine transform (2D-DCT) in order to reduce its dimensionality and retain only the most distinctive features. It is further localized in consecutive frames around its predicted position and its 2D-DCT representation is updated as the vehicle is approaching the camera. Trajectories of vehicles are modelled by cubic splines with certain constraints set on vehicles' position, speed, tangential and normal components of acceleration as well as their curvature. As the result of the entire process, trajectories of vehicles with an average position error of less than 10 cm in the area of the zebra crossing are generated.

4.2   Pedestrian Detection and Tracking

Pedestrians are detected and tracked only in the overview camera images. The first attempt of pedestrian detection involved using special Bosch cameras with built-in motion tracking algorithms. Unfortunately, it failed to provide accurate and time-deterministic results - the sampling rate was unpredictable and depended strongly on the contents of the video. This resulted in large gaps in pedestrian trajectories. What is more, the low sensitivity of the algorithm made it useless in non-perfect visual conditions. In the end, almost half of pedestrians were missed and many of those detected had short and jagged trajectories.

Due to the above, a PC-based algorithm was used. The requirements for this algorithm assumed its almost real-time performance, as it was also intended to control active signage in our experiments. Therefore, it was not possible to use the most sophisticated human identification and tracking methods but rather a well-known approach as described below.

Initially, a background/foreground separation is performed with a Gaussian Mixture Model (GMM). All the moving areas within the crossing are then normalized and parameterized with a 2D-DCT, similarly like for the vehicles, and tracked in consecutive frames. This preliminary trajectory can be very jagged and is iteratively refined by employing the likelihood probability test applied to the GMM models of pedestrian and background in the vicinity of the initial pedestrian position. As the result, in good visibility conditions, smooth trajectories of pedestrians are generated.

Since all the moving objects within the crossing that are not pedestrians (most often vehicles' headlights and reflections or shadows) are treated as potential pedestrians, a lot of false detections and false trajectories occur (approximately 10 % for Warsaw and even 50 % for Wrocław). These are, however, easily filtered out based on their characteristics that is quite different from a trajectory of a pedestrian crossing the street. To this end a random trees classifier (separate for each crossing) that was trained with over 1000 manually labelled trajectories was used. Its error rate was below 1 percent.

5 Selected Problems

Practically 100 % of vehicles carrying a clearly visible licence plate were correctly detected and nearly all of them were tracked properly (see below for details). Pedestrian detection and tracking was a much more difficult task due to the large variety of pedestrian appearances and behaviours as well as stronger influence of weather and visibility conditions.

5.1 Vehicle Detection and Tracking

As mentioned above, vehicle detection and tracking was a fairly easy task as long as a tracked car was not occluded too much by a truck or a bus. A more frequent problem was incorrect fitting of vehicles' fronts in consecutive frames. It was mainly caused by poor visibility resulting in improper front model adaptation or a rapid change of car dynamics (hard braking while yielding to a pedestrian). As a result, the front of the vehicle was slightly offset from its real position or sometimes the detected car seemed to go forward or reverse (occasionally rotating at the same time) while the real car was stopped or has already been gone (see Fig. 3). Fortunately, such cases were very rare (less than 0.5 %) and the latter case could be easily filtered out from further processing based on very unusual dynamics of the trajectories that would be extremely unlikely in real life.

5.2 Pedestrian Detection and Tracking

The first attempt of pedestrian detection with Bosch in-camera algorithms was rather unsatisfactory, but our own algorithm that was fine-tuned after initial experiments proved to be working correctly most of the time. In favourable conditions (daytime, overcast, no rain, no occlusions) it was able to correctly detect and track nearly 100 % of single pedestrians. However, in certain situations, pedestrian detection quality was compromised. At night, dusk and dawn, when captured images were dark, some pedestrians, especially wearing dark clothes were unnoticed or were detected only on the white strips of zebra, which resulted at best in short trajectories. Strong sunshine, on the other hand, caused clearly visible shadows that affected the motion detection part of the algorithm and resulted in highly distorted trajectories (see Fig. 4). Fog, rain or snow blurred the images and had some negative influence on pedestrian detection. Such days were removed from further processing.

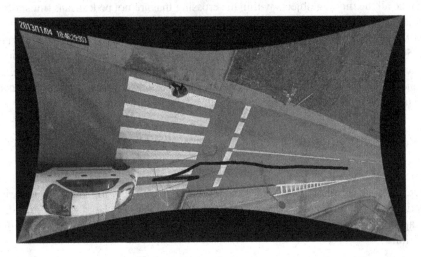

Fig. 3. Incorrect trajectory of a car which is about to leave the crossing, while its trajectory suggests that it remains in the middle thereof for a long time [own study]

Since people detection is based on motion analysis, many trajectories of pedestrians approaching the crossing and stopping at the curb for several seconds are divided. Trajectories also tend to split sometimes in the middle of the crossing, especially when people are dressed in dark or white clothes, which makes them disappear and reappear on the zebra. On the other hand, sometimes trajectories of two pedestrians that pass close by each other are merged into a single trajectory.

Fig. 4. Incorrect trajectories of pedestrians caused by sharp shadows (*left*) or crowd (*right*) [own study]

Detecting pedestrians walking in groups is the biggest challenge for the algorithm. Since it was required to run in real time, it was not possible to apply advanced people identification methods. Therefore, small groups of pedestrians are usually treated as one person, while large groups can be identified as two or three. In the latter case, the trajectories are usually short and/or not very smooth as the detection can jump from one pedestrian to another within the group (compare Fig. 4).

6   Detection Results and Statistics

During the study three people detection and tracking algorithms were used. The final, optimized PC-based version of the algorithm enabled correct detection of nearly 99 % of pedestrians (when small groups of pedestrians are counted as one) in favourable weather conditions (see Table 1). About 90 % of the generated trajectories are smooth and complete. This result is significantly better than the initially used in-camera detection and tracking module, which not only missed almost half of the pedestrians, but also produced very jagged and incomplete trajectories.

Table 1. Pedestrian detection rate for three algorithms used compared to manually labelled video recorded on October 24th, 2013 on both crossings in Warsaw [own study]

Pedestrian detection method	Individual pedestrians	Single and groups
Initial, in-camera motion detection	58 %	66 %
Early GMM background subtraction	78 %	88 %
Final GMM background subtraction	87 %	99 %

The distribution of pedestrians present on the crossing during the day that is divided into three parts roughly corresponding to the camera day and night switching times is given in Table 2. In the morning, when mostly single pedestrians are present, the individual detection is highest and it deteriorates with time as more and more groups of people arrive at the crossing. The lowest detection rate is recorded in the evening when there is still a large number of groups present and the visibility conditions are getting worse.

Table 2. Distribution of pedestrians on both crossings in Warsaw site on October 24th, 2013 [own study]

Hours	0:00–7:59	8:00–15:59	16:00–23:59	Total
Real no of pedestrians	1052	3710	1392	6154
Real no of groups	73	412	177	662
No of detections	971	3257	1140	5368
% of individual detections	92	88	82	87
% of detections of single and groups	99	100	97	99

Statistical analysis of average pedestrian speed during crossing the street for 25 selected days in Warsaw (POW direction, approx. 65.000 pedestrians detected) was performed (unusually fast bicycle, scooter and roller riders were excluded from the analysis). It shows that pedestrians walk slightly faster (1.46 m/s, stdev: 0.29) when vehicles are approaching them as compared to an empty street (1.43 m/s, stdev: 0.29). Average hourly distribution of pedestrian speed (see Fig. 5) also suggests that pedestrians walk faster in the evening than in the morning and slowest around noon. It is worth noting however that pedestrians walk clearly faster in the presence of vehicles only during weekdays – on weekends this difference is insignificant. Moreover, the average number of pedestrians per day of the week is almost constant with its lowest on Saturdays and highest on Sundays.

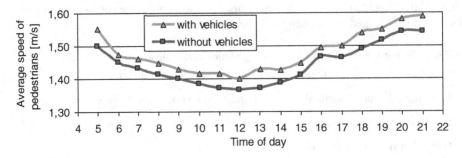

Fig. 5. Average hourly pedestrian speed during the street crossing based on 25 selected days for Warsaw site (POW direction). Standard deviation is nearly constant for both cases (0.29) [own study]

One can clearly see the shift of speed distribution with and without vehicles, which is depicted in Fig. 6. Median values are respectively: 1.44 and 1.41 m/s, which means over 2 % increase of pedestrian speed in the presence of incoming vehicles.

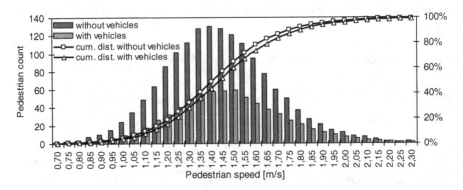

Fig. 6. Average daily histogram and cumulative distribution of pedestrian speed with and without vehicles [own study]

Average hourly pedestrian distribution shows vast differences in pedestrian count during the day, as expected. Two peak intensities were recorded: one around noon (195 pedestrians per hour, 30 % with vehicles) and the other around 17:00 local time (187 pedestrians per hour, 44 % with vehicles). The percent of pedestrians with vehicles did not fall below 20 % except for early morning and late evening hours.

7   Conclusion

The results obtained from video analysis of the material recorded at the pedestrian crossings in Warsaw and Wrocław show that the proposed system configuration and the performance of the detection and tracking algorithms used provide sufficient accuracy for the purpose of trajectory analysis in traffic conflict technique[2]. Although not all pedestrians in groups are correctly tracked, it has little influence on conflict detection in practice. The proposed solution can be successfully used for data acquisition necessary for the assessment of pedestrian crossing safety, however fully automatic methods of calculating some safety measures are yet to be developed, which is the objective of the ongoing research within the MOBIS project. The system also proved to be useful in real-time control of active signage, which warned drivers about the presence of pedestrians on the crossing and thus increased pedestrian safety.

Acknowledgments.   The research reported in this paper is a part of the project MOBIS which was funded by the Polish National Centre for Research and Development (NCBiR).

References

1. National Road Safety Council, National Road Safety Programme 2013–2020 (2013). http://krbrd.gov.pl/pl/narodowy-program-brd.html. Accessed on 20 June 2013
2. Szagała, P., et al.: Safety assessment of pedestrian crossings with video analysis. In: 27th ICTCT Workshop. Karlsruhe, Germany (2014)
3. Czajewski, W., Dąbkowski, P., Olszewski, P.: Innovate solutions for improving safety at pedestrian crossings. Arch. Transp. Syst. Telemat. **6**(2), 16–22 (2013)
4. Bishop, R.: Intelligent Vehicle Technologies and Trends. Artech House Inc, Norwood (2005)
5. Jones, W.: Building safer cars. IEEE Spectr. **39**(1), 82–85 (2002)
6. Vlacic, L., Parent, M., Harashima, F.: Intelligent Vehicle Technologies. Butterworth-Heinemann, Oxford (2001)
7. Kocur, D., Rovnakova, J., Urdzík, D.: Short-range UWB radar application: problem of mutual shadowing between targets. Elektrorevue **2**(4), 37–43 (2011)
8. Beckwidth, D.M., Hunter-Zaworski, K.M.: Passive pedestrian detection at unsignalized crossings. J. Transp. Res. Board **1636**, 96–103 (1998)
9. Markowitz, F., et al.: Automated Pedestrian Detection: Challenges and Opportunities, Walk21 Paper (2012)

---

[2] As of writing this paper, only one day of data from both crossings in Wrocław was available, so detailed statistics are not available, however early tests show that pedestrian tracking performance is on the same level as in Warsaw.

10. Kohler, S., et al.: Early detection of the pedestrian's intention to cross the street, In: 15th International IEEE Conference on Intelligent Transportation Systems, pp. 1759–1764 (2012)
11. Dollar, P., et al.: Pedestrian detection: an evaluation of the state of the art. IEEE Trans. Pattern Anal. Mach. Intell. **34**(4), 743–761 (2011)
12. Gandhi, T., Trivedi, M.: Pedestrian protection systems: issues, survey, and challenges. IEEE Trans. Intell. Transp. Syst. **8**(3), 413–430 (2007)
13. Geronimo, D., et al.: Survey of pedestrian detection for advanced driver assistance systems. IEEE Trans. Pattern Anal. Mach. Intell. **32**(7), 1239–1258 (2010)
14. Simmonet, D., et al.: Backgroundless detection of pedestrians in cluttered conditions based on monocular images: a review. Comput. Vis. IET **6**(6), 540–550 (2012)

Control of Coordinated Systems Traffic Lights.
Cloud Computing Technology

Elzbieta Grzejszczyk[✉]

Electrical Department, Warsaw University of Technology,
Pl. Politechniki 1, 00-661 Warsaw, Poland
elzbieta.grzejszczyk@ee.pw.edu.pl

Abstract. In area traffic coordination systems, both local and centralised databases play a very important role. They serve as massive historical and real-time data containers. Managing such a huge repository of information in on-line mode requires highly specialised tools embedded in tele-transmission solutions provided by CC (Cloud Computing) technology. The use of this tool become the basis of the traffic control systems in Intelligent Transport Systems presented and described in this paper as an example. This article shortly presents the database tools of Microsoft Azure technology (CC) and refers to well known database tools of Windows platform (i.e. MS SQL). The next presents database distributed management system supervising defined area traffic connections were take place a road traffic collision. The analyzed service is an example of a cloud computing application using an SQL Azure database to modify control parameters for a selected of intersections. Such modification occurs when a priority request for an event is handled (interrupt generated during a car traffic collision).

Keywords: Control telematics · CC as ITS technology · Smart database distributed management system

1 The Road Collision in GSM/GPRS Environment

1.1 Automobile on-Board Digital Networks

Ever stricter users' requirements concerning car safety and comfort made the producers install more and more complicated sensors and controllers of thereof.

Because of rapid information exchange within an ever more complex infrastructure, leading car companies started to introduce fast computer digital buses that had been used in telecommunication and information technology for a long time. Thus in the mid-1990s various types of on-board computer networks were introduced, which, depending on their function, met the required transmission data parameters.

Figure 1 shows modern information systems that now installed to control the work of individual automotive systems.

One of the most important microcontrollers uses for on-board system, connected with the safety of passengers are control units of air bags system/sensors - shown on Fig. 1. In simple terms, it can be assumed that the launch of airbag system is equivalent to a collision on the road. The aim of the handling of the collision from the view of the road control system, are exchanges parameters of traffic lights on neighbours intersection.

© Springer International Publishing Switzerland 2015
J. Mikulski (Ed.): TST 2015, CCIS 531, pp. 45–56, 2015.
DOI: 10.1007/978-3-319-24577-5_5

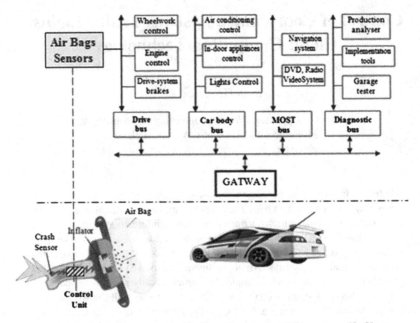

Fig. 1. Digital buses controlling run-time automobile systems [3, 8]

The essential role in above action performs real time operating system supervising all on-board network processes[1]. The on-board SIM/USIM card is supported by real time operating system as well. This functionality (SIM/USIM card plus real time operating system) was used in presented solutions [3, 6].

1.2 Wireless Transmission Data Over TCP/IP and GPRS Networks

Figure 2 presents the sequence of establishing a connection between MS (Mobile station i.e. SIM/USIM card) and IP Network (i.e. an IP number) [17]. Shown on Fig. 2 the schema of the establishing connection is typical for GPRS network and enables the assignation of the sender's and the receiver's addresses to each connected user (both in the IP and the GPRS network).

2 Database Systems in Intelligent Transport System (Road Systems)

In area traffic coordination systems, both local and centralised databases play a very important role. They serve as massive historical and real-time data containers.

---

[1] A proposition of just such a system branded OSEK/VDX Vehicle Distributed Executive was first presented in 1995. The architecture of the AUTOSAR (AUTomotive Open System ARchitecture) system acc. HIS (German Hersteller-Initiative Software).

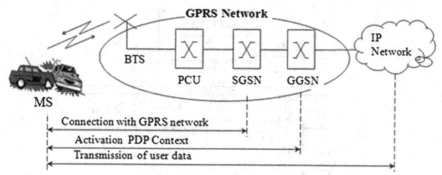

MS - Mobile Station, BTS - Base Transiver Station; PCU - Packet Control Unit;SGSN - ServingGPRS
Support Node; GGSN - GPRS Gatway Support Node;GPRS - General Packet Radio Service

Fig. 2. Packet data transmission over GPRS between a mobile station (MS) and the IP Network
[own study]

The kind of stored data was presented in [11]. Schema of the broad network
manages special kind of the data shown Fig. 3

Database Distributed Management System (DBDMS) is defined as a software
enables users to control distributed data without knowledge were they are physically
reside.

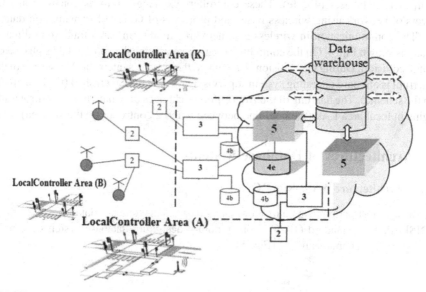

2 - LMT Local Manager of Data Transaction; 3 - GMT - Global Manager of Data Transaction (for Local
Area Identifiers); 5 - MC - Module of Communication (for Local Area Identifiers); 4b - Register of
crossroads for subarea of LA and their parameters 4e - Register of subarea of LA

Fig. 3. Database distributed management system [own study]

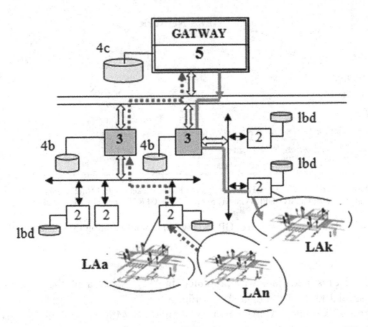

Fig. 4. Communication schema in wireless traffic area coordination systems. Wireless data transmission system. [own study]

In this schema (Fig. 3) - nodes of network data create controllers manages integrated with them databases (4b, 4e). These controllers exchanges information with another layers of network using wireless buses and protocols of GPRS of transmission data.

The communication in wireless data networks monitoring area traffic coordination systems shown Fig. 4. On the communication schema in local area LAn takes place a car traffic collision. During the collision is generated the system's interrupt. The source of this interrupt is onboard operating system supervising ones of the car crashed (the broken line on the schema). The handing of interrupt enforces changes of parameters of control traffic lights in local area LAk (the bold line between 5 and 2 controller on the schema).

3   Architectures of Database Systems

3.1   Architecture ANSI-SPARC

A basic abstraction standard for designing management database system is ANSI-SPARC[2] standard (1975). Contemporary designing database systems are references to this schema standard (Fig. 5).

---

[2] ANSI-SPARC - American National Standards Institute, Standards Planning And Requirements Committee).

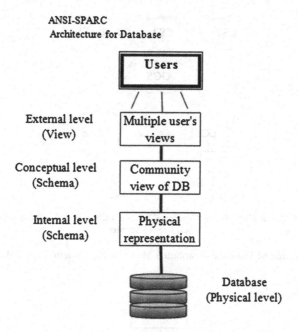

Fig. 5. Three layer schema of ANSI-SPARC architecture (Permission is granted to copy, distribute and/or modify this document under the terms of the GNU Free Documentation License,)

Three layers architecture. The standard defines three layers structure of the system, where presentation and manipulating data is independed from phisically location of the data. Three layers are defined as:

– **basic** layer - this is the layer of phisical storage data
– **conceptual** layer - is the manipulating data layer (conceptual level)
– **external** level - multiple user's views, level of users

3.2 Architecture of a Distributed Database System. An Federated Data Base System - FDBS

Architecture of a distributed database systems. Architecture of the system is rely on creating conception a global system - refers to local systems. (Figure 6) Inside distributed systems of data are distinguished schemas like: LIs -Local Internal Schema, LCS - Local Conceptual Schema, GCS Global Conceptual Schema and ES - External Schema. Dependency between schemas is shown on Fig. 6

An federated database system (FDBS) "is a collection of cooperating database systems that are autonomous and possibly heterogeneous" [18]. Schema of FDBS is shown on Fig. 7

The component DBSs are integrated to various degrees. The software that provides controlled and coordinated manipulation of the component DBSs is called a federated database management system (FDBMS). Both databases and DBMSs play important

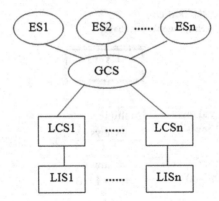

ES - External Schema **GCS** - Global Conceptual Schema **LCS** - Local Conceptual Schema **LIS** - Local Internal Schema

Fig. 6. Architecture of Database Distributed Management System – DBDMS [own study]

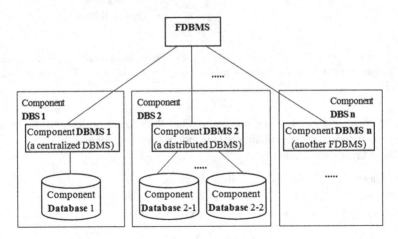

Fig. 7. An FDBS and its components [18]

roles in defining the architecture of an FDBS. Component database refers to a database of a component DBS. A component DBS can participate in more than one federation. The DBMS of a component DBS, or component DBMS, can be a centralized or distributed DBMS or another FDBMS. The component DBMSs can differ in such aspects as data models, query languages, and transaction management capabilities. One of the significant aspects of an FDBS is that a component DBS can continue its local operations and at the same time participate in a federation. [according to 18].

3.3   Heterogeneous Database Networks

Heterogeneous database networks integrated many solutions and concepts of database architecture. There are result of practice different systems and computer technology

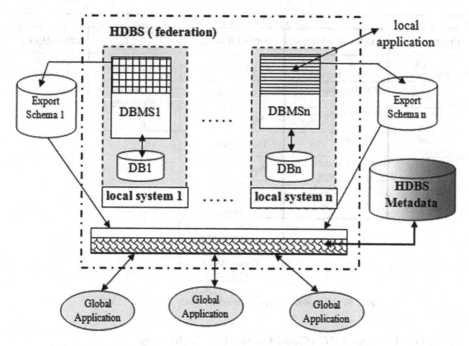

Fig. 8. HDBS (Heterogeneous Database System) architecture [own study]

(i.e. operating systems and data base software systems) in wide area networks. Figure 8 presents such network.

Management of the heterogeneous database networks become significant simplification as an result of progress IT technology. The newest solutions IT technology provides many integrated services supporting database systems. This services are defined as IaaS (Infrastructure as a Service - equipment provided), PaaS (Platform as a Service - licensed software as a service provided) and SaaS (Software as a Service - provided proprietary software from the provider) [13, 14, 16]. Above services are ones of the basic conceptions of Cloud Computing technology.

4 Cloud Computing Technology in Intelligent Transport System (Road Systems)

An efficient management of the information in coordinated traffic systems requires highly specialised tools embedded in tele-transmission solutions. Such solutions are provided by CC technology [1, 14, 16]. The SQL Azure technology plays an important role for the subjects discussed here. This technology is based on the well-known solutions of MS SQL Server. (It provides the same interface as SQL Server and familiar tools and libraries for that environment, though the environments are not identical) [14, 15].

Azure Management Portal				
COMPUTER	**DATA SERVICES**	**ASP SERVICES**	**NETWORK SEVICES**	**COMMERCE**
Virtual Machines	**Storage [Blobs, Tables, Queues]**	Notification Hubs	Virtual Network	Store & Marketplace
WebSites	**SQL Database**	Service Bus	**Traffic Mannager**	
Mobile Services	**SQL Data Sync**	Media Services	Express Route	
Cloud Services	HD Insight	BizTalkServices		
	Hyper-V-Recoovery Manager	Active Directory		
	Backup	Scheduler		
	Cache	ContentDelivery Network		
		Multi-Factor Authentication		
		Automation		
		Visual Studio OnLine		

Fig. 9. Microsoft Azure tools (own study based on [15])

4.1   SQL Azure as a CC (Cloud Computing) Technology

The **Relational DataBase as a Service** (highlighted in the Data Services chart) is based on MS SQL engine used in previous solutions.

Figure 9 shows a set of functionalities offered by Microsoft Azure cloud computing [15]. The SQL Azure environment provides the same tools (stored procedures, functions, triggers and other mechanisms found in T-SQL), as well as the same management environment - SQL Server Management Studio. Databases are accessed using well-known ODBS and JDBC SQL drivers, and applications can be developed using Visual Studio tools (ADO.NET and LINQ) [12]. In addition to its known functionalities, the Azure platform provides new and very useful solutions. These undoubtedly include the ability to program **distributed database systems**.

Depending on the needs, the application works on a pre-defined data repository (e.g. local, central or mixed)[3] (Figs. 3, 7 and 8). The data synchronisation operations cited here are performed using a dedicated special tool - Microsoft Sync Framework (Fig. 9). With regard to the issues discussed in the article, the implementation of RDBaaS (*Relational Database as a Service*) is shown in Figs. 3 and 4. RDBaaS (Ralation Database System as a Software) allows on-line programming/control of an area/distributed environment (objects/intersections defined in the system). An example programming diagram[4] was described in the Part 1 of this paper [11].

---

[3] This service is especially useful in centrally-controlled distributed traffic coordination system.

[4] for the main example in the article, i.e. a information message with collision information.

5   Case Study. Handling a Software Priority Request in Azure SQL Technology in Intelligent Transport System Applications

The service we are analysing is an example of a cloud computing application using an SQL Azure database to modify control parameters for a selected of intersections. Such modification occurs when a priority request for an event is handled. An example of an event is a road traffic collision.

Request handling involves changing the control parameters on neighbouring intersections, which experience heavier traffic as a result of such collision. Handling request can be done at any time. Priority handling information is reported by the system to the operator, along with the coordinates for the collision and a list of neighbouring intersections. The monitoring application/decision system calculates a new control strategy and displays it in the operator's interface. Operator's confirmation is equal to the remote update of control parameters in given intersections (Figs. 3 and 4).

It should be added that all data in SQL Azure solutions are stored in databases with specific address (http://dataBase.XX). A special storage and management strategy was developed for storing non-relational data (*e.g. measurements* or *video files*). This strategy is Azure Storage (Fig. 9) [14, 15].

Data transmission/saving from end-controllers is done automatically in the memory/http address assigned to the controller (Fig. 4), from which it can also be read at any moment. Processes supported by the Service require 3 defined roles (types of virtual servers), which communicate using Azure Queues [10, 13].

Business vision of the system. A service embedded in the cloud has in its system database complete information concerning traffic lights in all intersections in the area registered in the system. Such data include hour-by-hour (daily peaks in traffic intensity), month-by-month (weekend peaks) and year-by-year (vacation, holiday peaks, etc.) records. All data are uniquely identified by the so-called own and foreign keys typical for the relational model. Non-relational data are identified by solutions contained in Azure Storage [13] (*blob, container and EAV tables numbers*) (Fig. 9).

The supervising/operator's applications allows for:

a. Calling a list of local parameters[5] for all intersections in a given area (LA) at any time for a defined time span (year, day, month, hour),
b. Calling the data as in item above, but only for selected intersection (with a given id number),
c. Conducting simulation games for the intersection or a sub network of intersections [11].

In case of receipt of collision notification in a monitored area (with a given LA), the system takes 2 actions: - sends a warning text message to all users in the LA [5, 6]

---

[5] local data means stored data assigned to a single local controller in an area traffic management system in an intersection.

and - corrects/calculates the control parameters for the intersections in a selected subarea of one or several LAs.

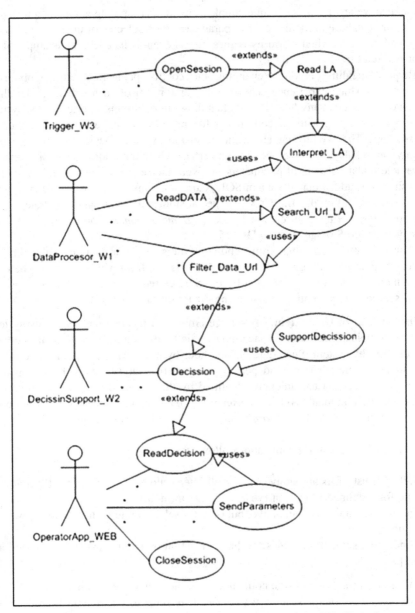

Trigger_W3 - Worker3; DataProcesor_W1- Worker1; DecissionSuport_W2 - Worker2; OperatorApp_WEB role

Fig. 10. Use cases for operator's application [own study]

During non-emergency operation, the Administrator chooses option a, b or c using an interactive form. After identifying the Operator's request, the system begins to handle it (including Azure Storage objects), thus generating a response presented in a feedback form. In the case of handling a priority request coming from a distributed network, the operator's interface switches into the emergency mode (choices are locked).

The feedback/information from the system can be presented as text or as processed data such as graphics or media[6]. This intelligent interaction is made possible by advanced telecommunications solutions included in the CC technology.

Project vision of the system. This service includes four roles (virtual servers): role **Web** (OperatorApp), **worker1** (DataProcessor), **worker2** (DecisionApp) and **worker3** (TriggerApp).

The **Web** (OperatorApp) role is responsible for downloading (from the operator UI) a link or links to http://stored data, which are then downloaded by the **worker1** (DataProcessor) to the local cache and stored in AzureBlobs (*special kind of the memory for non-relational data*). In the final phase, the OperatorApp (web) presents the associated files in the UI interface. The **worker2** (DecissionApp) role is responsible for the operation of and communication with the DS decision-making process (Deci-sionSystem). **Worker2** receives input parameters for DS from the system and passes them to DS. **Worker2** also receives the results of DS and passes these parameters to the Application.

The cooperation of these roles is shown in the UML cases (Fig. 10).

Worker3 (TriggerApp) is responsible for handling system interrupts/requests coming from a distributed network.

6 Conclusion

In the context of the issues described above, the **latest prototype** application solutions using 5G networks (with transmission speeds of up to 10/100 Gb/s) are especially noteworthy. Contemporary applications provide mobile users with on-demand TV services[7].(150 Mb/s) Considering the many applications of CCTV solutions in area traffic control systems (such as the CCTV subsystem [11]) it seems natural that the end users/on-board systems should be provided with video information. These could include clips/recordings showing the latest traffic changes (*especially considering the entries/exits from multi-level intersections*) or the situation on the planned route. (*Similar to municipal websites*). Video file support is becoming a standard practice in IT applications running in the CC environment[8]. However, the development of this type of specialised data in video format would require special engagement from the "area supervision services". Such involvement could of course be compensated by the potential users purchasing such videos/information.

---

[6] The form of presentation depends on an application.

[7] Horizon.tv video on-demand - as a service - for example provided by UPC Poland, iplainternet TV (including mobile devices).

[8] One of them was described in [13].

References

1. Cloud Application, Computer World, Nr 14/1029. ISBN: 0867–2334, www.computerworld. pl. Accessed 25 June 2014
2. Document OCIT-C_Protocol_V1_R1, Author: OCIT Developer Group (ODG) & Partner (Schlothauer & Wauer, PTV). http://www.ocit.org, Copyright © 2010 ODG & Partner
3. Fryskowski, B., Grzejszczyk, E.: Data transmission systems. Transport and Communication Publishers (2010)
4. GSM Phase 2 + General Packet Radio Service GPRS Architecture, Protocols and Air Interface - IEEE Xplore
5. Grzejszczyk, E.: Teleservice communication with motor vehicle. Electr. Rev. 94–98 (2011). ISSN: 0033-2097, R. 87 NR 12a/2011
6. Grzejszczyk, E.: Analysis of selected telematic services of the BMW service. Electr. Rev. 294–296 (2012). ISSN: 0033-2097, R. 88 NR 7a/2012
7. Grzejszczyk, E.: Selected issues of wireless communication over GSM with cars network computer system. GSTF J. Eng. Technol. 2(2), 106–109 (2013). ISSN: 2251-3701
8. Grzejszczyk, E.: The control on-line over TCP/IP exemplified by communication with automotive network. In: Federated Conference on Computer Science and Information Systems (FedCSIS), IEEE Xplore, vol. 1, pp. 807–810, Cracow (2013). ISBN: 978-1-4673-4471-5
9. Grzejszczyk, E.: The using of the satellite system GPS for the simulation of the identification of the car. Electr. Rev. 80(7–8), 718–722 (2004). ISSN: 0033-2097
10. Grzejszczyk, E.: Cloud computing as a tool in smart communication with a motor vehicle. Arch. Transp. Syst. Telemat. 7(4), 9–16 (2014). ISSN: 1899-8208
11. Grzejszczyk, E.: Control intelligent road transport systems. Coordinated traffic lights systems. In: TST 2015 - Transport Systems Telematics, April 2015, Wrocław, Poland (2015)
12. Grzejszczyk, E.: Introduction into Visual Web Developer Express 2008 and ASP.NET 2.0 Technology. Publishing House of Warsaw University of Technology, Warsaw (2010). ISBN 978-83-7207-853-7
13. Grzejszczyk, E.: Distributed database systems as a source of scientific/utility information in interactive intelligence systems. In: International Scientific Conference on Electronic publications in the Development of Science, Białystok (2014)
14. Microsoft Azure Platform, Computerworld Guide. www.microsoft.com/poland
15. Microsoft Library, Azure Management Portal. http://msdn.microsoft.com/en-us/library/azure/. Accessed 16 January 2015
16. Mateos, A., Rosenberg, J.: The Cloud at Your Service. Helion, West Midlands (2011)
17. Sanders, G., Thorens, L., Reisky, M., Rulik, O., Deylitz, S.: GPRS Networks. John Wiley & Sons Inc., England (2003)
18. Sheith, A.P., Larson, J.A.: Federated database systems for managing distributed, heterogeneous, and autonomous databases. ACM Comput. Surv. 22(3), 183–236 (1990)

Utility of Information from Road Weather Stations in Intelligent Transport Systems Application

Artur Ryguła[1]([⊠]), Krzysztof Brzozowski[1], and Aleksander Konior[2]

[1] University of Bielsko-Biala, 43-309 Bielsko-Biała, Poland
{arygula, kbrzozowski}@ath.eu
[2] APM PRO, 43-309 Bielsko-Biała, Poland
aleksander.konior@apm.pl

Abstract. In the article there were presented the results of information quality analysis for data recorded by the road weather stations in the aspect of the necessity to ensure road safety. The analysis was performed for the time horizon of several weeks including the period of time, during which there were both favorable and adverse weather conditions. The set of data about current road condition and the information about the particular meteorological parameters were collected for single road location with the redundancy of sensors in cross-section of the road.

Keywords: Road weather station · ITS control systems · Road traffic safety · Traffic user information

1 Introduction

Information about the current road condition is undoubtedly one of the elementary input data for a traffic management system. The results of conducted studies indicate that adverse weather does not only dramatically influence the level of traffic safety, but also determines the basic traffic conditions (e.g. by reducing the speed of the traffic free flow) [1]. Evaluation of the usefulness of meteorology systems is the subject of numerous research [2, 3]. From the point of view of the subject of this work, the utility of information is referred to the detection systems of dangerous road conditions whose exemplary algorithms were shown in the work [4].

Challenges, associated with the road safety improvement demanded from ITS systems that they will be able to be satisfying, providing that the quality of the input information enables the optimal traffic management under particular circumstances. Among series of information used in the control algorithms, there are also data characterizing the existing road conditions as well as in some solutions the forecast of weather situation. Therefore, the assessment of the quality can be applied both to the data collected by particular sensors as well as to information on the base of which, the assessment of forecast traffic conditions is done.

© Springer International Publishing Switzerland 2015
J. Mikulski (Ed.): TST 2015, CCIS 531, pp. 57–66, 2015.
DOI: 10.1007/978-3-319-24577-5_6

2 Road Weather Station

The subject of the analysis is the meteorological measurement system installed on II technical class of road (S69 two-lane expressway at kilometre 10+464 towards Żywiec). The diagram of the system is shown in Fig. 1.

At the specified location full redundancy system was installed, by placing sensors at both left and right lane of a roadway. Basic technical parameters of the sensors are described in Table 1.

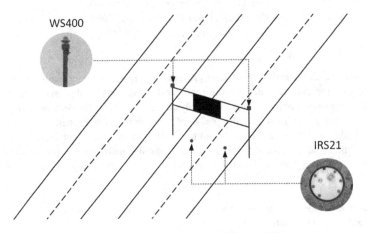

Fig. 1. Measurement system diagram [6]

Table 1. IRS21/WS400 technical parameter [5]

Measurement variable	Sensor	Accuracy	Principle
Air temperature	WS400	± 0.2°C (−20°C... +50°C), otherwise ±0.5°C (> −30°C)	NTC thermistor
Precipitation type and intensity	WS400	not available	Radar sensor measures the drop speed and calculates precipitation quantity and type by correlating drop size and speed
Road temperature	IRS21	±0.2°C (−10...10°C), otherwise ± 0.5°C	NTC thermistor
Freezing temperature	IRS21	±1°C for t > −10°C	Calculated from saline concentration (NaCl)
Water film height	IRS21	± (0.1 mm + 20 % of measurement)	Radar sensor
Saline concentration	IRS21	not available	Conductivity measurement

Measuring station consists of road sensors (IRS21) and compact weather stations (WS400). Road sensors are responsible for measuring parameters associated with the road surface (road temperature, water film height, saline concentration etc.) and the WS400 sensor registers air conditions.

3   Variable Message Sign Management Algorithm

The elementary task of the road sensors is to provide input information to sign control system of variable message. Data concerning the current road condition, supplemented with information derived from the compact weather stations, are used for the automatic generation of weather warnings (Fig. 2).

In this system VMS have three limited parts for displaying warning and speed limit sings and one free programmable area for text messages. The assumptions of the warning algorithm are described in Table 2.

Fig. 2. Variable message sign and road weather station [6]

Table 2. Warning algorithm [6]

No.	Weather conditions	Limited part between lanes	Limited part over lanes	Text field
1	Road condition= freezing rain/ ice /frost/wet snow/dry snow			SLOW DOWN
2	Road condition = wet/damp			SLOW DOWN
3	Road condition different from point 1 and 2 /sensor error/ lack of readings	not active		not active

According to the presented algorithm (Table 2) the priority levels are equal to algorithm number - the highest priority has the algorithm 1. In case, road conditions are different from specified in algorithm 1–2 or there are sensor/communication errors at VMS, only the speed limit signs are displayed.

4 General Characterization of Empirically Collected Set of Data

The set of data considered in this work, consists of different meteorological and road surface conditions recorded in the time period from 3rd November 2014 to 26th January 2015. The range of variation for parameters recorded during this period of time, i.e. air temperature, road surface temperature, water film height and saline concentration are presented in Table 3. The percentage of occurrence for particular road surface condition are presented as well.

Because redundant sensors are used for collecting meteorological and road parameters, the data recorded for sensor 1 and sensor 2 can be compared directly. This comparison enables us to characterize the difference in road conditions for two lanes of the road. Figure 3 presents the comparison of road surface temperatures T_S and temperatures of freezing point T_F recorded by sensors (sensor 1 – left line, sensor 2 – right line) in the same points of time.

The analysis of the data of road surface temperatures confirms differences in road surface temperature between both road lanes, according to the difference in traffic flow [7]. The value of median for this difference of road surface temperature equals to 0.3°C, while the maximum difference equals 2.9°C. It is worth noticing that the temperatures of freezing point T_F can be significantly different for both road lanes. The reason is different saline concentration as a result of winter road maintenance process. From this point of view one can make a conclusion that using the redundant sensor has its practical reason.

Table 3. Range of variation for parameters recorded and the percentage of occurrence for particular road surface condition [own study]

Parameter	Sensor 1	Sensor 2
Air temperature	−15.6 ÷ 19°C	−15.9 ÷ 18.8°C
Road surface temperature	−12.6 ÷ 24°C	−12.7 ÷ 23.2°C
Saline concentration	0 ÷ 6 %	0 ÷ 10.6 %
Water film height	0 ÷ 1.4 mm	0 ÷ 1.4 mm
Percentage of occurrence for particular road surface condition [%]		
Dry	57.6	63
Humid	28.1	23.9
Wet	2.2	1.1
Residual salt	0.3	0.8
Critical	11.8	11.2

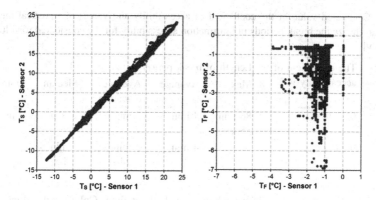

Fig. 3. The comparison of road surface temperatures T_S and temperatures of freezing point T_F recorded by sensors in the same points of time [own study]

5   Utility of Information from Road Weather Stations – An Evaluation

In the evaluation process of utility of information from road weather stations a few coefficients can be applied. Known values of these coefficients enable parameterization of the information utility with respect to meteorological and road surface condition. First, for a given time period the coefficient of accessibility w_a can be calculated. This coefficient characterizes a level of access to the data in terms of time and is calculated as follows:

$$w_a = \left(1 - \frac{\sum_{i=1}^{k} \Delta t_i}{t_t} \right) \cdot 100\% \tag{1}$$

where:

- k - number of periods of time in which the data is not recorded,
- Δt_i - length of i-th break period during recording data [min],
- t_t - the total analyzed periods of time [min] for which the coefficient of accessibility is calculated.

The value of this coefficient shows in percentage how often the data were accessible with interval of one minute, which means that the information of meteorological and surface conditions could be used in actual steering loop. The value of the coefficient of accessibility has to be analyzed in connection to values of some parameters characterizing breaks of information stream. The base parameters are statistical measures such as: average value, median value, dominant value and average deviation from average value. Formulated coefficient of accessibility and statistical measures mentioned above, supplemented with histogram presenting frequency occurrence of break periods, can be

Table 4. Calculated value of the coefficient of accessibility and values of statistical measures which characterize the break periods in information accessibility for the considered road location [own study]

Quantity	The coefficient of accessibility w_a	Length of break period				
		Max	Average	Average deviation	Median	Dominant
Sensor 1	93.3 %	86 min 55 s	4 min 41 s	3 min 8 s	3 min	2 min
Sensor 2	93.4 %		4 min 48 s	3 min 14 s	3 min 1 s	

used in order to analyze the time periods with lack of data. Calculated values of the coefficient of accessibility and statistical measures are presented in Table 4.

The difference in calculated value of the coefficient of accessibility w_a for analyzed sensor 1 and sensor 2 is a result of different number of break periods and different length of some time period. The lack of synchronic recording concerns respectively 0.3 % and 0.27 % of the total time t_t for sensor 1 and sensor 2. For majority of break periods there was no data from both sensors and it can be due to the fault of whole measurement system. The most frequent break periods were two minutes long. Histograms presenting frequency occurrence of break periods with different length respectively for sensor 1 and sensor 2 are presented in Fig. 4.

If we consider that the data in steering loop of VMS is actualized in ten minutes long intervals and break with length more than 20 min put the VMS off, analysis shows that this would happen only in 2 % cases. In order to complete the evaluation of information utility from continuity point of view, additional measures should be considered, such as: minimum and maximum length of an uninterrupted period, average value and median. Calculated values of these measures are presented in Table 5.

Analysis of the data presented in Table 5 leads to a conclusion that an average time separation between two break periods equalled the time needed for seven steering cycles. Moreover in 50 % of cases, the time separation between two break periods equaled the time needed for four steering cycles.

Taking into account the effectiveness of the steering algorithms, lack of the meteorological data has the same results as situation when the meteorological parameters were recorded but the road surface condition was not determined. Therefore, one can formulate the generalized coefficient of accessibility which additionally takes also into account these time periods, for which the road conditions are not determined.

The generalized coefficient of accessibility is calculated as follows:

$$\bar{w}_a = \left(1 - \frac{\sum_{i=1}^{k} \Delta t_i + \sum_{j=1}^{l} \Delta t_j}{t_t}\right) \cdot 100\% \qquad (2)$$

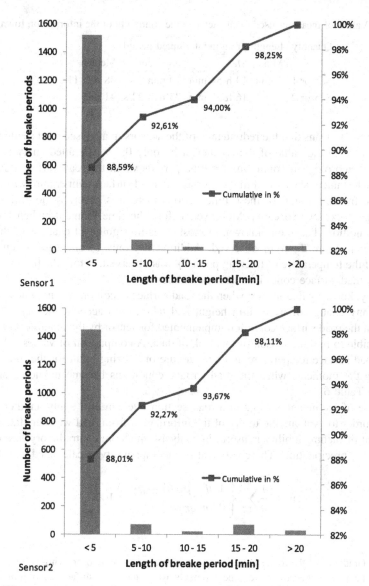

Fig. 4. Histogram presenting frequency occurrence of break periods with different length respectively for sensor 1 and sensor 2 [own study]

where:

- *l*- number of time periods for which the meteorological parameters were recorded but the road condition was not determined,
- Δt_j - length of j-th time period [min].

The value of the generalized coefficient of accessibility $\bar{w}_a$, calculated from (2) for the data analysed in this work equals 89.2 % for sensor 1 and 88.5 % for sensor 2

Table 5. Values of measures used to characterize the continuity of the information [own study]

Quantity	Length of an uninterrupted period			
	Min	Max	Average	Median
Sensor 1	2 min	19 h 54 min	70 min 3 s	38 min 11 s
Sensor 2		16 h 35 min	73 min 22 s	41 min

respectively. It means that the redundancy of the sensors in analysed road section leads to an increase in the value of the coefficient by only 0.7 %. Detailed analysis of the recorded meteorological conditions for time periods when the road surface condition was not determined, shows that in these cases the road surface temperature was always below the freezing point. In these time periods there was generally no atmospheric precipitation, except two cases. Moreover, before the time moments when the road surface conditions became unknown, in most cases no significant changes of the road surface temperature T_S were observed. Additionally, only in one case a significant change of the temperature of freezing point T_F was observed, before the time moments when the road surface conditions became unknown.

Finally, knowing that in case when the road surface condition was not known, there was not any change of water film height and taking into account the algorithm for prediction the road surface condition implemented for sensor by the manufacturer [5], it is impossible to find the reason of this lack of data. A comparison of values calculated for the road surface temperature and temperature of freezing point for the time period preceding the moments when the road surface conditions became unknown are presented in Table 6.

In case of redundant sensors in a road section one can also apply another coefficient, in order to evaluate the utility of the information from road weather station. The coefficient of incompatibility is useful in analysis which are contradictory in recorded data e.g. for precipitation. The coefficient of incompatibility is calculated as follows:

$$w_i = \frac{1}{n} \sum_{i=1}^{n} \begin{cases} 1 & if \quad p_1(t_i) \neq p_2(t_i) \\ 0 & otherwise \end{cases} 100\% \tag{3}$$

Table 6. Gradients of the road surface temperature and temperature of freezing point calculated for the time period preceding the time moments when the road surface conditions became unknown [own study]

	Range	Average	Dominant
ΔT_s [°C/min]	⟨-0.45;0⟩	-0.07	-0.15
ΔT_F [°C/min]	⟨-0.65;1.05⟩	0.08	0

where:

- n- number of time moments, for which synchronic recording from the two sensor has occurred,
- $p_j(t_i)$- value recorded for j-th sensor in time t_i.

The value of the coefficient of incompatibility equals 100 % in case of two absolutely different data time series and 0 % in case of two identical. In location considered in this work, sensors provide information about precipitation, using three discrete classes: no precipitation, rain and snow. A value of the coefficient of incompatibility w_i calculated for the data analyzed equals 6.76 %. If we consider incompatibility referring only to precipitation – no precipitation, i.e. without using distinction between kind of precipitation, the value of the coefficient is reduced by 0.1 %.

It is worth to notice, that this coefficient can by applied to measure incompatibility of air temperature recorded by redundant road station, as well. In this case the same measurement conditions have to be maintained and when comparing, the measurements accuracy should be taken into account.

6   Conclusion

In conclusion, the result of the analysis for the presented system with redundant sensors, indicates that:

- the validity of redundancy in the application to collect information about the variability of road condition for each lane,
- the lack of validity of redundancy in the context of increasing the availability of information used in the VMS management system.

The variability of road conditions between particular traffic lanes, results from a number of factors such as the roadway geometry, traffic flow rate or maintenance activities. The use of redundant sensors will be reasonable when we consider increasing the information availability only in case of using separated measuring channels and independent communication devices.

References

1. Ryguła, A., Maczyński, A., Piwowarczyk, P.: Evaluating the efficiency of road traffic management system in chorzow. In: Mikulski, J. (ed.) TST 2014. CCIS, vol. 471, pp. 424–433. Springer, Heidelberg (2014)
2. Maze, T.H., Agarwai, M., Burchett, G.: Whether weather matters to traffic demand, traffic safety, and traffic operations and flow. Transp. Res. Rec.: J. Transp. Res. Board, Management and Delivery of Maintenance and Operations Services, vol. 1948 / 2006, pp. 170–176 (2007)
3. Federal Highway Administration (FHWA). Road Weather Management Program. 556. http://ops.fhwa.dot.gov/weather/index.asp. Accessed on 2 Feburary 2015

4. Ryguła, A., Konior, A.: The integrated driver's warning system for weather hazards. Logistic No. 5/2014. The Institute of Logistics and Warehousing, Poznań (2004)
5. Lufft, G- Mess und Regeltechnik GmbH. http://lufft.com. Accessed 2 Feburary 2015
6. APM PRO sp. z o.o. materials
7. Chapman, L., Thornes, J.E.: The influence of traffic on Road surface temperatures: implications for thermal mapping studies. Meteorol. Appl. **12**, 371–380 (2005)

Computer Aided Implementation of Logistics Processes – Selected Aspects

Ilona Jacyna-Gołda[1(✉)], Konrad Lewczuk[2], Emilian Szczepański[2], and Jakub Murawski[3]

[1] Faculty of Industrial Engineering, Warsaw University of Technology, Warsaw, Poland
Jacyna.Golda@gmail.com

[2] Faculty of Transport, Warsaw University of Technology, Warsaw, Poland
{kle,eszczepanski}@wt.pw.edu.pl

[3] Faculty of Transport Doctoral Studies, Warsaw University of Technology, Warsaw, Poland
Murawski.Jakub@gmail.com

Abstract. The paper presents selected aspects of the application of information technology to support the implementation of logistics processes. The general discussion about optimization logistics processes precedes basics of designing procedure for logistics systems of different scale which are the foundation for three examples of applications tailored for micro-, and mezo-scale logistics systems. Applications are presented and discussed as tools to optimize logistics processes in aspect of their simultaneous usage to create advanced and comprehensive planning tools. Presented tools enable not only the design of selected elements of the logistics system but also allow assessing their effectiveness. An example of the possible use of applications LogMND to support shaping and dimensioning of point and linear logistic network elements and SCHED to support designing warehousing processes are given.

Keywords: Logistics processes · Decision support efficiency · Decision making process

1 Introduction

The business success is related to the implementation of logistics processes like warehousing, transhipments, transport and planning in general. The main objective is to implement logistics processes at the lowest cost, in high quality and efficiently. The role of logistics is of great importance regardless of business, so logistics departments are no longer reserved for large companies only, but also appear in the small companies with several workers. Essential elements of these departments are informatics systems and software tools tailored to the needs. Together with development, expansion and understanding of the logistics processes the set tools evolve and become more flexible, offer a wide range of integrated functionalities and stay an integral parts of logistics systems. The success or failure of business is often decided by a quality of informatics

© Springer International Publishing Switzerland 2015
J. Mikulski (Ed.): TST 2015, CCIS 531, pp. 67–80, 2015.
DOI: 10.1007/978-3-319-24577-5_7

system supporting taking rational decisions to increase productivity and effectiveness for both large corporations and small businesses.

One of the most important aspects of modern logistics is the use of multipurpose computer technologies. Special attention is given for supporting designing, control and management of complex logistic systems. The use of appropriate information systems significantly improves the logistics.

The analysis of comprehensive works like [3, 5, 6, 11] or [24] reveals that efficient and proper management of logistics processes of all scales and types is only possible with extensive use of information and telecommunications technology for (a) gathering and processing large amounts of logistics information, and (b)taking rational decisions on the base of those information. Many potential applications of computer science was pointed and discussed [8, 9, 14, 25]. They point basic modelling and optimization issues and name difficulties to be overcome by modern tools.

Selection of the right informatics tool is difficult. This is due to a wide and varied range of software developers, the overlap of functionalities and endless possibilities of configuration and modification. Therefore, it must be preceded by a thorough analysis of the business processes to identify standard elements of the processes to be covered by standard tools, custom items giving a competitive advantage, and the weakest areas to formulate expectations about the functionalities. Implementation of the informatics system should be comprised between constructing completely new solution fully matched to the business and re-adapting business to the system. The choice must be wise, because the tool unsuited to the needs not only improves its performance, but even makes it worse.

Designing logistics system requires solving subsequent logistics tasks in a way ensuring high efficiency and quality of a logistics system in total. To achieve this objective the individual elements of the system should be designed and linked up with a reliable and efficient way already at the stage of designing. The available programming languages and the rapid development of information technology provide great opportunities for dedicated, tailored computer applications suitable to support specific logistics processes.

2 Tools Supporting Decisions in Logistics Processes

Problems investigated in logistics business are in most cases complex multicriteria and multivariate issues attributed to the designing (modelling),management (operation) and controlling stage. Different objective functions can be built for these problems. Generally, the literature (compare [2, 6, 8, 10, 13] and [17, 19–22]) points three main groups of multi-criteria decision support methods:

- methods of multi-attribute utility theory,
- methods based on outranking relation,
- interactive methods, called dialog methods.

The first group is based on the aggregation of different criteria representing different points of view into one utility function to be optimized. After all, few criteria or attributes are reduced to one global parameter through the introduction of appropriate weights. Multi-attribute utility theory assumes that all variants of the problem are comparable. It means that for each pair of variants the decision maker will prefer one or accept them as equivalent.

In the second group of methods, modelling of decision maker preferences is done through outranking relationship, which permits non-comparable variants when decision maker is not able to indicate the better of the two variants. The methods of this group interleave the computational phase and the decision making phase forming a kind of dialogue with the decision-maker. In the first stage decision maker obtains a sample of compromise solutions. In the second, the sample is subjected to the assessment by introducing additional preferential information. Most of these methods are used within a multi-criteria mathematical programming. Dialog methods recently gain popularity. This is due to the fact that the decision maker has greater trust to the final result, thanks to their involvement in the process of solving the problem.

Today's information systems, despite being dedicated to specific areas of the business, embrace a wider area of interest. Integrated information systems consist of interconnected modules representing different groups of functions. Due to the variety of logistics processes throughout the supply chain, the implementation of these processes is supported by different solutions (selected instances) like:

Supplier Relationship Management – for the comprehensive management of purchasing and supply.

Enterprise Resource Planning – for the comprehensive management of purchasing and supply.

Warehouse Management System – for managing warehouse processes.

Customer Relationship Management – including all kinds of business processes related to the broader customer service.

Distribution Resource Planning – for managing distribution networks.

Supply Chain Management – for building a competitive advantage and integrating supply chains.

Transport Management System – for managing transport operations.

Advanced Planning Systems – specialized tools for planning in logistics.

The above-mentioned integrated information systems are used in different areas of logistics business and on different operational levels. These are the examples of typical solutions created on the base of best practices developed by business of different kinds. All businesses have their own requirements and specificities influencing informatics tools. Actually it is not possible to run a logistics business without those tools according to the rule that purchasing and distribution cycle is much shorter that production cycle. It means that some kind of planning is necessary at all levels of supply chain, and also these supply chains must be integrated into a global network for high efficiency, shorter response time, wider offer and lower costs.

Especially the last item – Advanced Planning Systems, is interesting for logistics planning, organization and designing. APS is a type of system tracking costs based on the activities that are responsible for driving costs in the production, distribution or even warehousing. An APS can allocate raw materials and production capacity optimally to balance demand and plant capacity or allocate handling and transport resources to the tasks. Advanced tools are in most cases tailor-made so include specific criteria and objective functions to support detailed processes.

The applications created for specific processes compete with market tools and systems. Own applications have advantage of full coverage of specific business processes and – plausibly – higher efficiency, but usually are not flexible, difficult to modify and need interfaces to other systems. Due to the very different requirements, companies are increasingly looking for computer tools prepared exclusively for their needs and combining features of specialized applications and standard systems based on best practices. Specialized tools for solving decision problems are based on algorithms that allow obtaining a solution in the acceptable time when using appropriate heuristics (like genetic programming) and hybrid algorithms. The following sections will discuss some original tools supporting the logistics process in different aspects.

3   Logistics Systems Designing Procedure

The logistics system is composed of subjects operating in production, supply, distribution and transport area. These elements are engaged according to material flow through superior and subordinated dependences, realizing various activities in order to supply products and services to the final consumer (see [5, 8, 10] or [17]). Logistic systems of different kinds and scales need different tools to be designed and operated, but there are some basic principles forming designing procedure[12].

Logistics system design should be carried out according to defined stages. Each stage should take into account analyse of logistics processes and burden of individual elements of the system, on the required level of detail necessary to identify actual situation, and to propose a cost and technologically effective solution. Full scope of design works of logistic system should contain (Fig. 1):

1. Analysis of the problem;
2. Identification of design data;
3. Formulation of logistics tasks;
4. The configuration (conceptualization) of design variants based on available data;
5. Dimensioning (counting) preferred variants;
6. Simulation of the logistics system operation in selected technological variants;
7. Selection of the best option in terms of specific criteria.

Presented procedure is a general conclusion made in terms of review of handbooks and fundamental publications like [5, 22] or [23]. Each step can be carried out at different levels of detail depending on the progress of the design work. Regardless of the size and complexity of designed (or analysed) logistics system, the first stage is dedicated to formulation of the logistics tasks carried out by the system. This allows getting qualitative and quantitative data about structure of material and information

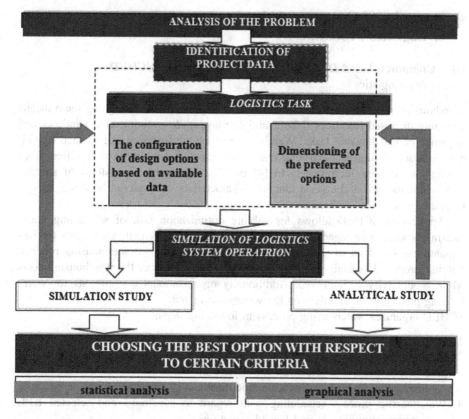

Fig. 1. Diagram of the procedure of logistics systems design [own study]

flows on entrance and on exit from the system and its surroundings. At this stage the evaluation criteria are set to reflect a point of view of decision makers.

The conceptualization means forming processes of material and information flows and selecting proper handling technologies to ensure the implementation of a specific logistics task in a few variants reflecting comparable alternatives. Conceptualized process is dimensioned to reveal necessary work forces, spaces, and time to perform logistics tasks in pursuance of selected evaluation criteria. The last stage is for selecting rational variant on the base of adopted criteria through multi-criteria evaluation.

As already mentioned, there are different areas of implementation that are characteristic for micro-, mezo- and macro logistics. On these three levels different applications can be used for logistics processes optimization. These application will cover more or less detailed processes, but when combined can be used as an engines for integrated tools of supply chain optimization.

4 Examples of Computer Aided Implementation of Logistics Processes

4.1 Computer Aided Design of Warehousing Process (SCHED) – Micro-logistics

Warehousing processes are crucial elements of supply chains. Designing them means assigning disposed resources (labour and equipment),determining time windows and sequence of warehousing tasks. Warehouse process organization can be then considered as a scheduling problem with many processors, but it significantly differs from classic formulations (compare[1] to [4] or [7]), especially the systems of specific technical constrains and criteria functions characteristic for material handling subsystems are difficult for application.

Application SCHED allows for solving optimization task of scheduling warehousing process with regard to complex of KPIs, especially realization costs for formulated cases and set of specified constrains characteristic for warehousing process. Solving proposed task allows finding rational schedule to cut the warehousing costs while productivity is improved. Additionally organizational assumptions for warehousing process have an effect on the warehouse layout.

SCHED organizes warehousing process in following steps:

1. Defining tasks emerging from client's orders and warehousing technology.
2. Defining the sequence of cause and effect for warehousing tasks with resultant of process constrains and priorities.
3. Assigning optional resources to identified tasks.
4. Warehousing process scheduling with regard to constrains and selected KPIs (genetic programming to find feasible solution).

The main criteria function minimizes daily labour consumption normalized by work costs. The final measure of the quality of warehousing process is total realization cost.

Having data about warehouse tasks and their duration, disposed labour and technical resources and technological constrains a decision makers can use a SCHED application to set and manage efficient and economical warehousing process which is base for capacity planning in supply chains. The following example shows the point.

For a warehousing process consisting of nine tasks one compared different variants of organization. Facility works for 290 days per year for a one working shift per day. Daily work time is divided into twelve 40-minute time intervals. The task parameters and constrains are presented in Table 1.

There are four types of resources assigned to tasks presented in Table 2. Resources have been detailed into labour categories and types of handling equipment.

Warehousing process was organized with regard to task constrains presented in Table 1. Variants of schedule are characterized by different values of criteria function and are classified in Table 3. All calculations were performer with application SCHED. Table 3 gathers appropriate characteristic for each solution.

Figure 2 presents chart of reduced workload for the process in solution no. 2.

Table 1. The parameters and constrains of warehousing process tasks [own study]

Task	Daily number of cycles	Time of single cycle (h)	Task workload (work-hours)	Resource type	Constrains
1	302	0,028618	8,643	1	Minimal realization time 80 min*) Schedule granulation 2 × 40 min. Must be finished before task $i = 2$
2	302	0,036387	10,989	2	Can't be realized in 1,2,3 time period Schedule granulation 2 × 40 min. Must be finished before task $i = 1$
3	218	0,00543	1,184	4	Schedule granulation 3 × 40 min. Non-parallel with $i = 4$
4	145	0,021138	3,065	1	Schedule granulation 3 × 40 min. Non-parallel with $i = 3$
5	314	0,033953	10,661	1	Schedule granulation 1 × 40 min.
6	338	0,034575	11,686	3	Can't be realized in 11,12 time period Schedule granulation 1 × 40 min.
7	160	0,013862	2,218	4	Can't be realized in 1,2,3,4 t. period Schedule granulation 2 × 40 min.
8	110	0,019397	2,134	1	Schedule granulation 2 × 40 min.
9	198	0,025693	5,087	2	Schedule granulation 2 × 40 min.

*) mandatory for all tasks

Table 2. Resources for warehousing process realization [own study]

Resource type	Handling equipment type	Unit cost of equipment work k^u ($/h)	Labor category	Unit cost of labor category k^u ($/h)	Utilization of working time for a resource
1	1	7,00	1	6,19	0,81
2	2	4,00	2	4,54	0,765
3	2	4,00	1	6,19	0,765
4	0 (manual work)	–	3	7,01	0,9

Table 3. Results gained in SCHED application [own study]

Solution no.	Number of people (labor category)			Number of equipment (type of equipment)		Number of resources (resource = equipment + labor category)				Reduced workload (work-hours)	Annual operational costs ($/year)
	1	2	3	1	2	1	2	3	4		
1	8	5	2	6	7	7	6	3	2	17,377	203775,9
2	8	4	2	6	7	6	5	3	2	16,127	193038,4
3	7	4	2	5	7	6	5	3	2	15,046	178442,2
4	7	4	1	5	7	6	5	3	1	15,046	161782,8
5	7	4	1	5	6	6	4	3	1	14,823	161782,8
6	7	3	1	5	5	5	4	3	1	13,141	151045,2
7	6	3	1	4	5	5	4	3	1	12,632	136449,1
8	6	3	1	4	5	4	4	3	1	11,856	136449,1

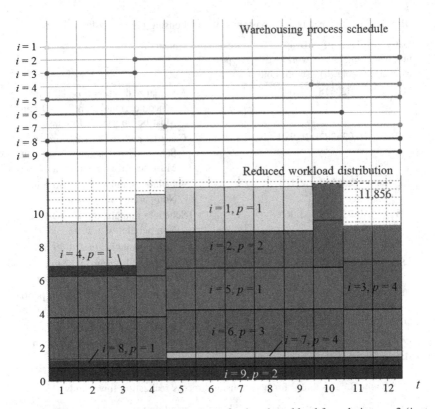

Fig. 2. Warehouse process schedule with chart of reduced workload for solution no. 2 (i – task number, p – resource number) [own work]

4.2   Computer Aided Organization of Logistics Network for Supply and Distribution of Production Companies by LogMND – Mezo-Logistics

LogMND application supports design of logistics network for production with the location and designing of storage facilities. The algorithm of the application is presented in Fig. 3 and discussed in [15, 16, 18].

Application offers optimization module consisting of two procedures designating the optimal locations of storage facilities and designating rational transportation plan, module for dimensioning of storage facility–can operate independently of other parts of the application and set cost and productivity characteristics, and module of modification storage facility location – a modification of network configuration, to realize logistic tasks with minimum resources. The flow volumes on distribution network are estimated by Busacker-Gowen algorithm.

The LogMND application uses variant data about production needs with detailed information on particular assortments, capacity of suppliers, potential locations of

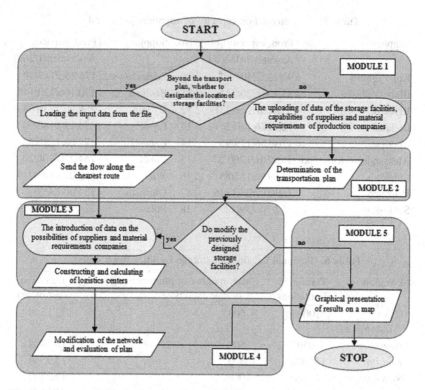

Fig. 3. The overall block diagram of the LogMND computer application [own study]

Table 4. Material needs of production companies in variant approach [own study]

No.	Production company	Variant I	Variant II
		Assortment 1/2/3/4 in option W1	Assortment 1/2/3/4 option W2
1	Baborów	240/140/220/140	300/150/220/180
2	Kamienica Polska	250/340/180/230	380/300/200/300
3	Lipnica Murowana	350/190/250/209	180/400/50/220
4	Kowal	150/270/190/150	250/330/220/100
5	Solec-Zdrój	190/336/320/250	400/500/20/90
6	Stopnica	120/310/230/270	120/80/100/300

storage facilities with terrain limitations and minimum material flow volumes to run a storage facility and transition cost assigned to flow volumes.

The application is used to set potential locations of storage facilities on the logistics network and to set a capacity of those facilities. Additional parameters like warehouse capacity, daily incomes and outcomes, basic dimensions of functional areas of the warehouse, number of equipment and employees, technical and efficiency cost parameters and investment expenditures are set. The program allows for graphical

Table 5. The production capacity of suppliers [own study]

No.	Supplier	Prod. capacity [plu] Assortment1/2/3/4	No.	Supplier	Prod. capacity [plu] Assortment1/2/3/4
1	Kołczygłowy	90/135/250/330	10	Zdzieszowice	176/155/147/70
2	Biała Podlaska	85/133/220/244	11	Bochnia	170/166/220/148
3	Brzozów	117/167/218/231	12	Dydnia	286/90/223/101
4	Bielawa	120/276/150/261	13	Lipsk	275/120/180/90
5	Chodzież	170/156/119/95	14	Czeladź	177/68/128/292
6	Aleksandrów Kujawski	182/201/126/120	15	Łobez	164/230/90/220
7	Lubiszyn	112/150/155/85	16	Wieliczki	103/223/120/219
8	Drużbice	169/197/340/245	17	Oleśnica	134/30/84/90
9	Siedlisko	155/70/239/129	18	Puławy	224/169/137/170

Table 6. Potential locations of storage facilities [own study]

Lp.	Location	Terrain limitations	Min. number of plu required to run a storage facility	Transition cost of plu
1	Czarna Dąbrówka	10000	600	12,15 zł
2	Augustów	9500	500	15,74 zł
3	Korczyn	150000	300	15,33 zł
4	Siewierz	12000	1000	12,22 zł
5	Braniewo	10000	800	41,67 zł
6	Drelów	10000	500	23 zł
7	Santok	9000	600	34,23 zł
8	Zelów	10000	400	17,06 zł

Table 7. Selected parameters of storage facilities obtained from the **LogMND**, variant I/II [own study]

	Variant I/II	Variant I/II	Variant I/II	Variant I/II
Parameter	Drelów/Augustów	Korczyn/Korczyn	Siewierz/Siewierz	Zelów/Zelów
Warehouse capacity (pallets)	1014/1220	4921/4077	2883/3406	2544/2424
Daily pallet input	152/183	739/612	433/511	382/264
Daily pallet output	178/214	862/714	505/596	446/425
Daily return of empty pallets	21/25	100/83	59/69	52/50
Total expenditures	1843036/2100012	6781062/5543274	4010110/4833476	3794504/3560540
Annual exploitation costs	359854/415565	1477849/1176019	814639/1045014	793078/739669
Total cost of labour	329280/403760	1540560/1211280	807520/1062320	807520/733040
Average transition cost per pallet	19,43/19,19	17,53/16,73	16,08/17,68	17,98/17,36
Cubature per pallet	6,11/5,83	4,5/4,53	4,77/4,6	5/4,9

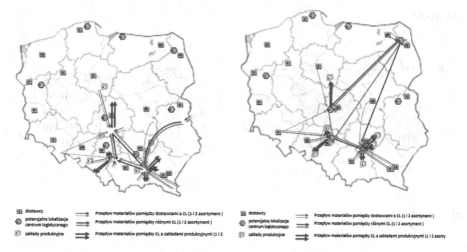

Fig. 4. Flow volumes between elements of logistics network in variant I in assortment structure 1 and 2 [own study]

Fig. 5. Flow volumes between elements of logistics network in variant II in assortment structure 1 and 2 [own study]

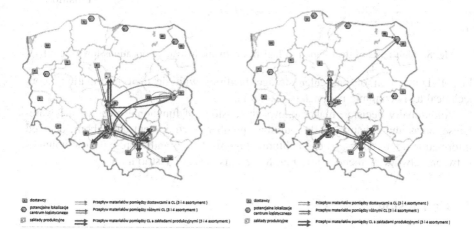

Fig. 6. Flow volumes between elements of logistics network in variant I in assortment structure 3 and 4 [own study]

Fig. 7. Flow volumes between elements of logistics network in variant II in assortment structure 3 i 4 [own study]

illustration of material flows, locations and characteristics of designed system. Detailed examples of usage are presented in [17].

The implementation of the LogMND can be presented on the example. Table 4 presents material needs of production companies. The locations of suppliers and their supply possibilities are given in Table 5. Locations of potential storage facilities, including terrain limitations, unit costs of transition and minimum number of required units are presented in Table 6. As a result of the optimization decision maker gets from

a) variant

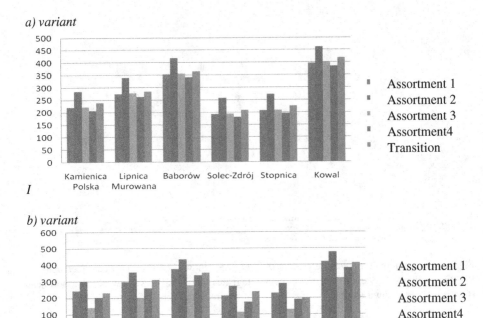

b) variant

Fig. 8. Unit costs of distribution in logistics network for variant locations [own study]

LogMND location of particular storage facilities with detailed information about technical and economic parameters (Table 7).

Additionally decision maker knows dimensions of functional areas of the warehouse, areas and cubature of the building, number of equipment and labour, detailed information about costs and expenditures. Figures 4, 5, 6 and 7 present flow volumes between network elements while Fig. 8 presents costs of distribution.

5   Conclusion

Presented tools are tailored to special applications, therefore can be extremely useful for decision makers in studying complex logistics systems starting from defining their elements up to the systems influencing regional economy. They allow quickly and without lot of work to determine whether the newly designed system will operate without interruption and ensure the implementation of assumed logistics tasks. Tailor-made tools are an important condition of analysis variants of logistics system organization and technology.

Presented tools enable not only the designing of selected elements of the logistics system but also allow assessing their operational effectiveness. Decision support with computer techniques for companies of TSL market is necessitated by searching for optimal solutions, while increasing productivity and trading of their companies. This applies to both large and small companies.

Applications can support designer's work in solving problems of different level. Detailed example touches the problems of logistics network configuration for transport and warehousing services with particular emphasis put on the location of objects like distribution centres, hubs, and intermodal terminals.

Presented applications allow solving problems on different levels of difficulty and complication. These kinds of solutions can be a base for advanced planning applications prepared for specified usage by network developers.

References

1. Ambroziak, T., Lewczuk, K.: A method for scheduling the goods receiving process in warehouse facilities, Total Logistic Management. Annual no.1, pp. 7–14. AGH University of Science and Technology Press, Kraków (2008)
2. Ballou, R.H.: DISPLAN: a multiproduct plant/warehouse location model with nonlinear inventory cost. J. Oper. Manage. 5(1), 75–90 (1984)
3. Bechtel, C., Jayaram, J.: Supply chain management: a strategic perspective. Int. J. Logist. Manage. 8(1), 15–34 (1997)
4. Błażewicz, J., et al.: Handbook on Scheduling. From Theory to Applications. Springer, Heidelberg (2007)
5. Bowersox, D.J., Cross, D.J., Cooper, M.B.: Supply Chain Management. Mc Graw-Hill, New York (2002)
6. Bramel, J., Simchi-Levi, D.: The Logic of Logistics: Theory, Algorithms, and Applications for Logistic Management. Springer Series in Operations Research. Springer-Verlag New York, Inc., New York (1997)
7. Bruckner, P.: Scheduling Algorithms. Springer, Heidelberg (2007)
8. Dolgui, A., Soldek, J., Zaikin, O.: Applied Optimization: Supply Chain Optimization, Produkt/Process Design, Facility Location and Flow Control. Springer Scence + Business Media Inc., Boston (2005)
9. House, R.G., Karrenbauer, J.J.: Logistics system modelling. Int. J. Phys. Distrib. Mater. Manage. (IJPD & MM) 8(4), 189–199 (1978)
10. Jachimowski, R., Żak, J.: Vehicle routing problem with heterogeneous customers demand and external transportation costs. J. Traffic Logist. Eng. 1(1), 46–50 (2013)
11. Jacyna, M., Wasiak, M. (eds.): Simulation Model to Support Designing a Sustainable National Transport System. Index Copernicus International, Warsaw (2014)
12. Jacyna, M.: Distribution warehouses and realisation of logistic processes of logistic in supply chains. Arch. Transp. Polish Acad. Sci. Com. Transp. 20(3), 5–20 (2008). ISSN 0866-5946
13. Jacyna, M., Szczepański, E.: An approach to optimize the cargo distribution in urban areas. Logist. Transp. 17(1), 53–62 (2013). ISSN: 1734-2015
14. Jacyna, M., Żak, J.: Computer Techniques as Innovative Tool Supporting Decision Making Process Within Waste Collection in Cities. Logist. Transp. 19(3), 13–25 (2013)
15. Jacyna-Gołda, I.: Chosen aspects of logistics network design method for production service companies. Int. J. Logist. Syst. Manage. 15(2–3), 219–238 (2013)

16. Jacyna-Gołda, I., Żak J.: Selected aspects of the optimization the structure of logistic system. In: Proceedings - 21st International Conference on Systems Engineering, ICSEng, pp. 438–441 (2011)
17. Jacyna-Gołda, I.: Evaluation of operational reliability of the supply chain in terms of the control and management of logistics processes. In: Nowakowski T. et. al. (eds.) Safety and Reliability: Methodology and Applications. CRC Press Taylor & Francis Group, pp. 549-558 (2015). ISBN 978-1-138-02681-0
18. Jacyna-Gołda, I.: Logistics network design for production service companies. In: Proceedings of International Conference on Industrial Logistics, ICIL 2012, pp. 219-224, Brazil, Finland, Croatia, Zadar (2012). ISSN 978-953-7738-16-7
19. Lewczuk, K., Wasiak, M.: Transportation services costs allocation for the delivery system. In: Proceedings of 21st International Conference on System Engineering, 16–18 August 2011, Las Vegas, Nevada, USA (2011). DOI:10.1109/ICSEng.2011.84
20. Lewczuk, K.: Selected aspects of organizing order-picking process with dynamic assignment of material to locations. In: Carpathian Logistics Congress, CLC 2012, pp. 565–571 (2012)
21. Lewczuk, K.: Wybrane aspekty projektowania terminali cross-dockingowych, Prace Naukowe PW Transport 97, pp: 327–336, OWPW, Warsaw (2013)
22. Stadtler, H., Kilger, C.: Supply Chain Management and Advanced Planning. Concepts, Models, Software and Case Studies, 3rd edn. Springer, Heidelberg (2005)
23. Sule, D.R.: Logistics of Facility Location and Allocation. Marcell Dekker Inc., New York (2001)
24. Szczepański, E., Jacyna-Gołda, I., Murawski, J.: Genetic algorithms based approach for transshipment HUB location in urban areas. Arch. Transp. 31(3), 73–82 (2014)
25. Wasiak, M.: Simulation model of logistic system. Arch. Transp. 21(3–4), 189–206 (2009)

Algorithm for Analysis of Road Surface Degradation

Marián Hruboš[(⊠)], Aleš Janota, and Igor Miklóšik

Department of Control and Information Systems,
University of Žilina, Univerzitná1, 01026 Žilina, Slovakia
{Marian.Hrubos,Ales.Janota,
Igor.Miklosik}@fel.uniza.sk

Abstract. The paper presents results obtained by the algorithm designed to analyze road surface degradation based on a 3D model. The model is generated from measured data collected by the mobile measurement platform. Results of the analysis help to estimate further development of different types of degradations of road surface such as cracks, pot-holes, rutting and shoving, deterioration, local deformations or beaten longitudinal tracks. The advantage of the solution is the knowledge of the precise GPS position coordinates of all defects identified in the road surface. Estimation of progress of further damaging process of road surface and the future state of its degradation then can be utilized for better determination of the time frame for road repairs. The proposed algorithm respects and considers regulations and procedures actually used by the Slovak Road Administration and applied for the road I and II classes as well as for motorways and expressways.

Keywords: Point cloud · 3D model · Road surface · Degradation · Data processing · Analysis

1 Introduction

The ever-increasing intensity of road transport has adverse effects on the quality of communications. Different types of disturbances resulting from road surface damages such as cracks, longitudinal and transverse bumps, local declines, potholes, wavy surface or beaten longitudinal gauge may negatively influence ride comfort [1].

To measure deformations of road surface many methods and measuring equipment have been developed so far. One large group of measuring devices utilizes unique properties of laser measurement systems. These contactless methods are based on measurement of the time-of-flight of laser pulses and make possible to measure a distance between the laser measuring device and the object on road surface.

In our research we have focused on measurement of macrotexture up to unevenness. The laser measuring device enables us to make precise measurement of the road surface and then create its 3D model formed by the cloud of points. Generally, point clouds may be acquired with stereo cameras, monocular systems or laser scanners. There are many methods and approaches available such as those discussed in [2] and based on extraction of so called "feature points"; or others [3] that define the surface as

© Springer International Publishing Switzerland 2015
J. Mikulski (Ed.): TST 2015, CCIS 531, pp. 81–89, 2015.
DOI: 10.1007/978-3-319-24577-5_8

the isosurface of a trivariate volume model, or many others. Once all the points have been processed, we get a model which is ready for application of the texture. Thus our algorithm is able to analyze degradation of the road surface based on this 3D model.

Thanks to results of analysis it is then possible to develop a system capable of alerting drivers who are approaching an inequality or potentially any other defect found in the road surface. On the basis of long-term measurements it is also possible to estimate the next evolution of disturbances in the road surface. Measurements could be automated and performed for example by robots and thus one could monitor existing disorders, their size, and in the case of improper and/or alarming conditions to schedule a repair of the damaged road surface.

This paper was written with motivation to take up the previously published findings on measurement and visualization of road surface degradation [1] and to present new knowledge resulting from our recently continued research.

1.1 Equipment Used in Slovakia

Every country has a certain competent institution which is responsible for operation and maintenance of its road network. For example, in the Czech Republic it is the Road and Motorway Directorate which operates several diagnostic vehicles (ARAN, ARGUS, TRT and SKM). As far as Slovakia is concerned, at present the Slovak Road Administration uses the Profilograph GE [5] - a multifunctional measuring device designed to measure road surface degradation with the help of 16 laser scanners. Its movement is recorded by three accelerometers and two gyroscopes. Subsequently data can be exported into the output file of the pg2 type (Fig. 1).

1.2 Technical Specifications Used in Slovakia

In 1994 Slovakia began the process of systematic construction of its road database (known under abbreviation CDB) necessary for collection, processing and evaluation of data on the state road network. This step has made possible to provide objective information about conditions of the roads and facilities, phenomena and circumstances affecting their quality. For the purpose of assessment of the qualitative status of the road a clear definition of the technical road condition is important. This is the summary of the quantities of the selected criteria determining the level, function and road transport needs. Following data analysis, it determines operational capacity of the road as a summary of the characteristics of the road depending on the instantaneous value of the variable parameters, i.e. of roughness, equality and surface condition. Provided that the prescribed values are kept, continuous, rapid, economical and safe driving of motor vehicles may be ensured.

Technical parameters of roadway scan be divided into two groups:

- Fixed parameters: they vary only by conscious intervention or natural disaster. (Width arrangement of communication, geometric routing, etc.)
- Variable parameters: they indicate the physical-mechanical properties of roads changed by weather and transport effects.

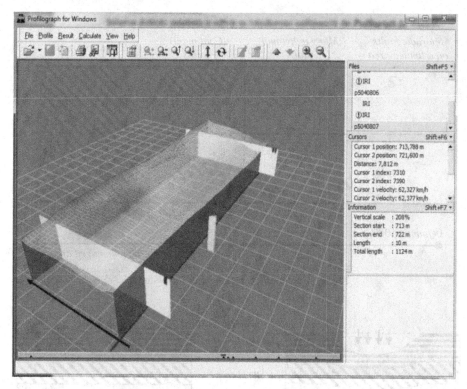

Fig. 1. A sample model of road surface generated by the profilograph GE [5]

Equality of road surface is a prerequisite for ensuring road safety, passenger comfort and comfort of other road users, efficient cost of operation (fuel economy) and resource savings in maintenance (less wear on vehicles and road).

There are two basic types of inequalities in relation to maintenance (Fig. 2):

– Local inequalities that arise from breaches of road surface. With good maintenance, these disorders did not occur on the road.
– Persistent inequalities that occur during the life of the road. They cannot be removed by normal maintenance.

Inequalities may further be divided into:

– Periodic inequalities - consist of either a sine wave around or cosine shape or recurring inequalities,
– Local inequalities - potholes, bumps, drops inlets, …
– Stochastic inequalities – they have a random character.

Permanent deformations occur most frequently in the form of waves, which may have the form of ruts. There are two basic types of permanent deformations (Fig. 3):

– Deformation in the whole structure of the road,
– Ruts which are formed in the upper layers of asphalt.

Faults:

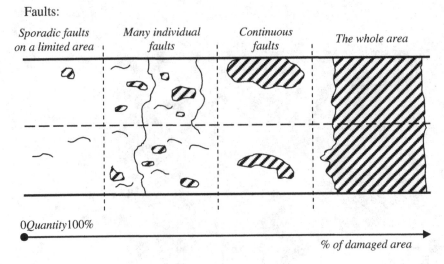

Fig. 2. Evolution of disturbances [own study]

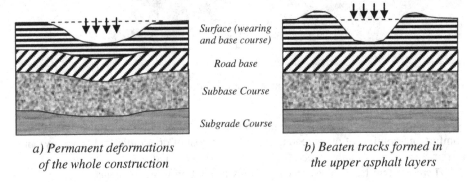

*a) Permanent deformations
of the whole construction*

*b) Beaten tracks formed in
the upper asphalt layers*

Fig. 3. Basic types of permanent deformations [own study]

The fault that occurs on the road surface has tendency to expand in time to all directions or even in depth. The intensity of development disorders in depth depends on the qualitative development disorders (Fig. 4).

2 The Algorithm for Detection of Road Surface Degradation

To process a cloud of points we use our own algorithm that incorporates a real position of the measurement equipment and tilts in all axes. The algorithm makes data fusion possible for data obtained by the Global Positioning System (GPS) receiver, Inertial Navigation System (INS) and the laser scanner. A similar algorithm for calculation of trajectory was presented in the paper [7]. We are able to calculate trajectory of the measurement platform using video information. More details about the method can be

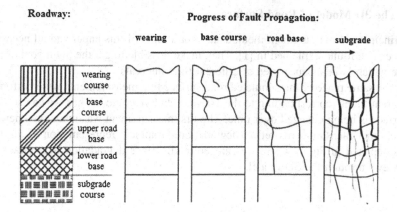

Fig. 4. Evolution of road surface deformations [own study]

found in the publication [8]. To be compatible with many of the common visualization approaches (such as MeshLab, Blender, CloudCompare), our preferred format type of the output data file is *. OBJ since it is suitable for display of objects in the three-dimensional space.

2.1 The Mobile Measurement Platform

The concept of our mobile measurement platform (Fig. 5) is based on getting and fusing data obtained by the specified devices and their fast processing. The primary data are obtained by 2 two-dimensional (2D) laser scanners. The measurement platform integrates them with seven cameras, GPS and INS receivers, server, switch and UPS. The SPAN CTP navigation system helps to get precise position of the measurement platform itself [4, 6].

All the equipment was obtained within the project "ITMS-26220220089 New methods of measurement of physical parameters and dynamic interactions of motor vehicles, traffic flow and road conditions" financed from the European regional development funds.

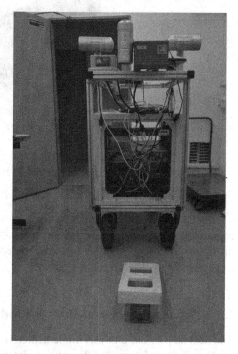

Fig. 5. The mobile measurement platform captured in the laboratory conditions [photo by authors

2.2   The 3D Model of Road Surface

The principles of measurement methods are not a topic of this paper and all necessary details can be found explained in [1]. They make possible to get the 3D model of road surface which is being measured at different time intervals.

At the same place of the simulated road surface five measurements were performed in different times (corresponding to the 1st year, 2nd year, etc.). Thus we can see how the surface is being changed over time. The first measurement was made on a new flat surface, other measurements reflect degradation. Graphical representation of this process is depicted in Fig. 6 where we can see road surface degradation over time (negative view) through the 3D model.

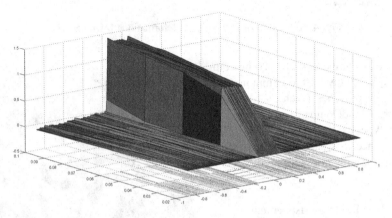

Fig. 6. The 3D model of (simulated) road surface degradation [own study]

Figure 7 shows the gradual deepening of the degradation profile (Note: there is a negative and therefore enlarged representation). For a better understanding of the displayed cross section of the measured object, the algorithm shows each section of the measurement.

2.3   The Algorithm for Analysis of Road Surface Degradation

The next step of our analysis implemented in our algorithm is calculation of the rate of change of degradation at different time intervals. In the figure we can see the gradual deepening of road surface degradation (shown inverted - increasing). The algorithm calculates the increase of degradation depth over time, and this information is displayed in Fig. 8.

After calculation of gains in each of the measured sections the algorithm calculates the largest increase in a section and then the data are plotted in Fig. 9.

Based on these increments we can determine the rate of change of the surface and also whether the rate of change is in accordance with the technical rules used by the

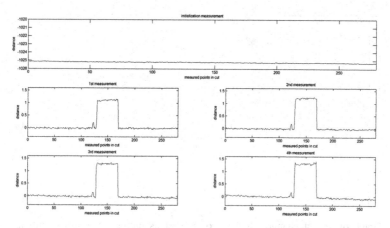

Fig. 7. The 3D model of road surface degradation in each cut [own study]

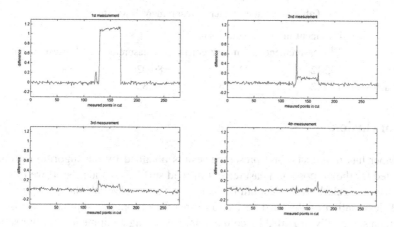

Fig. 8. Increment in each measurement [own study]

Slovak Road Administration. In their technical rules the maximum rate of change of depressions is set to 1 mm depth for one year. This parameter is implemented in our algorithm. In the picture we can see two stages displayed as two horizontal lines. From the graph, we can also see how much this limit was exceeded. For a better understanding of the evolution of degradation, we have integrated into the algorithm the calculation of exceeding the boundaries of each year and the sum of years. In the table we can see the value (in percentage) of exceeding the limit 1 mm/1year and how much (in percentage) the threshold for each year (1st year - 1 mm; 2nd year - 2 mm; 3rd year - 3 mm...) was exceeded (Table 1).

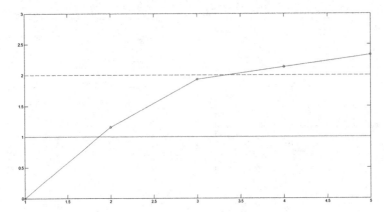

Fig. 9. Graph of rate of change where x-axis represents individual measurements and y-axis deformation depth in mm [own study]

Table 1. Value of each measurement [own study]

	Increment in one measurement [%]			
	1st measurement	2nd measurement	3rdmeasurement	4th measurement
One year	15,312	−22,108	−80,026	−80,16
Each year	15,312	−6,796	−86,822	−266,982

3 Conclusion

This paper has introduced and presented results obtained by our algorithm proposed and tested for the purpose of measurement of road surface degradation. If we measured road surface regularly with a certain frequency, we could also calculate and provide the rate of degradation of the road surface in time. The proposed approach seems to be better than standardly provided by commercial measuring equipment since our solution also provides higher resolution (the number of measured points per scan). The advantage of this solution is the precise knowledge of the GPS position coordinates of the defect in the road surface. The estimation of the future state of degradation of road surface then can be used to determine and plan the time frame for repairs of the road. Implementation of our algorithm considers actually valid regulations and procedures used by the Slovak Road Administration for road classes I and II and also for motorways and expressways. Based on our analysis, it is then possible to create a system that would be able to alert drivers when approaching inequalities about conditions of the road surface.

Acknowledgments. This work has been supported by the Educational Grant Agency of the Slovak Republic (KEGA) within the project "KEGA 010ŽU-4/2013 Modernization of didactic equipment and teaching methods with a focus on the area of robotics".

References

1. Hruboš, M., Janota, A.: Road surface degradation – measurement and visualization. In: Mikulski, J. (ed.) TST 2014. CCIS, vol. 471, pp. 1–10. Springer, Heidelberg (2014)
2. Toll, B., Cheng, F.: Surface reconstruction from point clouds. In: Olling, G.J., Choi, B.K., Jerard, R.B. (eds.) MIS. IFIP, vol. 18, pp. 173–178. Springer, Heidelberg (1999)
3. Huang, A., Nielson, G.M.: Surface approximation to point cloud data using volume modeling. In: Post, E.H., Nielson, G.M., Bonneau, G.P. (eds.) Data Visualization. SISEC, vol. 713, pp. 333–343. Springer, Heidelberg (2003)
4. Halgaš, J., Janota, A.: Technical devices cooperation to obtain data for 3D environment modelling. In: Mikulski, J. (ed.) TST 2011. CCIS, vol. 239, pp. 330–337. Springer, Heidelberg (2011)
5. Hruboš, M.: Nástroj na zistenie stavu degradácie vozovky v čase (A Tool to Detect Status of Road Degradation in Time). MSc. thesis No. 28260220122010, Dept. of Control & Information Systems, University of Žilina, Slovakia, p. 77 (2012)
6. Halgaš, J., Hruboš, M., Pirník, R., Janota, A.: determination of formulas for processing of measured points representing road surface deformations. In: Mikulski, J. (ed.) TST. CCIS, vol. 329. Springer, Heidelberg (2012)
7. Šimák, V., Nemec, D., Hrbček, J., Janota, A.: Inertial navigation: improving precision and speed of euler angles computing from MEMS gyroscope data. In: Mikulski, J. (ed.) TST 2013. CCIS, vol. 395, pp. 163–170. Springer, Heidelberg (2013)
8. Bubeníková, E., Franeková, M., Holečko, P.: Security increasing trends in intelligent transportation systems utilising modern image processing methods. In: Mikulski, J. (ed.) TST 2013. CCIS, vol. 395, pp. 353–360. Springer, Heidelberg (2013)

Safety Analysis of Accidents Call System Especially Related to In-Land Water Transport Based on New Telematic Solutions

Tomasz Perzyński[✉], Andrzej Lewiński, and Zbigniew Łukasik

Faculty of Transport and Electrical Engineering,
University of Technology and Humanities in Radom,
Malczewskiego 29, 26-600 Radom, Poland
{t.perzynski,a.lewinski,z.lukasik}@uthrad.pl

Abstract. In the paper the analysis of e-call system informing about accidents in land transport with application of public standards GSM and GPS is shown. Based on Markov processes the two models are introduced: reliability model for hardware and behavioral model describing man-system co-operation (including level of equipment and environmental conditions together with weather). The reliability and maintenance parameters correspond to typical reliability characteristics of GPS/GSM devices and time characteristics related to service, monitoring and management of critical events using such devices. Presented results (probabilistic and time) may be also adapted to another applications such mountain tourism and extreme sports, but even in railway transport with GPS positioning in the regional lines (without typical centralized railway control infrastructure).

Keywords: Transport safety · Telematic transport systems · Markov models

1 Introduction

One of the elements of the use of modern telematics solutions in land transport is among other thing improvement the functionality and increasing the safety level. The influence of new solutions is a part of the safety studies in transport [5], including driver behavior [8, 9]. Modern ICT (*Information and Communication Technologies*) solutions take information from sensors and cameras and allow for safer movement of objects (cars, trains, boats). In addition, in the event of an incident (a road traffic collision, capsizing the boat) allows to faster their localization and sending the appropriate emergency services. One of the priorities, when it comes to road transport, is to build an appropriate infrastructure to receive reports of traffic accidents (ang. *Public Safety Answering Point* - PSAP).In Poland the function of PSAP fulfil the *Rescue Notification Center "112"* (pol. CPR).Such projects are part of the European Commission's strategy, and its part is *e-Call* system. The paper presents an analysis of the notification system about an accident in land transport, using GSM and GPS standard. Information about the location of the transport object with a number of passengers at the time of the dangerous event (immediately life-threatening) getting from the GPS together with additional data is transmitted to the monitoring center

© Springer International Publishing Switzerland 2015
J. Mikulski (Ed.): TST 2015, CCIS 531, pp. 90–98, 2015.
DOI: 10.1007/978-3-319-24577-5_9

on the GSM connection. For cars it is the extension of the *e-Call* system, but similar system is proposed to the yachts on inland waters [4, 5]. It is the authors' original concept, designed to show how the combination of this type of equipment can significantly improve safety. In the rail transport such solution is based on GSM-R, [2, 3]. In this case GSM-R cooperate with typical identification train devices (for example – balise, insulate rail section). In order to determine probability, characterizing safety of such type of the notification systems (with respect to devices used in the proposed system), authors applied the analysis of stochastic processes. These processes describe the events, also critical, connected with mobility of objects (vehicles, boats, etc.) in different conditions. On the basis of Markov processes the models were proposed: reliability model for electronic devices, and exploitation model for system including an influence of a man. The second model takes into consideration a degree equipment object in system, but also the typical environmental conditions, including weather. Reliability and exploitation data are based on typical reliabilities characteristics of popular devices GPS/GSM and temporal characteristics connected with services, monitoring and crisis management using such ICT systems. The results (probabilistic and time) can be adapted to other uses, mountaineering and extreme sports, but also in rail transport that can make use of GPS positioning on regional lines (usually such lines are not equipped with centralized rail control systems) [7].

2   E-Call System

E-Call is designed first of all to improve the effectiveness of emergency services. In its own assumption it can to contribute to a reduction in the number of victims and to alleviate ailment of injuries sustained during road accidents. *E-Call* system was developed based on a three-dimensional approach [1]. The system consists of: the system of in- vehicle, communication network (GSM) and points PSAP. Diagram of the system is shown in Fig. 1.

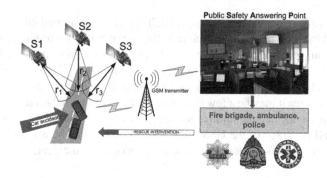

Fig. 1. Scheme of *e-Call* system [own study]

In motor vehicles *e-Call* system consists of GSM /GPS. Currently in Poland it is possible to make a call to the emergency number "112" without having registered and active GSM module SIM card. Thus, even foreign vehicles that have the module can use the emergency notification system. System module can be integrated with the airbag in the car. In the event of a traffic incident, shot in a car airbag module initiates the connection *e-Call*. The basic idea of the system is shown in Fig. 2.

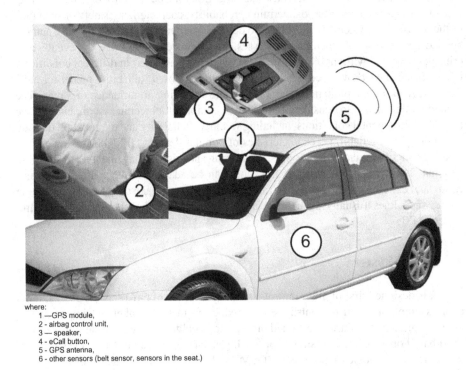

where:
1 —GPS module,
2 - airbag control unit,
3 — speaker,
4 - eCall button,
5 - GPS antenna,
6 - other sensors (belt sensor, sensors in the seat.)

Fig. 2. Scheme of *e-Call* system [own study based on [10, 11]]

In case of car accident to the emergency call center is transmitted information about the event and location data. During the call, the operator will try to talk to the victims in order to obtain the details of the event. In the absence of GPS signal, vehicle position is determined on the basis of data from the GSM base station (BTS). In this case, the discrepancy between the actual locations can be up to several hundred meters. In the case of built-up area it may be a few streets away. In addition, in the vehicle is installed emergency button for manual notifications (e.g. we are witnessed the incident). Due to the lack of full coverage of the GSM network in Poland, may be a situation in which there will not be possible to notify the rescue services about incident.

3   Emergency Notification System for Tourists Yachts

Another solution based at telematics systems is proposed by the authors [4, 5], emergency notification system about dangerous incident in inland waters. Proposed system is similar to the *e-Call* system (systemis at the stage of building a prototype) and will be equipped in GSM and GPS modules. The system also based atthree-dimensional approach: the system-board (modules GPS /GSM), the GSM network, and center of emergency services (pol. Aquatic Volunteer Emergency Corps). In the case of an event (capsizing the boat) tilt sensor installed in the system will activate the module and will send the *sms* with the appropriate information and geographical location. In the absence of actual GPS position, the system will read the last saved position (buffer - last 15 min.). System diagram is shown in Fig. 3.

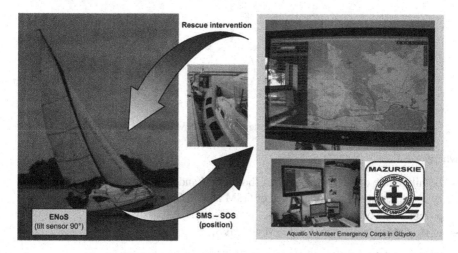

Fig. 3. Scheme of proposed ENoS [own study]

4   Markov Models

There is a group of physical phenomena, which owing to their complexity there is no possible description of deterministic. Carrying out in the same test conditions give different results. In such cases, we are dealing with random phenomena. To the group of these phenomena includes all kinds of events on the road or on the waters. Hence the authors decided to use Markov processes, which are one of the ways of safety analysis. Random process $\{X_t\}$ is called a Markov process, if, for each time t_0 the probability of any position in the future $(t > t_0)$ depends only on the position at time $t = t_0$ and does not depend on the course of the past. Because the proposed to the safety analysis models have countable states, and it is possible to accidentally move between them, thus we have deal with the process with discrete states. For the analysis assumed stationary, ergodic and homogeneous character of Markov processes. Figure 4 shows the model of the system with respect to the transmission of GPS and GSM. The proposed model is a tool for analysis of the solutions presented in Sects. 2 and 3. The model assumes that the most undesirable state is 1 and 3. It was assumed, that in states 1 and 3 is not possible to send any messages concerned event due to lack of GSM network, and also position based at GPS. In the event of such a situation, the rescue services will be informed by the victims or by accidental witnesses. Due to lost a GSM connection it is possible, that in many places the time of waiting for help may take longer (up to several hours).

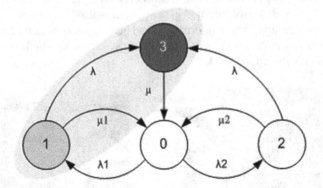

Fig. 4. Markov model for GPS/GSM [own study]

where:

- λ- failure rate of electronic devices (both GSM and GPS),
- λ_1, λ_2 - intensity of disappearance of GSM and GPS signals,
- μ- repair rate of electronic devices,
- μ_1, μ_2 - intensity of service in GSM and GPS,

   In the model from Fig. 4 we can distinguish the following states:

- 0 –state of safety. In the event of danger situation system is correctly working and sending the messages.
- 1 –no GSM signal.
- 2 –no GPS signal.
- 3 –no GPS and GSM signal.

   We can also ascribe, for model from Fig. 4, transition matrix:

$$M = [p_{ik}] = \begin{bmatrix} p_{00} & p_{01} & p_{02} & p_{03} \\ p_{10} & p_{11} & p_{12} & p_{13} \\ p_{20} & p_{21} & p_{22} & p_{23} \\ p_{30} & p_{31} & p_{32} & p_{33} \end{bmatrix} \tag{1}$$

where $0 \le p_{jk} \le 1$, and $\sum_{k=1}^{j} p_{jk} = 1 \, \mathrm{j,k} = 1,2, \ldots, \mathrm{n}.$

   In order to solve the equations used mathematical apparatus in the form of operator equations (Laplace equation), and also computer aided - the *Mathematica* software. The window of the analysis is shown in Fig. 5.

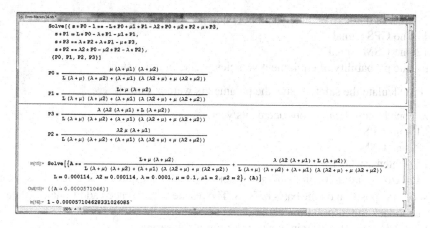

Fig. 5. The window of analysis [own study]

To calculate the values, the parameters were assumed: $\lambda_1 = 0{,}000114$, $\lambda_2 = 0{,}000114$, $\lambda = 0.0001\,h^{-1}$, $\mu = 1/t_1 = 0, 1\,h^{-1}$, $\mu_1 = 1/t_1 = 2\,h^{-1}$, $\mu_2 = 1/t_2 = 2\,h^{-1}$. Based at assumption, the estimated value of safety S is equal:

$$S = 1 - (P_{danger}) = 1 - (P_1 + P_3) = 0.999943 \tag{2}$$

Figure 6 shows the model takes into consideration the addition reactions of the emergency services.

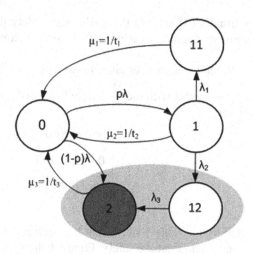

Fig. 6. Markov model for vehicles/yachts with notification system [own study]

In the model form Fig. 6 we can distinguish:

- 0 –state of correct work. System is working,
- 1 –state of danger. Vehicle/yacht equipped with system,

- 2 –state of danger. Vehicle/yacht not equipped with system,
- 11 –no GPS signal,
- 12 –no GSM signal,
- p – the probability of equipment vehicles/yachts in the system.

To calculate the safety value, the parameters were assumed:

- λ – one hundred dangerous accidents/year.
- $\lambda 1$ – no GPS - 1 h/y.
- $\lambda 2$ – no GSM- 1 h/y.
- $\lambda 3$ – intensity 60/1 h
- $\mu 1 = 1/t_1$, t_1 –after 30 min. emergency service arrives (in spite of GPS defects, system sends the position on the basis of BTS. The rescue services need additionally 10 min. due to lack the information about correct position).
- $\mu 2 = 1/t_2$, t_3 – after 20 min. arrive the emergency service,
- $\mu 3 = 1/t_3$, t_3 – after 2 h arrive the emergency service.

The model assumes that the most dangerous state is 2 and 12 (there is no possibility to send information about accident). To calculate the value of safety S, the probabilities P2 and P12 were estimated:

$$P2 = \frac{\lambda\lambda_3\mu_1\cdot(\lambda_1-p\lambda_1+\lambda_2+\mu_2-p\mu_2)}{(\lambda_3\mu_1\cdot(\lambda_1+\lambda_2+\mu_2)\mu_3+\lambda\cdot(\lambda_1\lambda_3(\mu_1-p\mu_1+p\mu_3)+\mu_1\cdot(\lambda_2\cdot(\lambda_3+p\mu_3)+\lambda_3(\mu_2-p\mu_2+p\mu_3))))} \qquad (3)$$

$$P12 = \frac{\lambda_2\cdot(p\cdot\lambda\cdot\mu_1\cdot\mu_2)}{(\lambda_3\mu_1\cdot(\lambda_1+\lambda_2+\mu_2)\mu_3+\lambda\cdot(\lambda_1\lambda_3(\mu_1-p\mu_1+p\mu_3)+\mu_1\cdot(\lambda_2\cdot(\lambda_3+p\mu_3)+\lambda_3(\mu_2-p\mu_2+p\mu_3))))} \qquad (4)$$

According to the formula (3) and (4) the analysis of safety depending on the percentage of the equipment of vehicles/yachts in the system, is shown in the Table 1.

Table 1. Analysis of safety [own study]

L.p.	% vehicles/yachts with the system	Safety S = 1–(P2 + P12)
1	10	0,990201762
2	50	0,994541877
3	80	0,997809408

The results presented in the Table 1 show, that the equipment of vehicles/boats in automatic notification system increase safety. Figure 7 shows the number of critical events per 10 000 occurred, depending on the percentage fitment of the system.

Lack notification system causes, that in 10000 events with 10 % participation vehicles with installed system there are average 98 critical events, and with 80 % participation there are only 22 critical events.

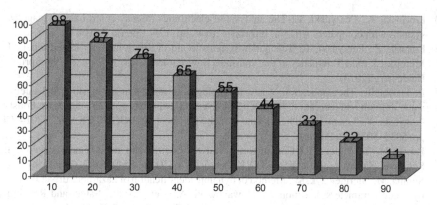

Fig. 7. Number of critical events in 10000 of all events as a function of the equipment in the system [own study]

5   Conclusion

Systems described in the paper can speeds up time of reaction emergency services in case of event, thus in this way have an influence on reducing the number of victims. Analysis of safety rate introduced in the paper shows, how the probability of a critical events depends on the equipment of vehicles (yachts), but also on the timing related to the availability of GPS and GSM. In the case of *e-Call*, system is already used in many countries. Currently in Poland points CPR "112" are already prepared to receive information in the form of *sms*. The CPR Radom in 2014 registered only two such application, but with increase the number of devices installed in vehicles, such application may be more. Thanks to telematics solutions, additionally information about the incidents and traffic jams may be transferred to road managers. This may cause changes in the organization of movement, but the movement will be continual, [6]. Should also be taken into consideration reduction the probability of secondary accidents. In the case of the concept of the system described in Sect. 2, such solutions are not yet applied in inland water. The system is in the process of construction and verification. In this solutions type, the problem can be absence in many places GSM network. Therefore, suggested in Sect. 3 Markov models reflect the typical behaviour of the system (no signals, failures). On the basis of proposed models the safety analysis has been done. The analysis allows for estimate the numerical values of safety, and to determine an influence of the system on the quantity of critical events. Analysis shows, that with the increase of installed systems significantly decreases the number of critical events.

References

1. COM/2013/0315. Decision of the European Parliament and of the Council on the Deployment of the Interoperable EU-wide e-Call
2. Lewiński, A., Łukasik, Z., Perzyński, T., Ukleja, P.: The future generation of railway control systems for regional lines including new telematic solutions. In: Mikulski, J. (ed.) Telematics in the Transport Environment, CCIS 471, pp. 13–17. Springer, Heidelberg (2014)

3. Lewiński, A., Perzyński, T.: The analysis of electronics railway control and management systems with computers AID. In: Infraszyn 2014', pp. 125–139. (in Polish)

4. Łukasik, Z., Perzyński, T.: Telematics systems to aid of safety in water inland turists. In: Mikulski, J. (ed.) Telematics in the Transport Environment CCIS 395, pp. 89–96. Springer, Heidelberg (2013)

5. Perzyński, T.: The application of new technologies in management, logistics and safety in water tourism and recreation. In: LOGISTYKA nr. 3/2014, CD pp. 1231–5478. (in Polish)

6. Perzyński, T.: Telematics in management of city transport. In: LOGISTYKA nr. 3/2014, CD pp. 5030–5035. (in Polish)

7. Perzyński, T., Ukleja, P.: Contemporary railway control and management systems. In: Solutions, Safety, Logistic. LOGISTYKA nr. 6/2014, CD pp. 8542–8547. (in Polish)

8. Sumiła, M., Siergiejczyk, M.: Method of dynamic identification of hazardous driver behavior by traffic parameters detection. In: Nowakowski, A.F., et al. (eds.) Safety and Reliability Methodology and Applications, pp. 109–114. CRC Press Taylor & Francis Group, London (2015). ISBN 978-1-138-02681-0

9. Sumiła, M.: Evaluation of the drivers' distraction caused by dashboard MMI interface. In: Mikulski, J. (ed.) Telematics in the Transport Environment CCIS 471, pp. 396–403. Springer, Heidelberg (2012)

10. Crash test prověřil e-Call. www.motorinfo.cz. Accessed on 2nd December 2015

11. CAN communication and e-Call. www.can-cia.org. Accessed on 2nd December 2015

Modeling of Process of Maintenance
of Transport Systems Telematics with Regard
to Electromagnetic Interferences

Mirosław Siergiejczyk[1]([⊠]), Jacek Pas[2], and Adam Rosinski[1]

[1] Warsaw University of Technology, 00-662 Warsaw, Poland
{msi,adro}@wt.pw.edu.pl
[2] Warsaw Military University of Technology, 00-908 Warsaw, Poland
JPas@wat.edu.pl

Abstract. Transport systems telematics are used in a variety of conditions surrounding it electromagnetic environment. Occurring over a wide transport area electromagnetic interferences, intentional or unintentional (stationary or mobile), can cause disruption of this system. The article presents the issues related to the modelling of the process of maintenance of transport telematics systems. It is taken into account not only the type of reliability structure, but also the effect of electromagnetic interferences on the analysed system. Through mathematical analysis, the obtained equations allow to calculate the probability of a complete system suitability $R_0(t)$ and the probability of failure $Q_0(t)$ for the selected maintenance situations. It is also taken into account the impact of the electromagnetic interferences, both additive and multiplicative, on the analysed system.

Keywords: Electromagnetic compatibility · Transport · Maintenance

1 Introduction

Transport telematics systems operate under various maintenance conditions. They need to be reliable as they are required for transport processes to be uninterrupted [1]. Providing the appropriate usability and maintenance parameters is one of the key problems. So far, the authors conducted usability and maintenance analyses of the entire system [12] as well as its individual subsystems (e.g. power systems [11, 18], navigation systems [13, 14, 17]). Electromagnetic interference is not included. Therefore, it is important to conduct the usability and maintenance analysis of transport telematics systems with regard to electromagnetic interference.

The paper presents the issues related to the influence of electromagnetic interference of the low frequency range on the transport telematics system, which is used in a variety of conditions surrounding electromagnetic environment [4]. Interference is produced intentionally or unintentionally in the transport area [9, 23]. It may cause improper operation (functioning) of the system – Fig. 1 [10]. The transport telematics system (STT) is responsible, among others, for the transport safety, that is, implementation of the process of the movement of people and/or freight [19].

© Springer International Publishing Switzerland 2015
J. Mikulski (Ed.): TST 2015, CCIS 531, pp. 99–107, 2015.
DOI: 10.1007/978-3-319-24577-5_10

2 Basic Issues Concerning Electromagnetic Compatibility in the Transport Environment

Electromagnetic compatibility is the ability of a given device (e.g. the SST transmitter) or a telematics system, as a whole, to operate in the certain electromagnetic environment in a satisfactory manner and without producing intolerable interference by everything that is in this environment – other systems or subsystems, e.g. SRK, safety.

Transport telematics systems can include, e.g. traffic control systems, as well as increasingly installed safety transport systems (surveillance), (e.g. fire alarm system, closed-circuit television system CCTV [15, 16], intrusion and panic alarm system, etc.).

According to the definition of electromagnetic compatibility 50(161), the telematics system which is installed on the moving or stationary means of transport (Fig. 1) should have:

- Installations – consist of spatially distributed systems – e.g. telematics, safety, SRK, etc., devices, one or more of the supporting structural elements and spatially located connections with systems and devices treated as terminal equipment (telematics system transmitter cooperating with the safety system), operated in functional relation to each other;
- component – each element that is intended to be built into the device, but does not have the functional independence and is not designed for direct use by the user (e.g. safety system detector, camera, GPS antenna);
- system – according to the EMC Directive, it is defined as a number of devices interconnected for a specific purpose that are placed into circulation as only one functional unit – e.g. electronic safety system, vehicle location monitoring system, etc.;
- a system consists of functionally related to each other devices that are operated using the supporting structure (open or closed – Fig. 1) and spatially distributed connections (wires used to power supply, electromagnetic fields – for wireless communications, optical connection – linear fire and mechanical detectors – housing of devices and subsystems).

Due to the complex structure of the electromagnetic field and the difference of its properties in the vicinity of the interference source, e.g. wire, antennae (near field) and a certain distance from the source of interference (far field – the distance depends on frequency) coupling by the electromagnetic field is divided into inductive coupling or capacitive coupling (in the near field) and electromagnetic radiation (in the far field). The interfering signals parameter determining the type of coupling, in which the energy associated with interference "attacks" the sensitive device is frequency of signals. For frequencies less than 30 MHz, the dominant are interference of the device (system) via wires coming into it, while for higher frequencies, the signals transmitted via electromagnetic field are becoming increasingly important.

The electromagnetic interference existed within the railway area has an impact on transport telematics systems using couplings [2, 6, 8]:

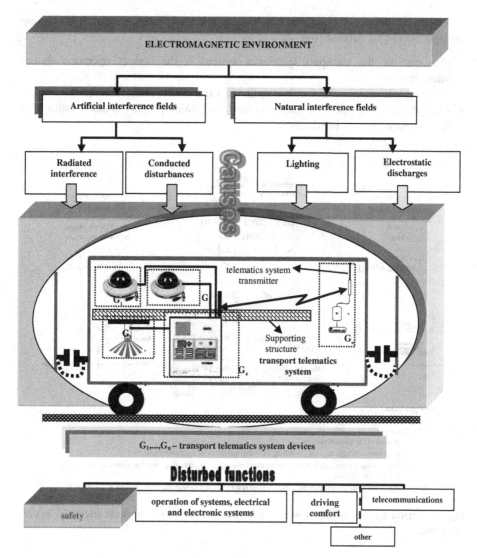

Fig. 1. The impact of electromagnetic interference on the basic functions performed by the transport telematics system [own study]

- radiated, a frequency range from 30 MHz - the size of interference is proportional to parameters of the electromagnetic field, i.e. the intensity of the electric field E and the magnetic field H;
- conducted – proportional to the value of the current I [A], the interference U [V] voltage;
- induction (amplitude distortion proportional to the rate of change of the current over time);
- capacitive (amplitude distortion proportional to the rate of change of voltage over time) [2, 6, 8].

Due to the impact of interference on the transport telematics system, the following concepts should be defined (Fig. 2):

- resistance of the transport telematics system is the correct operation during interference;
- transport telematics system vulnerability is a reaction to interference;
- strength of the transport telematics system is retaining primary characteristics after the disappearance of interference.

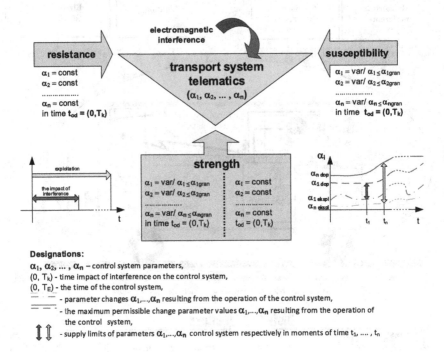

Fig. 2. Criteria for the electromagnetic interference effects on the transport telematics system [own study]

3   Modeling of Transport Telematics Systems Maintenance with Regard to Additive and Multiplicative Electromagnetic Interference

Models of the maintenance process of transport telematics systems require an analysis of particular types of conditions encountered in actual conditions of devices [3, 21, 22]. In the paper, the analysis with regard to electromagnetic interference will be conducted.

As a result, we obtain relationships, which allow to determine values of probabilities of considered systems' staying in the distinguished maintenance states [5, 7, 20].

Below, the system with one transmission bus and modules (a central processing unit and n-modules) of a serial structure was presented. Failure to the module or the impact of interference on the operation of various elements in the system causes the transition of the system from the state of complete usability $R_0(t)$ to the state of safety unreliability $Q_B(t)$ (Fig. 3).

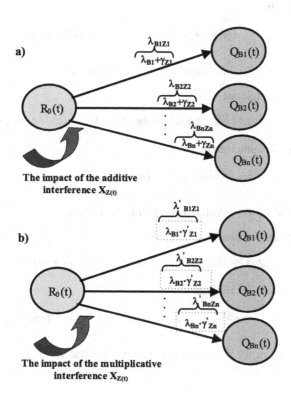

Fig. 3. Relationships in the transport telematics system with one transmission bus [own study]: (a) the impact graph of additive interference; (b) the impact graph of multiplicative interference. Markings in fig.: $R_0(t)$ – the probability function of the system staying in the state of complete usability, $Q_B(t)$ – the probability function of the system staying in the state of safety unreliability, λ_{B1} – intensity of transitions of the central processing unit, λ_{B2}, ..., λ_{Bn} – intensity of the modules transitions, γ_{Z1}, γ_{Z2}, ..., γ_{Zn} – indicators determining the impact of the A, B1, B2 interference types respectively to the central processing unit and modules, λ_{B1Z1} – intensity of the central processing unit transitions for additive interference, λ_{B2Z2}, ..., λ_{BnZn} – intensity of transitions of the modules for additive interference, λ'_{B1Z1}– intensity of transitions of the central processing unit for multiplicative interference, λ'_{B2Z2}, ..., λ'_{BnZn} –intensity of transitions of the modules for multiplicative interference.

Considering the system distributed with one transmission bus and modules in terms of the usability and maintenance aspect, the following relationships on the impact of interference on the system can be put down:

(a) The impact of the A interference type on the system, sample projects (Fig. 4):

  – additive

$$\lambda_{ZB} = (\lambda_{B1} + \gamma_{Z1})\mathrm{lub}(\lambda_{B2} + \gamma_{Z2})\mathrm{lub}(\lambda_{Bn} + \gamma_{Zn}) \tag{1}$$

  – multiplicative

$$\lambda_{ZB} = (\lambda_{B1} \cdot \gamma'_{Z1})\mathrm{lub}(\lambda_{B2} \cdot \gamma'_{Z2})\mathrm{lub}(\lambda_{Bn} \cdot \gamma'_{Zn}) \tag{2}$$

(b) the impact of the B1 interference type on the system:

  – additive interference

$$\lambda_{ZB} = (\lambda_{B1} + \gamma_{Z1}) + (\lambda_{B2} + \gamma_{Z2}) + \ldots + (\lambda_{Bn} + \gamma_{Zn}) \tag{3}$$

  – multiplicative interference

$$\lambda_{ZB} = (\lambda_{B1} \cdot \gamma'_{Z1}) + (\lambda_{B2} \cdot \gamma'_{Z2}) + \ldots + (\lambda_{Bn} \cdot \gamma'_{Zn}) \tag{4}$$

(c) the impact of the B2 interference type on the system:

  – additive interference

$$\lambda_{ZB} = (\lambda_{B1} + \gamma_{Z1}) + (\lambda_{B2} + \gamma_{Z2}) + \ldots + (\lambda_{Bn} + \gamma_{Zn}) \tag{5}$$

  – multiplicative interference

$$\lambda_{ZB} = (\lambda_{B1} \cdot \gamma'_{Z1}) + (\lambda_{B2} \cdot \gamma'_{Z2}) + \ldots + (\lambda_{Bn} \cdot \gamma'_{Zn}) \tag{6}$$

(d) in the absence of the interference impact on the system

$$\lambda_B = \sum_{i=1}^{n} \lambda_{Bi} \tag{7}$$

Knowing intensity $\lambda(t)$ of failure and indicators $\gamma(t)$ of the impact of different types of interference on the individual modules of the system, it is possible to determine the probability of complete usability of the system $R_0(t)$ and the probability of failure $Q_0(t)$ (Table 1).

Received relationships allow to determine the probability of the transport telematics system staying in the state of complete usability R_O.

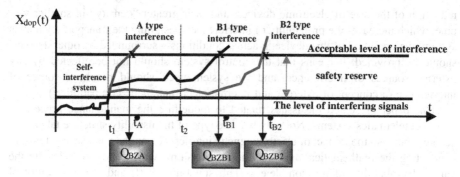

Fig. 4. Exemplary implementation of the impact of the A, B1, B2 interference types on the electronic system [own study] – where: t_1, t_2 – moments of the interference occurrence, x – exceeding the acceptable level of interference, Q_B –the probability function of the system staying in the state of safety unreliability, t_A, t_{B1} t_{B2} – the time of transition of the system from the state of complete usability $R_0(t)$ to the state of safety unreliability Q_{BZ} under the influence of interference of a specific type

Table 1. Exemplary calculations of the probability of complete usability of the system $R_0(t)$, and the probability of failure $Q_0(t)$ for the selected maintenance situations [own study]

Type of interference affecting the system	Reliability of the electronic system	The probability of system failure
No interference	$R_0(t) = \exp[-\int_0^t \lambda_B(\tau)d\tau]$	$Q_0(t) = 1 - R_0(t)$
A type interference	$R_{0A}(t) = \exp[-\int_0^t (\lambda_{B1} + \gamma_{Z1})(\tau)d\tau]$	$Q_{0A}(t) = 1 - R_{0A}(t)$
A type interference	$R'_{0A}(t) = \exp[-\int_0^t (\lambda_{B1} \cdot \gamma'_{Z1})(\tau)d\tau]$	$Q'_{0A}(t) = 1 - R'_{0A}(t)$
B1 type interference	$R_{0B1}(t) = \exp[-\int_0^t (\lambda_{B1} + \gamma_{Z1} + \lambda_{B2} + \gamma_{Z2})(\tau)d\tau]$	$Q_{0B1}(t) = 1 - R_{0B1}(t)$
B1 type interference	$R'_{0B1}(t) = \exp[-\int_0^t [(\lambda_{B1} \cdot \gamma'_{Z1}) + (\lambda_{B2} \cdot \gamma'_{Z2})](\tau)d\tau]$	$Q'_{0B1}(t) = 1 - R'_{0B1}(t)$
B2 type interference	$R_{0B2}(t) = \exp[-\int_0^t (\lambda_{B1} + \gamma_{Z1} + \lambda_{B2} + \gamma_{Z2} + \lambda_{B3} + \gamma_{Z3})(\tau)d\tau]$ $R'_{0B2}(t) = \exp[-\int_0^t [(\lambda_{B1} \cdot \gamma'_{Z1}) + (\lambda_{B2} \cdot \gamma'_{Z2}) + (\lambda_{B3} \cdot \gamma'_{Z3})](\tau)d\tau]$	$Q_{0B2}(t) = 1 - R_{0B2}(t)$ $Q'_{0B2}(t) = 1 - R'_{0B2}(t)$

4 Conclusion

The widespread use of electric and electronic systems of transport telematics systems results in the necessity of a variety of systems to work on their setting close to each other. The use of integrated circuits in the transport telematics system results in reduction of the size of electronic devices, and their greater "density" in smaller volume, which increases the probability of interference. Designing the transport telematics system, the operation of this device in actual conditions – surrounded by other devices, should be provided. It means that the control system should not be affected by any external sources of interference, and the system itself should not be a source of interference (a concept of external and internal electromagnetic compatibility).

This paper presented the issues related to modelling the maintenance process of transport telematics systems. Not only was the type of the usability structure taken into account, but also the impact of electromagnetic interference on the analysed system. By conducting the mathematical analysis, the relationships, which allow to calculate the value of probability of the complete system suitability $R_0(t)$ and the probability of failure $Q_0(t)$ for the selected maintenance situations, were determined. The impact on the analysed system of electromagnetic interference, both additive and multiplicative, was taken into consideration. In the further research, conducting analyses with regard to other types of structures of transport telematics systems is foreseen.

References

1. Będkowski, L., Dąbrowski, T.: The basis of exploitation, Part II: The basis of exploational reliability. Military Academy of Technology, Warsaw (2006)
2. Charoy, A.: Interference in electronic equipment. WNT, Warsaw (1999)
3. Dabrowski, T., et al.: The method of threshold-comparative diagnosing insensitive on disturbances of diagnostic signals. Przeglad Elektrotechniczny - Electrical Review **88**(11A), 93–97 (2012)
4. Dyduch, J., Pas, J., Rosinski, A.: The basic of the exploitation of transport electronic systems. Technical University of Radom, Radom (2011)
5. Epstein, B., Weissman, I.: Mathematical models for systems reliability. CRC Press / Taylor & Francis Group, Boca Raton (2008)
6. Koszmider, A.L.: Practical guide to electromagnetic compatibility. ALFA – WEKA (1998)
7. Laskowski, D., et al.: Anthropotechnical systems reliability. In: Nowakowski, T., et al., (eds) Safety and Reliability: Methodology and Applications - Proceedings of the European Safety and Reliability Conference ESREL 2014, pp. 399-407. CRC Press/Balkema, London (2015)
8. Ott, H.W.: Methods of reducing interference and noise in electronic systems. WNT, Warsaw (1979)
9. Paś, J., Duer, S.: Determination of the impact indicators of electromagnetic interferences on computer information systems. Neural Comput. Appl. **23**(7–8), 2143–2157 (2013)
10. Pas, J., Dyduch, J.: Impact of electromagnetic interference on transport security systems. Measurements Automatics Robotics no 10 (2009)
11. Rosinski, A., Dąbrowski, T.: Modelling reliability of uninterruptible power supply units. Eksploatacja i Niezawodność – Maintenance and Reliability **15**(4), 409–413 (2013)
12. Rosiński, A.: Rationalisation of the maintenance process of transport telematics system comprising two types of periodic inspections. In: Selvaraj, H., Zydek, D., Chmaj, G. (eds.) Progress in Systems Engineering. AISC, vol. 330, pp. 663–667. Springer, Heidelberg (2015)
13. Siergiejczyk, M., Krzykowska, K., Rosiński, A.: Parameters analysis of satellite support system in air navigation. In: Selvaraj, H., Zydek, D., Chmaj, G. (eds.) Progress in Systems Engineering. AISC, vol. 330, pp. 673–678. Springer, Heidelberg (2015)

14. Siergiejczyk, M., Krzykowska, K., Rosiński, A.: Reliability assessment of cooperation and replacement of surveillance systems in air traffic. In: Zamojski, W., Mazurkiewicz, J., Sugier, J., Walkowiak, T., Kacprzyk, J. (eds.) Proceedings of the Ninth International Conference on DepCoS-RELCOMEX. AISC, vol. 286, pp. 403–412. Springer, Heidelberg (2014)

15. Siergiejczyk, M., Paś, J., Rosiński, A.: Application of closed circuit television for highway telematics. In: Mikulski, J. (ed.) TST 2012. CCIS, vol. 329, pp. 159–165. Springer, Heidelberg (2012)

16. Siergiejczyk, M., Paś, J., Rosiński, A.: Evaluation of safety of highway CCTV system's maintenance process. In: Mikulski, J. (ed.) TST 2014. CCIS, vol. 471, pp. 69–79. Springer, Heidelberg (2014)

17. Siergiejczyk, M., Rosiski, A., Krzykowska, K.: Reliability assessment of supporting satellite system EGNOS. In: Zamojski, W., Mazurkiewicz, J., Sugier, J., Walkowiak, T., Kacprzyk, J. (eds.) New results in dependability and computer systems. AISC, vol. 224, pp. 353–363. Springer, Heidelberg (2013)

18. Siergiejczyk, M., Rosiński, A.: Analysis of power supply maintenance in transport telematics system. Solid State Phenom. 210, 14–19 (2014)

19. Siergiejczyk, M.: Operational effectiveness of transport telematic systems. Scientific papers of Warsaw University of Technology, Transport, No. 67, Warsaw (2009)

20. Stapelberg, R.F.: Handbook of Reliability, Availability Maintainability and Safety in Engineering Design. Springer, London (2009)

21. Stawowy, M.: Model for information quality determination of teleinformation systems of transport. In: Nowakowski, T., et al, (eds) Proceedings of the European Safety and Reliability Conference ESREL 2014, pp. 1909–1914. CRC Press/Balkema (2015)

22. Sumiła, M.: Selected aspects of message transmission management in ITS systems. In: Mikulski, J. (ed.) TST 2012. CCIS, vol. 329, pp. 141–147. Springer, Heidelberg (2012)

23. Mikulski J., Analiza zagrożeń pól magnetycznych w transporcie. Logistyka nr 3, CD-ROM (2009)

Model of the Hierarchical Process
of Managing the Approaching Air Traffic
in the Terminal Area

Jacek Skorupski[✉]

Faculty of Transport, Warsaw University of Technology, Warsaw, Poland
jsk@wt.pw.edu.pl

Abstract. Air traffic in the airport controlled area is carried out according to standard procedures. However, they are disturbed by random factors, so the traffic is stochastic in nature and requires ongoing monitoring by the air traffic controller that operates in the approach control sector (TMA). One of his/her goals is to form the landing aircraft queue so as to maximize the airport capacity. The task is difficult because there are multiple entry points to the TMA and many points at which the individual aircraft streams merge. The paper presents the model of the process of forming landing aircraft queue. The model has been implemented as a coloured Petri net. It has a hierarchical structure corresponding to the actual multi-level structure of the merging aircraft streams process. The study shows an example of modelling of the approaching air traffic consisting of aircraft landing at the Warsaw Chopin airport on the RWY 11 runway. The developed software system SECRAN can be used to support the approach controller in the planning process and in the current control of approaching air traffic in TMA area.

Keywords: Air traffic · Airport arrival management · Hierarchical sequencing · Petri nets · Air traffic controller support

1 Introduction

Air traffic within a Terminal Area (TMA) is planned and controlled by the approach control service (APP). Traffic volume is especially high around the airport - the nodal point in air transportation network. Many aircraft perform complicated manoeuvres: the approach and landing and also climbing after the takeoff. Therefore, typical APP controller tasks are extremely difficult [15]. In recent years, another task - to prepare the aircraft sequence for landing is becoming increasingly important. This sequence should allow a smooth and timely landing of any aircraft in such a way as to maximize the available capacity of the airport, which in most cases is the bottleneck of the air transport system. The aircraft scheduling task is a hierarchical one, with respect to each aircraft it consists of a number of decisions over the time.

An air traffic controller is assisted in his/her tasks by the appropriate intelligent systems that allow one to remotely obtain information about the aircraft positions. Then, they work out control decisions using the available flight plans and control algorithms in use [5]. At the end, they transmit control clearances to the aircraft to

© Springer International Publishing Switzerland 2015
J. Mikulski (Ed.): TST 2015, CCIS 531, pp. 108–120, 2015.
DOI: 10.1007/978-3-319-24577-5_11

execute [1]. Works towards the establishment of efficient algorithms for controller support in the process of forming a queue of landing aircraft is conducted in many research centres (e.g. in Europe as a SESAR programme [9]).

Arriving aircraft traffic management support is the subject of this paper. The outline of the mathematical model in the form of Petri net, its implementation in the form of a computer system SECRAN (SEquence CReator and ANalyser), and some examples of simulation experiments that show the applicability of the proposed solution are presented. Creating a schedule of landings in accordance with a predetermined landing control algorithm and evaluation of the control algorithm in terms of different parameters (e.g. the capacity or punctuality) can be assigned to the main areas of application. In this paper both of these areas will be presented.

2   Landing Aircraft Scheduling as a Part of the Air Traffic Management in the Airport Area

2.1   General Principles of Planning the Traffic Incoming to the Airport

Incoming air traffic is organized according to the runway in use. The decision on its choice shall be taken with taking into account the meteorological conditions (especially the strength and direction of the wind), navigational equipment, traffic situation, etc. [6]. For airports with multiple runways many variations are possible, especially when we assume the configuration in which one runway is used for the take-off and another for the landing. The choice of the runway in use determines the end point of the arriving aircraft trajectory.

The starting point of the arrival trajectory is dependent on the direction of the approaching aircraft and air route used previously. Arrival procedures, the so-called STARs, are predefined between the starting and the end points. Their names are derived from the names of the starting points of the procedure [7]. They are designated by a list of waypoints, for which also recommended cruising altitude and speed limit can be determined. The APP controller can modify STAR procedures. Most often the modification consists in bypassing some waypoints and flying directly between any two navigational waypoints [2]. The so-called *direct* may lead even from the starting point to the end point without changing direction.

2.2   Airport Capacity and Air Operations Safety

A problem of landing aircraft scheduling is in fact the problem with two conflicting objectives. On the one hand, we seek to maximize the airport capacity [16]. This can be achieved by organizing the queue for landing in such a way that the aircraft are densely packed (the distance between them is small). This makes it possible to realize a lot of landings per unit time. Dense packing is obtained when the aircraft sequence is suitable with respect to the weight categories and the APP controller uses the minimum separation allowed by the regulations [4].

The second goal of the scheduling process is to ensure punctuality of landings and also safety and high reliability of a planned sequence execution. When the aircraft are densely packed, even a small distortion of their movement (for example due to wind or inaccuracies in the navigation) could lead to an infringement of the separation. This must not happen. Therefore, in such a situation, it is necessary to perform the special procedure by which one or more aircraft move to the end of the queue. In this case, the execution time of a series of landings increases. Such unexpected manoeuvres may also be relevant for the traffic safety [14].

It is easy to see that the APP controller should use a scheduling algorithm in which both criteria are taken into account. The task is difficult, multi-criteria, therefore it is necessary to support him/her with a kind of an intelligent system [13]. The importance of both criteria may vary over time. Therefore, one cannot provide the optimal solution, and should seek a solution appropriate for the current traffic situation and the status of the environment.

2.3   Multi-level Process of Forming the Landing Aircraft Queue

Forming a landing aircraft queue is usually performed in the TMA region directly related to the aerodrome where the landing is to take place. However, traffic streams overlap in the areas with a big number of airports. Therefore, solutions are sought in which the planning horizon is greater [8]. In such a situation one can propose a solution in which the individual streams are partly coordinated and merged in earlier stages of flight. This concept results from the analysis of STAR procedures. It is also advantageous from the safety point of view. Uncertainty about the punctuality of arrivals would be very large if all aircraft are directed to one merging point. In the case of disturbances we would have to deal with the situation of many aircraft performing complex manoeuvres in a limited airspace. Therefore it is more convenient to merge streams of aircraft arriving from similar direction earlier. On the one hand this makes the decomposition of the scheduling process; on the other hand the uncertainty as to the punctual arrival is lower.

3   The Model of Hierarchical Process of Landing Aircraft Scheduling

The structure of the model of approaching aircraft queue creation process adopted in this paper is somewhat similar to the concept presented in [3]. In their paper an attempt to apply a so-called "list algorithm" for APP controller decision support was undertaken. The model in the form of Petri net proposed here extends the capabilities of that approach. The flight time is treated here as dynamic and random variable. Additionally flight time measurements and shortcuts (*directs*) that are actually used by air traffic controllers have been taken into account.

3.1   Subject of Modelling - the Area of Analysis and Assumptions

The paper analyzes the hierarchical process of creating the arriving aircraft schedule for STAR procedures leading to a landing on the RWY 11 runway at the Frederic Chopin Airport in Warsaw. STAR routes are presented in Fig. 1, and Table 1 presents a brief description of all procedures available in this case.

In the basic version of the model we assume that *directs* are not used and all aircraft perform the full STAR procedure. This assumption has been adopted to better take into account the multi-level hierarchy of landing queue creation process. In most cases, the *directs* are routed to the end point of the STAR procedure or in its immediate vicinity. This causes that many intermediate merging points are omitted. This may bring the multi-dimensional problem to a one-dimensional problem. Because of the practice, the effect of using *directs* will be examined in the experimental part of this work.

The nature of the scheduling algorithm used by the APP controller is the second major assumption of this model. Based on the considerations in Sect. 2 it is assumed that aircraft are sequenced according to the scheduled time of their appearance at the TMA border, without changing their order (FIFO principle). In addition, it is assumed that the controller does not apply redundant space between aircraft, and they are scheduled in such a way as to keep the separation required by international regulations, in particular related to the turbulence behind the aircraft [2].

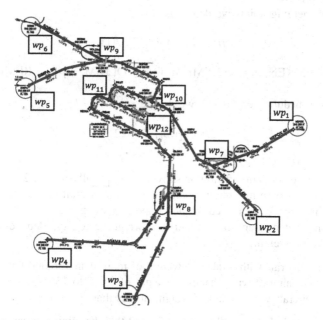

Fig. 1. Arrival trajectories for Warsaw Chopin airport RWY 11 [own study]

Table 1. STAR procedures for RWY 11 [own study]

Procedure	NEPOX	LIMVI	LOGDA	AGAVA	BIMPA	SORIX
Length [km]	158.9	143.3	179.1	200.8	149.6	148.5
Sequencing stages	3	3	2	2	3	3
Waypoints number	16	15	15	17	15	17

3.2 Model of Hierarchical Scheduling Process

The analysis of the structure of all RWY 11 STAR procedures shows that in the scheduling process one can distinguish 12 important waypoints. These are: TMA input points, which are also starting points of the scheduling process, first, second and third level merging points, and one end point. We denote

$$WP = \{wp_i\}, i = 1, 2, \ldots, w \tag{1}$$

the set of important waypoints, $w = 12$.

The set of entry points we define as

$$EP = \{wp_i\}, i = 1, \ldots 6 \tag{2}$$

where $wp_1 = $ NEPOX, $wp_2 = $ LIMVI, $wp_3 = $ LOGDA, $wp_4 = $ AGAVA, $wp_5 = $ BIMPA, $wp_6 = $ SORIX.

The set of merging points we define as

$$MP = \{wp_i\}, i = 7, \ldots 11 \tag{3}$$

where $wp_7 = $ EMKEN, $wp_8 = $ BEMRA, $wp_9 = $ OLDIM, $wp_{10} = $ REMDI, $wp_{11} = $ WA413.

The set of scheduling end points we denote

$$LP = \{wp_i\}, i = 12 \tag{4}$$

where $wp_{12} = $ FAP/FAF.

The structure of the aircraft flow is shown schematically in Fig. 2.

The compliance with minimum separation between aircraft in accordance with the rules shown in Table 2 is checked in each important waypoint.

Separation is dependent on the aircraft weight category, depending on their maximum take-off weight:

- heavy (H) – aircraft with a take-off weight of more than 136,000 kg,
- medium (M) - aircraft with a take-off weight of 7,000 to 136,000 kg,
- light (L) – aircraft with a take-off weight of less than 7,000 kg.

In cases not included in Table 2 it is assumed that the minimum separation is one minute.

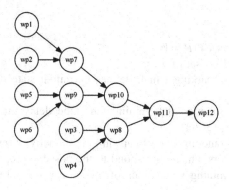

Fig. 2. A scheme of the aircraft flow in the model [own study]

Table 2. Minimum separation between arriving aircraft [own study]

Lead aircraft	Follower aircraft	Minimum separation
heavy (H)	light (L)	3 min.
heavy (H)	medium (M)	2 min.
medium (M)	light (L)	3 min.

3.3   Coloured Petri Net for Evaluation of the Process of Managing the Approaching Air Traffic in the Terminal Area

The structure of the aircraft flow shown in Fig. 2 was the basis for the creation of a model in a form of hierarchical, coloured Petri net. This approach allows us to achieve several goals.

First, it is possible to determine (plan) the aircraft sequence according to the accepted scheduling algorithm. We can thus obtain a fully intelligent telematic solution. Aircraft positions (and therefore the time they appear in the waypoints from the *EP* set) can be obtained automatically from the air traffic surveillance systems [10]. The SECRAN system works out the solution of the scheduling problem. This solution and the expected distance between the aircraft can be transmitted from the APP controller on board the aircraft by means of voice communication or by using a digital air data link (e.g. CPDLC).

On the other hand, the use of this model and the computer tool SECRAN allows for simulation analysis of the air traffic in the TMA. One can analyse the traffic quality indicators (e.g. punctuality, reliability) of the obtained sequences in the absence of disturbances, but also in the presence of various non-nominal situations. Analysis of the results of such simulations allow for optimization of the scheduling algorithm.

To carry out research and experiments the hierarchical coloured Petri net with the following structure was used [11, 12, 14]

$$S_{AM} = \{P, T, A, M_0, \tau, X, \Gamma, C, G, E, R, r_0, B\} \tag{5}$$

where:

P – set of places,

T – set of transitions $T \cap P = \emptyset$,

$A \subseteq (T \times P) \cup (P \times T)$ – set of arcs,

$M_0 : P \rightarrow \mathbb{Z}_+ \times R$ – marking which defines the initial state of the system that is being modeled,

$\tau : T \times P \rightarrow \mathbb{R}_+$ – function determining the static delay that is connected with carrying out activity (event) t,

$X : T \times P \rightarrow \mathbb{R}_+$ – random time of carrying out an activity (event) t,

Γ – finite set of colors which correspond to the possible properties of tokens,

C – function determining what kinds of tokens can be stored in a given place: $C : P \rightarrow \Gamma$,

G – so-called "guard" function which determines the conditions that must be fulfilled for a given event to occur,

E – function describing so-called weights of arcs, i.e. the properties of tokens that are processed,

R – set of timestamps (also called time points) $R \subseteq \mathbb{R}$,

r_0 – initial time, $r_0 \in R$.

$B : T \rightarrow \mathbb{R}_+$ – function determining the priority of a given event, i.e. controlling the net's dynamics when there are several events that can occur simultaneously.

One of the most important components of this structure is the set of colours, which in the case of this model takes values $\{GI, AC, SEQ\}$. *GI* colour represents the consecutive numbers and times of appearance of aircraft in the system. Colour *AC* contains information on the parameters of moving aircraft, and the colour *SEQ* represents the sequence of aircraft appearing in the waypoint.

4   Simulation Analysis of the Hierarchical Process of Arrivals Management

The model of approaching aircraft scheduling, discussed briefly in Sect. 3, has been implemented in CPN Tools 4.0 package as SECRAN program. The developed Petri net is coloured and hierarchical. The net's hierarchy corresponds to the hierarchy of the scheduling process and is being implemented by the mechanism of pages that allows one to separate parts of the model. The synchronization of pages in this case is implemented by a mechanism of fused places. These places are marked with ellipses with a label in the lower left corner (Figs. 3, 4 and 5). In the basic version of the presented model six pages have been created. Due to the limitation of the paper's volume only some of them will be presented.

The first page presented is *Merge 1–2 to 7*. It has two important functions in the model:

- implements the input of the aircraft into the analysed TMA, including checking the separation on input waypoints wp_1 NEPOX and wp_2 LIMVI
- combines traffic streams approaching from wp_1 and wp_2 in the merging point wp_7 EMKEN, also with separation checking function.

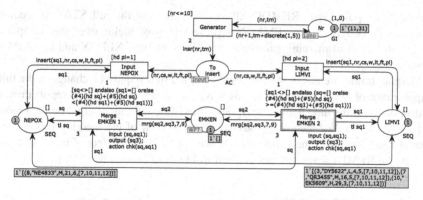

Fig. 3. Page *Merge 1–2 to 7* in the model of scheduling traffic approaching RWY 11 [own study]

Petri net implementing *Merge 1–2 to 7* page is shown in Fig. 3.

On Fig. 3 in places NEPOX and LIMVI we can notice a sequence of aircraft appearing in the navigation waypoint. The sequence is shown in the box below the place. Every single aircraft is described by the token having the following structure:

$$ac = 1\text{'}(nr, cs, w, lt, ft, pl) \tag{6}$$

where:

  nr – aircraft's number in the system,
  cs – identification mark of the aircraft, so-called call sign,
  w – weight category of the aircraft,
  lt – planned time of the aircraft's appearance in the merging point,
  ft – random time of flight to the next merging point,
  pl – further planned route, written as a series of numbers of important waypoints.

Examples of the generated data shown on Fig. 3 demonstrate that at the LIMVI waypoint three aircraft are going to appear: DY5622 at time 4, QR3455 at time 16 and EK5609 at time 29.

Figure 4 shows the page *Merge 7–9 to 10*. It contains the model of the flight, which begins in waypoints wp_7 EMKEN and wp_9 OLDIM, and ends with merging these two

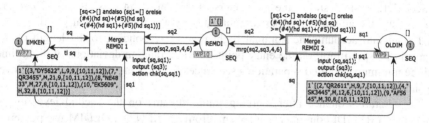

Fig. 4. Page *Merge 7–9 to 10* in the model of scheduling traffic approaching RWY 11 [own study]

streams at the point wp_{10} REMDI. All aircraft carry out the full STAR procedure. Tokens in the waypoint wp_7 EMKEN represent plan of flights over this waypoint, which is the result of merging streams starting in points wp_1 NEPOX and wp_2 LIMVI shown in Fig. 3.

Merging traffic streams in the waypoint wp_{10} REMDI required a change in the time of appearance of DY5622 aircraft in this waypoint. It was scheduled to report there at the time of 18 (at the time 9 in the waypoint EMKEN and 9 min of flight on the section EMKEN-REMDI). For the sake of separation as a result of the merging process, the planned flight time over the point REMDI was set to 21. The effect of merging traffic flows in the REMDI waypoint can be seen in Fig. 5 (a box on the right).

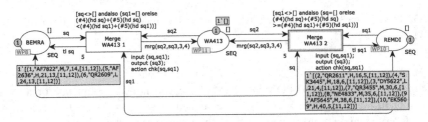

Fig. 5. Page *Merge 8–10 to 11* in the model of scheduling traffic approaching RWY 11 [own study]

4.1 The Module for Determination of the Landing Sequence

As was already indicated, by using the concept of hierarchical (distributed) aircraft scheduling we decompose this task. This makes the proper synchronization of aircraft arrival times easier for a single merging point. However, in return, to predict the situation in further merging points is more difficult. The mathematical model and the computer tool SECRAN, used in this work, allow for the determination of the final sequence, together with planned (expected) times of appearance over the subsequent waypoints. Developed solutions (decisions) can be transmitted remotely to the aircraft crew through the voice communication or data link. The crew, in turn, can programme their onboard flight management systems (FMS) to meet the expectations of air traffic control services.

Landing sequence for a sample set of 10 aircraft will now be presented. Aircraft arrivals to the entry points *EP* were generated according to the assumptions presented in Sect. 3.1. Table 3 shows the parameters of the entries in these points. These are respectively: the aircraft's number, weight category and time of arrival [min].

Taking into account: the nominal flight time corresponding to the length of the segment, the speed limit on the entry point, possible random deviations of flight time and the minimum required separation - sequences for merging points of the first level are shown in Table 4.

The aircraft sequence after merging traffic streams on the second level in the hierarchy (at REMDI point merging streams from EMKEN and OLDIM waypoints) is as follows (weight categories omitted):

Table 3. Aircraft arrivals to TMA [own study]

Entry point	NEPOX	LIMVI	LOGDA	AGAVA	BIMPA	SORIX
First aircraft	4, H, 7	5, H, 12	2, M, 3	1, L, 0	9, H, 26	
Second aircraft	8, L, 24		3, L, 6	6, L, 17	10, L, 30	
Third aircraft				7, L, 20		

Table 4. The results of the first-level merging [own study]

Merging point	EMKEN	BEMRA	OLDIM
First aircraft	4, H, 13	1, L, 10	9, H, 32
Second aircraft	5, H, 15	2, M, 11	10, L, 35
Third aircraft	8, L, 29	3, L, 14	
Fourth aircraft		6, L, 28	
Fifth aircraft		7, L, 29	

$$\langle (4, 20), (5, 22), (8, 36), (9, 38), (10, 43) \rangle \tag{7}$$

The sequence on the third level of merging (in WA413 point merging streams from REMDI and BEMRA waypoints) is as follows:

$$\langle (1, 24), (2, 25), (4, 26), (5, 27), (3, 30), (8, 42), (9, 43), (6, 46), (7, 47), (10, 48) \rangle \tag{8}$$

The final sequence in FAP/FAF merging point is as follows:

$$\langle (1, 28), (2, 29), (4, 30), (5, 31), (3, 34), (8, 45), (9, 46), (6, 49), (7, 50), (10, 52) \rangle \tag{9}$$

4.2 Scheduling Algorithm Evaluation - Simulation Experiments

The second possible application of the solution presented in this paper is the evaluation of the scheduling algorithm used by the APP controller. A good indicator for this assessment is the average interval between landings. This indicator assesses both scheduling objectives, which were mentioned in Sect. 2.2 - capacity and punctuality. In this section, two scheduling strategies will be compared. First, the reference one, was described in Sect. 3.1. It consists in: aircraft perform full STAR procedure, and FIFO rule is used. The second strategy will be modified in a way that *directs* will be used in selected waypoints.

Average interval between landings is a random value. Among other things, it is very dependent on the arrival traffic stream characteristics. To eliminate individual variability, a simulation experiment was conducted in which 10^4 sequences were tested. Average interval between landings for the strategy without the use of *directs* and for the strategy with *directs* used in three waypoints AGAVA, NEPOX and BIMPA are presented in Table 5.

Table 5. Scheduling strategies comparison [own study]

Strategy	Average interval between landings [min]
No *directs*	5.14
Direct: AGAVA-REDSA	4.93
Directs:AGAVA-REDSA and NEPOX-NIMIS	4.89
Directs: AGAVA-REDSA, NEPOX-NIMIS and BIMPA-REDSA	4.82

The structure of the aircraft flow in the experiment is shown in Fig. 6. In this experiment, a set of important waypoints consists of $w = 14$ elements. Additional waypoints, which are targets of *directs* will be denoted as

$$ADP = \{wp_i\}, i = 13, 14 \tag{10}$$

where wp_{13} = REDSA, and wp_{14} = NIMIS.

As one can see, the use of *directs* improves the assessment that can be attributed to the analyzed scheduling strategies. The average distance between landings translates directly into airport capacity. The observed difference of more than 6% between strategy without *directs* and strategy with three *directs*, in relation to the airport capacity can be considered significant.

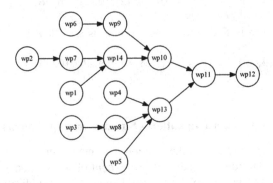

Fig. 6. A scheme of the aircraft flow in the simulation experiment No 3. [own study]

5 Conclusion

In the paper a model in the form of coloured Petri net, together with a computer tool SECRAN created with the use of CPN Tools 4.0 package is presented. They allow for the analysis of the problem of multi-stage, hierarchical scheduling of aircraft approaching for landing. This issue is very important from a practical point of view, and the necessity of its solution is strongly emphasized recently in European research projects.

The model and software presented in this paper allows one to determine the detailed sequence of aircraft, in accordance with adopted scheduling strategy, over all merging points. The schedule contains both the sequence and the aircraft flight times on particular waypoints. Even for simple scheduling algorithm, as presented in this paper, this question is difficult, especially since the flight times are random variables.

The second important application area of the presented SECRAN system is the evaluation of scheduling algorithms used in practice. Through their comparison we can search for better solutions. The paper proposes and presents the evaluation in terms of the average interval between landings, which is inversely proportional to the airport capacity. The results of experiments show that even at very simple scheduling algorithms it is possible to significantly increase the capacity of the airport area.

References

1. Finke, C., et al.: Enhancing the security of aircraft surveillance in the next generation air traffic control system. Int. J. Crit. Infrastruct. Prot. **6**, 3–11 (2013)
2. ICAO. Procedures for Air Navigation Services - Rules of the Air and Air Traffic Services, International Civil Aviation Organisation DOC 4444-RAC/501, ed. 15th. (2007)
3. Kwasiborska, A., Markiewicz, K.: Methods of list scheduling landing aircraft as control support system in decision-making, scientific works of warsaw university of technology. Transp. **104**, 21–32 (2014)
4. Lieder, A., Briskorn, D., Stolletz, R.: A dynamic programming approach for the aircraft landing problem with aircraft classes. Eur. J. Oper. Res. **243**, 61–69 (2015)
5. Murça, M., Müller, C.: Control-based optimization approach for aircraft scheduling in a terminal area with alternative arrival routes. Transp. Res. Part E: Logist. Transp. Rev. **73**, 96–113 (2015)
6. Netjasov, F.: Fuzzy expert model for determination of runway in use case study: airport zurich. In: 1st International Conference on Research in Air Transportation, ICRAT 2004, Zilina, Slovakia, pp. 59–64 (2004)
7. PANSA. AIP Poland, Flight Information Services (2015). http://www.ais.pata.pl/aip
8. Schuster, W., Ochieng, W.: Performance requirements of future Trajectory Prediction and Conflict Detection and Resolution tools within SESAR and NextGen: Framework for the derivation and discussion. J. Air Transp. Manage. **35**, 92–101 (2014)
9. SESAR. Annual Report 2012, SESAR Joint Undertaking, Brussels (2013)
10. Siergiejczyk, M., Krzykowska, K., Rosiński, A.: Reliability assessment of cooperation and replacement of surveillance systems in air traffic. In: Zamojski, W., Mazurkiewicz, J., Sugier, J., Walkowiak, T., Kacprzyk, J. (eds.) Proceedings of the Ninth International Conference on DepCoS-RELCOMEX. AISC, vol. 286, pp. 403–412. Springer, Heidelberg (2014)
11. Skorupski, J.: Airport traffic simulation using petri nets. In: Mikulski, J. (ed.) TST 2013. CCIS, vol. 395, pp. 468–475. Springer, Heidelberg (2013)
12. Skorupski, J.: Traffic Incidents as a Tool for Improvement of Transport Safety. In: Weintrit, A. (ed.) Navigational Problems – Marine Navigation and Safety of Sea Transportation, pp. 101–108. CRC Press/Taylor & Francis/Balkema, Leiden (2013)
13. Skorupski, J.: Multi-criteria group decision making under uncertainty with application to air traffic safety. Expert Syst. Appl. **41**(16), 7406–7414 (2014)
14. Skorupski, J.: The risk of an air accident as a result of a serious incident of the hybrid type. Reliab. Eng. Syst. Saf. **140**, 37–52 (2015)

15. Skorupski, J., Stelmach, A.: Model of air traffic in terminal area for ATFM safety analysis. In: Safety, Reliability and Risk Analysis: Theory, Methods and Applications - Proceedings of the Joint ESREL and SRA-Europe Conference, vol. 3, pp. 2191–2198. Taylor and Francis/Balkema, London (2009)
16. Stelmach, A., Malarski, M., Skorupski, J.:Model of airport terminal area capacity investigation. In: Proceedings of the European Safety and Reliability Conference 2006, ESREL 2006 - Safety and Reliability for Managing Risk, pp. 1863–1868 (2006)

Innovative Control System for High Efficiency Electric Urban Vehicle

Karol Cichoński[✉] and Wojciech Skarka

Institute of Fundamentals of Machinery Design,
Silesian University of Technology,
Konarskiego 18A, 44-100 Gliwice, Poland
karolcichonski89@gmail.com, wojciech.skarka@polsl.pl

Abstract. Designers faces many problems while designing and constructing prototype of special purpose car and this is what happens in case of high-efficient electric city car named Bytel, which was especially built for Shell eco-marathon competition. Bytel takes part in Urban Electric category and its drive consists of two brushless DC motor (BLDC) mounted directly in wheels. Smart Power team which carries the task comes from the Silesian University of Technology in Gliwice. One of the assignments which required individual approach was the innovative control system of the car and it is the main topic of this article. The core task of the control system is receiving steering signals from the driver, signal processing and sending them to drivers. It is equipped with many additional functions like e.g. visualization, measurement and storage system as well as safety systems. All of these facilities serve the purpose of improving driver's safety and enable delivery of a lot of data to analyze which has a huge influence on power consumption. The paper shows the whole process of forming the systems from design assumptions, construction to tests in labs.

Keywords: Control system · BLDC motor · Shell Eco-marathon · High efficiency electric car

1 Introduction

Nowadays electric cars become more and more popular. Many factors influence the current situation, which are for example widespread environmental policies, technological growth of electric drives and electric energy storage, marketing activities of car producers. Driving range is constantly growing and charging time is still decreasing. All this results in the fact that electric cars are more and more cheaper and thus more widely available. Every bigger automotive producer has in his offer cars with full electric or hybrid drive [7, 12].

The need to promote environmentally friendly vehicles is also recognized by Shell, and Shell Eco-marathon competition. This competition is organized every year in three editions- Europe, Asia and Americas. This is competition for students from all over the world. They design and build high-efficiency vehicles whose main goal is to run over the greatest distance using one unit of energy, depending on the type of fuel that is used to supply vehicle. There are several categories to choose from [18].

© Springer International Publishing Switzerland 2015
J. Mikulski (Ed.): TST 2015, CCIS 531, pp. 121–130, 2015.
DOI: 10.1007/978-3-319-24577-5_12

The innovative control system that is described in this paper is intended to vehicle named Bytel (Fig. 1). Bytel competes in Urban Electric category- small city car that is equipped with electric drive. It was built within the project Smart Power [3], at the Institute of Machinery Design at the Faculty of Mechanical Engineering of the Silesian University of Technology. The control system is one of the most important components affecting the energy consumption of the vehicle [3, 6]. During design, the individual components have been optimized in order to reduce energy consumption and the team refined a complex methodology to optimize the characteristics of the vehicle in this regard [14, 16].Around the world, intensive research are currently carried out on control systems for both battery-electric vehicles [1, 2, 6, 8, 9, 17] as various other types of drives [7, 11–13].

The control system was described in this article in context of huge requirements for this system and cooperation with other vehicle systems. It is one of the components that give possibility to achieve revolutionary low power consumption. The main task of the control system is receiving steering signals from the driver, signal processing and sending them to drivers [3]. It is equipped with many additional functions like e.g. visualization, measurement and storage system as well as safety systems [5, 15]. All of these facilities serve the purpose of improving driver's safety and enable delivery of a lot of data to analyze, which has a huge influence on power consumption.

Fig. 1. Bytel race vehicle [own study]

2   Concepts

Figure 2 shows general scheme of the control system. It consists of the following modules and functionalities:

- receiving acceleration and brake signals from driver and transmitting it to motors controllers,
- measuring current consumption of BLDC motors (every motor independently),
- measuring propulsion battery voltage,
- measuring the movement parameters like speed, average speed, distance, race time, lap number,

– measuring temperature of motor controllers and propulsion battery,
– checking for the presence of smoke and combustible gases,
– checking for the correct operation of motors controllers,
– storing data on SD card,
– displaying all necessary information for driver on LCD display,
– sending data to telemetry module,

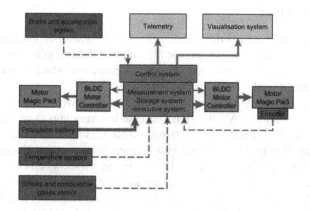

Fig. 2. General scheme of control system [own study]

Below are presented design assumptions that are imposed by the organizers of Shell Eco-marathon which are necessary to pass technical inspection and be allowed to start in the competition [18]:

– maximum voltage on board of any vehicle at any point must not exceed 48 Volts nominal and 60 Volts max,
– only one propulsion battery and one accessory battery is allowed,
– all batteries must maintain a negative ground,
– negative outputs from propulsion battery and accessory battery cannot be connected,
– all cases for electronics must be made of transparent materials,
– drive system should have terminal to plug joule meter for measurement result
– the motor controller must be tailor-built for the Shell Eco-marathon. One or more single printed circuit boards (PCB) need the text "SEM" to be included in the mask of the PCB etching,
– it is allowed to use single board computers for the design of motors controllers.

Others design assumptions:

– drive system consists of two BLDC motors which are embedded in the rear wheels hubs,
– every motor is controlled by independent motor controller,
– driver gives an acceleration signal through the Hall-effect pedal,
– driver gives a braking signal through the switch on steering wheel,
– galvanic isolation is necessary between control system and motors controllers,

- all elements through which propulsion current flows must be optimized of losses occurring at them,
- main element of control system is one board computer the Arduino Due.

3   Project and Realization

3.1   The Control Unit

Single board computer named the Arduino Due has been selected as control unit. It is based on microcontroller Atmel SAM3 × 8E with 32 bit ARM core. The main reason why this computer has been selected is very fast processor which provides the right amount of computational power.

The Arduino has many peripherals embedded and hardware support of communication buses (for example CAN BUS). In this case it is very important because control system cooperates with many other systems which are in vehicle (like an additional equipment controller, safety systems). Fast communication without noise is of paramount importance. On Fig. 3 we can see the scheme which shows all electronic devices and communication signals. Additional advantages of the Arduino are large number of libraries which are for free, approachable programming language, possibility to test particular functionality without the need to make printed circuit. The authors have known Arduino platform from previous projects.

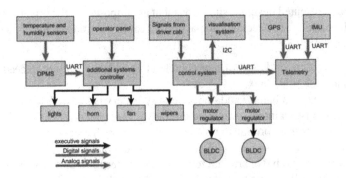

Fig. 3. Data flow scheme in Bytel [own study]

3.2   Driver Interface

The driver interface with visualization system is the most important element which is used for communication between driver and the control system. The driver should receive information in a clear and unambiguous way without any problems. The access to movement parameters and diagnostic warnings is very important for Driver as thanks to them it is possible to drive according to the previously calculated strategy [10, 16]. This results in repeatability of lap and better outcome in the competition. Diagnostic information allows driver to react to irregularities immediately after their occurrence.

The main element of driver interface is alphanumeric LCD display 4 × 20, which is able to display 20 signs in 4 rows and is equipped with RGB backlight. Backlight color change can be used to transmit some diagnostic information and warnings (for example to indicate low battery voltage). The interface is equipped also with five red LED indicators which can be programmable according to purpose. The visualization of system during tests is shown in Fig. 4.

Fig. 4. Driver interface during test [own study]

3.3 Data Measurement and Storage System

The measurement system is the most extensive part of the control system which is described in this article. This is due to the fact that the data that is collected by the control system is used for such purposes as:

- sending correct signals to motors controllers,
- protecting the vehicle and the controller itself,
- protecting motor controllers,
- providing the driver with all information which is necessary to drive according to the strategy.

Measurement of Vehicle Motion Parameters. Vehicle motion parameters are calculated based on the interrupt from the incremental optical encoder. The encoder consists of perforated disc and slotted opt coupler TCST1103. The encoder resolution is 16 pulses per revolution of the wheel. This is sufficient to calculate vehicle speed, race distance and any others motion parameter. Every rising edge triggers the interrupts program in the microcontroller, which counts the number of interrupts per time unit and based on this calculates vehicle speed.

Measurement of Electrical Parameters. The electrical parameters are determined to calculate the amount of energy consumed by the vehicle. Power is calculated as the product of current on the motors and voltage on propulsion battery. The vehicle is equipped with two drive motors. The control system is able to measure current consumption on every motor independently. Two current sensors ACS756 are used to measure current which work based on Hall effect. Their measuring range is +-50 A. They are characterized by high accuracy (total measurement error is less than 1 %) and small dissipation- sensor resistance is 130 mOhm. Sensor output is analog signal in the range of 0–5 V and with resolution of 20 mV/A. Sensor reply is measured by the built-in microcontroller ADC with the resolution of 12 bit. Voltage of sensor output is higher than is allowed on the microcontroller input therefore it is reduced by resistor voltage divider with a value of 1.5.

Battery voltage is measured directly by the microcontroller ADC after reduced by resistor voltage divider with a value of 20. This method allows for the safe measure voltage in the range 0–66 V.

Temperature Sensors. Digital temperature sensors that are used in the control system are named DS18B20. They are used to measure the temperature of motors controllers and propulsion battery. These sensors allow the measurement of temperature in the range $-55°C - +125°C$ with the resolution of $0.5°C$. Communication with the control system is by the 1-Wire bus.

Smoke and Combustibles Sensor. Smoke and combustibles sensor is used to alert the driver in the event of fire risk. The sensor as used in the control system is module MQ2. It allows for the detection of smoke and gases such as hydrogen, LPG, methane, carbon monoxide, alcohol or, propane-butane.

The sensor is equipped with 0–5 V analog output and digital output. Switching threshold of digital output can by adjust of the built-in potentiometer.

Storage System. Control system as data storage system uses SD card module. SD cards allows to store large amounts of data and are also relatively cheap and safe.

4 Laboratory Tests

4.1 Test Bench

The test bench shown in Fig. 5, has been done because simultaneously the body chassis of vehicle was made. For this reason access to a car was difficult and testing the car directly was impossible. These tests helped to refine the control system software, to test most of functionality and to detect potential errors. The test bench was created based on a chassis dynamometer described in [4]. It consists of the control panel Fig. 5, the control system with motor drivers, two direct motors MagicPie3. These are the same as the motors used in the vehicle.

The operation panel consists of the following components:

1. visualization system
2. acceleration pedal
3. regenerative braking button
4. button to increment a number of laps
5. data reset button
6. emergency switch
7. switch to turn on/off control system

Fig. 5. Operation panel and test bench [own study]

4.2 Test on the Bench

The first stage of the tests was to check initialization procedure and reaction of control system for motor controller damage and SD card damage or its lack. Damage of motor controllers was simulated by disconnecting the power from them whereas the damage of the memory card by pulling it out of the slot. The tests confirmed the correctness of the procedure in the control system initialization. In case of detection of any of the above-described defects, the procedure was interrupted until the error was approved by the user (driver). The next tests were intended to map the conditions during the race. The system was supplied from the car battery to allow verification of regenerative braking. Regenerative braking generates high reverse currents, which in the case of the laboratory DC power supply could result in the power supply damage. The test plan assumed completing 10 starts which simulate rides on a distance of 500 m. Each of the runs was ended by regenerative braking, as it is during the Shell Eco-marathon. During the tests all the necessary data was recorded and motors worked without any additional load. Figure 6 shows the graph representing the instantaneous velocity and the race distance. The maximum speed that was registered is consistent with the characteristics from producer.

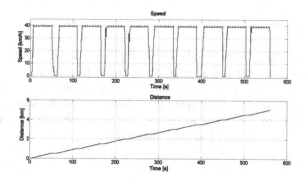

Fig. 6. Velocity and distance in time domain [own study]

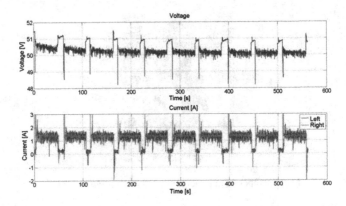

Fig. 7. Current and voltage in time domain [own study]

Figure 7 presents a chart that shows voltage and currents at the controllers in the time domain. The increase in current consumption causes a voltage drop that is visible on the chart. Short-term current peaks with a value below zero result from regenerative braking. Short braking time and small current value is due to the low inertia of wheels with motors. There was no temperature increase of motor controllers. This is due to low load on test bench. During operation a rise in temperature will be noticeable in the vehicle.

4.3 Verification of Smoke and Combustible Gases Sensor

The smoke and combustible gases sensor was tested outside the test bench. The reason for this was the safety considerations. The main purpose of the tests was verification of operation and determination of the characteristics. Based on characteristics alarm thresholds were appointment for the diagnostic system.

During the tests response of sensor have been measured against the following extortions:

– smoke
– butane
– acetone vapors

The measurement results are shown in Fig. 8. The chart shows the answer recorded at the ADC (Analog to Digital Converter) in time domain.

The sensor allows to detect extortions from all tested substances. In electric vehicle reaction to smoke is the most important. Fire is the main danger when vehicle is supplied by the LiFePo4 battery. Alarm threshold with value of 1200 allows to detect smoke even at low concentration.

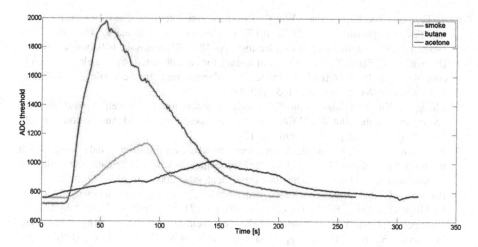

Fig. 8. Response of smoke and combustible gases sensor in time domain [own study]

5   Conclusion

The system has been programmed and tested in The Laboratory of Mobile Systems at the Silesian University of Technology. The tests confirmed the proper working of all functionality which were described at design assumptions. The implementation in the vehicle and the final verification will be possible after the finished work with car chassis. After the implementation the control system in the car should be determined with new alarm thresholds. This will also improve its performance and minimize the number of false alarms.

The control system has hardware support to the CAN BUS communication. When software support of CAN BUS will be available in Arduino IDE, the use of this BUS will increase the reliability and the speed of communication.

References

1. Bimal, K., Bose, A.: Microprocessor-Based Control System for a Near-Term Electric Vehicle, IEEE transactions on industry applications 17(6): 626–631 (1981)
2. Bimal, K., Bose, A.: DC motor control system for electric drive. IEEE Trans. Ind. Appl. **Ia-14**(6), 565–572 (1978)
3. Sternal, K., Cholewa, A., Skarka, W., Targosz, M.: Electric vehicle for the students' shell eco-marathon competition. design of the car and telemetry system. In: Mikulski, J. (ed.) TST 2012. CCIS, vol. 329, pp. 26–33. Springer, Heidelberg (2012)
4. Cichoński, K., Jezierska-Krupa, K., Gleń, M., Skarka, W.: The comparative study of drivetrain of high-performance electric vehicle. Diagnostyka **15**(2), 65–70 (2014)
5. Cichoński, K., Otrębska, M., Skarka, W., Zamorski, P.: Designing safety systems for electric race car. In: Mikulski, J. (ed.) TST 2013. CCIS, vol. 395, pp. 162–165. Springer, Heidelberg (2013)

6. Yu Han, G., Chee, Ken L., Kuew Wai, C.: Electric vehicle intelligent control system hardware modules configurations. In: 2012 IEEE Conference on Sustainable Utilization and Development in Engineering and Technology, pp. 187–191, Malaysia, 6–9 October 2012
7. Dhadyalla, G., Snell, T.: Combinatorial testing for an automotive hybrid electric vehicle control system. In: 2014 IEEE International Conference on Software Testing, Verification, and Validation Workshops, pp. 51–57 (2014)
8. Cheng, L., Xu, Y.: Design of intelligent control system for electric vehicle road train. In: Proceedings of the 10th World Congress on Intelligent Control and Automation 6–8 July 2012, Beijing, China, pp. 3958–3961 (2012)
9. Xu, P., Guo, G., Cao, J., Cao, B.: A novel fore axle whole-turning driving and control system for direct-wheel-driven electric vehicle. In: Proceedings of the IEEE International Conference on Automation and Logistics, Qingdao, China September 2008, pp. 705–709 (2018)
10. Przystałka, P., et al.: Velocity planning of an electric vehicle using an evolutionary algorithm. In: Mikulski, J. (ed.) TST 2013. CCIS, vol. 395, pp. 171–177. Springer, Heidelberg (2013)
11. Huang Qi, Q., Chen, Y., Li, J.: Control of electric vehicle, urban transport and hybrid vehicles. In: Soylu, S., (ed.) InTech. pp. 163–192 ISBN: 978-953-307-100-8 (2010). http://www.Intechopen.Com/Books/Urbantransport-And-Hybrid-Vehicles/Control-Of-Electric-Vehicle. Accessed on Accessed on 15th July 2014
12. Zhang, R, Chen, Y.: Control of hybrid dynamical systems for electric vehicles. In: Proceedings of the American Control Conference, pp. 2884–2889, Arlington, VA, USA, June 2001
13. Saeks, R., Cox, C.: Design of an adaptive control system for a hybrid electric vehicle. In: Accurate Automation Corporation. Chattanooga, TN 37421 USA, pp. 1000–1005 (1999)
14. Skarka, W.: Application of numerical inverse model to determine the characteristic of electric race car. In: Tools and Methods of Competitive Engineering (TMCE) Symposium. 19 – 23 May 2014. pp. 263–274, Budapest, Hungary (2014)
15. Skarka, W. et al,: Advanced driver assistance systems for electric race car. In: Tools and Methods of Competitive Engineering (TMCE) Symposium. 19 – 23 May 2014. pp. 1487–1494, Budapest, Hungary (2014)
16. Targosz, M., Skarka, W., Przystalka, P.: Simulation and optimization methodology of prototype electric vehicle. In: Marjanović D., Štorga, M., Pavković, N., Bojčetić, N. (eds.) Proceedings of the 13th International Design Conference DESIGN 2014. pp. 1349 – 1360. Dubrovnik, Croatia (2014)
17. Zhao, Y., Zhang, Y., Zhao, Y.: Stability control system for four-in-wheel-motor drive electric vehicle. In: 2009 Sixth International Conference on Fuzzy Systems and Knowledge Discovery, pp. 172–175 (2009)
18. Shell Eco-marathon (2014) Official Rules - chapter 1. http://www.shell.com/global/environment-society/ecomarathon/for-participants/general-information/rules.html. Accessed on 15th July 2014

Information System for Drivers Within the Integrated Traffic Management System - TRISTAR

Jacek Oskarbski[✉], Marcin Zawisza, and Michał Miszewski

Gdansk University of Technology, 80-233 Gdansk, Poland
{joskar,marcin.zawisza,micmisze}@pg.gda.pl

Abstract. Advanced traveler information systems (ATIS) for drivers are a very important element of modern traffic management. In recent years ITS infrastructure is being developed also in Poland. It allows for delivering to drivers information related to the conditions in the road network through, inter alia, dedicated Variable Message Signs (VMS). Such information enables drivers to take decisions, contributing to improving the efficiency and safety of the transport system. They also allow to manage the traffic speed dynamically, taking into account weather conditions hazards, temporary disruptions or incidents. Paper provides an overview of different solutions for Advanced Traveler Information Systems in Poland. The place of ATIS in architecture of Tri-City TRISTAR system is described as well as the use of data, functions and algorithms that allow them to be implemented. Furthermore ATIS development plans and plans for research to be carried out to improve the functioning of the system are presented.

Keywords: Intelligent transport systems · Traffic management · Information systems

1 Introduction

Due to the rapid growth of mobility and individual motorisation of residents of Polish cities there are more and more problems related to ensuring proper operation of transport. Road networks are becoming more and more congested, resulting in increased waste of time and reduced reliability of the transport network. As demonstrated by the experience of many cities in the US and Europe the expansion of the road system has rarely seen a long-term improvement of traffic conditions. Nowadays, the key issue is the deployment of Intelligent Transport Systems (ITS), with special emphasis on traveler information systems (ATIS).

ATIS is strongly correlated with various factors. These factors can be classified in the following five main categories [1]:

- drivers' socioeconomic characteristics, such as age, gender, driver familiarity with the network, etc.,
- VMS characteristics, such as VMS information content and location,
- trip characteristics, such as trip purpose and departure time,

© Springer International Publishing Switzerland 2015
J. Mikulski (Ed.): TST 2015, CCIS 531, pp. 131–140, 2015.
DOI: 10.1007/978-3-319-24577-5_13

- drivers' attitudes and perceptions, such as drivers' risk preferences, perceived usefulness of VMS, etc.
- network characteristics, congestion levels and road weather conditions.

Many studies examined the impact of traffic information. For instance, a study was conducted on how travelers would respond to different traffic information. Research was based on a questionnaire survey of commuters in California Bay Area [2]. Results indicated factors affecting travel decision changes due to delays on the usual route, travel time on alternative routes, perceived level of congestion on alternative routes and information sources. Delay information on alternative routes was found to be significant to diversion decision. A bivariate model to examine the endogenous dependency of the use of radio traffic information and VMS for the Amsterdam region was presented in [3]. The authors found that drivers who were influenced by radio traffic information were more likely to be also influenced by VMS information. Drivers responses to VMS information were studied in [4]. The data was analyzed using logistic regression models. Results showed that information provided by VMS were perceived to be useful but only 20 % of the respondents made a route diversion. A multinomial modeling analysis of Dutch samples collected from internet survey [5] showed that suggestion on alternative route was the most preferred content by drivers (next were location, length and cause of traffic delay). The effects of VMS on route choice, speed and drivers behavior were investigated in [6]. An empirical analysis of the field data confirmed that VMS were effective in rerouting of traffic. A study results to determine user awareness and perception of VMS on Wisconsin's freeways [7] showed that route diversion was considered if the VMS displayed information on time increase due to an accident, road works or traffic congestion for at least 15 min. The main task of ATIS is the communication of the following information to drivers [8]:

- travel times between known destinations,
- traffic conditions along a road corridor,
- construction notices,
- special event notices and instructions for drivers,
- maintenance operation schedules,
- severe weather announcements,
- incident notifications.

1.1 Advanced Traveler Information Systems in Poland

We can observe development of ITS systems in Poland both in urban areas and on motorways currently. One of the main information communicated to drivers in urban systems are travel times between two points in a city with an indication of alternative routes. Such systems were implemented in cities of Szczecin and Wroclaw. Traffic management entities uses VMS also to displays other information e.g. information on temporary changes in traffic system or new road layout, incidents in street network as well as messages promoting safe behavior on the roads. Another solution of Information System for drivers without installing dedicated devices (VMS) in road infrastructure can be found in the city of Bialystok, where the existing signposts are equipped with electronic modules for displaying numerical values.

An example of a rural ATIS is Intelligent Traffic Control System of Podhale Region (ISSRRP). It is a territorial system (on national and regional roads), using measures of ITS for traffic control based on the information from the devices in the system, with use of communication and information channels such as GSM/GPS, Internet and by providing - via variable message boards - messages about travel time on a specific route to the destination (Zakopane, Rabka Zdroj, Krakow, Myslenice, Nowy Targ) with graphical information showing traffic conditions on a specified route [9]. ISSRRP provides the following functions:

- traffic measurement stations using RTMS (Remote Traffic Microwave Sensor) technology carry out measurement of vehicles speed, vehicle classification and the measurement of the volume of traffic on the sections assigned to the station. Each station has a built-in camera which enables to view a road surface (video image or a sequence of pictures),
- meteorological stations carry out the measurement of air temperature, pavement temperature, wind speed and direction, air transparency, surface condition, rainfall and generate warnings about weather conditions,
- CCTV (closed-circuit television) cameras allow to view traffic conditions on the road,
- traffic information boards (Variable Message Boards - VMB) provide drivers with information about alternative routes during the journey, and provide information on the types of difficulties,
- ANPR (automatic number plate recognition) cameras support system in the calculation of travel times between selected points of road network.

ISSRRP effectiveness analysis in conditions of random incidents (road accidents) were developed in [10] on the basis of the analysis of traffic assignment during periods of traffic accidents that result in limiting the capacity of the road network elements. The closure or narrowing of the road in the scene was taken into account in the simulation network model. Analysis showed a positive impact of the system on the dispersion and improving traffic conditions in the road network in case of an incident.

ATIS are also implemented on motorways (e.g. A2 motorway). Information for drivers provided with variable message signs and variable message boards focuses primarily on managing speed simultaneously with the communication of information about the difficulties and dangers (accidents, vehicle queues, dangerous condition of the road surface, road works), additional information is provided about alternative routes to avoid traffic disturbances.

One of the major ITS projects implemented currently in Poland is the TRISTAR Integrated Traffic Management System. Its range covers the main road system of three adjacent cities - Gdansk, Sopot and Gdynia. The system supports actions related to traffic management and public transport for the optimal use of road infrastructure, improvement of traffic safety and reduction of the negative impact of urban traffic on the environment. Among the main modules of the TRISTAR system the following can be distinguished: Traffic Control System with the module to provide Public Transport vehicles with prioritization in traffic, Monitoring and Traffic Surveillance System, Video Surveillance System,

Transport Planning System (supported by Multilevel Transport System Model), Public Transport Management System and information systems: Advanced Traveler Information System for drivers and Public Transport Passenger Information System [11].

All the TRISTAR system components use numerous vehicle detection devices, which consist of inductive loops and video image processors positioned throughout the entire area of the system operation as well as GPS transmitters installed in vehicles of public transport and receivers to detect the location of mobile devices. The Traveler Information System uses the data collected by other modules of the System in order to provide reliable information about traffic. With the application of dedicated algorithms, these data are processed and presented to drivers using the devices installed on the road. This article outlines the operation of the ATIS implemented in the TRISTAR System based on the example of the city of Gdynia.

2   Traveler Information System for Drivers in TRISTAR

The Advanced Traveler Information System has been designed for the presentation of the collected and processed traffic data from detection devices of the TRISTAR system. Drivers are provided with information about traffic disturbances via Variable Message Boards and Variable Message Signs installed at strategic locations throughout the Gdynia street network. Access to the presented information will be also possible via the website. The data from ATIS presented on the variable message boards and signs provide a source of information in the following areas:

– current travel time for major sections of the road network;
– current incidents and traffic congestion, including accidents, breakdown of traffic signals, failure of road or technical infrastructure, road works carried out, closed roads, mass events;
– planned events and obstructions including road works, repairs, closed roads, mass events;
– current weather conditions on the roads (e.g. temperature, humidity, wind strength and direction etc.);
– warnings of hazardous weather conditions (e.g. a slippery surface, side wind, fog, etc.) coming from automatic weather stations integrated within the System.

The information displayed on Variable Message Boards (VMB) is designed to give recommendations as to specific behavior on the road, but they are not mandatory and the decision to comply is the responsibility of the driver (e.g. a recommendation to use a detour). If there are no incidents on the network, basic information presented on the signs is the travel time in a given direction through two alternative routes. Due to the diversity of travel goals and motivations this information is only complementary for drivers, as they often do not have the ability to change their decision on the choice of the route and destination of the journey.

Variable message signs (VMS) are part of the traffic organisation and information presented obliges drivers to comply with the displayed information, e.g. change of the speed limit. Signs have full force and failing to adhere to them has consequences stipulated by the provisions of road traffic law. The main aim of the Traveler Information System for Drivers is to ensure smooth and safe traffic flow within the road network covered by the Traffic Management System. As in every area of life, adequate and reliable information allows for proper plans of action, thus reducing the risk of incurring additional losses (e.g. time or costs). In an increasingly saturated road network, current traffic information allows for the minimisation of time loss by choosing the optimal route or changing the mode of transport.

2.1 System Infrastructure

The operative elements for ATIS are the Variable Message Boards and Signs. The effectiveness of the system depends largely on the proper location of the devices. The boards should be located so to enable change of decision on the selection of an alternative route in advance before the intersections. The Variable Message Signs in Gdynia are located on the sections of roads with fast moving traffic, where the information about the change of the speed limit or the occurrence of potential hazard in traffic is more important.

In Gdynia 8 variable-message boards were installed in three main locations: the intersection of Morska St. and the Tri-City Bypass (Fig. 1), the intersection of Morska St. and Trasa Kwiatkowskiego Rd. and on the Droga Gdyńska St. route and its intersection with the Wielkopolska St. Information for drivers is displayed on large-format LED screens. The messages displayed on the devices are initiated automatically. The system proposes content depending on the situation on the road automatically, semi-automatically or is fed manually by operators at the Traffic Management Centre. The VMB shown in Fig. 1 enables the provision of information on the selection of an alternative route towards Gdansk via the Tri-City Bypass or the main artery running through Tri-City centers. In recent years the bypass has been used as a road within the agglomeration. In the summer, it serves very heavy tourist traffic in the direction of the Hel Peninsula, which often causes obstructions in traffic fluidity. These factors dictate the location of the VMB in the described location.

The most extensive system of Variable Message Boards is located at the intersection of Morska St. and Trasa Kwiatkowskiego Rd. (Fig 2). Each entry of the intersection is equipped with a board, which enables the display of information about alternative routes in different directions and possible incidents on each of the exit roads. Trasa Kwiatkowskiego Rd. leads to the Port of Gdynia and has a significant share of heavy freight vehicle traffic. Susceptibility and difficulties associated with this is one of the criteria justifying the location of the boards at this intersection.

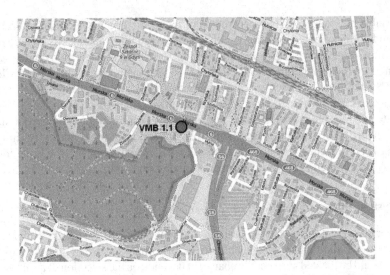

Fig. 1. Location of Variable Message Boards within the intersection of Morska St. and the Tri-City Bypass in Gdynia [own study].

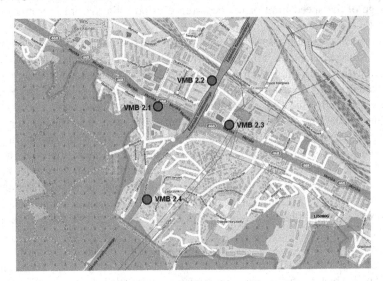

Fig. 2. Location of Variable Message Boards within the intersection of Morska St. and the Tri-City Bypass in Gdynia [own study]

Variable Message Signs are devices that consist of several LED screens, each of which acts as an independent sign, having the same legal implication as the vertical sign, they are elements of permanent traffic organisation equipment. The signs form complies with the Minister of Infrastructure Regulation of the 3 July 2003 on detailed technical specifications for road signs and signals and road traffic safety equipment and their placement on the road. According to the Regulation they match the color and shape of the corresponding permanent signs. However, some simplification of the symbol form is applied and exchange the background color from white (yellow) to black and black symbols to white (yellow). The edges of prohibition and warning signs are red.

As in the case of the VMB, the signs are displayed automatically by the master system or an operator at the Traffic Management Centre. In order to maintain the continuity and coordination of operation, the scenarios and procedures have been prepared which, in the event of certain conditions (e.g. weather), display speed limit with additional appropriate sign or text message. Five structures with Variable Message Signs have been installed in Gdynia – on the Trasa Kwiatkowski Rd. (one in each direction) and the Droga Gdyńska St. (one on the lane in the direction of the Gdynia centre and two in the direction of Gdansk).

2.2 Messages on VMS and VMB Devices

The location of devices in strategic positions on the road network of Gdynia have been described above. The main criteria for their selection was the ability of directing to alternative routes. As a result in the case of an incident on any of the routes, it is possible to indicate a diversion. The TRISTAR system allows for displaying information on Variable Message Boards in three modes. In standard mode (automatic)VMB displays travel times between alternative routes and VMS displays the speed limit which, in case of detection of dangerous weather (e.g. black ice) is reduced and also appropriate warning sign and text message appears.

In the case of an incident detection by the system, a message is sent to the operator for approval (semi-automatic mode). Variable Message Boards in this mode display information about disruption in the network and location of incident (the system estimates travel times on defined sections of the network and responds to time exceeding the warning threshold).Variable Message Signs display the appropriate speed limit with the A-33 warning sign in the case of detection of a vehicle queue at the first junction before the sign, as in the automatic mode.

In the case of planned events (e.g. road works or mass event), the operator feeds the event on the map (manual mode) which is interpreted appropriately by the system, Variable Message Boards display information about planned events, and along with Variable Message Signs about incidents occurring within area of the system for which the impact time on the transport network is clearly defined.

2.3 Relationship Between ATIS and Other TRISTAR Subsystems

Automatic and semi-automatic modes of ATIS are based on data obtained from other TRISTAR subsystems. All information from the system is stored in dedicated databases. One of these databases is the Integrated Database (IDB), where all the latest information from each of the TRISTAR modules are transferred. Any information from the subsystem to the IDB is then simultaneously downloaded by the respective modules. For the correct operation, the ATIS needs the following information:

– road surface condition, visibility and wind speed –from module measuring meteorological parameters (Weather Parameters Measurement System);
– travel times on road sections in the Tri-City –from Travel Time Calculation Module,

– information about the detection of a potential road incidents–from Traffic Incident Detection Module and Travel Time Calculation Module,
– queue lengths at intersections entries –from Traffic Control System,
– road incidents detected by the TRISTAR system operators –from Monitoring and Traffic Surveillance System.

The figure below (Fig. 3) shows the relationship of individual components of the TRISTAR system with the ATIS system.

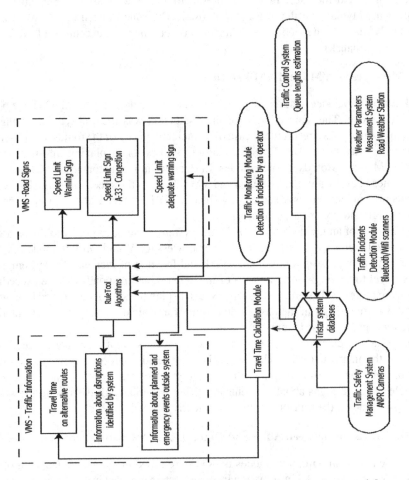

Fig. 3. ATIS relationship with other Tristar System modules [own study]

2.4   ATIS Algorithms

Gevas Software implemented in the TRISTAR System consists of multiple components. One of them is RuleTool. It is a tool for algorithm designing on the basis of data contained in the TRISTAR databases. With the use of this tool, the engineer can set the boundary conditions which should be fulfilled to display a certain type of message (automatic and semi-automatic mode). A calculation step of each algorithm stored on a RuleTool is one minute. During each step of the calculation data are retrieved from the corresponding components of the IDB, then they are checked with the boundary conditions of particular algorithms. In the case when all the conditions are met, the workflow is activated, which displays defined messages on the devices assigned to the particular algorithm. Workflow is active until one of the necessary conditions is no longer met. At the same time several workflows may be running, in this case a message of higher priority workflow is displayed. An example of an algorithm associated with weather conditions is presented in the figure below (Fig. 4).

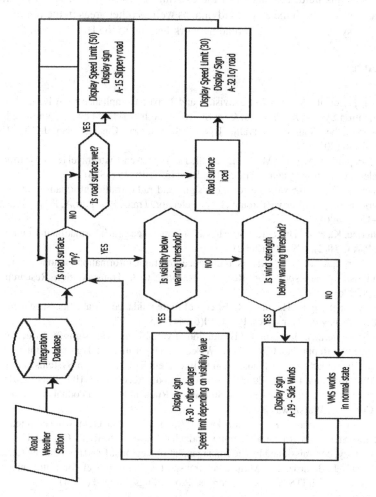

Fig. 4. Exemplary ATIS algorithm for Variable Message Signs [own study]

3   Conclusion

The positive aspects of the impact of ATIS to improve traffic conditions and safety indicate the need to develop the system in the Pomeranian Region, both in terms of functionality and area. Algorithms implemented within TRISTAR system can be the basis for further development of information system for drivers. One of the areas on which the research will be conducted is to determine the methodology of speed limit estimation due to weather conditions. Further studies are necessary for VMS and VMB location as well as provided information both in terms of content and graphic form. At present, there are no legal regulations, guidelines or methodology containing boundary conditions in this field. Expansion of the existing infrastructure of ATIS is expected. Such plans refer to both the city of Gdynia, as well as other areas in the region (e.g. an information system for drivers in road network leading to the Hel Peninsula).

References

1. Kattan, L., et al.: Information Provision and Driver Compliance to Advanced Traveller Information System Application: Case Study on the Interaction between Variable Message Sign and other Sources of Traffic Updates in Calgary, Canada. Can. J. Civ. Eng. **38**, 1335–1346 (2011)
2. Polydoropoulou, A., et al.: Modeling revealed and stated en-route travel response to advanced traveler information systems. Trans. Res. Rec. **1537**, 38–45 (1996)
3. Emmerink, R., et al.: variable message signs and radio traffic information: an integrated empirical analysis of drivers' route choice behavior. Trans. Res. Part A, Policy Pract. **30**(2), 135–153 (1996)
4. Chatterjee, K., et al.: Driver response to variable message sign information in London. Trans. Res. Part C **10**(2), 149–169 (2002)
5. Muizelaar, J., Arem, B.V.: Drivers' preferences for traffic information for non-recurrent traffic situations. In: Transportation Research Record 2018, Transportation Research Board, 72–79(2006)
6. Erke, A., Sagberg, F., Hagman, R.: Effects of route guidance variable message signs (VMS) on driver behavior. Trans. Res. Part F **10**(6), 447–457 (2007)
7. Ran, B., Barrett, B., Johnson, E.: Evaluation of variable message signs in Wisconsin: driver survey. Final Report No. 0092-45-17, Wisconsin Department of Transportation (2004)
8. Wisconsin Department of Transportation Intelligent Transportation Systems (ITS) Manual (2000). http://www4.uwm.edu/cuts/itsdm/chap6.pdf. Accessed on 10 February 2015
9. Zakrzewski, P.: Inteligentny System Sterowania Ruchem Regionu Podhalanskiego. V Polish ITS Congress, Warszawa (2012)
10. Oskarbski, J., Jamroz, K., Oskarbska, I.: Analiza i ocena efektywności Inteligentnego Systemu Sterownia Ruchem Regionu Podhalanskiego – ISSRRP, Gdansk University of Technology, commissioned by the Management of Regional Roads in Krakow (2013)
11. Oskarbski, J., Jamroz, K.: Multi-level transport systems model for traffic management activities. In: 10th ITS European Congress Proceedings. Finland (2014)

Software Quality Assurance in e-Navigation

Adam Weintrit[✉]

Gdynia Maritime University, 81-226 Gdynia, Poland
weintrit@am.gdynia.pl

Abstract. The International Maritime Organization (IMO) has decided that e-Navigation should be 'User Need' led and take into account the Human Element. In this paper the Author, which is a member of the IMO expert group on e-Navigation since 2006, will describe the IMO guideline on software quality assurance in e-Navigation. The guideline highlights that software in support of e-Navigation may be a standalone product or part of a larger more complex system incorporating data and information management. The guideline introduces quality models to assist in identifying the characteristics of system software which allows for the successful harmonization, integration, exchange, analyses and presentation of maritime data and information to meet user needs.

Keywords: e-Navigation · IMO · ITS · Marine navigation · MSI · Transport telematics · Safety of sea transportation · Software Quality Assurance (SQA)

1   Introduction

The International Maritime Organization IMO expert group led by Australia is preparing the draft Guidelines on Software Quality Assurance (SQA) [3], developing standards to harmonize ship and shore e-Navigation. However, everything indicates that it will be a part of a larger document containing three previously separately considered guidelines on Human Centred Design (HCD) for e-Navigation systems, on Usability Testing, Evaluation and Assessment (UTEA) for e-Navigation systems and on Software Quality Assurance (SQA) in e-Navigation.

SQA is a set of processes that ensures software meets and complies with required quality specifications. The IMO guideline on SQA highlights that software in support of e-Navigation may be a standalone product or part of a larger more complex system incorporating data and information management. The guideline introduces quality models to assist in identifying the characteristics of system software which allows for the successful harmonization, integration, exchange, analyses and presentation of maritime data and information to meet user needs.

e-Navigation is a current international initiative that is intended to facilitate the transition of maritime navigation into the digital era, is a vision for the integration of existing and new navigational tools, in a holistic and systematic manner that will enable the transmission, manipulation and display of navigational information in electronic format [1, 7].

© Springer International Publishing Switzerland 2015
J. Mikulski (Ed.): TST 2015, CCIS 531, pp. 141–150, 2015.
DOI: 10.1007/978-3-319-24577-5_14

2   The IMO Guideline on Software Quality Assurance

Navigation systems increasingly provide a variety of information and services for enhancing navigation safety and efficiency. These systems require the connection and integration of onboard navigational systems as well as shore-side support systems and involve the collection, integration, exchange, presentation and analysis of marine data and information.

The merits of navigation systems can be found not only in their range of functions but also underpinned by their trustworthy software and overall usability. The IMO guideline is intended to complement and support the principle requirements as specified under SOLAS regulation V/15 [3].

Achieving trustworthy software and usability in the development of complex systems requires a disciplined and structured approach. The IMO guideline encourages such an approach in the development and management of e-Navigation systems, with a particular focus on Software Quality Assurance (SQA) and Human Centred Design (HCD) that includes Usability Testing (UT). Systems so designed, developed and managed throughout their life cycle deliver improved user performance, being stable and resilient, and most importantly support users in low and high workload environments; such as during challenging navigation and environmental conditions when users are most vulnerable to making mistakes and when error management and recovery is essential. Other important benefits include limiting the amount of operator familiarisation training that is needed and the time and resources required for system maintenance and support.

There are some significant challenges associated with digital data and software quality, including the use of both existing and new forms of digital data and the software required to operate the various types of e-Navigation-related systems and equipment. Most likely, software-related issues will become a significant challenge for achieving harmonized ship borne and shore-based e-Navigation. For this to occur, an established means/process for software quality assurance (SQA) is needed.

SQA focuses on defining and testing software quality and how that helps meet user requirements to ensure that high quality, robust, testable and stable software is used in e-Navigation systems. e-Navigation software quality needs to be evaluated to ensure relevant quality characteristics meet the requirements of the system.

The basic premise of HCD is that systems are designed to suit the characteristics of intended users and the tasks they perform, rather than requiring users to adapt to a system. UT is a key component of HCD and uses methods that rely on including users to test the ability of systems to support user needs. UT helps to identify potential problems and solutions during design and development stages by using an iterative approach to testing where the design evolves through rounds of prototyping, testing, analysing, refining and testing again.

The combination of SQA and HCD (including UT) provides opportunities to guide system design and development to improve data quality and information analysis, and to generally meet user needs and enhance safety.

The IMO developed guideline is not intended to be the sole source of guidance for SQA and HCD and associated activities. Rather, it is intended to provide a general understanding of SQA and HCD for the effective design and development of e-Navigation systems. It draws extensively on existing relevant international standards.

3   Scope of the IMO Guideline on SQA

The scope of the IMO guideline on SQA is to provide an overarching document to ensure that e-Navigation quality design attributes are included in the development of e-Navigation systems. Figure 1 provides an overview of the quality design attributes that should be considered and includes "product and data quality", "meet user needs", "security" and "functional safety". This guideline mainly addresses software quality which incorporates "product and data quality" and "meet user needs". Consideration of all the design attributes will help ensure that software and human-based risks are addressed. Figure 1 also provides information on relevant standards that developers and designers of e-Navigation systems should consider in ensuring all quality attributes are addressed ensuring overall system quality.

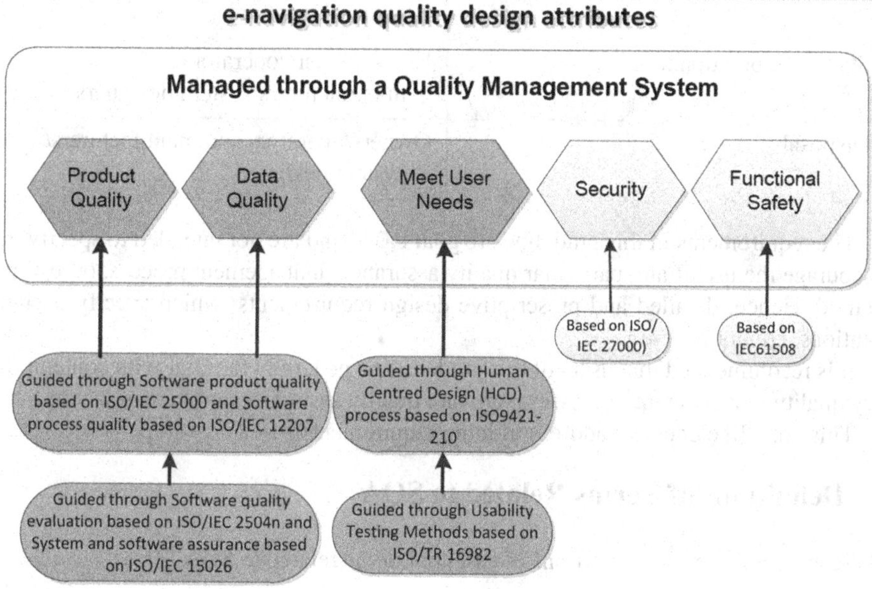

Fig. 1. Concepts and standards for e-Navigation quality design attributes [3]

This guideline is intended to be used by all stakeholders involved in the design and development of e-Navigation systems, with its primary users being those that develop and test e-Navigation systems. Stakeholders include equipment designers and manufacturers, system integrators, maritime authorities and regulators, shipbuilders, ship owners, operators, Vessel Traffic Service authorities and Rescue Coordination Centres, and other relevant international organizations such as the International Association of Marine Aids to Navigation and Lighthouse Authorities (IALA) and the International Hydrographic Organization (IHO).

Table 1 provides a summary of stakeholder involvement in the application of this guideline at each of the e-Navigation system life cycle stages.

Table 1. Stakeholder involvement [3]

Life cycle Stage	Stakeholder
Analysis Operational System Feedback	Manufacturers/system designers, users, ship owners/operators, regulatory authority
Stage 1: Concept development	Manufacturers/system designers, users
Stage 2: Planning and Analysis	Manufacturers/system designers, users
Stage 3: Design	Manufacturers/system designers, users
Stage 4: Integration and Testing	Manufacturers/system designers, users, approval authority (regulator), owners/operators
Stage 5: Operational	Users, owners/operators and manufacturers/system designers
Disposal	Owners/operators and manufacturers/system designers

The requirements in this guideline are goal based and are not intended to specify or discourage the use of any particular quality assurance, management process, or testing method. Hence, detailed and prescriptive design requirements, which specify design solutions, are not covered.

It is recommended that users of this guideline be generally familiar with contemporary quality management processes, software quality assurance and human factors.

This guideline does not address training requirements.

4   Definitions of Terms Related to SQA

There are the following definitions of essential terms related to SQA [3]:

e-Navigation: The harmonized collection, integration, exchange, presentation and analysis of marine information on board and ashore by electronic means to enhance berth-to-berth navigation and related services for safety and security at sea and protection of the marine environment [1, 7–9].

Human Factors: The scientific discipline concerned with the application of validated scientific research about people, their abilities, characteristics and limitations to the design of systems they use, environments in which they function and interact, and jobs they perform to optimize human well-being and overall system performance [6].

Human Centred Design (HCD): An approach to system design and development that aims to make interactive systems more usable by focussing on the use of the system; applying human factors, ergonomics and usability knowledge and techniques.

The term "human-centred design" is used rather than "user-centred design" in order to emphasize that this process also addresses impacts on a number of stakeholders, not just those typically considered as users. However, in practice, these terms are often used synonymously.

Software Quality Assurance (SQA): A set of processes that ensures software meets and complies with required quality specifications. Designated SQA processes align with a system design life cycle.

Usability Testing (UT): Evaluation methods and techniques used to support Human Centred Design (HCD) and used for the purpose of increasing the usability of a system.

5   Quality Management System

It is recommended that SQA, HCD and associated activities are performed using a quality management system such as ISO/IEC 90003:2014 or relevant standards to ensure that quality requirements are embedded in the development life cycle process to achieve software quality, meet user needs and enhance safety of e-Navigation systems.

This guideline can be applied to the design of systems with varying levels of complexity, regardless of whether a new system is being developed or an existing system is being modified.

Figure 2 shows a typical generic life cycle [3] with the stages recommended as a minimum for the application of this guideline to the development of e-Navigation systems:

- Analysis of operational system feedback;
- Stage 1: Concept development;
- Stage 2: Planning and analysis;
- Stage 3: Design;
- Stage 4: Integration and testing;
- Stage 5: Operation; and
- Disposal.

The aim of SQA, HCD and associated UT activities is to ensure that for each stakeholder, user and task requirements are considered in the development process. This takes into account interactions between people, technology and the physical and organisational environments within which they work. Outcomes can be maximised if SQA, HCD and associated activities are applied by teams with relevant multi-disciplinary skills and experiences.

SQA and HCD are performance and risk based processes. Hazards are identified, associated risks assessed and if necessary, risk reduction and control measures are implemented to ensure an acceptable level of quality, usability and safety. Because they are performance-based processes, validation is based on how the outcomes are achieved.

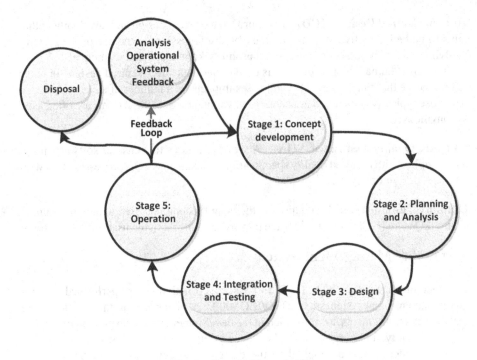

Fig. 2. Generic life cycle [3]

6   Software Quality Assurance

Key to ensuring software quality in e-Navigation is to address the quality attributes that need to be considered in the development and design of e-Navigation systems as highlighted in Fig. 1. Software in support of e-Navigation can be a product on its own, or part of a larger system and includes data and information. A key function of e-Navigation software is to harmonize, integrate, exchange, present and analyse maritime data and information to meet user needs.

Functional Safety: The performance of systems related to e-Navigation software should be assured in terms of required functions and level of integrity. The reliability and availability of safety related functions should be specified based on stakeholder requirements and traceable through documentation. Functional safety requirements should be defined, implemented and managed throughout the life cycle. The required level of functional safety can vary depending on the designed functionality and intended use, and should be determined by an appropriate risk based process. Guidance for ensuring functional safety is provided in IEC61508 [2] or relevant standards.

Security: It is important to consider and properly address security to prevent cyber-attacks, hacking or other illegal intrusions. Any e-Navigation implementation should provide a secure digital environment, in particular addressing avoidance, prevention and detection of any cyber security threats, locally, regionally and internationally. ISO/IEC 27000 [5] or relevant standards provides guidance on software and cyber security.

Software Quality Models for e-Navigation: This section introduces three types of quality models for e-Navigation software systems that are defined by the ISO/IEC 25000 series [4]: product quality, data quality and quality-in-use.

The product quality model categories are: functional suitability, performance efficiency, compatibility, usability, reliability, security, maintainability and portability. It should be noted that ISO 25010 [4] uses "usability" to describe the attributes that confer quality-in-use. The usage of usability in this guideline is different but very close to quality-in-use.

Software quality is also dependant on the quality of input data, which should conform to relevant international standards. As shown in Fig. 1, data quality is one of the key attributes of e-Navigation systems. Data quality requirements and data quality characteristics should be based on ISO/IEC 25012 [4] and related standards (i.e. International Hydrographic Organization (IHO) standards for nautical information including Electronic Navigation Charts (ENC)). These standards propose a general data quality model to support organizations to acquire, manipulate and use data with the necessary quality characteristics.

A systematic approach to ensure data quality is recommended, and can include:

- defining and evaluating data quality requirements in data production, acquisition and integration processes;
- identifying data quality criteria, also useful for re-engineering, assessment and improvement of data; and
- evaluating the compliance of data with legislation and other relevant requirements.

Producers of input data should have life cycle management practices in place to handle possible data format changes during the life cycle. These life cycle management practices should include timely announcements to software producers and end users about such changes. As part of the DQA producers of input data should test all data in service for conformance with relevant international standards.

The quality in use of a system characterizes the impact that the product (system or software product) has on stakeholders, measuring effectiveness, efficiency, freedom from risk and satisfaction in specific contexts of use. It is determined by the quality of the software, hardware and operating environment, and the characteristics of the users, tasks and social environment. All these factors contribute to the quality in use of the system. Examples of quality in use measures are given in ISO/IEC ISO/IEC 25024 [4].

Software quality evaluation: The required software quality depends on the intended use or objectives of the system of which the software is a part. Software products need to be evaluated during design, implementation and integration to determine whether the relevant quality characteristics are met.

Software quality evaluation processes are defined in relevant international standards, such as ISO/IEC 25040 which contains the following activities [3]:

- define the purpose and scope of the evaluation and identify software quality requirements;
- specify and develop the quality measures and establish decision criteria;
- develop the evaluation plan;

- carry out the evaluation applying quality measures and the decision criteria; and
- review the evaluation results and prepare an evaluation report and provide feedback.

For each activity identify applicable measurement tools, constraints, inputs and outputs. Outputs of previous activities can be used as inputs to subsequent stages. The first activity may include output from previous evaluations as an input.

When an evaluation is performed concurrently with software product development, associated activities can be performed as part of software life cycle processes (ISO/IEC 12207 or relevant standards) and/or system life cycle processes (ISO/IEC 15288 or relevant standards).

Figure 3 outlines the main activities that should be undertaken in the software life cycle, as below [3]:

- Pre-activity: Conduct preliminary hazard analysis;
- Activity 1: Stakeholder and system requirements definition;
- Activity 2: System requirement analysis;
- Activity 3: Software architecture design and implementation;
- Activity 4: Software testing, installation and acceptance;
- Activity 5: Software operation and maintenance; and
- Activity 6: System disposal.

Activity 1: Stakeholder and system requirements definition
This activity involves specifying the required characteristics and identifying the context of use of the system being developed. During this activity validation and conformance requirements of the system will also be identified.

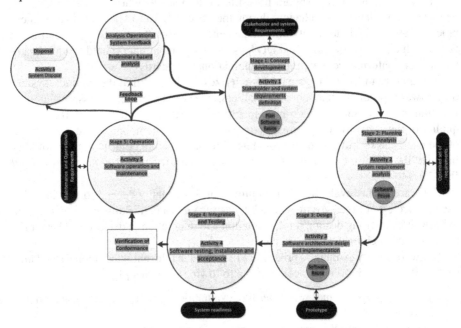

Fig. 3. Overview of Software Quality Assurance activities [3]

Activity 2: System requirements analysis
This activity involves defining a set of functional and non-functional system requirements with various configurations developed in order to ensure an optimized solution. This activity results in a prioritized, approved and updated set of system requirements including SQA requirements which are consistent and traceable.

Activity 3: Software architecture design implementation
This activity involves defining and structuring the elements of the system, ensuring it meets defined software quality requirements. The verification between the system requirements and the system architecture should also be carried out during this stage. A strategy for software integration based on the priorities of the system requirements needs to be developed with criteria to verify compliance.

An important aspect to be considered during the early stages of software design is software reuse. This needs to be considered during stages 1 to 3 of the software life cycle. Software reuse is the use of existing software assets in some form within a software development process. Software assets include products from prior developments such as components, test suites, designs and documentation. Software assets may be modified as needed to meet new system requirements.

Activity 4: Software testing, installation and acceptance
This activity ensures that the integrated software is compliant with the system requirements. Appropriate methods and standards for testing software should be developed to ensure the reliability and validity of the software qualification test and as much as possible conformance to expected results. Software qualification testing should take place in its intended operational environment. As previously mentioned, appropriate test data sets provided by relevant international organizations such as IALA, IHO, etc. should be used to ensure conformance with shore based data. An important pre-condition is to ensure that the use of shore and ship based data has been subject to a DQA process. This activity also involves evaluating and testing the integrated system using pre-defined criteria with evidence produced demonstrating quality assurance.

Verification of conformance: It is recommended that certificates of conformance with existing software and data quality should meet relevant standards to ensure the verification of software systems.

It is recommended that the verification process for e-Navigation SQA be carried out by reviewing the related documents on e-Navigation software system or data, by inspecting the implementation of the e-Navigation software system and testing the software functions. It is recommended that the testing environment covers berth-to-berth operation, ship-to-ship communication, ship-to-shore communication as well as shore-to-shore communication.

Activity 5: Software operation and maintenance
This activity involves the identification and evaluation of conditions for correct operation of the software in its intended environment. An operation and maintenance strategy needs to be developed in consultation between the software developers and users. This will ensure that any software and system modifications, upgrades, changes to the existing system interface and updating of system and software documentation are appropriately managed and do not compromise product requirements or safety.

Activity 6: System disposal
A system disposal strategy should be developed to facilitate knowledge retention and analysis of long-term impacts. A hardware disposal strategy should also be developed to promote the use of non-hazardous materials during manufacturing.

7 Conclusion

The combination of the five e-Navigation solutions, and the three guidelines, Guidelines on Human Centred Design (HCD) for e-Navigation, Guidelines on Usability Testing, Evaluation and Assessment (U-TEA) for e-Navigation systems and Guidelines for Software Quality Assurance (SQA) in e-Navigation, proposes an e-Navigation implementation that facilitates a holistic approach to the interaction between shipboard and shore-based users.

To provide the benefits for all stakeholders, regarding on software/system/software service and data used in software through the life cycle Customers can be served qualified software/data. Providers can verify their qualified software/data. e-Navigation SQA will support the two types of viewpoints by how to dealing with.

SQA process will be designed in detail. Key activities will be developed for the SQA process. Practices will be developed for support the SQA process.

References

1. Amato, F., et al.: e-Navigation and future trend in navigation. TransNav Int. J. Mar. Navig. Saf. Sea Transp. **5**(1), 11–14 (2011)
2. IEC 61508. Functional Safety of Electrical/Electronic/Programmable Electronic Safety-related Systems. International Electrotechnical Commission (2010)
3. IMO NCSR2/6. e-Navigation Strategy Implementation Plan. Report of the Correspondence Group on Harmonization of Guidelines related to e-Navigation, submitted by Australia. Sub-Committee on Navigation, Communications and Search & Rescue, International Maritime Organization, London, 5 December 2014
4. ISO/IEC 25000-series - Systems and software engineering - Systems and software Quality Requirements and Evaluation (SQuaRE) - Guide to SquaRE (2014)
5. ISO/IEC 27000-series (also known as the ISMS Family of Standards) - information security standards published jointly by the International Organization for Standardization and the International Electrotechnical Commission (2013)
6. Patraiko, D., Wake, P., Weintrit, A.: e-navigation and the human element. TransNav Int. J. Mar. Navig. Saf. Sea Transp. **4**(1), 11–16 (2010)
7. Weintrit, A.: Telematic approach to e-Navigation architecture. In: Mikulski, J. (ed.) TST 2010. CCIS, vol. 104, pp. 1–10. Springer, Heidelberg (2010)
8. Weintrit, A.: Development of the IMO e-navigation concept – common maritime data structure. In: Mikulski, J. (ed.) TST 2011. CCIS, vol. 239, pp. 151–163. Springer, Heidelberg (2011)
9. Weintrit, A.: Technical infrastructure to support seamless information exchange in e-Navigation. In: Mikulski, J. (ed.) TST 2013. CCIS, vol. 395, pp. 188–199. Springer, Heidelberg (2013)

Software Simulation of an Energy Consumption and GHG Production in Transport

Tomas Skrucany[✉], Martin Kendra, Branislav Sarkan, and Jozef Gnap

Faculty of Operation and Economics of Transport and Communications, University of Zilina,
Univerzitna 1, 01026 Zilina, Slovakia
tomas.skrucany@fpedas.uniza.sk

Abstract. Simulation of an energy consumption in transport is often used due to satisfactory accuracy and cost efficiency. The simulation is not influenced by many surrounding factors which are acting during the measurements in real operation. This paper due to the simulation of energy consumption an GHG production of two similar trains which use different types of drive and energy wells in the same chosen railway with more variants of capacity utilization. The software Dynamics of Train is used for the simulation.

Keywords: Simulation · Energy consumption · GHG production · Transport vehicle

1 Introduction

Mobility is one of the most important human needs in this century. Average number of trips and the average traveled distance per man is constantly rising. Transport is becoming a very important element of human existence which has very negative impact on the environment by noise, vibration, accidents, areas needs, congestions and energy intensity.

During the transportation process energy entering transforms in to the movement of vehicles which provide the required transfer of goods and people in the area. Therefore, the transport depends on the supply of energy. Today transportation is largely dependent on oil, as the vast majority of vehicles are driven engines combusting petroleum products - hydrocarbon fuels.

Railway transport is representative mode of transport where most railway vehicles are now powered by electric traction motors, so the rate of dependence on oil is lower than previous modes. But the fact is that in most countries the electricity is produced through petroleum products or coal. All of these are non-renewable natural resources and their stocks have steadily declined.

Proper selection of traction in the railway transport can help implement the objectives of the White Book to minimize the energy consumption of transport and create a sustain able environmentally friendly mobility.

© Springer International Publishing Switzerland 2015
J. Mikulski (Ed.): TST 2015, CCIS 531, pp. 151–160, 2015.
DOI: 10.1007/978-3-319-24577-5_15

2   Model Study

In this case study we consider the transport along one chosen valley in Slovakia. There is a railway track without an electrical trolley. Nowadays small trains run at this track regularly several times a day. There are two modes of passenger transport in the valley – train and bus. Tracks of both transport modes are situated along the river Rajcanka. This track connects Zilina (administrative capital city of northern territorial unit of Slovakia) and a small town Rajec situated in the southern part of valley with amenities for people lived in valley villages. Routing of track is North – South with distance of 21.3 km.

Difference of the altitudes between Zilina (340) and Rajec (450) causes the track slope which reaches the highest value 13 ‰, except a small hill before the railway station in Zilina where is the slope 17 ‰ but only on a short distance. Average slope between end stations is 5 ‰ (Fig. 1).

There are 12 stops (stations) on the track, Zilina is the first one on the beginning and the last one is Rajec at the end of the track. Between them there are 10 other stops. The highest track speed limit is 60 km/h but on some sections there are the speed limits only 50 or 40 km/h. Travelling time between the end stations is 37 min.

The average number of transported passengers for the year 2014 is 32 passengers on one train.

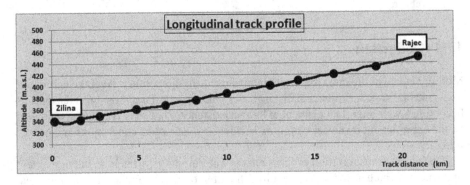

Fig. 1. Elevation track profile with stations [own study]

2.1   Vehicle Technical Parameters

Simulation of the energy consumption was done for two railway vehicles used in Slovak republic in a regional passenger transport (Fig. 2, Table 1). The choice of the railway vehicles was done due to similar capacity and construction size of these railway vehicles. They are:

- electric three units railway vehicle with the series number 425.95,
- diesel two units railway vehicle with the series number 813-913.

The electric vehicle was made by consortium EMU-GTW High Tatras (Adtranz, nowadays Bombardier Transportation; Stadler Fahrzeuge, nowadays Stadler; ŽOS Vrútky). This railway vehicle was made in the years 2000, 2001 and 2002.

Fig. 2. Railway vehicles [own study]

The diesel vehicle was made by ZOS Zvolen as a reconstruction of an old diesel one unit railway vehicle with series number 810. ŽOS Zvolen has been making this diesel railway vehicle since 2007.

Table 1. Basic technical parameters of railway vehicles [own study]

Series number of railway vehicle	425.95	813-913
Drive arrangement	2'´Bo' 2"	1´A´ + 1'1'
Power system	1.5 kV DC	diesel
Power transmission	–	hydromechanical
Maximum speed	80 km/h	90 km/h
Combustion engine	–	MAN D 2876 LUE 21
Design rate	602 kW	257 kW
Tare weight	41 t	39 t
Gross weight	56 t	53 t
Vehicle length	32 984 mm	28 820 mm
Number of seats	88 + 20	78 + 5
Maximum number of Standing passengers	92	120

3   Calculation of Energy Consumption and Emission Production

Software Railway dynamics has been used to calculate the energy consumption of the train. The power consumption of the train has been calculated on the basis of predefined and selected values on the defined route. The software works with imported maps and elevation profile of railway routes. Based on these defaults and selected parameters (locomotive type, train weight, train length, axle load, number and location of stops) power consumption was calculated in kWh. This software can be used to calculate energy consumption and operational or driving time of some arbitrary train on some arbitrary railway track. It is needed to import data of train and track for calculation (Fig. 3) [2, 3].

It is necessary to use the principle well-to-wheels for relevant comparison of the results for different types of consumed energy.

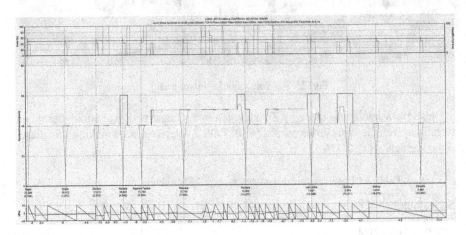

Fig. 3. Output data from the software Railway dynamics [own study]

3.1 Standard EN 16258: 2012 and Its Using in Calculations

This European Standard specifies general methodology for calculation and declaration of energy consumption and greenhouse gas emissions (GHG) in connection with any services (cargo, passengers or both). It specifies general principles, definitions, system boundaries, methods of calculation, allocation rules (allocation, assignment) and recommendations on information to support standardized, accurate, reliable and verifiable declarations regarding energy consumption and greenhouse gas emissions associated with any freight services. It also contains examples of these principles use.

The calculation for one given transport service must be performed using the following three main steps [1]:

- Step 1: Identification of the various sections of the service;
- Step 2: Calculation of energy consumption and greenhouse gas emissions for each section;
- Step 3: Sum the results for each section

The standard does not consider only the production of the secondary emissions and energy consumed during the combustion of the fuel (energy conversion from fuel to mechanical energy) but as well as primary, incurred in the extraction, production and distribution:

- e_w well-to-wheels energetic factor for defined fuel,
- g_w well-to-wheels emissions factor for defined fuel,

- e_t tank-to-wheels energetic factor for defined fuel,
- g_t tank-to-wheels emissions factor for defined fuel.

Well-to-wheels is "well on wheels" and also covered primary and secondary emissions and consumption. This factor is somewhere also called as LCA (life-cycle-analysis).

Tank-to-Wheels factor is thinking only of secondary emission and consumption.

This Standard specifies general methodology for calculation and declared value for the energetic factor and factor in greenhouse gas emissions must be selected in accordance with Annex A [1].

Emission gases are composed of several individual components (gas) [6, 7]. Each of them have different chemical and physical properties, so they otherwise participate in environmental degradation. In order to compare emissions from different activities, fuels, vehicles where emissions have different impact, one representative unit used in the comparison must be designated. This is the CO_2 equivalent which is a measure of the impact of specific emissions and likens it to the impact of CO_2. The label is CO_2e (equivalent).

3.2   Electric Energy Consumption

Calculated energy is the mechanical work needed to move the train. If is it transformed into units of MJ, it can be subsequently converted to total consumed energy by an overall energy efficiency of Eq. (1). It means that the well-to-wheels principle is used- factors e_w, g_w (EN 16 258:2012) or f_{LCA}, or total energy efficiency η_{TE}.

$$E_{TE} = \left(E_{ME}.3,6 \right).\eta_{TE} \text{ [MJ]} \tag{1}$$

where:

- E_{TE} total energy consumed by electric traction (wtw) [MJ]
- E_{ME} mechanical energy consumed by the movement of the train (train dynamics software result) [kWh]

Energy and emission factors (e_W, g_W) or overall energy efficiency (η_{TE}) reflect a partial losses of production and distribution of power energy in the chain [4]:

1. energy mixture used in electric energy production,
2. the efficiency various energy sources (depending on the source),
3. transfer efficiency (distribution) el. supply to the final consumer (circa 0.93).

These fact simply that the effectiveness (efficacy) of the el. energy is directly related to power production technology, the composition and proportions of individual resources and the effectiveness of its distribution [4].

$$\eta_{TE} = \eta_P.\eta_T.\eta_V \tag{2}$$

where:

- η_{TE} overall energy efficiency [-]
- η_P efficiency of energy production (sources mixture)[-]

- η_T power transfer efficiency[-]
- η_V efficiency of vehicle system [-]

The value of overall energy efficiency is 0.34 in Slovak republic. This value is calculated on the basis of statistical data (efficiency and ratio of each primary energy source).For comparison this value is the same in Germany and the average value of EU is 0.35 [1].

This calculation of energy consumption is applicable only for the electric train. The procedure is another for the diesel train. We do not consider the energy source mixture. It is appropriate to use the factors and procedure form of the EN 16 258:2012 for diesel train. The amount of consumed fuel should be multiplied by energy factor for that fuel from Appendix A of the standard to calculate the total energy consumption.

$$E_{TF} = FC_V \cdot e_W = [(E_{ME} \cdot m_{Pe}) \cdot 1/\rho_F] \cdot e_W \ [MJ] \tag{3}$$

where:

- E_{TF} total energy consumed by diesel vehicles [MJ]
- FC_V fuel consumption of vehicle [1, dm^3]
- E_{ME} mechanical energy consumed by the movement of the train (train dynamics software result) [kWh]
- m_{Pe} vehicle engine specific fuel consumption [g/kWh]
- ρ_F fuel (diesel) specific weight (density)[g/dm^3]
- e_W energetic factor "wtw" for defined fuel [MJ/dm^3]

3.3 GHG Production

The emission factor LCA was used to calculate the amount of produced emissions of the electric train. The consumed energy [MJ] is computed by mechanical work and efficiency of the vehicle. This value is multiplied by LCA factor which takes the energy source mixture into account, too [5].

$$G_{TE} = [(E_{ME}/\eta_V) \cdot 1000] \cdot f_{LCA} \ [tCO_2e]$$
$$G_{TE} = [(E_{ME}/\eta_V) \cdot 3,6] \cdot f^g_{LCA} \ [gCO_2e] \tag{4}$$

where:

- G_{TE} the total amount of emissions produced by electric traction [tCO$_2$e]
- f_{LCA} emission factor for electric energy in Slovakia [tCO$_2$e/MWh]
- $f_{LCA}{}^g$ emission factor for electric energy in Slovakia [gCO$_2$e/MJ]

For the GHG production calculation, the consumed amount of diesel fuel should be multiplied by an emission factor for that fuel from Appendix A of the EN standard.

$$G_{TF} = FC_V \cdot g_W = [(E_{ME} \cdot m_{Pe}) \cdot 1/\rho_F] \cdot g_W \ [gCO_2e] \tag{5}$$

where:

- G_{TF} the total amount of emissions produced by diesel vehicles [gCO_2e]
- g_W emission factor for defined fuel [tCO_2e/MWh]

The basic units of MJ and gCO_2 were chosen for the calculation because they are declared units in the standard. However, for better comparison and expression, it is possible to expressed individual amounts in other units, for example GJ, KJ, tCO_2, $kgCO_2$eora combination of them, in the case of proportional expressing of quantities (see the evaluation) [4].

4   Evaluation

The calculation for this model study was done on the track in bidirectional ways, so one way down the hill and the other way up the hill. This elevation is seen in the energy consumption which is higher for uphill track, from Zilina to Rajec. Only the numbers as the results from transport in both directions are in the evaluation table and graphs.

Table of the final evaluation shows the advantage of the large capacity which the electric train nr. 425 has (Table 2). This unit is the most similar alternative to the unit nr. 813. It is often used on the railway with higher slope (mountains) in Slovakia thank to its higher power value. But this fact causes higher total energy consumption. However, the capacity of the unit is up to 108 passengers, thus converted consumption per transported passengers at full occupancy is less than the diesel train consumption. But it is not possible to apply for the real operation because the average number of traveled passengers in train is much less.

The simulated fuel consumption of the diesel train was compared to the real consumption of this train operated on this track. This simulated result was validated because the simulation error was only −8 %. So every consumption results were increased of the value 8 % to be closer to the reality.

Table 2. Final evaluation [own study]

State	Train	Fuel	Energy (MJ)	Emissions (kg CO₂e)	Pas.N r.	Energy (MJ/prs)	Emissions (kgCO₂e/prs)
Full loaded	425	electric	1 086.1	36.2	108	10.06	0.34
	813	diesel	982.1	74.5	83	11.83	0.90
Real pas. nr.	425	electric	899.8	30.0	32	28.12	0.94
	813	diesel	822.0	62.4	32	25.69	1.95

The electric train is not always the most environmental friendly transport mode. If we consider the energy consumption as the most important parameter, the diesel train reaches better results with lower energy intensity. The energy consumption of the electric train is not dependent only on the efficiency of the vehicle systems, but also on the efficiency of the electric energy production in the country [8, 9].

In the case of real passenger number the diesel train reaches higher value of efficiency than the electric train, it consumed only circa 90 % of the electric train energy consumption (MJ/prs). But if the trains would be loaded fully, more efficient is the electric train. Diesel train consumption is now 118 % of the electric train consumption (Fig. 4).

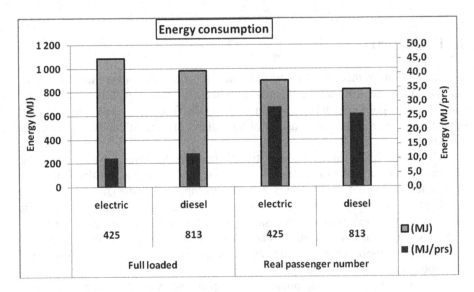

Fig. 4. Evaluation of the energy consumption [own study]

The emissions production has the opposite result as the energy consumption. In this case the electric train is more friendly to the environment then the diesel train (Fig. 5). However, it is not possible to reach this scenario neither in all EU countries, nor in developing countries. Emissions production of electric traction is more dependent on the energy source mixture than the energy consumption. This study was calculated for Slovakia. Slovak energy source mixture is very friendly to the environment (production of the CO_2e) because of 50 % nuclear energy, 17 % water energy and only small share of energy from fossil fuels. The LCA factor in Slovakia is only 0.353 tCO_2e/MWh, while the EU average is 0.578. GHG production per capita of the electric train is 50 % of the diesel train in Slovakia. The electric train is not the "green" choice of transport everywhere, it would produce more GHG than the diesel train in countries with other source mixture, like Poland or Estonia (they use the fossil fuels as the biggest source of electric energy) with LCA factor up to 1.593 tCO_2e/MWh (almost 5-times more of the Slovak factor) [5].

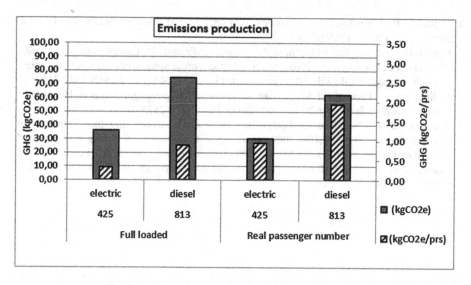

Fig. 5. Evaluation of the GHG production [own study]

5   Conclusion

The results of this simulation do not determine which traction is better, greener or more friendly to the environment. It is not possible to do it, because the energy efficiency and GHG production is not dependent only on the type of fuel or traction but also on the capacity usage and electric energy sources. It is necessary to load the trains with the adequate number of passengers (suitable choice of the train according to the transport flow) and to use ecological produced electric energy. The transport efficiency with the low level of passengers is decreasing and without "green" electric energy the electric trains are not ecological.

References

1. European standard EN 16 258:2012. Methodology for calculation and declaration of energy consumption and GHG emissions of transport services (freight and passengers)
2. Klinko, M., Grencík, J.: Tilting body vehicles on Slovak railways - potential for use and parameters to be considered. Commun. Sci. Lett. Univ. Zilina **10**(3), 45–49 (2008). ISSN 1335-4205
3. Zvolensky, P., et al.: Evolution of maintenance systems of passenger and freight wagons from the ECM certification point of view. Commun. Sci. Lett. Univ. Zilina **16**(3A), 40–47 (2014)
4. Skrucany, T., Gnap, J.: Energy intensity and greenhouse gases production of the road and rail cargo transport using a software to simulate the energy consumption of a train. In: Mikulski, J. (ed.) TST 2014. CCIS, vol. 471, pp. 263–272. Springer, Heidelberg (2014)
5. Technical annex to the SEAP template instructions document: The emission factors. Document of the European Commission

6. Vaishnav, P.: Greenhouse gas emissions from international transport. Issues Sci. Technol. **30**(2), 25–28 (2014). ISSN 0748-5492
7. Garcia-Alvarez, A., Perez-Martinez, P.J., Gonzalez-Franco, I.: Energy consumption and carbon dioxide emissions in rail and road freight transport in Spain: a case study of car carriers and bulk petrochemicals. J. Intell. Transp. Syst. **17**(3), 233–244 (2013). ISSN 1547-2450
8. Dolinayova, A.: Factors and determinants of modal split in passenger transport. Horizons of railway transport. Sci. Paper **2**(1), 33–39 (2011). ISSN 1338-287X
9. Nedeliakova, E., Nedeliak, I.: Comparison of transport modes and their influence to environment. In: TRANSCOM 2009 8th European Conference Of Young Research and Scientific Workers: Žilina June 22–24, 2009, Slovak Republic. Section 2: Economics and Management - part 2 (M-Z). – Zilina, pp. 43-46, University of Zilina (2009) ISBN 978-80-554-0040-2

Traffic Processes Models in Traffic Water Engineering Systems

Piotr Majzner[✉]

Akademia Morska w Szczecinie, ul. Wały Chrobrego 1-2,
70-500 Szczecin, Poland
p.majzner@am.szczecin.pl

Abstract. The presented models represent phenomena occurring in waterway subsystems - at fairway intersections and within a fairway. The measures of traffic processes under consideration are the number of vessels waiting to enter a waterway subsystem and delay time of these vessels. The applicability of specific models is discussed along with their usefulness as a function of input intensity of vessel stream flowing into the subsystem.

Keywords: Intersection · Fairway · Delay · Waiting

1 Introduction

The fairway is the major, most frequent component of waterway infrastructure. Fairways are established in a variety of water areas:

- open sea areas, where fairway boundaries are defined by local regulations and/or marked by aids to navigation,
- dredged river stretches and other natural bodies of water,
- canals.

The fairway may be recti- or curvilinear. In terms of traffic management, we can consider one-way and two-way fairways. Passage by vessels is the primary function of fairways.

Vessel streams move along a fairway. There exist certain relations between proceeding vessels, and relevant research problems include fairway capacity, safety of vessels, and disturbances of traffic flow.

An intersection of fairways is a major element of waterway infrastructure. The area of intersection may be affected by such phenomena as excessive approach of vessels or delayed traffic. Two fairways crossing each other is the most common type of intersection. Its specific type is the one where a fairway is cut by a ferry shuttle route with ferry traffic moving across the fairway. Research problems related to the safety at an intersection are discussed in studies [2, 5, 6], and the time of delay that occurs in the traffic process has been analysed in the works [4, 5] and others.

Problems of delays in fairway intersection traffic directly affect safety. Vessels which have to give way at an intersection must either reduce their speed or stop before an intersection.

© Springer International Publishing Switzerland 2015
J. Mikulski (Ed.): TST 2015, CCIS 531, pp. 161–171, 2015.
DOI: 10.1007/978-3-319-24577-5_16

Analyzing traffic processes on a fairway and fairway intersections and taking into consideration relevant publications, we should draw out attention to the phenomena related to:

- times of delay that occur in the traffic process,
- the number of vessels waiting to enter the intersection.

Measures describing the above phenomena may be defined analytically [1, 4, 6] using the method of deterministic analysis, or by the determination of characteristics using computer simulation. Because in the publications parameters such as delay times and the number of waiting vessels have been determined separately for each waterway subsystem, this article attempts to synthesize solutions used so far and verifies the applicability of individual methods.

2 Formulation of the Problem

A schematic vessel traffic on a fairway is illustrated in Fig. 1. The fairway capacity μ can be calculated from this formula [2, 6]:

$$\mu = \frac{v}{\Delta l + L_s} \qquad \left[\frac{1}{h}\right] \tag{1}$$

where v– vessel speed, Δl– interval between vessels, L_s – vessel length.

If we analyze the meaning of the term fairway capacity, we can see it directly depends on the distance maintained between vessels in the stream and on their speed, while the dependence on vessel length is much weaker. In considerations so far the attention has been paid only to the fairway traffic process. It turns out, however, that due to the probabilistic nature of traffic, the resultant fairway capacity is also affected by phenomena taking place within fairway approaches. Repeated studies of the process of vessel reporting before fairway entry have revealed random character of time intervals between reports, described by an exponential distribution.

This renders a sufficient approximation of reality if we assume that vessels approach the fairway from a wide range of directions. Vessels proceeding an approach channel have to maintain speeds and distances as provided by local regulations, or at least observing the rules of COLREGs.

A graph of vessel traffic process within a fairway approach and on the fairway is shown in Fig. 2.

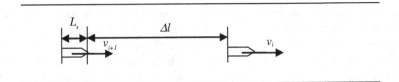

Fig. 1. Schematic diagram of vessel traffic on a fairway [own study]

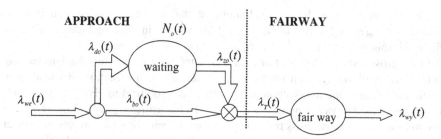

Fig. 2. A graph of vessel streams in the approach and the fairway [own study]

Vessels moving in the fairway approach area make up a stream with intensity $\lambda_{we}(t)$. Vessels that can enter the fairway without delay form a stream with intensity $\lambda_{bo}(t)$. Vessels reaching the fairway entrance form a stream with intensity $\lambda_T(t)$, while at the fairway exit we can observe a stream with intensity $\lambda_{wy}(t)$. When there is a vessel already in the fairway at a distance shorter than allowable, or there are vessels waiting to enter the fairway, a reporting vessel gets a waiting status (principle "first in, first out"). Vessels acquiring waiting vessel status make up a stream with intensity $\lambda_{do}(t)$. At the same time some vessels terminate the waiting status, forming a stream with intensity $\lambda_{zo}(t)$. We can assign the waiting status to a number of vessels $N_o(t)$. Parameters of the $N_o(t)$ function are essential for fairway capacity.

An example diagram illustrating vessel traffic process at a fairway intersection is shown in Fig. 3.

Vessels proceeding in the fairway make up a stream with intensity $\lambda_w(t)$, herein referred to as the longitudinal stream. At the right angle to that fairway some vessels are crossing the fairway make up a stream with an intensity $\lambda_p(t)$, called here the cross stream. Vessels move at a speed v_w in the longitudinal stream and v_p in the cross stream. Analysing traffic processes in real systems we can observe that generally one of the fairways is constantly privileged at an intersection. In the examined case we assume that vessels of the longitudinal stream have the right of way relative to the cross stream

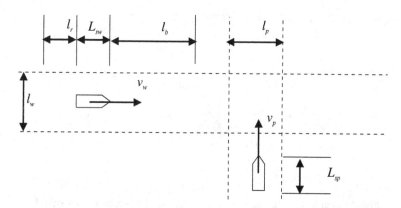

Fig. 3. Schematic traffic process at an intersection [own study]

vessels. The intensity of longitudinal traffic at the intersection subsystem input is denoted as $\lambda_{wwe}(t)$, and at its output $-\lambda_{wwy}(t)$. As vessels in the longitudinal traffic are privileged, this relationship holds $\lambda_{wwe}(t) = \lambda_{wwy}(t)$.

In the cross traffic a stream of vessels with intensity $\lambda_{pwe}(t)$ enters the intersection, while a stream of vessels with intensity $\lambda_{pwy}(t)$ leaves the intersection. Because these vessels cannot enter the intersection at any time, being obliged to give way to vessels moving along the fairway (longitudinal stream), the intensities $\lambda_{pwe}(t)$ and $\lambda_{pwy}(t)$ do not have to be equal. Because cross traffic vessels have to wait for a fairway vessel to clear the intersection, there may be a number of vessels of the cross stream– $N_o(t)$.

The distance covered by a fairway vessel along the intersection is denoted l_p, while l_w is the distance covered by a crossing vessel. The section l_p for the privileged (stand-on) vessel plays a warning role only. The section l_w for the subordinate vessel is of major importance. A vessel can find itself within this section only when adopted safety requirements have been satisfied.

Let us assume that a crossing vessel may enter the intersection (section l_w), if all the conditions given below are satisfied:

- the stern of a fairway vessel is at least at a distance l_r away from the point of intersection of vessel routes,
- a crossing vessel will be able to leave the section l_w before a fairway vessel reaches a point defining the distance l_b from the point of route intersection;
- preceding vessel of the same traffic stream is at a minimum admissible distance Δl_{min}.

Figure 4 presents a graph of the traffic process at an intersection.

Models of traffic processes in the fairway and fairway intersection show essential conformity in terms of delays and number of vessels with waiting status, as illustrated by the graphs of traffic processes. There is only a difference in the interpretation of

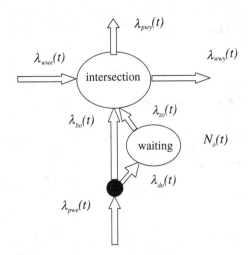

Fig. 4. Graph of the traffic process at a fairway intersection [own study]

fairway and intersection models. The fairway occupation time relating to a moving vessel is a quotient $(\Delta l + L_s)/V$, while the intersection occupation time is a sum of occupation by two vessels: privileged (stand-on) and subordinate (give-way) vessels.

3 Analytical Research

The authors of [5, 6] use a method with kinematic equations of vessel stream traffic to solve traffic process related problems. Their method is deterministic to the extent that random variables are represented by expected values. Elements of probability calculus have been used in the analysis and the construction of some measures. There is a simplification in assuming only a uniform distribution as a stochastic model.

One of the main assumptions of that method is description of vessel stream traffic by kinematic equations and an observation that a vessel on the fairway occupies a certain section (domain) determined by its dimensions, and by distances ahead and astern where no other vessels should be present. The resultant assessment measure determined in [6] is the mean delay time t_{op} falling on one passage of a vessel in the examined stream, expressed by the formula:

$$t_{op} = \frac{1}{2} \cdot \lambda_{we} \cdot T_z^2 = \frac{\lambda_{we}}{2\mu^2} \quad [\text{s}] \tag{2}$$

On the other hand, the delay time of an ingoing vessel is equal to the number of waiting vessels N_o multiplied by the time T_z, equal to the inverse of subsystem capacity μ for the examined stream. After transformations, the number of vessels N_o waiting to enter the fairway has this form:

$$N_o = \frac{t_{op}}{T_z} = \frac{\lambda_{we}}{2 \cdot \mu} \quad [\text{vessels}] \tag{3}$$

Naturally, both formulas have a physical sense for $\lambda_{we} < \mu$.

To sum up, we can state that a model developed by the above method is characterized by the deterministic interval between vessels in the stream, deterministic time of subsystem occupation by a vessel and random character (limited uniform distribution) of positions of the two time intervals on the time axis. After the name of the model's author let us call it Piszczek's model. The model is applicable to the fairway intersection and the fairway as such.

The study [4] presents another analytical method which takes into account the random character of time intervals between vessels (limited by exponential distribution), assuming the determinism of time of subsystem occupation by a vessel and random relations of positions of the two sections on the time axis. The developed Olszamowski's model, also named after its author, has been used for the determination of the mean waiting time for river vessels on crossing routes.

The model assumes that vessels in the exciting stream are moving at time intervals τ, realizing Poisson's process. Vessels are treated as material points. Let T_z denote a time of subsystem occupation by a vessel of the examined stream for a fairway, or two vessels for an intersection. A vessel to enter the fairway (intersection) has to wait until the time interval τ is greater than T_z. Delay time is a random variable of three random variables with the same exponential distributions, provided that each of them separately is less than T_z.

Finally, the mean time t_{op} of vessel delay in the examined stream has this form [5]:

$$t_{op} = \frac{1}{\lambda_{we}} \cdot \left(e^{\frac{\lambda_{we}}{\mu}} - 1 - \frac{\lambda_{we}}{\mu} \right) \text{ [h]} \tag{4}$$

where:

λ_{we}– input intensity of the exciting stream, [1/h],

μ– subsystem capacity for the examined stream λ_b, [1/h]

The number of vessels waiting to enter the intersection, after transformation similar to that for formula (3), has this form:

$$N_o = \frac{\mu}{\lambda_{we}} \cdot \left(e^{\frac{\lambda_{we}}{\mu}} - 1 - \frac{\lambda_{we}}{\mu} \right) \text{ [vessels]} \tag{5}$$

To sum up, we can state that the model developed by the above method has a random character (exponential distribution) of the time interval between vessels, deterministic time of subsystem occupation by a vessel and random positions of the two intervals on the time axis.

Another analytical method is the method of mass service applied to a classical model presented in publication [1]. The model known as Gutenbaum's model named after its creator, takes into account the random character of time interval between vessels (exponential distribution), random time of subsystem occupation by a vessel (exponential distribution) and random relations of the positions of two time intervals on the time axis. The degree to which the processes are random is in this case the greatest. Exponential distributions are without a memory, because random realizations are independent.

Finally, the expected number of vessels with the waiting status N_o gets a value as per this formula [1]:

$$N_o = \frac{\lambda_{we}}{\mu - \lambda_{we}} \text{ [vessels]} \tag{6}$$

where:

λ_{we} – input intensity of the exciting stream [1/h],

μ – subsystem capacity [1/h].

After transformation reverse to that for formula (3), the mean delay time t_{op} due to waiting for the entry to the subsystem falling on a vessel is expressed by this formula:

$$t_{op} = \frac{N_o}{\mu} = \frac{\lambda_{we}}{\mu(\mu - \lambda_{we})} \quad \text{[h/vessels]} \tag{7}$$

where:

λ_{we} – input intensity of exciting stream [1/h],
μ – subsystem capacity [1/h],
N_o – mean number of waiting vessels.

Phenomena occurring in transport systems are random phenomena. Nevertheless, analyzing complex processes we often represent random variables taking its expected, or mean value. For the input intensity value λ_{we} lower than the capacity μ the traffic on the fairway and within the intersection proceeds without delays:

$$\begin{aligned} t_{op} &= 0 \quad \text{[s]} \\ N_o &= 0 \quad \text{[1]} \end{aligned} \tag{8}$$

When the value of input intensity λ_{we} reaches the value of capacity μ, both mean delay time falling on a vessel and the number of vessels with waiting status tend to infinity:

$$\begin{aligned} t_{op} &\to \infty \quad \text{[s]} \\ N_o &\to \infty \quad \text{[1]} \end{aligned} \tag{9}$$

4 Examples

In [3] the author has compared the mean waiting time and the number of vessels with waiting status for Piszczek's, Olszamowski's and Gutenbaum's models, deterministic analysis method and simulation method. Due to restrictions applied in deriving analytical relationships, the simulation method uses only an exponential distribution of vessel occurrence intervals in the privileged stream.

On the fairway, occupation time is the resultant of intersection occupation by both privileged and subordinate vessels. Hence substantial restrictions introduced in the models, e.g. concerning the privileged vessel length, cease to matter so much. That is why we can extend the scope of distributions of vessel appearance periods.

It has been assumed that the period of vessel appearance is a random variable T_{we} from one of the alternative distributions:

- exponential,
- uniform,
- Weibull,
- normal, when the standard deviation was

$\sigma = 33$ % of mean value,
$\sigma = 20$ % of mean value.

The capacity of the model fairway is adopted from real measure values [6, 7] and was equal to:

$$\mu = 17,43 \quad [1/h] \tag{10}$$

We have performed a series of simulation experiments for the above determinants. In the tests the input intensity of exciting streams was gradually increased from zero to the value of capacity μ.

Figure 5 presents relationships of the mean number N_o of vessels waiting to enter as a function of input intensity λ_{we}, obtained by:

– using computational analytical relations (3), (5), (6) for the capacity μ with the value (10) and formulas (8), (9),
– computer-based simulation for above mentioned distributions of the random variable T_{we}.

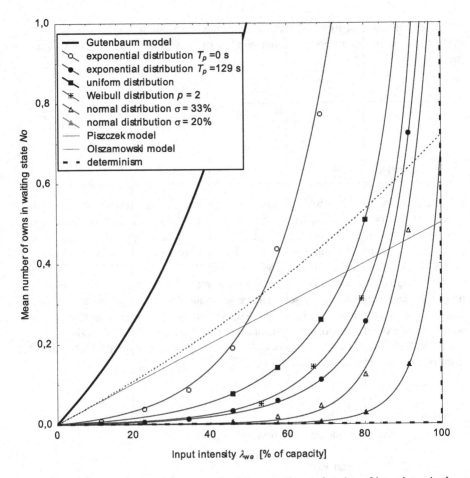

Fig. 5. Number of vessels waiting to enter the fairway – N_o as a function of input intensity λ_{we} expressed as % of the capacity [own study]

For simpler generalization of conclusions, the input intensity on the axis x is referred to capacity μ percentage.

The chart has a deliberately extended vertical scale to show clearly differences between the models. The plots of mean numbers of waiting vessels have been approximated by the least squares method. Substantial differences can be observed between the results obtained by various methods. The extremely deterministic analysis (dash line) does not permit to reflect phenomena taking place in the system – number of waiting vessels assumes the zero value for subcritical states or ∞ for supercritical states.

The results from Gutenbaum's model are on the other extreme. The greatest randomness, independence of the realization of random variables results in the fastest

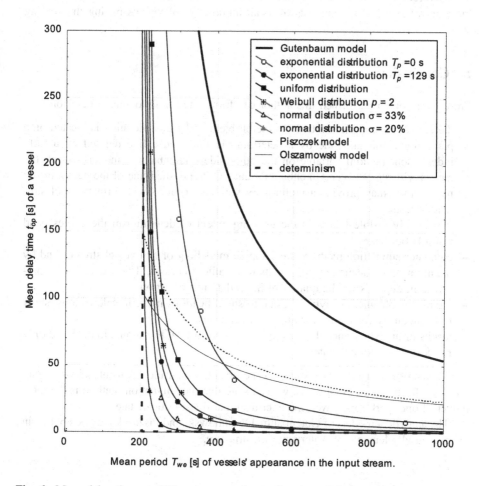

Fig. 6. Mean delay time t_{op} falling on a vessel as a function of the mean period of vessels appearance in the input stream [own study]

increase of the number of waiting vessels as a function of input intensity, tending to infinity for $\lambda_{we} \rightarrow \mu$. The results from respective analytical relationships of Olszamowski and Piszczek are characteristic. Their models differ from Gutenbaum's, but what they have in common is the deterministic character of the time of system occupation by vessel. There is a 90 % similarity of their results to the 40 % capacity. The finite value of N_o for $\lambda_{we} \rightarrow \mu$ makes them different from the other models, which in real conditions and system operation time tending to infinity is practically impossible, as well as practically unstable.

Figure 6 presents relationships of the mean delay time falling on one vessel t_{op} as a function of input period T_{we}, obtained by computer simulations for various distributions of the random variable T_{we}, obtained analytically after substitution to the formulas (2), (4), (7) of the capacity determined by (10) and from formulas (8), (9).

Interpretation of the results of mean delay time t_{op} of a vessel confirms observations made in reference to the analysis of mean number N_o of vessels having the waiting status.

5 Conclusion

From the research performed this author can formulate the following conclusions:

- the area of acceptable solutions to the problem under consideration is located on a plane bound on one side by a deterministic line, and a line defined by a fully independent random variable on the other side (Gutenbaum's model). As all the curves will run between Gutenbaum's line and the dashed line of the deterministic nature, they may provide a preliminary verification of logical correctness of simulation tests,
- it is clearly visible that with the growing extent of determinism the curves bend towards both axes,
- computer simulation method offers simple modelling of real vessel streams and by definition more accurately represents real traffic processes. The accuracy of representation depends on the quality of input data identification,
- the results obtained analytically, due to simplifications made in calculations, show little adequacy for reality for quasi-critical states,
- results of analytical models are similar to the results of the simulation method only for deeply subcritical states.

The choice of a model depends on the objective and the input intensity-capacity ratio, but from a wide perspective we can state that the simulation method is the most universal one, performing well in subcritical and quasi-critical states.

The analytical models of Gutenbaum, Olszamowski and Piszczek may be applied in examining all elements of waterway infrastructure.

References

1. Gutenbaum, J.: Modelowanie matematyczne systemów Akademicka Oficyna Wydawnicza EXIT, Warszawa (2003)
2. Majzner, P.: Metoda oceny akwenów ograniczonych z wykorzystaniem symulacji ruchu strumieni jednostek, rozprawa doktorska, Szczecin (2008)
3. Majzner, P.: Fairway Traffic Intersection Processes Models Zeszyty Naukowe AM w Szczecinie Nr 38(110). Szczecin (2014)
4. Olszamowskij, S.B., Zemlakowskij, D.K., Scepetow, I.A.: Organizacja bezopasnosti plawanija sudow, Transport Moskwa (1979)
5. Piszczek, W.: Modele miar systemu inżynierii ruchu morskiego. Studia nr 14, WSM Szczecin (1990)
6. Piszczek, W.: Model bezpieczeństwa ruchu promów na skrzyżowaniu toru wodnego i przeprawy promowej, Zeszyt Naukowy WSM nr 59, Szczecin (2000)

Motor Vehicle Safety Technologies in Relation to the Accident Rates

Ján Kapusta and Alica Kalašová[✉]

The Faculty of Operation and Economics of Transport and Communications,
University of Žilina, Univerzitná 1, 01026 Žilina, Slovakia
{jan.kapusta,Alica.Kalasova}@fpedas.uniza.sk

Abstract. The increasing need for human mobility is one of the indicators of wealthy society and economic success of human behaviour. Development of transportation in all its sectors is also connected with the evolution of society. Negative aspects caused by this development are the occurrence of road accidents, energy efficiency and traffic congestions. The response to these major challenges cannot be limited to traditional measures. It is important to present and evaluate the impact of intelligent vehicle systems on road transportation safety. Therefore, it is necessary to change and modify the current situation that would lead to decrease in number of accidents that occur on the roads every year. Number of accidents is a good safety indicator. This paper identifies and presents different safety technologies used in modern motor vehicles. Use of such technologies and vehicle to vehicle communication as a part of cooperative systems is crucial in achieving this goal. The aim is to build a common understanding of the asset that cooperative systems and new safety features provide in road transportation and later create a proper environment for their deployment on European roads.

Keywords: Transport safety · Motor vehicles safety · Cooperative systems

1 Introduction

Road transportation today faces enormous challenges. Demand for personal mobility is increasing while imposing a high cost on society. Road transportation safety refers to the methods and measures used for reducing the risk of a person using the road network being killed or seriously injured. Road traffic crashes are one of the world's largest public health and injury prevention problems. The problem is all the more acute because the victims are overwhelmingly healthy prior to their crashes. Numerous initiatives by European Commission are underway, for example, to raise awareness and to make motor vehicles technically safer. High-tech in-vehicle safety and efficiency features represent an opportunity to improve this situation. Their potential to bring a positive impact on transportation safety is well known. These technologies have not penetrated the market, solely due to a lack of understanding about the potential benefits to driving behaviour [1].

© Springer International Publishing Switzerland 2015
J. Mikulski (Ed.): TST 2015, CCIS 531, pp. 172–179, 2015.
DOI: 10.1007/978-3-319-24577-5_17

2 Road Transportation Accident Rates

Road traffic accident also known as traffic collision or motor vehicle collision takes place when a vehicle collides with another vehicle, pedestrian, animal or other stationary obstruction such as a tree or utility pole. Road traffic accident may have many different results. Few of them are injury, death, vehicle damage and property damage. Road accidents are caused mainly by humans when they neglect or refuse to follow laid down rules, signs and regulations concerning the use of roads. An estimate of over 1.2 million people are killed in road crashes each year and as many as 50 million are injured [2].

Smeed's Law is an empirical rule relating traffic fatalities to traffic congestion as measured by proxy of motor vehicle registrations and country population. Smeed interpreted his law as a law of human nature. The number of deaths is determined mainly by psychological factors that are independent of material circumstances. People will drive recklessly until the number of deaths reaches the maximum they can tolerate. When the number exceeds that limit, they drive more carefully [3]. This law provides a good example on how people think while driving.

A study by Rumar using crash reports from the United Kingdom and U.S. as data, found that 57 % of crashes were due solely to driver factors, 27 % due to combined roadway and driver factors, 6 % due to combined vehicle and driver factors, 3 % due solely to roadway factors, 3 % due to combined roadway, driver and vehicle factors, 2 % due solely to vehicle factors and 1 % due to combined roadway and vehicle factors.

Human factors in vehicle collisions include all factors related to drivers and other road users that may contribute to a collision. Examples of such factors include driver behaviour, visual and auditory acuity, decision making ability and reaction time. Driver impairment describes factors that prevent drivers from driving at their normal level of skill. Common impairments are for example alcohol, physical impairments such as poor eyesight, age, fatigue (sleep deprivation), drug use and distraction such as conversations and operating a mobile phone while driving. Road design is crucial for safe driving [4].

Fatal injuries include all the victims who die within 30 days of the accident as a result of injuries sustained. Injuries are not always correctly classified by severity in police accident reports. Definitions of injuries are often not clear and there is no standardization whether in EU or U.S. Long term impacts of traffic injuries are poorly documented. There are reasons to believe that a number of people living with lasting impairments as a result of traffic injury is likely to be increasing [5]. Property damage only (PDO) is the most common type of accident. The only negative aspect of such an accident is financial loss without any injuries.

Figure 1 shows that number of fatal accidents is decreasing in EU and Slovakia. On the other side, in 2012 the number increased in both, USA and in the state of Texas. It shows that actions of European Union led to the improvement in terms of safety for all network users.

One approach to understand accident severity is to investigate the relative frequency of accident severity. This concept can be visualized as a pyramid, where fatal accidents stand at the top of such a pyramid. These accidents are relatively rare. At the base of the

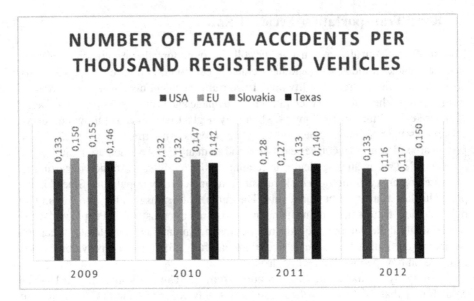

Fig. 1. Number of fatal accidents per thousand registered vehicles [own study based on [6–9],

pyramid there are traffic conflicts such as interactions between road users which do not result in an accident. The levels in between consist of accidents resulting in severe and slight injuries, as well as accidents that only result in property damage [10].

Road traffic accidents generally fall into one of four common types:

- Lane departure crashes, which take place when a driver leaves the lane they are currently in and collide with another vehicle or a roadside object (these include head-on collisions and run-off-road collisions)
- Collisions at junctions (rear-end collision and angle or side impacts)
- Collisions involving pedestrians and cyclists
- Collisions with animals

Despite this division of types of accidents there are other types that occur and are important to mention. Rollovers are not very common, but lead to greater rates of severe injuries and deaths. Some of these are considered to be secondary events that occur after a collision with a run-off-road crash or a collision with another vehicle.

3   Safety Systems in Motor Vehicles

Evolving technological advancements have great potential for improving the safety of road transportation. Number of safety and security proposals are developed by motor vehicle producing companies. These technologies are being developed in order to protect drivers as well as other users of the network. Their impact is not noticeable right now. In the next years to come most of them will become a routine part of all the new vehicles built worldwide. Some of the functions that assist the driver in detecting hazards and avoiding most types of accidents are:

- Lane departure warning systems (LDW) which monitor the position of a vehicle within a lane and are set to warn the driver if the vehicle deviates or is about to deviate outside the lane unexpectedly. The system maintains the vehicle position by detecting lane markings or street boundaries via a video sensor. A warning occurs only above a certain minimum speed (Fig. 2).

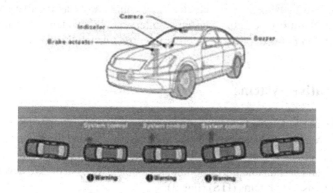

Fig. 2. Lane departure warning system [17]

- Collision warning system (CWS) monitors the roadway ahead and is supposed to warn a driver via sound and light signals when potential danger such as another vehicle or object is detected in the same lane and thus can help avoid rear-end impacts or minimize the effects of these type of collisions. The brakes are pre-charged to prepare for efficient braking if the risk of a collision increases despite the warnings.
- Adaptive cruise control (ACC) systems are in-vehicle electronic systems that can be integrated with CWS and can automatically maintain a minimum following interval to the vehicle in front in the same lane. If there is no vehicle ahead it works as a conventional cruise control so the speed is set by the driver.
- Rear object detection systems which detect moving and stationary objects located within a specific area behind the vehicle can be integrated with other sensors such as side object detection sensors to cover other blind spots around the vehicle. European Commission estimated that blind spot problem causes about 500 fatalities a year on Europe's roads. Because of this problem a directive that requires rear-view mirrors to be upgraded in order to reduce this blind spot was implemented [11].
- Safe human machine interaction for navigation systems. All in-vehicle information and communication systems intended for use by the driver while the vehicle is in motion, for example navigation systems, essential safe design and use aspects for the human/machine interface need to be taken into account. Several different types of system with different display positions and technologies such as head-up or separate detachable display are currently on the market [13].
- Fuel efficiency advisor is a transportation information system that provides in real time the current location of motor vehicles, their fuel consumption, driver times, service intervals and much more. Fuel efficient driving is supported through on-board functions for the driver as well as follow-up reports in the back office system [13].

- Impairment warning (IW) alerts tired and distracted drivers. A camera monitors the movements of the car between the lane markings and calculates the risk of the driver losing control of the vehicle. A message on the display advises the driver to take a break [13].
- Vehicle stability systems (VSS) monitor lateral acceleration from on-board sensors to reduce rollovers due to excessive speed in a curve and prevent loss of control crashes due to instability of a vehicle. They can be used as passive (warning of potential instability) or active systems (intervene by reducing the throttle and applying different brake pressure in order to correct instability) [12].

4   Cooperative Systems

The main goal of cooperative systems is to increase road safety using wireless communication among vehicles and also between the vehicles, drivers and the roadside infrastructure. This is an attractive solution contributing to the European goal of safer, cleaner and more efficient and sustainable traffic solutions. Cooperative systems are new generation of intelligent transport systems (ITS) (Fig. 3).

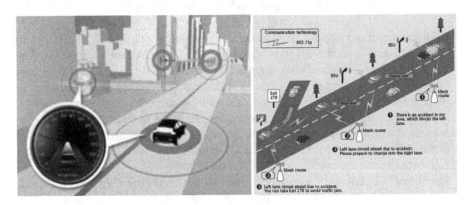

Fig. 3. Cooperative system working principle [18]

ITS is still a young discipline, varying from country to country in levels of acceptance, take-up and local applicability. It is a generic term for the integrated application of communications, control and information processing technologies to the transportation system. The resultant benefits save lives, time, money, energy and the environment. The term "ITS" is flexible and capable of being interpreted in a broad or narrow way. "Transport telematics" is a term used in Europe for the group of technologies that support ITS. ITS covers all modes of transport and considers all elements of the transportation system – the vehicle, the infrastructure, and the driver or user, interacting together dynamically. The overall function of ITS is to improve decision making, often in real time by transport network controllers and other users, thereby improving the operation of the entire transport system. The definition encompasses a broad array of techniques and approaches that may be achieved through stand-alone technological applications or as enhancements to other transportation strategies. Information is at the core of ITS whether it is static or real time traffic data or a digital map. Many ITS tools are based on the collection, processing, integration and supply of information. Data generated by ITS may provide real-time information about current conditions on a network, or on-line information for journey planning, enabling highway authorities and agencies, road operators, public and commercial transport providers and individual travellers to make better informed, safer, more coordinated and more 'intelligent' decisions or 'smarter' use of networks. Safety benefits include safety systems such as adaptive speed control, collision detection and avoidance, enhanced vehicle safety systems and cooperative vehicle highway systems (CVHS). European Union have invested massive public funds in research and technological development of this system. The path to widespread deployment of ITS is not without its challenges. Much of the technology is well proven but increasingly there is a realization that the more difficult issues are social, institutional and political [14].

5   Vehicle - to - Vehicle Communication

Vehicle-to-vehicle (V2V) communications comprises a wireless network where automobiles send messages to each other with information about their actions. This data include speed, location, and direction of travel, braking and loss of stability. Vehicle-to-vehicle technology uses dedicated short-range communications standard (DSRC). The range is up to 300 meters or 1000 feet or about 10 s at highway speeds. On the first cars, V2V warnings might come to the driver as an alert, perhaps a red light that flashes in the instrument panel, or an amber then red alert for escalating problems. It might indicate the direction of the threat. All that is fluid for now since V2V is still a concept with several thousand working prototypes or retrofitted test cars. Most of the prototypes have advanced to stage where the cars brake and sometimes steer around hazards [15] (Fig. 4).

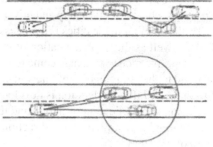

Fig. 4. Vehicle to vehicle communication [19]

The goal of V2V communication is to prevent accidents by allowing vehicles in transit to send position and speed data to one another over an ad hoc mesh network. Depending upon how the technology is implemented, the vehicle's driver may simply receive a warning should there be a risk of an accident or the vehicle itself may take pre-emptive actions such as braking in order to slow down. V2V technology enables an ubiquitous 360 degree awareness of surrounding threats. V2V is an important part of the intelligent transport system (ITS). An intelligent transport system will use the data from vehicle-to-vehicle communication to improve traffic management by allowing vehicles to also communicate with roadside infrastructure such as traffic lights and signs. The technology could become mandatory in the not-too-distant future and help put driverless-cars on the roads [16].

6 Conclusion

Cooperation of all drivers is crucial for the prevention of accidents. From this situation comes a need for control of road transportation by all the responsible authorities. Road traffic safety refers to the methods and measures for reducing the risk of a person using the road network being killed or seriously injured. The relatively low level of fatalities in rail, sea and air transport accidents stands in sharp contrast to the number of road fatalities that occur every year. Major progress has however been made in road safety, having as a result a noticeable yearly decrease in road fatalities throughout the years. Numerous initiatives are underway, for example to raise awareness and to make motor vehicles technically safer. The number of accidents is a good safety indicator. There is still a need to enforce innovative rules, regulations and systems into the vehicles to minimize this number. Once the vehicles will be equipped with the newest technologies and they will be able to communicate with each other there is a strong belief that number of accidents will decrease rapidly. These technologies help drivers in critical situations and when they pass for example a collision site they are able to send information about their occurrence to the vehicles approaching a dangerous place in the network. It means that almost 30 % of driver based collisions could be avoided by the use of cooperative systems. [18] In 2012 there were 28126 fatal accidents on European roads. With the use of vehicle to vehicle (V2V), vehicle to infrastructure (V2I) and vehicle to other type of device (V2X) communications this number could be lowered to as low as 19688 fatalities. To be sure about this potential decrease we need to gain a better understanding of the short and long term socio-economic impact of such systems on safety and driver comfort.

Traffic calming in the cities is a process reflecting the efforts to achieve new quality of life as well as the implementation of modern transport policy at European level. In practice, traffic moderation may come in various forms according to the type of area and road, and to the requirements of relevant citizens. It is appreciated that after many years of hesitation, traffic moderation is developing in Slovakia too. The common task is the advertising and edification of public and the presentation of good practices. Nevertheless, the trend is definitely in the direction of joining the European efforts for humanisation of transport system.

References

1. EUROFOT: Vision. Ertico – ITS Europe (2015). http://www.eurofot-ip.eu/en/about_eurofot/vision/
2. Ubani, A.T.: Road Accidents: Causes, Consequences and Prevention (2013). http://ubanichijioke.hubpages.com/hub/road-accidents-causes-consequences-and-prevention

3. Dyson, F.: Part II: A Failure of Intelligence. MIT Technology Review (2006). http://www.technologyreview.com/news/406948/part-ii-a-failure-of-intelligence/
4. Lum, H.: Interactive Highway Safety Design Model: Accident Predictive Module (1995). Office of Corporate Research, Technology, and Innovation Management (2011). http://www.fhwa.dot.gov/publications/publicroads/95winter/p95wi14.cfm
5. Masniak, D.: Social and economic costs of road accidents in Europe. Gdanska Wysza Szkola Administracji, Poland (2008). http://www.law.muni.cz/sborniky/dp08/files/pdf/financ/masniak.pdf
6. Statista: Number of vehicles registered in the United States from 1990 to 2011. Statista, Inc., New York (2013). http://www.statista.com/statistics/183505/number-of-vehicles-in-the-united-states-since-1990/
7. The State of Texas: The Texas Automotive Manufacturing Industry. Texas: Office of the Governor, Economic Development and Tourism (2013). http://governor.state.tx.us/files/ecodev/Texas-Automotive-Industry-Report.pdf
8. MV SR: Celkovy pocet evidovanych vozidiel v SR. Ministerstvo vnutra Slovenskej republiky (2014). http://www.minv.sk/?celkovy-pocet-evidovanych-vozidiel-v-sr
9. European Commission: EU transport in figures: Statistical Pocketbook 2012. European Union (2012). http://ec.europa.eu/transport/facts-fundings/statistics/doc/2012/pocketbook2012.pdf
10. Volvo Trucks: European accident research and safety report. Volvo Trucks, Goteborg (2013). http://www.volvotrucks.com/SiteCollectionDocuments/VTC/Corporate/Values/ART%20Report%202013_150dpi.pdf
11. European Comission: Open roads across Europe. European Commission, Energy and Transport DG, Brussels (2006). http://ec.europa.eu/transport/road/doc/road_transport_policy_en.pdf
12. Burks, S.V., et al.: Transportation Research Circular E-C146: Trucking 101. Transportation Research Board, Washington, DC (2010). http://onlinepubs.trb.org/onlinepubs/circulars/ec146.pdf
13. EUROFOT: Intelligent Vehicle Systems. Ertico – ITS Europe (2015). http://www.eurofot-ip.eu/en/intelligent_vehicle_systems/
14. World Road Association: PIARC ITS Handbook. World Road Association, France (2011). http://road-network-operations.piarc.org/index.php?option=com_content&task=view&id=32&Itemid=65&lang=en
15. Howard, B.: V2V: What are vehicle-to-vehicle communications and how they work? ExtremeTech (2015). http://www.extremetech.com/extreme/176093-v2v-what-are-vehicle-to-vehicle-communications-and-how-does-it-work
16. Haughn, M.: Vehicle-to-vehicle communication (2014). TechTarget (2015). http://whatis.techtarget.com/definition/vehicle-to-vehicle-communication-V2V-communication
17. Lane departure prevention: The National Roads and Motorists (2015). http://www.mynrma.com.au/motoring-services/buy-sell/buying-advice/features/lane-departure-prevention.htm
18. SRP: Aktuální trendy v ITS s ohledem na bezpečnost silničního provozu. Praha: SDT (2014)
19. Ingram, A.: NHTSA Moving Forward With Vehicle-To-Vehicle Communication. MotorAuthority (2014). http://www.motorauthority.com/news/1094064_nhtsa-moving-forward-with-vehicle-to-vehicle-communication

Concept of a Telematics System
Model in Crisis Management

Andrzej Bujak and Mariusz Topolski[✉]

Wroclaw Schools of Banking, Fabryczna 29-31, Wroclaw, Poland
{Andrzej.Bujak,Mariusz.Topolski}@wsb.wroclaw.pl

Abstract. The paper is about the concept of a telematics system model in crisis management. It presents current telematics solutions in crisis management. The authors show that there are many telematics domain systems ranging from monitoring, traffic management, and ending with the exchange of information. However, there is the lack of a solution that will connect them together. In this paper the authors present the concept of an integrated telematics system. The elaboration discusses organizational issues, risk analysis, structural specifics, the specifics of the components, costs and benefits, and an implementation plan. The purpose of this solution is to improve a rapid response to emergency situations, i.e. public events, traffic accidents, disturbances and other situations. That concept takes into account current needs arising from the topic.

Keywords: Telematics system · Crisis management

1 Introduction

Everyday there is a likelihood of risk posed by the forces of nature or human activity. Every year, all over the world, we have to deal with ever more unpredictable in the effects weather anomalies. Occurrence of floods, hurricanes or blizzards often takes the form of natural disasters resulting in casualties. Moreover, we live in a time of conflict, war, ethnic unrest and terrorism daily consuming millions of lives.

A characteristic for of the existing threats is not impossible to determine, namely, the time, place and geographical scope of their occurrence in order to prevent and minimize the effects of risks and to save lives of victims involved in crisis management. The crisis management process can be divided into four phases: prevention, preparation, response and recovery. Prevention and preparation phase is to minimize the possibility of an emergency. The main purpose of the organization is to respond to rescue and emergency assistance to the injured. Reconstruction and aims to restore the state of a crisis situation before it occurs involves the reconstruction of the damaged infrastructure [1, 3].

© Springer International Publishing Switzerland 2015
J. Mikulski (Ed.): TST 2015, CCIS 531, pp. 180–187, 2015.
DOI: 10.1007/978-3-319-24577-5_18

Each of these phases is characterized by the need to process large amounts of information. The processing of information in the event of emergency response consists primarily of collecting, updating and transferring information. The information collected include potential sources of risk, a database of available forces and means that can be used in case of emergency. The information collected will help to develop procedures to be followed by aggregating data, analyzing the effectiveness of emergency response plans, simulating possible scenarios for emergency events.

Information and communications systems can accelerate the speed of information transmission between rescue groups and command centers. The smooth operation of telematics systems allows for quick and effective aid organization which directly affects the lives and health of victims.

The crisis management telematics systems use [2]:

- monitoring subsystem,
- fixed communications subsystem,
- subsystem management and maintenance.

A monitoring center is a place of collective representation of events. Its location is dictated by a locational and organizational solution adopted in the city government. Regardless of the location, monitoring is required within easy reach of the authorities responsible for crisis management and information it mapped and processed. Monitoring centers have a monitoring large monitor screens, the server and the database of monitored events. An example of the use of monitoring in crisis management may be cameras on the dams, so you can continuously monitor water levels and warn the impending danger. Another application of monitoring is to put it in places in big groups of people such as railway stations, shopping malls, movie theaters or places of a religious nature that may be exposed to terrorist attacks.

For the purposes of crisis management centers in the region (provincial and district/ municipal and local) the following networks should be organized [1]:

- telephone communications,
- radio,
- information (local and WAN), providing access to a variety of decision support applications and information management.

A telephone communication subsystem is a fixed backhaul network using fiber optic cable routes usually and metal, and as backup tracks - radio lines. ICT network created MAN (Metropolitan Area Network) provides physical and logical connection management positions communications nodes and the transmission of information in accordance with the needs. During the routine activities of crisis management they are mainly used for telecommunications services provided by local operators. Fixed telephony is used daily for communication between crisis management units. It is the fastest way to provide information about the threat [2].

Telephone communication between users of fixed telephony and mobile users (radiotelephone) enables quick contact e.g. with facility security personnel or with the services directly working in the area during the rescue. With this service, a user logs on to the system using a stationary terminal, and after authentication to communicate with the radio network users [2].

The analysis of the communication system requirements for crisis management to monitor changes in the electronic communications market shows that the most appropriate technology to organize the system is used in the IP network (Internet Protocol) and the corresponding control operation of the network nodes (soft switch), according to the architecture of IMS (IP Multimedia Subsystem). The IMS architecture can provide a variety of services such as voice, video and data. The proposed technology makes it possible to build a logically uniform for all users communication system with its own addressing. The main advantage of this architecture is the ability to create a system using previously used the infrastructure and equipment i.e. the public telecommunications networks, telephone internal networks, data networks and the Internet [1, 4].

The computer network uses the IP protocol for the purposes of transmitting a VoIP signal (Voice over Internet Protocol) in order to more quickly respond to threats to safety of people and fixed assets.

The telephone network enables the provision of telephone services and fax transmission to all its users and tele- and video-conferencing services users selected at regular and backup jobs. An ability to perform video conferencing allows for a more realistic image of the enormity of the disaster and to present its range. It is possible to have a reciprocal access to the services users and data. This way, all users of the system have constant access to the list of forces and resources that can be committed, emergency procedures, emergency response plans. In this way an access is ensured to databases of the crisis management system, electronic mail, electronic exchange of documents (EDI - Electronic Data Interchange), as well as the access to the Internet and its services, data networks (e.g. The police, the state fire brigade, ambulance) [1].

An additional service and convenience is a teleconference which relies on the statement of a telephone call between more than two telephones. A teleconference eliminates the problem of changing the details of the original information, which is possible in the case of a multiple transmission of information to the next caller. This can occur if the effect of "deaf phone" and information such as the number of victims modified.

The communication system should be managed and maintained in accordance with the recommended by the ITU-T layered model of management for telecommunications, which includes the following layers of management: network elements, network, services and business management. This subsystem should allow for the continuous management of the network, including monitoring, recording and reproduction of the events with the use of geographic information system GIS (Geographic Information System). Management and maintenance of the communication system should correspond to the recommendations of the international and national levels. The function of management and maintenance should be possible in all phases of the system, such as system planning, compiling and running interconnection, operation and reconfiguration and recovery communication system.

Moreover, in the context of developing, mobile and additional services used by the authorities of crisis management, emergency services and public safety consist in:

- user number portability to other end of the telephone network and set its telephone and permissions (i.e. Nomadic landline users), so profile and slogan (PIN) used by the user to log on to the network,
- prioritizing calls, enabling the user a higher priority, indicating a high priority call, or even disconnecting lower priority,

- voicemail, allowing users to leave and listen to messages on the functioning telephone system with voice messages left, browsing a voice mail using a web browser,
- notifying information services, providing selected users (senior command) with transmit subordinate short, urgent text messages or voice,
- telephone communication between users of fixed-line and mobile users (radiotelephone),
- telephone service through the Internet or a network of cooperation,
- it is also possible to use a set of e-mail services and its integration with cameras,
- access to the central book of contacts in order to obtain information on telephone numbers, e-mail addresses and other useful data, for example a department, a supervisor, a position,
- access to a central application, which means that the user may have access to the same data in the place of residence as in the workplace,
- services and severance virtual meetings are useful for management teams and crisis management and other management groups at central and provincial levels.

There is no doubt that modern telematics systems contribute significantly to improvement of communication between emergency services and affect the response time in the event of an emergency. Hopefully, a continuous development of technology will create an ideal system of early warning and alert in the future and unify the crisis management system for the whole country [1].

2 Regional Warning System RSO

The Regional Warning System is a service alerting the general public about local hazards. On August 31, 2014 r. RSO pilot testing ended in all provinces. Its implementation was made possible thanks to the implementation of Terrestrial Digital Television, as well as cooperation between the Polish Television, the Ministry of Administration and Digitization and Institute of Meteorology and Water Management (IMGW).

RSO covers the entire country. Implementation of the project as of 1 January 2015 was done by a pilot in the period of December 2013 - August 2014 in all provinces: the first stage by the end of December 2013 (Lubusz, Mazovia, Podlasie, Greater and West), the second stage by the end of March 2014 (Lower Silesia, Lublin, Lesser Poland and Subcarpathian), the third stage by the end of June 2014 (Lodz, Opole, Silesia and Świętokrzyskie), the fourth stage by the end of August 2014 (Bydgoszcz, a Pomeranian and Warmia Masurian).

Messages/warnings disseminated within the RSO include the following thematic categories:

- overall,
- meteorological
- hydrological,
- water levels (water gages).

A free mobile application of the Regional Warning System is available in stores with applications for each operating system (Android, iOS, Windows Phone). The application can found in stores under key words "RSO" and "Regional Warning System". It provides access to messages generated by the provincial disaster management centers provincial offices throughout the country (each province). In order to familiarize yourself with the specific error simply "download" RSO app, and then select any region. Moreover, the "drivers" of RSO may contain traffic information. The application is also provided in the section containing the guides of conduct in emergency situations.

Action of RSO. A message (warning) is generated by the provincial disaster management center on the website of the office of the provincial and digital terrestrial television (Regional TV), and telephone applications.

Messages appear on the TV screen in the form of inscriptions. They briefly inform and refer the details, for example a specific page teletext. The TVs customized hybrid TV (i.e. connecting TV to the Internet), you can switch to a site that offers such movie information on the threat.

RSO Mobile application provides access to messages generated throughout the country.

3   The Concept of the Telematics System Model

Intelligent Transportation Systems are a wide collection of various technologies (telecommunications, information technology, and automatic measurement) and the management techniques used for transport in order to protect lives of road users and to improve efficiency of the transport system and to protect natural resources (Fig. 1.).

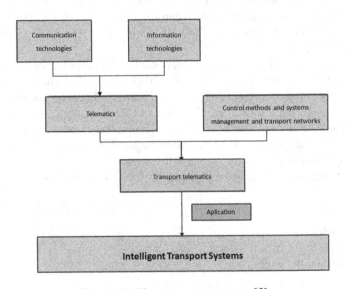

Fig. 1. Intelligent transport systems [5]

Intelligent Transportation Systems are a combination of information and communications technology for a transport infrastructure and vehicles in order to improve safety, increase efficiency of transport processes and environmental protection. ITS improves conditions in the field of multi-modal travel, dealing with private and public means of transport by road, air and maritime transport. Results of the research on the benefits of using intelligent crisis management system are provided in Fig. 2.

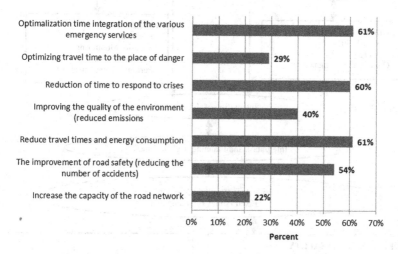

Fig. 2. The impact of the crisis management ITS [own study]

One of the most important tasks of the state aims to introduce intelligent transport solutions to establish the ITS architecture, which is a series of links (logical, physical and communication) between the elements that make up systems of Intelligent Transport Systems in order to create a scalable, easy to maintain and manage solution.

A domestic architecture does not indicate a specific technology or a vendor, thereby becoming open systems that increase competitiveness of the implemented solutions. Currently in Poland ITS solutions are "islands", it means that they individually meet the predetermined role but when combined they can lead to a situation when these systems are not compatible and will not be able to work together without bringing the same potential benefits. Figure 3 is the physical architecture of ITS.

The model shows the concept of regional integration with an intelligent warning system transport system. Regional integration and ITS warning system are the source of knowledge that can take full advantage of the crisis.

The results of subjective evaluation by the user of the ITS system is shown in Fig. 4. The research area is divided into 14 areas in Wroclaw. The study was conducted among 147 people. Surveys were carried out in Wroclaw in the area of major and minor interchanges, at bus stops and public transport. It assesses the main assumptions that are made in the project implementation of intelligent transport system in Wroclaw.

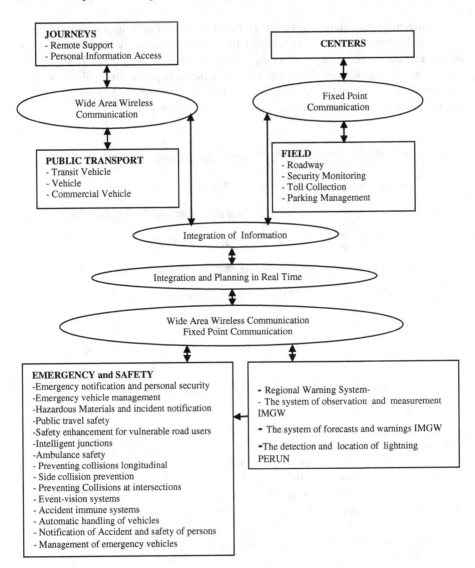

Fig. 3. The model of the crisis management system [own study]

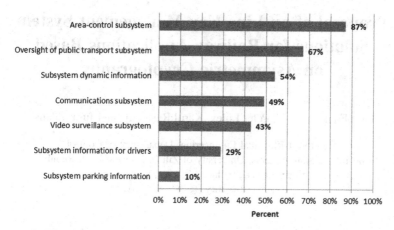

Fig. 4. The model of the crisis management system [own study]

4 Conclusion

According to studies into crisis management attention should primarily be paid to an area-control subsystem, the oversight of public transport subsystem and subsystem dynamic information. According to the research cited above, areas require continuous improvement. As far as crisis management is concerned, the least important subsystems are subsystem of parking information and an information subsystem for drivers. The authors present the concept of crisis management system. Only through the use of the full measurement information, security can be efficiently managed locally and globally.

References

1. Hendler, Z., Kowalewski, M., Kowalczyk, B.: System łączności na potrzeby służb bezpieczeństwa publicznego i zarządzania kryzysowego w aglomeracji miejskiej, Telekomunikacja i techniki informacyjne, pp. 3–4 (2008)
2. Kowalewski, M., Kowalczyk, B., Parapura, H.: Sieci i usługi telekomunikacyjne w zarządzaniu kryzysowym, Telekomunikacja i techniki informacyjne, pp. 1–2 (2011)
3. Markusik, S.: Infrastruktura logistyczna w transporcie; t.I. Środki transportu, Wydawnictwo Politechniki Śląskiej, Gliwice (2009)
4. Tundys, B.: Logistyka Miejska – teoria i praktyka, Warszawa (2014)
5. http://www.itspolska.pl/?page=11. Accessed on 22 May 2015

Proposal of on-Line Key Management System Solutions for Railway Applications Based on Asymmetric Cryptography

Mária Franeková[⊠], Peter Lüley, Karol Rástočný, and Juraj Ždánsky

Faculty of Electrical Engineering, Department of Control
and Information Systems, University of Žilina, Žilina, Slovak Republic
{maria.franekova,peter.luley,karol.rastocny,
juraj.zdansky}@fel.uniza.sk

Abstract. This article is devoted to the transmission of safety-related messages via open transmission system in application with ETCS (European Train Control System) system Level - L2 using cryptographic protocol Euroradio. Authors in this article describe conceptual proposal of on-line key management system managing the keys of all entities included in communication in the range of domains in safe manner. Proposed KMS (Key Management System) assumes the use of asymmetric cryptography. In practical part are analyzed ideological solutions of the use of public keys within the communication of ETCS system entities in two neighboring domains. Generated keys of proposed KMS hierarchical architecture were simulated for the ECC (Elliptic Curve Cryptography) algorithm, specifically for Koblitz curves in the software tool Cryptool.

Keywords: Safety-related system · European Train Control System · Key management system · Identification · Asymmetric cryptography · ECC · Simulation

1 Introduction

During the control of safety-related processes should be given the greatest attention to the design and implementation of control system safety protection in order to eliminate threads both from inside of the system as well as from external environment. Such processes are for example in railway traffic control. There was created project ERTMS (European Rail Traffic Management System) as a response to the need of railway traffic mutual interoperability. This project includes the development of a unified railway traffic control system ETCS (European Train Control System) [1] which allows simple and fast train transfer through the whole Europe. The ETCS development is divided into three levels (L). LevelL2, which is currently under development, uses also communication via open transmission system GSM-R (Global System for Mobile Communications – Railway) [2]. Because of the sensitivity of transmitted messages on railway operation, transfer of such information must be properly secured. Since there is possible unauthorized access to open transmission system it is necessary to use also cryptographic techniques. According to standard STN EN 50159 [3] there are two recommended models of messages for the open transmission systems: B0 (message

J. Mikulski (Ed.): TST 2015, CCIS 531, pp. 188–197, 2015.
DOI: 10.1007/978-3-319-24577-5_19

encryption) and B1 (cryptographic redundancy). Essential part of the cryptographic algorithms is the key management system, which is the most important part in all sub-phases of cryptographic system development.

In order to secure the communication ETCS system L2, on which we focus in the article, is using the cryptographic protocol Euroradio (ER) Fig. 1. Euroradio is multi-purpose transmission method which will be in the near future creating connections on all European railways between the stationary centers TsE (Trackside Element) and all mobile units RBC (Radio Block Central) and if necessary also among mobile units themselves controlled by centre TCC (Traffic Control Centre). Information about train location, availability of railway sections and other information necessary for the ETCS L2 operation are obtained through the station and railway safety equipment IL (InterLocking). All functions necessary for train speed control are carried out onboard of the train by EVC (European Vital Computer) and the transmission is carried out by MS (Mobile Station). As reference points to determine the distance for trains and to determine the direction of the trains serve non-switching balises. ER system needs for the key management of used cryptographic algorithms the KMS (Key Management System).

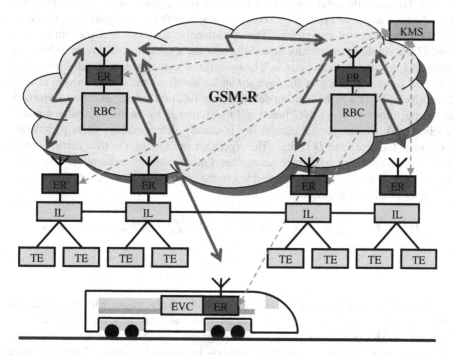

Fig. 1. Messages transmission among entities of stationary and mobile part of the system in architecture ETCS L2 [own study]

In terms of the architecture the ER system is based on the seven-layer reference model RM OSI with the safety layers as main parts, which are added between transport and application layer in RM OSI [4, 5]. Those safety layers are ESL (Euroradio Safety

Layer) and SAI (Safety Application Interface). The function of the ESL is to protect messages from being modified during the transmission (corruption, insertion, and masquerade). Next safety procedures of ESL includes message authentication during transmission and ensuring of message integrity. Both these procedures are carried out by keyed hash function MAC (Message Authentication Code) what is function of the message (M) and shared key K_c during the application of hash function H:

$$MAC = H_{Kc}(M).$$ (1)

Protocol additionally guarantees the identification of sender's identity [6] based on the imprint (of authorization code) which could be performed only by the entity owning the key. The key is known only the sender and receiver. The second safety layer SAI provides protection against threats caused by wrong sequence of messages (repetition, loss, delay and incorrect sequence). Protection against these threats is achieved by added serial numbers and time stamps to the messages. The basic requirement on the cryptosystem used in Euroradio is on the implemented cryptographic mechanisms, which must withstand cryptographic attacks throughout the whole lifetime of the system. To assess the safety and effectiveness of used cryptographic algorithm can be used the approaches to express the computational complexity of algorithms, which are based on the theory of complexity. The operational complexity of algorithm is determined by asymptotic complexity describing how the algorithm will change its behavior depending on the input data size n. The operational complexity is usually referred as O (called *Landau notation* or *Bachmann-Landau notation*) and it is a function of input data O(f(n)) [6]. This is the limiting description of function course, so called asymptotic upper magnitude gradient MG function f(n) expressed by another (usually sampler) function g(n). Computational complexity is usually determined by three parameters: S (Space), T (Time) and D (Data). The algorithm optimization is then carried out by minimization of one of these three parameters. Let's assume the existence of functions f (n) and g(n). If these functions are defined in the sub-set of real numbers then (2) and (3) are valid and are equivalent to:

$$f(n) = O(g(n)); \ n \to \infty \Leftrightarrow \exists n_0, \exists MG > 0 : |f(n)| \le MG|g(n)|; \forall n > n_0$$ (2)

$$f(n) = O(g(n)); n \to \infty \Leftrightarrow \exists MG > 0 : \lim_{n \to \infty} \frac{f(n)}{g(n)} = MG$$ (3)

As computationally secure are currently considered algorithms with exponential or combinatorial complexity which are breakable in real time only for small values of input data n. This article deals only with cryptographic mechanisms in ESL safety layer in terms of effective key distribution methods in the on-line mode. The conceptual proposal is based on asymmetric cryptography algorithms.

It should be emphasized that there do not exist comprehensive proposal of ETCS L2 on-line key management system for the purpose of safety procedures based on cryptography and it is necessary to solve this issue.

2 Key Management System for Safety-Related Applications

Key management is set of processes and mechanisms which support exchange of keys and reflect relations among entities. This system incorporates phases from key generation through key transmission and key archiving to the key removal. For the safety-related applications must be all phases of KMS (Key Management System) handled in a safe manner in accordance with required SIL (Safety Integrity Level). General requirements applicable to the key management system are defined in the standards for railway applications, especially in [3] where can be found links to standards e.g. ISO/IEC 1170-1, 2, 3 and ANSI X9.1 dealing with key management systems and their application switch symmetric and asymmetric cryptographic systems in COTS (Commercial-Off-The-Shelf) technology. These standards, however, are focusing on different group of safety-related processes in the field of banking and finance. But there also exist specifications specifically dedicated to the recommendations for key managements system of ETCS system and for its sub-systems. These recommendations are developed with the support of research teams working in UNISIG group. This group of companies was founded on the initiative of the EU (European Union) in 1999. Members of this group are nowadays companies as Alstom, Ansaldo STS, Bombardier, Invensys, Siemens, Thales, AŽD Praha and MERMEC. Subsets, as are named aforementioned specifications, include a wide range of issues related to various equipment and systems used in ETCS. For the purposes of KMS is the most important subset 038 – off-line key management [7]. Important is also subset 037 – Euroradio FIS [8].

There exist two main approaches in the development of key management systems during the development of ETCS. The main difference is the distribution media. If the key is distributed physically we recognize the off-line key management. If the key is distributed in the system by software we recognize on-line key management. Other approaches in the development of KMS can be distinguished according to the type of the cryptographic algorithm used in safety procedures, either based on symmetric or asymmetric cryptography. Currently the KMS system in ETCS railway system works in off-line mode. According to [9] the KMS location is in so-called KMC (Key Management Centre) where are also defined procedures for key exchange among KMC centers in various domains. The term KMC represents list of railway (RBC) and train (OBU) entities, definition of the rules for keys assignment, identification of other domains where domestic OBU is allowed to drive and identification of the domains of which OBU's are accepted by the domain. From the perspective of keys generation is enforced generation of not a single but a hierarchy of keys, similarly as in the COTS technology. One key (master) is generated and stored (with longer duration) and from this key are derived so-called relation keys (session keys) which are deleted after the connection is terminated.

The hierarchy of keys is divided into three levels:

Level 3 - KTRANS transport keys used to secure the control communication between the KMC (Key Management Centre) and ERTMS entity RBC (Radio Block Centre) or OBU (On Board Unit) of the train to obtain or renew the authentication keys. Keys to secure the connection between the KMCs are called K-KMC.

Level 2 - KMAC authentication keys used to determine the connection keys and ETCS entities authentication.

Level 1 -KSMAC session keys used to secure data during the transmission among entities.

The use of particular keys according to the type of communicating entities within the ETCS system is explained in Table 1. First option describes allocation of unique KMAC to each OBU valid in particular domains. Second option describes the allocation of various KMAC keys for OBU in different domains. This reduces the impact on the domain in case of KMAC disclosure resulting in unauthorized access to RBC area. Since there are assigned different keys to the unit in different RBC's the impact is only on domain with compromised key. In other domains can be the railway operation without influence.

The K-KMC key should be distributed among domains before start of any transactions. It consists of two parts with length 192 bits. First part K-MAC1 is used to ensure the integrity and authenticity of the transaction by the use of CBC-MAC algorithm. Detailed calculation of MAC code is described in subset 037 – Euroradio FIS [8]. Second part of the key K-MAC2 is used to provide the data confidentiality during the transmission what means KMAC key encryption. For this reason is the K-KMC2 key divided into three sub-keys K_1, K_2, K_3, each with length 64 bits (8 parity bits). Each block is then encrypted and decrypted by 3DES [10].

Table 1. Definition of keys and their use in off-line KMS system [own study]

Involved entities	Key usage			Note
	Identification and authentication	Message authentication	Encryption	
RBC – OBU	KMAC	KSMAC	-	Interoperability
KMC - RBC/OBU	-	-	-	Domain-specific
KMC – KMC	-	K-KMC1	K-KMC2	Communication

3 Proposal of on-Line KMS Based on Asymmetric Cryptography

Authors built this proposal on the use of asymmetric cryptography system ECC (Elliptic Curve Cryptography) based on algebraic structure of elliptic curves over the finite field with security ensured by ECDLP (Elliptic Curve Discrete Logarithm Problem). Discrete logarithm problem in elliptic curves has currently more than 10 years of investigation and yet remains hard problem with exponential complexity what can lead to the use of shorter keys and better performance of the communication system.

Let's assume the same settings of elliptic curve for all domains of KMS system. This setting will be generated only once during the introduction of KMS into the force. The domain parameters of elliptic curve was set based on FIPS 186-3 [11] recommendation:

K-409: $m = 409$, $f(z) = z^{409} + z^{87} + 1$, $a = 0$, $b = 1$, $h = 4$

n = 0x 007FFFFF FFFFFFFF FFFFFFFF FFFFFFFF FFFFFFFF FFFFFFFF FFFFFE5F 83B2D4EA
    20400EC4 557D5ED3 E3E7CA5B 4B5C83B8 E01E5PCF

x = 0x 0060F05F 658F49C1 AD3AB189 0F718421 0EFD0987 E307C84C 27ACCFB8 F9F67CC2
    C460189E B5AAAA62 EE222EB1 B35540CF B9023746

y = 0x 01E36905 0B7C4E42 ACBA1DAC BF04299C 3460782F 918EA427 E6325165 E9EA10E3
    DA5F6C42 E9C55215 AA9CA27A 5863EC48 D8E0286B

Unlike in the KMS concept based on symmetric cryptography, where every individual entity has assigned one key, in the proposal for KMS based on EEC will be for all entities introduced key pairs (public and private key). In Table 2 is shown the proposed key hierarchy, recommended keys lengths in bits and their use.

Table 2. Proposal for a key hierarchy for asymmetric KMS cryptosystem [own study]

Key (key length)	Use
$\{PK_{AKT},\ SK_{AKT}\}$ [416 b]	Public and private key used for encryption/decryption of messages between two TCC
K_{TRANS} [192 b]	Secret symmetric key used for encryption/decryption of messages between two entities
$\{PK_{MAC}, SK_{MAC}\}$ [416 b]	Public and private key used for encryption/decryption of message: between train and RBC station $\{PK_{MAC-R}, SK_{MAC-R}\}$, between TCC and RBC station (within one domain) $\{PK_{MAC-T}, SK_{MAC-T}\}$, between modified end station RBC and KMS $\{PK_{MAC-K}, SK_{MAC-K}\}$.

In Fig. 2 is shown the use of PK_{MAC} keys during communication with KMS 1 between two domains A and B. In Fig. 3 is shown the use of PK_{AKT} keys.

Modified end station RBC (in Fig. 2) performs also communication with relevant KMS subjects and provides service for other domains in its range.

In Fig. 3 is shown the conceptual proposal of key architecture between two domains and the method of communication between the train and station within communication of ETCS entities in two domains. Other parts of the KMS system: generation, distribution, archiving and interface are in [12].

All public keys will be stored and published in a shared DB (Database) system accessible for all entities belonging to the KMS domains. After each successful key pair distribution the key distribution systems ends the public part of the key with the subject identification to CDVK (central database of public keys). CDVD makes the public key

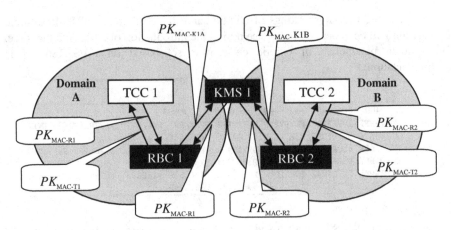

Fig. 2. Proposal of public keys PK_{MAC} usage in communication of ETCS system entities between domains A and B with modified end station RBC [own study]

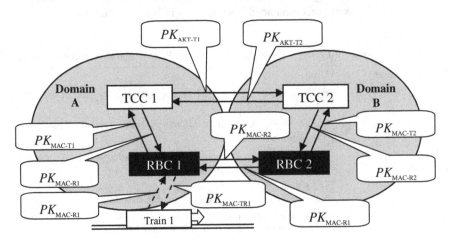

Fig. 3. Proposal of the use of public keys between two domains in train - station communication [own study]

accessible for other subjects in KMS domains. We assume that each RBC station is provided with its identification and its communication key pair. In Fig. 4 is shown more detailed example of train communication with RBC station in domain A.

Let's assume that the DB in train contains individual identification numbers of RBC stations through which has the train planned route and their public keys PK_{MAC-R}(see Table 3). Train knows also its identification number id_{TR} and key pair $\{SK_{MAC-TR}, PK_{MAC-TR}\}$.

In the shown example:

id_{TR} = TR0569

SK_{MAC-TR} = 8FAD4A30 654F06A0 91E6FE2A D24E4151 F00D86BB EF8BCC46 82F285E5 0E6BDE39 EDFAEBE6 0E3F07D9 A8FF79A1 067ADB12 182E160E

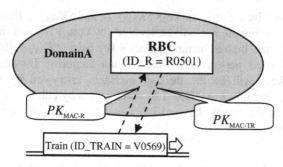

Fig. 4. Example of train communication with RBC station in one domain [own study]

PK_{MAC-TR} = E38580AE 97A4CFB3 C2E380BC 26FD9FEF B70BD69F 7998CEB0 6CD062D9 ACB91BF7 4C7435B6 4A02DD98 45BF83E9 663EDFB2 02BBB312

Note: All keys in the shown example were generated in SW tool Cryptool for selected type of ECC curve.

Table 3. Example of the DB content for one train TR [own study]

ID_RBC	SK_{MAC-T}[Hex]
R0125	5334A317 EE30134E 3BDB54D6 82B4DC2E ACE8FAA8 F4D0FE8A DCBF0475 6440FE19 41D6BB5A 0BE10B65 467CBD04 7A087ACA 7824F4B7
R0501	64A8CC51 F2BE8CC5 ECC3FE7F 934E76BC F5FC7968 90C13C0A 5304A044 80F87DB9 D4D07736 51E19006 0BF9E135 26F685B0 DD9FB5FC
R2177	F13C89D7 FCF9A32B 60ADF856 0129397C B68F4816 AAE1A335 0F29A1CE 19EA4F6B 8E0C5AEA 8A8A2152 7BBA5079 CDAEB58F 56B7AAC9

Database DB of RBC station will contain individual identification numbers of trains having planned routes through the area of RBC station and their public keys PK_{MAC-TR} (see Table 4). RBC station knows its identification number id_{RBC} and its private and public key {SK_{MAC-R}, PK_{MAC-R}}.

In the shown example:
id_R = R0501
SK_{MAC-R} = F71271DA 6D4FDB9C E8EFBC11 7B6A87EF C00C5EF8 41429E20 9F261AA8 1ABECBD9 FB2F2CEF CEBDCBA6 74D9D7AA 2ED0F6A4 1F0CC5AC
PK_{MAC-R} = 64A8CC51 F2BE8CC5 ECC3FE7F 934E76BC F5FC7968 90C13C0A 5304A044 80F87DB9 D4D07736 51E19006 0BF9E135 26F685B0 DD9FB5FC

As seen both databases DB contain necessary identification data (ID_TR and ID_R) for sending encrypted messages by public keys PK_{MAC-TR} and PK_{MAC-R} and for messages decryption by their private keys SK_{MAC-TR} and SK_{MAC-R}. Received messages unable to decrypt by private key will be ignored (by both RBC and train).

Distribution of new highest hierarchical level key pairs (PK_{AKT} and SK_{AKT}) must be realized by authorized person or by certification authority. Distribution of lower hierarchy level keys will be the through messages encrypted by the public key PK_{MAC-K1} (in the direction from TCC 1 to KMS 1) and by public key $PK_{MACK-T1}$ (in the opposite direction). Private keys of individual key pairs will be used to decrypt received messages.

Table 4. Example of the DB content for one RBC station [own study]

ID_TR	PK_{MAC-TR}[Hex]
V0569	E38580AE 97A4CFB3 C2E380BC 26FD9FEF B70BD69F 7998CEB0 6CD062D9 ACB91BF7 4C7435B6 4A02DD98 45BF83E9 663EDFB2 02BBB312
V1112	85C915AE A0AD9E88 4F62DFFC D4CD1FAC E34CFEC7 FCCEB7C9 3BEC6265 2ADBB09A 7843C10D AADC8F08 5AE476E2 C58BBBBA BB20C83B
V0798	A5FA5AD0 E756BEA9 3B69E9B1 4A55F147 6150906F FCEF05D2 EF15634F 3379FB88 3742C78C 6FD2C356 13CA885A A028B030 4C4AD010

4   Conclusion

For authorized transmission of messages among entities of mobile and stationary parts of ETCS L2 System is necessary to have efficient and computationally secure KMS System. At present is for the purpose of Euroradio protocol used off-line KMS System based on symmetric cryptography, where the authenticity is ensured by CBC-MAC supported by 3DES algorithm [13]. Described proposal of on-line KMS System is based on perspective asymmetric cryptographic algorithm ECC for which today do not exist efficient algorithm able to solve discrete algorithm problem in exponential time when followed the recommended key length [14]. During the implementation of KMS is necessary to securely distribute first generated key pars to each entity of ETCS after the public key is validated by certification authority [15]. Advantage of this solution is that all public keys are stored and accessible for all entities belonging to the KMS domains in shared DB system.

Acknowledgement. This work has been supported by the Educational Grant Agency of the Slovak Republic (KEGA) Number: 008ŽU-4/2015: Innovation of HW and SW tools and methods of laboratory education focused on safety aspects of ICT within safety critical applications of processes control.

References

1. Mikulski, J.: Telematic technologies in transportation. In: Janecki, R., Sierpiński, G. (eds.) Contemporary Transportation Systems. Selected Theoretical and Practical Problems. New Culture of mobility, pp. 131–143. Publishing House of the Silesian University of Technology. Monograph no. 324, Gliwice (2011)
2. Franeková, M., Rástočný, K., Janota, A., Chrtiansky, P.: Safety analysis of cryptography mechanisms used in GSM for railway. In: International Journal of Engineering: Annals of Faculty Engineering Hunedoara. Romania. Tome III, ISSN 1584-2665 (2011)
3. EN 50159: Railway applications: Communication, signalling, andprocessing systems. Safety-related communication in closed and open transmission systems, CENELEC (2010)
4. Zahradník, J., Rástočný, K.: Safety of railway interlocking systems. In: Slovak, EDIS, ISBN 80-8070-546-1, Žilina (2006)
5. Franeková, M., et al.: Safety communication of industrial networks. Monograph. In: Slovak, EDIS - ŽU Žilina, ISBN 978-80-8070-715-6 (2007)
6. http://www.cs.cas.cz/portal/AlgoMath/MathematicalAnalysis/Inequalities/ BachmannLandauNotation.htm. Accessed 16 January 2015
7. UNISIG Subset 038 v2.1.9. Off line key management FIS (2005)
8. UNISIG Subset-037 v2.3.0: Euroradio FIS (2005)
9. Franeková, M., Voštenák, M.: Proposal of key management system for ETCSLevel 2. In: Scientific International Journal Mechanics, Transport, Communications, Sofia, Bulgaria. Issue 2/2010. UK 7.1-Uk.7.7. ISSN 1312-3823 (2010)
10. ANSI X9.52: Triple Data Encryption Algorithm Modes of Operation (1998)
11. FIPS 186-3: Digital Signature Standard (2012)
12. Voštenák, M.: Key management for ETCS system. Diploma work, University of Žilina (2010)
13. Sachin, M., Kumar, D.: Implementation and analysis of AES, DES and Triple DES on GSM Network. IJCSNS Int. J. Comput. Sci. Netw. Secur. **10**(1), 298–303 (2010)
14. Gallo, P.: Enhanced authentication mechanisms based on elliptic curves, Ph.D. work, TU Košice, Slovakia. In: English (2014)
15. Mikulski, J.: Analiza zagrożeń pól magnetycznych w transporcie, Logistyka nr 3, 2009 (2009) CD-ROM

Transformations in the Ticket Distribution Network for Public Urban Transport in the Processes of Implementation of Electronic Fare Collection Systems

Grzegorz Dydkowski[✉]

University of Economics in Katowice, 40-287 Katowice, Poland
dydkowski@onet.pl

Abstract. In many cities in Poland and worldwide, systems of electronic collection of fares for the use of public urban transport are implemented ever more widely. The most common starting point for assessing the efficiency of such systems is the comparison of costs of the currently functioning system with those of a system using electronic cards. Using the example of the Silesian Public Services Card project, implemented in the central part of the Provence of Silesia, by municipalities that form the Municipal Transport Union of the Upper Silesian Industrial District an attempt has been made to compare the costs of existing system of sale and distribution of paper tickets, and the system of electronic fare collection based on the electronic Silesian Card of Public Services (ŚKUP). Attention should be paid to the fact that modern systems, which are based on electronic tickets, give much wider possibilities of efficient management of process and transport service offer, hence they are related to obtaining greater external advantages, which is of much importance for investments financed using public funds.

Keywords: Electronic tickets · Electronic payment systems · Public urban transport · Ticket distribution system

1 Introduction

With the development of public urban transport systems, also systems for selling and distributing paper tickets were developed, initially those tickets were sold by conductors, later external points of sale and stationary sales networks were developed. The implementation of information technologies for electronic toll collection - besides the development of suitable infrastructure, purchase of hardware, and implementation of software – requires transformation of the existing network of ticket sale and distribution. The paper discusses those issues and attempts to assess and compare costs of distribution in the system based on paper tickets and electronic toll collection systems based on electronic cards. Making such an analysis extends the knowledge concerning cost generation and cost structure, it is also a starting point for examining the efficiency of solutions assumed.

© Springer International Publishing Switzerland 2015
J. Mikulski (Ed.): TST 2015, CCIS 531, pp. 198–209, 2015.
DOI: 10.1007/978-3-319-24577-5_20

2 System of Paper Tickets Sales and Distribution in Municipal Transport Union of the Upper Silesian Industrial District (KZK GOP)

At present, the share of private wholesalers in the single ticket segment is some 71 %, while in the segment of season tickets is some 26 %. At present, KZK GOP is a party in 200 contracts signed with counterparties that deal with distribution of urban transport tickets. The network of sales points comprises nearly 3500 points of sale, including over 1000 ticket offices (points of sale where season tickets can be purchased) [1]. The number of points of sale managed by the biggest counterparties is presented in Table 1.

One of the biggest partners distributing KZK GOP tickets is "RUCH" S.A. By the end of 2011 it used to supply a network of 440 ticket offices and some 150 points of ale distributing single tickets. Its market share at that time (according to the value of tickets collected from the warehouses of KZK GOP) amounted to some 41 % in the group of season tickets and some 34 % in the group of single tickets. In the early 2012 "RUCH" S.A. commenced the procedure of re-organizing the firm. Due to changes, the number of ticket offices and points of sale selling single tickets, - through which "RUCH" S.A. distributes tickets – dropped to: 306 ticket offices and 40 points of sale, respectively. Entities which had been previously supplied with tickets by "RUCH" S.A. changed their suppliers for other big distributors [1].

Besides the stationary points of sale, the territory served by KZK GOP also contains 53 vending machines, which sell public transport tickets round the clock and since April 2014 also 40 Stationary Card Top-up Machines, under the ŚKUP project. Revenues from the sale of tickets via vending machines amounted to more than 2.9 million zloty in 2013, their monthly sales value was from about 200 thousand zloty in winter months, to more than 300 thousand zloty in summer holiday months. Between January

Table 1. The number of points of sale managed by the biggest counterparties of KZK GOP (as of 31.12.2014) [2]

Counterparty (name)	Total number of points of sale	Points of sale distributing single tickets	Ticket offices
"RUCH" S.A.	306	40	266
Poczta Polska S.A.	297	6	291
SERVICE FMCG Sp. z o.o.	86	0	86
PKM Sp. z o.o. w Gliwicach	69	10	59
KAR-TEL Sp. z o.o. S.k.	185	125	60
Kolektura Biletowa Kawka Irena	181	159	22
MZKP Tarnowskie Góry	26	4	22
Total	**1150**	**344**	**806**

Table 2. Monthly average number and value of tickets sold via mobile phones, in the years 2011–2014 [2]

Year	2011	2012	2013	2014
Monthly average number of tickets sold via mobile phones	4 115	10 785	16 788	25 856
Monthly average value of tickets sold via mobile phones (in złoty)	10 958	30 385	50 497	77 970

and September 2014, the sale of tickets in all vending machines amounted to more than 2.6 million zloty, and varied from some 220 thousand zloty in January to over 350 thousand zloty in September [1].

In order to make it easier for passengers to contact KZK GOP, namely to exchange correspondence, to obtain complex information concerning the functioning of Urban transport in the region, as well as to enable them purchase tickets of all kinds, KZK GOP launched the network of Passenger Service Points (POP). At present, in the area served by KZK GOP there are five such Points, located in: Sosnowiec, Bytom, Gliwice, and Katowice. In a relatively short time, a new Point is planned to be opened in Chorzów. Another new Point is also planned to be opened at the modernized bus station in Piekary Śląskie [1].

Taking into account the ongoing progress in information Technologies, and the growing importance of modern distribution channels, KZK GOP signed agreements with CallPay, and the company Projekt & Parking Serwis Polska, (currently moBilet), by the virtue of which sales of single tickets via mobile phones have been launched [2]. Thanks to it, passengers may choose the system of ticket purchasing and making settlements, which is the most convenient for them. The possibility of purchasing tickets via mobile phones has been ever more popular among passengers, which is shown in Table 2.

At present, the distribution network for paper tickets covers some 3500 stationary points of sale, ticket vending machines, Passenger Service Points (POP) and sales of tickets via mobile phones. Moreover, by virtue of agreements concluded with service providers, tickets are also additionally sold by drivers on board of municipal public transport vehicles [2].

3 Functioning of the System of Ticket Sales and Distribution After Implementation of the Silesian Card of Public Services (ŚKUP)

After the implementation of the ŚKUP tickets for the urban transport organized by KZK GOP will be sold mainly via personalized and non-personalized ŚKUP cards. A personalized card will contain data identifying the user, and only that owner will be able to use the card. The card will enable the passenger also to encode her/his rights to pay reduced fares. A non-personalized card will not contain personal data, any current holder will have the right to use it (see [3, 4]).

A personalized card will be available only in the Customer Service Points (POK). Issuing the first personalized card, as well as its replacement for reasons for which the user is not held responsible (e.g. expiry of the card) will be free of charge. The application for issuing a personalized card may be filled and submitted in person in any POK or via Internet, by means of the Customer Portal [5]. When submitting the application, in the POK, the user will have to have her/his ID, in order to verify the personal data, as well as a photograph. It will be also possible to take the photograph at the POK. When submitting the application via Internet, it will be necessary to fill in a suitable form in the Customer Portal, as well as to pay a fee the amount of which shall correspond with the costs of card production. That amount will be paid to the account linked with the ŚKUP card. The card owner will be able to use it, after collecting it, after its activation. A personalized ŚKUP card will be available for collection from the POK indicated in the application, after signing the agreement concerning the use of personalized card, with KZK GOP and the bank, that is the entity responsible for issuing cards. It is assumed that the agreement concerning the use of a personalized card will be concluded upon reception of the application for issuing a card, by the bank and KZK GOP, as well as payment of the fee (if the latter is required). When collecting the personalized ŚKUP card, the passenger should present her/his ID card [6].

It will be possible to purchase a non-personalized card at POK, POP, points of sale provided with the module for fee collection/card top-up, as well as stationary card top-up devices. A cash deposit is required for issuing a non-personalized card. The user of a non-personalized card will obtain a confirmation for issuing the card. That document is to be stored throughout the card use period, as it is indispensable for receiving the deposit back, when the card is returned. The agreement concerning the use of non-personalized card will be concluded upon the reception of the card by the user [6].

The ŚKUP card shall hale the following main functions: electronic money/purse and electronic ticket carrier. The Electronic Money/Purse Instrument (IPE) of ŚKUP shall enable making transactions with the use of electronic money [7]. The ŚKUP card shall contain information concerning the amount of funds available. The contract on issuing the electronic money shall be concluded when the first crediting of IPE takes place, which is similar to the user having been acquainted with the suitable regulations, and the user's approval of their provisions, as regards issuing and using, as well as settlement of transactions with the use of electronic money/purse. It will be possible to use the card for making payments for public services rendered by merchants/service providers that accept ŚKUP cards. Crediting the card (purse) with electronic money will be possible [6]:

- via execution of a money transfer order or making a cash deposit on the IPE account,
- via execution of a money transfer order to the IPE account, through Customer Portal,
- in Customer Service Points (POK) or Passenger Service Points (POP).

The electronic purse function shall allow making payments for single trips using urban public transport directly from the ŚKUP card account. One will be able to select between the tariff where fares depend on the distance travelled, and the tariff where zones and travel time are considered. In the tariff depending on distance, the correct fare will be collected automatically when the service is used. Upon boarding the vehicle, the passenger shall apply the ŚKUP card to the charging module, and the fare, in the maximum amount (as for travelling to the end of route defined individually for each vehicle) will be automatically collected. Then, when leaving the vehicle, the passenger shall again apply the ŚKUP card to the charging module, and then part of the fare will be paid back to the card. As a result, the passenger shall only pay for the section which she/he actually travelled. In case of selecting the zone-travel time tariff, the passenger, after entering the vehicle, will be able to select a proper single ticket in the vending machine and pay the fare using the electronic purse [8]. Thanks to this functionality it will be possible to integrate with other carriers [3, 9].

Topping-up the ŚKUP cards with electronic season ticket will be possible in POK, POP, sales points provided with a module for collecting fares/topping-up cards, and in stationary machines for topping-up cards. It will also be possible to purchase a season ticket via Internet using the Customer Portal. After purchasing a season ticket via Internet, its activation will take place by attaching it to the reader of the module for collecting fares/topping-up cards in POK, POP, as well as sales points or module for collecting fares in vehicles. The ŚKUP card distribution network will consist of 40 POK, 6 POP, 800 sales points, 109 stationary machines for topping-up cards, and Customer Portal [6]. The functionalities of specific points in the distribution network are presented in Table 3.

Drivers shall sell tickets in accordance with the currently binding Tariff of KZK GOP, and shall distribute zero fare tickets to persons authorized to travel free, in case they do not hold a card. Issuing a "zero fare" ticket shall take place after the driver checks the document that authorizes the passenger to ride free of charge [8]. The person selling tickets will not be authorized the accept a return of ticket already printed. Tickets will be sold and issued by the vehicle driver from a printer coupled with universal on-board computer installed under the ŚKUP project [6].

In line with the original assumptions, after launching the ŚKUP Project all the currently valid paper tickets – both single and season ones – shall remain, being distributed by the network currently functioning, as well as by stationary card topping-up machines. Validation of single paper tickets will be possible solely via the one module for fare collection, installed by the first door from the front of vehicle. Single tickets will remain available for purchase via mobile phones.

4 Comparison of Distribution Costs for Urban Transport Tickets Before and After Introduction of the ŚKUP Card

At present, the distribution of paper tickets for services of local collective transport may be organized by external entities, after signing a suitable contract with KZK GOP, which contract authorizes such an external entity to sell tickets directly, as well as to distribute tickets further, that is to re-sell tickets to other entities. The subject matter of contract for the sale of tickets may comprise only single tickets, or single and season tickets. The distributor, when purchasing tickets from KZK GOP, gets a specific rebate from the face value of the ticket, which is defined in the Tariff for transport of passengers and luggage by urban transport organized by KZK GOP. The rebate depends

Table 3. Functionalities of ŚKUP card distribution points [6]

no.	Functionality	POK	POP	Stationary machine for topping-up cards	Sales points	Customer Portal
1	applying for a personalized card	X				X
2	issuing a personalized card	X				
3	issuing a non-personalized card	X	X	X	X	
5	topping-up the card with electronic money	X	X	X	X	X
6	encoding a season ticket on the card	X	X	X	X	X
7	encoding rights for reduced fares on a personalized card	X	X			
8	change/amendment of card user personal data	X				X
9	updating the data saved on the card	X	X	X	X	
10	blocking cards	X	X			X (personali-zed card)
11	removing the authorization hold for a card/unblocking	X				
12	cancellation of a card	X				
13	returning a card	X				
14	making available the billing for topping-up cards with electronic money	X	X			X
15	dealing with complaints concerning cards	X				
16	dealing with complaints concerning urban public transport		X			

upon the number and type of tickets, and amounts from 5 % to 7 % for single tickets, and from 3 % to 5 % for season tickets. Thus, the remuneration for the distributor is the difference between the face value of the ticket, stipulated in the tariff, which is the price paid by the passenger when purchasing the ticket at the point of sale, and the value of the ticket after rebate [10].

The contract for distribution of tickets issued by KZK GOP may be signed with any business entity, there are no additional criteria concerning access to the market. It is the market that will verify the location of sales points. The contract imposes an obligation upon the distributor to offer, without interruptions, all the tickets that are in the tariff, while KZK GOP has the right to check the stock, as well as proper marking of tickets; in case of finding shortcomings or discrepancies, the transport organizer also has the right to impose pecuniary penalties (fines) [6].

The ŚKUP project is co-financed by the European Union, thus the period of 65 months has been assumed for calculations, as minimum project sustainability, which needs to be guaranteed to obtain funding from the European Fund for Regional Development [4]. Moreover, due to the depreciation of fixed assets that are included in the undertaking, the period of 10 years has been assessed and analysed, as concerns the comparison of distribution costs [11]. Table 4 contains the costs of distribution system for paper tickets issued by KZK GOP. The following assumptions have been made for the calculation:

Table 4. Costs of sales and distribution of paper tickets issued by KZK GOP (net values, in million Polish zloty) [own study]

Years	Ticket punchers	Ticket vending machines (60 pcs.)	Cost of ticket distribution (rebates and discounts)	Costs of maintenance and management, of which:			Total
				Costs of operation	Costs of labour	Other costs	
(million Polish zloty)							
Investment	9.6	1.8					**11.4**
1			17.5	0.5	2.1	0.7	**20.8**
2			17.7	0.5	2.1	0.7	**21.1**
3			17.9	0.5	2.2	0.7	**21.4**
4			18.1	0.5	2.2	0.7	**21.7**
5			18.4	0.5	2.3	0.8	**21.9**
6			18.6	0.6	2.3	0.8	**22.2**
7			18.8	0.6	2.4	0.8	**22.5**
8			19.0	0.6	2.4	0.8	**22.8**
9			19.3	0.6	2.5	0.8	**23.1**
10			19.5	0.6	2.5	0.8	**23.4**
Total	**9.6**	**1.8**	**184.8**	**5.5**	**23.0**	**7.7**	**232.0**

- in the period analysed, the existing form of sales and distribution of tickets has been maintained,
- the net ticket sales value has been assumed at the level of plan for 2015 (253.3 million zloty) and for each year that follows the increase of ticket sales has been assumed by 1.2 % per year; that increase influences the amount of rebates, thus also the increase of distribution costs,
- the average rebate for selling tickets assumed for calculation has amounted to 6.4 %,
- the average yearly increase of costs maintenance and management of the distribution system has been at 2 %,
- unchanged level of employment in the unit responsible for sales and distribution of tickets has been assumed,
- continuity of sales via 60 ticket vending machines has been assumed.

The existing distribution system, based on sale of paper tickets, has the average cost of about 22.1 million Polish zloty a year. That cost comprises mainly of:

- costs related to purchase and replacement of ticket vending machines,
- costs of ticket distribution, that is costs of providing discounts to distributors, as well as costs of rebate for the common ticket with regional railway transport provider Koleje Śląskie,
- costs of maintenance and management of the present system, that is costs of operation (among others: purchase of paper for painting tickets and information materials, e.g. information stickers placed in urban public transport vehicles), costs of labour, and other costs (among others: costs of running the office, office space maintenance).

The implementation of ŚKUP system shall enforce change of organization of the distributors' market, as the network of distributors shall consist of 800 card topping-up points, selected via tender procedure. The application of tender procedure will allow to verify in market conditions the commissions for selling tickets. The remuneration of the distributor, for the sale of electronic tickets in ŚKUP system, will be the commission, being a percentage of the sales value [6]. Irrespective of the expenditures incurred during implementation of the project, a cost assessment has also been made, as regards costs to be incurred after the implementation, during operation of the system [11]. Table 5 lists the costs of sales and distribution of electronic tickets in the system of ŚKUP.

For assessing the costs of distribution after implementation of ŚKUP, the following assumptions hale been made:

- complete change of the form of sale and distribution of tickets has been assumed – only electronic tickets,
- commission for sales of electronic tickets in the ŚKUP has been assumed to amount to 2 % (800 points of sale),
- the commission value has been assessed in reference to the value of net ticket sales assumed in the plan for 2015 (253.3 million Polish zloty), increased by the rebates granted to entities which presently sell paper tickets (17.3 million Polish zloty),
- an increase of the sales value has been assumed, by 1.2 % a year,

Table 5. Costs of sales and distribution of electronic tickets in the ŚKUP system (net values, in million Polish zloty) [own study]

Years	Individual infrastructure of KZK GOP and shared/joint infrastructure	Commission for sales (800 points)	Costs of management and maintenance of the sales and distribution system in ŚKUP project				Costs for KZK GOP (costs of labour and other costs)	Total
			Card replacement and data transfer	Renumeration of the settlement agent	Operation of ticket vending machines	Costs of maintenance of the ŚKUP system		
in million Polish zloty								
Investment costs during implementation	71.7							71.7
Other costs	34.6							34.6
1		5.4	5.3	2.0	0.7	4.4	3.6	21.4
2		5.5	5.3	2.0	0.7	4.4	3.7	21.5
3		5.5	5.3	2.0	0.7	4.4	3.7	21.7
4		5.6	5.3	2.0	0.7	4.4	3.8	21.8
5		5.7	5.3	2.0	0.7	4.4	3.9	22.0
6		5.7	5.8	2.3	0.8	4.8	4.0	23.3
7		5.8	5.8	2.3	0.8	4.8	4.1	23.5
8		5.9	5.8	2.3	0.8	4.8	4.1	23.6
9		6.0	5.8	2.3	0.8	4.8	4.2	23.8
10		6.0	5.8	2.3	0.8	4.8	4.3	24.0
Total	**106.3**	**57.1**	**55.3**	**21.5**	**7.2**	**46.0**	**39.4**	**332.9**

- the implementation of the ŚKUP system will enforce increase of the costs of maintenance of the system for KZK GOP, in particular the costs of personnel and other costs related to the functioning of the office, by about 0.8 million Polish zloty,
- at the same time, for the years to come an average yearly increase of the costs of maintenance and management of the distribution system, by 2 %, has been assumed.
- the costs of card replacement, data transfer, remuneration of the settlement agent, operation of ticket vending machines, and well as of the maintenance of the ŚKUP system have been assumed on the basis of project cost calculation,
- it has been assessed that the costs of distribution and sales of electronic tickets account for 80 % of the costs of functioning of the shared/joint infrastructure of the ŚKUP project, during the project durability (5 years),
- after the project durability period, in subsequent years (6-10) increase of costs of management and maintenance of the system of electronic ticket sales and distribution by 10 % has been assumed, due to possible change of the system operator, and increase of costs connected with the functioning of the system,

Implementation of the project concerning fare collection with the use of electronic cards requires investment expenditures, mainly for the purchase of suitable equipment for operation, issuing, and topping-up of cards, devices in vehicles and for ticket inspection, as well as suitable software. It has been assessed that in case of the ŚKUP system, the investment expenditures to be incurred during the implementation period, for the delivery of the electronic ticket distribution system amount to some 106.3 million Polish zloty, thus about 56 % of the entire value of the project. One should keep in mind that the actual costs may differ from data presented in the tables, as they are the results of propounding specific assumptions for making a certain simulation and comparing the costs of functioning of both systems.

On the basis of data presented it can be seen that the yearly costs of operation of the electronic fare collection system are pretty close to those of the paper ticket distribution system, and amounts – in the studied period to the average of 22.7 million Polish zloty a year. Hence, from the point of view of operating costs of the distribution system, it is definitely more advantageous for the organizer of urban collective transport, implementing electronic fare collection is to totally give up paper tickets, and replace them with electronic tickets. Simultaneous maintenance of both systems would significantly increase the costs of ticket distribution. However, such a situation cannot – in principle – be avoided completely, mainly due to social reasons, as it is necessary to provide a transitory period, which would allow all passengers to get acquainted with the new system.

5 Conclusion

On the basis of the comparison made it can be stated that the maintenance of electronic fare collection system in urban public transport is not significantly more expensive than the operation of a distribution system based on paper tickets. Of course, the implementation of such a system requires purchasing of hardware for issuing and handling cards, devices installed in vehicles, as well as implementation of suitable software, yet costs of maintenance of both systems in specific years are comparable. One should bear in mind here that the advantages for the organizer of collective urban transport, which result from electronic fare collection are incomparably greater than in case of paper tickets. They are connected, first of all, with the possibility of collecting complex data from the market, and more efficient as well as dynamic management of the transport services offer. Moreover, the implementation of fare collection system with the use of electronic cards enables – to a much larger extent - differentiation of prices and more flexible development of transport services tariffs. The advantages of implementing an electronic system of payments for collective urban transport services have a financial dimension, of course, as they allow to reduce the costs of services provided, due to more efficient management of the transport offer, as well as generating more revenue from the sales of tickets. One should not forget, at the same time, that the results obtained may differ, depending on the system of electronic fare collection system being implemented, as well as the technology applied, still the ŚKUP project may serve as an example of a justified investment.

References

1. Sale and distribution of tickets in KZK GOP, KZK GOP, Katowice (2014)
2. Internal data of KZK GOP, Accessed from 10 February 2015. http://www.kzkgop.com.pl
3. Lubieniecka - Kocoń, K., Kos, B., Kosobucki, Ł., Urbanek, A.: Modern tools of passenger public transport integration. In: Mikulski, J. (ed.) TST 2013. CCIS, vol. 395, pp. 81–88. Springer, Heidelberg (2013)
4. Dydkowski, G.: Koszty i korzyści wynikające z wprowadzania elektronicznych systemów pobierania opłat za usługi miejskie. Innowacje w Transporcie. Organizacja i Zarządzanie. Zeszyt Naukowy nr 602. Problemy Transportu i Logistyki nr 12, pp. 29–42. Uniwersytet Szczeciński, Szczecin (2010)
5. Kos, B.: Rozwój e-administracji w lokalnym i regionalnym transporcie zbiorowym na przykładzie Śląskiej Karty Usług Publicznych. Europejska przestrzeń komunikacji elektronicznej. Zeszyty Naukowe Uniwersytetu Szczecińskiego Nr 763. Ekonomiczne Problemy Usług Nr 105, pp. 117–130, Szczecin (2013)
6. The contract for the supply, implementation and maintenance of the Silesian Public Services Card between KZK GOP, Asseco Poland S.A. and BRE Bank S.A. (2012)
7. Dydkowski, G.: Rozwój płatności za usługi komunalne na przykładzie projektu Śląskiej Karty Usług Publicznych. In: Michałowska, M. (ed.) Efektywność transportu w teorii i praktyce, pp. 243–253. Akademia Ekonomiczna w Katowicach, Katowice (2010)
8. Urbanek, A.: Directions of broadening the range of tariff systems functionalities in urban transport. Arch. Trans. Syst. Telematics 7(4), 50–54 (2014)
9. Tomanek, R.: Funkcjonowanie transportu. pp. 47–59. Wydawnictwo Akademii Ekonomicznej w Katowicach, Katowice (2004)
10. The Act no LXXXII/6/2007 of KZK GOP Assembly on the rules for granting discounts for ticket sales (2007), Access from 10 February 2015. http://bip.kzkgop.pl/pdf/uchwaly/2007/uchwala_LXXXII_6_2007.pdf

11. Dydkowski, G.: Effectiveness of the urban services electronic payment systems on the example of silesian card of public services. Arch. Trans. Syst. Telematics **7**(4), 3–8 (2014)
12. Karoń, G., Mikulski, J.: Problems of ITS architecture development and ITS implementation in upper-silesian conurbation in poland. In: Mikulski, J. (ed.) TST 2012. CCIS, vol. 329, pp. 183–198. Springer, Heidelberg (2012)

Safety Management System in the Railway Board Activity - An Outline of Issues

Jerzy Mikulski[1], Beata Grabowska–Bujna[2], and Sonia Wieczorek[2(✉)]

[1] University of Economics in Katowice, 40-287 Katowice, Poland
jerzy.mikulski@ue.katowice.pl
[2] Jastrzębska Spółka Kolejowa sp. z o.o., 40-335 Jastrzębie Zdrój, Poland
{bbujna,swieczorek}@jsk.pl

Abstract. Accession of Poland to EU structures resulted in need to take a number of adjustment adaptation steps. One of them is the transposition of the European Union regulations into national legislation. This applies to a variety of areas, including railway safety. The problem is relatively new and it requires both the knowledge of the specifics of the railway sector and a number of regulations. The article brought the objective railway market structure closer, paying attention to the role of the government administration authorities and railway boards in shaping of the security postulate. Basic legislation defining the direction of improving safety in rail transport were systematized, and an exemplary model of a safety management system was presented.

Keywords: Safety · Safety management system · Risk assessment

1 Introduction

The rail transport safety[1] belongs to important and at the same time complicated issues, both from the application and empirical point of view. The complexity of those issues results from a specific nature of the railway system, which is strongly and significantly connected to many entities and processes. The existing interfaces and their variability substantially differentiate the railway safety perception, which makes that this category should be considered in many dimensions.

Because of the extent of undertaken issues the paper focuses on the presentation of general requirements for designing a system for safety management by the infrastructure manager with special emphasis on modern institutional conditions. The consideration of railway safety in such an approach requires taking into account the role fulfilled by the national and EU entities in creating and implementing solutions used to improve the described postulate. The study pays also attention to the key element of safety management system, which is the risk assessment.

---

[1] Numerous safety definitions operate in the subject literature, which are transferred onto the ground of transport theory. For the needs of the paper in question the definition used in the aviation sector has been used, i.e. safety is the state, in which a possibility of damage to people or property occurrence is minimised and maintains on a permissible level or below this level due to intentionally carried out continuous process of hazards identification and safety risk management.

© Springer International Publishing Switzerland 2015
J. Mikulski (Ed.): TST 2015, CCIS 531, pp. 210–219, 2015.
DOI: 10.1007/978-3-319-24577-5_21

2   Elements of the Safety Management System

Issues related to the rail traffic safety occupy a special place in the European Union transport policy. This aspect has made that the railway sector achieved elaborate regulation instruments, which set priorities and directions of action in the field of safety. The existing mechanisms make that solutions prepared and implemented to improve safety are frequently of an obligatory nature. This situation creates specific conditions on the railway market, characterized by the fact that the process of safety improvement involves many entities of varying organizational - legal forms.

Figure 1 presents an example of a model showing the place and role of selected entities in the railway system environment in the context of safety.

The systematization of railway sector participants presented in Fig. 1 shows that entities operating on the EU and national level are closely interrelated and enter into interactions.

Those relations result in developing a uniform approach to safety in the rail transport designing. Especially a correct performance of tasks, realizing functions assigned to the specified units, makes that the arrangement of this environment has a significant impact on the final shape of railway safety. Summing up, each of those entities bears responsibility for safety in accordance with the fulfilled role.

In the described system the European Parliament has a considerable importance in determination of safety priorities, passing directives and regulations defining general rules of railway safety operation and determining the path to achieve unified detailed solutions.

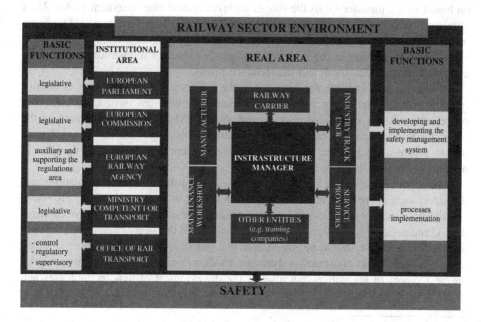

Fig. 1. Simplified model of railway sector environment from the safety point of view [own study]

The European Commission, basing on European Parliament and European Council acts, specifies detailed conditions of railways operation, resolving inter alia: decisions, regulations, recommendations and directives amending provisions of annexes to European Parliament and Council directives.

The European Railway Agency (ERA) plays a significant role in the system of creating instruments ensuring the rail transport safety. This institution guards the correctness of railway market operation, among others supervising the implementation of recommendations in the field of safety. It should be emphasized that the scope of this institution activity is quite broad. Basic tasks of the Agency comprise a technical support in the community legislation implementation aimed at development of a uniform approach to safety in the European railway system, guaranteeing a high safety level [1]. The remaining tasks performed by the Agency for safety may include: providing independent and impartial expertise, promoting innovation, facilitating cooperation and information exchange between all entities of the railway sector, giving recommendations to the Commission on a common method for safety assessment and on common safety requirements.

The implementation of safety paradigm in the railway sector, at so elaborated EU regulations, forces establishing a structure coordinating actions on the level of each Member State.

The basic authority in Poland is the Ministry competent for transport[2], which powers comprise primarily the legislative function, consisting in creating and amending legal regulations, including the implementation of EU safety-related standards to the national legislation. From the safety point of view the State Commission for Railway Accidents Examination is an important unit operating within this entity structure, which on behalf of the minister fulfils the role of an investigation body pursuant to Art. 21 of Directive 2004/49/CE. On the national level the Office of Rail Transport (UTK) is the next important unit, which ensures safety, performing regulatory, control, and supervisory tasks in relation to the real area entities, in particular infrastructure managers, carriers, industry track users and maintenance plants.

A separate non-institutional category of the rail transport area consists of entities running business, including infrastructure managers, who are obliged to carry out processes based on the safety management system (SMS), which is defined as the organization and measures taken by the infrastructure manager and railway undertakings to ensure safety [2]. The framework of this document is determined by the EU and national regulations (Fig. 2).

The model presented in Fig. 2 shows basic relationships between regulations and the safety management system. It has been designed in such a way as to provide a possibility to modify it and expand with additional elements. The scheme systematizes the EU and national legislation and basic components of the safety management system formed based on it. It should be emphasized that this system structure is more complex and the process of its construction dynamic. Its directions are determined not only by the next pieces of legislation, but also by the development of new technologies and

---

[2] Since 27 November 2013 the function of minister for transport has been fulfilled by the Ministry of Infrastructure and Development.

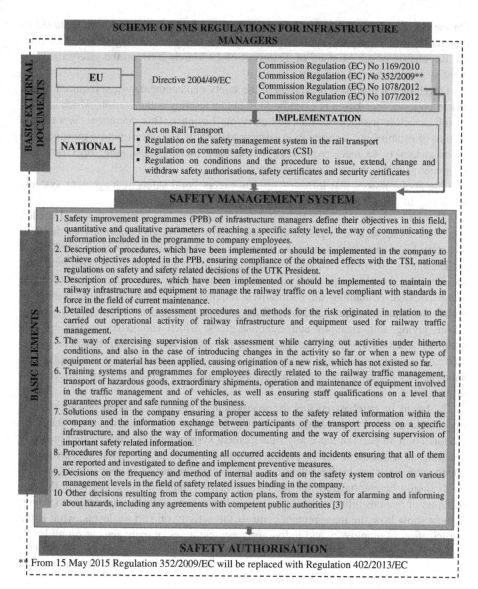

Fig. 2. Simplified scheme of SMS regulations applicable to infrastructure manager [own study based on [3]]

management theories. Variability of those determinants makes that the safety management system must be systematically adapted to currently binding conditions and permanently improved.

The Directive of the European Parliament and of the Council on safety on the Community's railways [4] is the most important instrument, which determines a common regulation framework in the field of railway safety ensuring, imposing on each infrastructure manager the obligation to establish a safety management system.

On the Polish ground the obligation resulting from this directive has been included in the Act on Rail Transport [2] and in several secondary pieces of legislation, including the Regulation of the Minister of Transport of 19 March 2007 on the safety management system in the rail transport.

Development and implementation of the safety management system required by the aforementioned legislation is a condition to obtain a safety authorization, which entitles an infrastructure manager to start and carry out business. This documents is a confirmation of establishing a safety management system by the infrastructure manager and of its capability to meet requirements necessary for safe designing, operating and maintaining of the railway infrastructure [2].

The above makes that infrastructure managers build safety management systems according to strictly specified criteria.

Then this system is subject to verification by the national safety authority. Detailed requirements applicable to performing assessment of systems conformity in the field of safety have been included in the Commission Regulation (EC) No 1169/2010 of 10 December 2010 on a common safety method for assessing conformity with the requirements for obtaining a railway safety authorization. This act is a part of legislation package containing all harmonized requirements and methods, by means of which the national safety authority shall perform assessment of safety conformity before giving authorizations and establish rules, which should be applied by this authority when exercising supervision once the safety authorization. has been given. After the system verification and positive assessment, depending on the application submitted by the infrastructure manager, the President of UTK gives the authorization or extends it.

It should be emphasized that the assessment is carried out based on the existing documentation and procedures. To obtain and then to maintain and extend the authorization all parts of the safety management system must be documented in a way enabling its assessment before giving the authorization, in the course of performing supervision activities by the safety authority and in the period of recertification.

It should be emphasized that the documentation must comprise primarily the distribution of responsibility in the organizational structures of the infrastructure manager. It must show how the management controls the activity on various levels, what is the participation of employees and individual representatives of management on all levels and how a continuous improvement to the safety management system is ensured [4].

3   Risk in the Rail Transport

The main goal to develop and implement a safety management system, as mentioned earlier, is to ensure safety on an appropriate level by taking actions aimed at preventing and reducing probability of railway accidents occurrence.

Postulates defined this way justify situating the risk assessment in the central part of the safety management system, forcing at the same time the necessity of developing risk handling instruments. One of solutions consists in designing a risk management system understood as a planned use of policies, procedures and management practices within tasks related to the risk analysis, evaluation and supervision [5].

From the risk management possibility point of view, it is necessary to classify the existing risks. The analysis of the subject literature shows that there are numerous breakdowns of this category, both in theory and in practice. Depending on the adopted breakdown criterion, those systematizations substantially differ from each other. The determination of risk origination in a specific activity is a frequently used categorization determinant. In the rail transport a breakdown prevails, which takes into account their following types:

- own risk - originating directly due to activities of the infrastructure manager, comprising a professional[3] and operational risk,
- common risk - related to activities within the interface, e.g. between the infrastructure manager and service providers and carriers,
- the other risk - related with third party contacts, which are not directly related to the infrastructure management process, but affect the system safety.

The infrastructure manager is obliged to define assessment procedures and methods for each of aforementioned risks. This standard implementation is subject to a strict control of the national authority supervising the railway safety. Procedural studies enable systematic resolution of problems related to the risk resulting from the carried out activity. The formalization of described process allows also creating a transparent structure of safety improvement measures.

Legal requirements do not indicate explicitly risk assessment methods or risk management standards, which would be used in the rail transport. Nevertheless, regulations impose on the infrastructure manager the duty to identify hazards, to evaluate them, accept, determine risk control measures, monitor as well as to exchange information between interested parties.

The above catalogue provides practical guidelines to establish risk management procedures and methods by a specific infrastructure manager. However, the lack of risk assessment method indication at permanently increasing safety requirements forces the necessity to skillfully use in practice the existing risk management methods. It seems that only such approach will allow optimizing the risk management process.

Considering a broader risk assessment context, that is previously presented notional scope of risk management, legal requirements [5, 6] and the risk assessment methods used in the railway sector, it is possible to distinguish significant components of the process - Fig. 3.

The proposal of risk management system in the rail transport presented in Fig. 3 is an integrated structure, taking into account risk assessment components required by the railway legislation, elements of the Failure Mode and Effects Analysis (FMEA) method, which is a voluntary and widespread standard of risk assessment in the railway sector, and also chosen assumptions of the risk analysis process defined in the ISO 31000 standard.

Determination of risk management rules, transparent and adapted to the needs of specific organisation, and their application in practice condition effectiveness of this process, allowing thereby ensuring an appropriate safety level.

---

[3] There are numerous professional risk assessment methods. In the rail transport the RISC SCORE method is most frequently used, more on that.

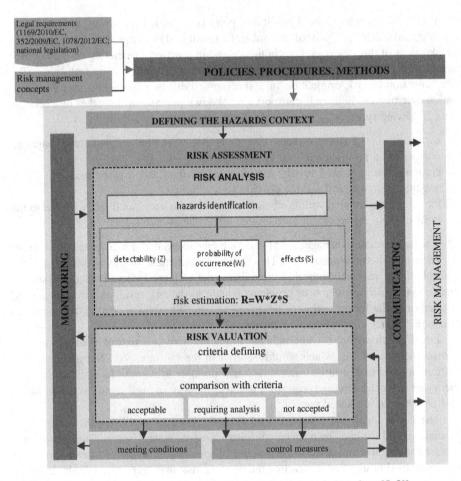

Fig. 3. Risk management in the rail transport [own study based on [5–8]]

When starting the management process, first it is necessary to define the context and the scope of carried out risk assessment. Then it is necessary to move to the risk assessment phase, which in accordance with the terminology adopted in regulation 352/2009 means a holistic process comprising risk analysis and evaluation.

A systematic use of all available information to identify hazards and to estimate the risk is the basis of the analysis. The hazards identification consists in a formal way of detecting, recording, analyzing and gathering information on hazards, which influence the organization activities. The scope of identification should comprise all processes carried out in the company, taking into account such factors as: people, procedures, the technical condition of technical infrastructure etc.

The ensuring of the process repeatability is the condition of identification effectiveness, which is dictated by a high variability of conditions, in which railway sector entities operate, and also by the complexity of interactions between them.

The FMEA method integrates properly with this context due to its basic assumption of continuous improvement. It consist in analytical determination of causalities of risk origination. Three stages are distinguished within this method: preparation, the analysis itself and introduction and supervision of preventive measures.

The first stage consists in detailed determination of analysis goal and subject and in defining areas, in which hazards should be identified.

The analysis of defined hazards' causes and effects is important in the second stage. To this end a list of potential hazard occurrence reasons and their probable effects is determined. Then the probability of a hazard occurrence (W), its detectability (Z) and effects (S) are determined by assigning quantified values to those parameters. The assigned values range from 1 to 10, acc. to rules adopted by the given infrastructure manager. It should be emphasized, that unified tables of values have been elaborated in Poland, which are used by entities from the railway sector [9].

Then, to obtain a measurement of the analyzed risk, they are estimated using so-called risk index (R), which is a product of the aforementioned parameters (W, Z, S). In accordance with the adopted assessment scale from 1 to 10, index R may take values from 1 to 1000. This approach enables the risk valuation because of its criticality, which is one of important assumptions of the FMEA method.

After index R estimation the risk is evaluated, with the basic assumption to determine, whether a permissible risk level has been achieved.

In Poland the level of risk tolerated in the railway sector is not regulated by legal requirements. However, a risk matrix was prepared for this sector needs, defining acceptability thresholds, which have been adopted by most of railway entities, including infrastructure managers.

The definition of acceptability criteria for the rail transport sector enables determination of the risk profile, i.e. whether it is acceptable, requires analysis or is not accepted.

In Poland most entities assume, that the risk is permissible, when $R \leq 120$; requires analysis, when it is within the range of $120 < R \leq 150$; and above 150 it is considered significantly threatening the safety of the whole railway system and considered not accepted.

Further actions are taken depending on the range, to which the given risk falls. In the case, when the risk falls in the 'requires analysis' or 'not accepted' category it is necessary to start stage three, consisting in determination, introduction, and supervision of control measures, i.e. correcting and/or preventive actions aimed at reducing the risk index. These measures should comprise specific tasks, the implementation time, the responsible person and the risk estimation assuming the effectiveness of recommended actions performance.

It should be emphasized that the essence of proper risk assessment in the rail transport consists in its performance with respect to all permanent processes, taking into account the own, common and the other risk and in the case of introducing organizational, operational and technical changes[4].

---

[4] In the case of change introduction by a railway manager, the risk assessment is only one of elements of overall change analysis. Because of the need to meet numerous requirements specified in Regulation 352/2009, this issue requires a separate broader discussion.

The risk management process, to be effective, must take into account also elements of permanent risk monitoring and communicating[5].

The risk monitoring should consider mechanisms, which will allow assessing the effectiveness of risk handling, i.e. whether the risk assessment, including the risk identification proceeds properly, whether proper measures and solutions are used and whether they have provided the intended outcome, whether the hazard still exists or new ones have occurred, whether the risk probability and influence has changed. The monitoring ensures also updating of adopted solutions, which is necessary in a changing environment.

When defining a risk management system it is also necessary to determine and develop procedures, which will ensure that the risk management rules and their modifications are appropriately communicated. It is necessary to determine appropriate information exchange channels with interested parties and to implement mechanisms providing a possibility of hazards consulting with individual participants of the railway system.

4   Conclusion

The rail transport safety ranks among most important issues of the EU policy. This attitude is reflected in a consistent and integrated approach, which determines frameworks for infrastructure managers in the context of safety. These conditions make that many entities are involved in the process of ensuring safety, which implement initiatives for improvement to this postulate. The current scheme of safety management system is definitely a solution, which allows adopting safety improvement mechanisms to the economic practice. The system, to be effective, should be adapted to the size of the organization, the type and complexity of carried out processes and accompanying risks.

It is also of key importance that the structure of railway sector entities would be favorable to implementation of innovative solutions, minimizing the risk of carried out business, via creation of solutions supporting the raising of safety level.

It should be emphasized that the approach presented in this paper is only an outline of addressed issues. Because safety is a complex function, consisting of staff competence, of scope and intensity of carried out business, of railway infrastructure quality and of external factors. So a complex presentation of safety issues in the rail transport requires a separate and more extensive consideration of each of those contexts.

---

[5] In the railway sector there is a number of legal requirements in the field of risk monitoring and communicating. These are very extensive issues. This paper presents only basic assumptions in this area.

References

1. Regulation (EC) No 881/2004 Of The European Parliament And Of The Council of 29 April 2004 establishing a European railway agency, 164/1 (2004)
2. Ustawa z dnia 28 marca 2003 r. o transporcie kolejowym, (tekst jednolity: Dz. U. z 2013 r., poz. 962 z późniejszymi zmianami)
3. Rozporządzenie Ministra Transportu z dnia 19 marca 2007 r. w sprawie systemu zarządzania bezpieczeństwem w transporcie kolejowym, Dz. U. nr 60, poz. 407 (2007)
4. Directive 2004/49/Ec Of The European Parliament And Of The Council of 29 April 2004 on safety on the Community's railways and amending Council Directive 95/18/EC on the licensing of railway undertakings and Directive 2001/14/EC on the allocation of railway infrastructure capacity and the levying of charges for the use of railway infrastructure and safety certification (Railway Safety Directive), L. 164/44 (2004)
5. Regulation (EC) No 352/2009 of 24 April 2009 on the adoption of a common safety method on risk evaluation and assessment as referred to in Article 6(3)(a) of Directive 2004/49/EC of the European Parliament and of the Council, L 108/4 (2009)
6. Regulation (EU) No 1078/2012 of 16 November 2012 on a common safety method for monitoring to be applied by railway undertakings, infrastructure managers after receiving a safety certificate or safety authorization and by entities in charge of maintenance, L 320/8 (2012)
7. Sitarz, M.: Bezpieczeństwo na polskich kolejach – teoria i praktyka, TTS, nr 5–6, s. 56 (2012)
8. ISO 31 000:2009 Ed. 1.0: Risk Management- Principles and guidelines on implementation, pp. 13 (2009)
9. Chruzik, K., Drzewicki, A., Wachnik, R.: Wykorzystanie metody FMEA do oceny ryzyka w MMS, Zeszyty Naukowe Politechniki Śląskiej, seria Transport, No 81, pp. 19–22, Katowice (2013)

Performance Analysis of Authentication Protocols Used Within Cooperative - Intelligent Transportation Systems with Focus on Security

Ján Ďurech$^{(\boxtimes)}$, Mária Franeková, Peter Holečko, and Emília Bubeníková

Faculty of Electrical Engineering, Department of Control and Information Systems, University of Žilina, Žilina, Slovak Republic
{jan.durech,maria.franekova,peter.holecko, emilia.bubenikova}@fel.uniza.sk

Abstract. The authors of this contribution focus on analysis of V2V communication security solutions in Cooperative - Intelligent Transportation Systems (C-ITS). They emerge from the current state of risks and potential security incidents within communication between moving nodes. In more detail, they focus on the service of message nonrepundation and message recency, which utilises the cryptographic digital signatures techniques in combination with timestamps. The experimental part analyses security solutions with three types of cryptographic digital signatures techniques for two traffic scenarios based on actual traffic data from the D1 highway. The results are studied in dependence on the most frequent required application parameters for the transmission of safety relevant messages, like message length, cryptographic header length, message processing time and delay in relation to network throughput.

Keywords: Cooperative-intelligent transportation system · VANET · V2V · V2X · Security architecture · Authentication protocols · Cryptography algorithms · Traffic scenario · Modelling

1 Introduction

Cooperative - Intelligent Transportation Systems belong to a new generation of Intelligent Transportation Systems providing drivers information directly into vehicle through transmission of various warning messages [1].

The communication happens between vehicles (mobile nodes, V2V) without the need to pass a fixed infrastructure, or between a vehicle and a fixed infrastructure (V2I) which is referred to as *Dedicated Short Range Communication*(DSRC) [2].

The fundamental components of C-ITS comprise of C-ITS units integrated in passenger vehicles, trucks and public transport vehicles - so called On-Board Units (OBU), units located fixed in communication infrastructure -*Road Side Unit*(RSU) and a central system monitoring and managing C-ITS units in the transport infrastructure.

Communication between the individual C-ITS components is provided by a *Vehicular ad–hoc Network* (VANET), which is currently considered one of the most important wireless communication technologies in the area of intelligent transport

© Springer International Publishing Switzerland 2015
J. Mikulski (Ed.): TST 2015, CCIS 531, pp. 220–229, 2015.
DOI: 10.1007/978-3-319-24577-5_22

systems. The communication security solutions in VANET are being developed progressively and the problem is of high attention also because of increasing number of risks related to wireless transmission between mobile nodes [3]. In the last ten years, many projects, consortia, associations have been established worldwide to cover international fundamental as well as applied research projects in cooperation with reputable car manufacturers, like for example [4, 5]. In Europe, a prominent position is represented by the *Car 2 Car Communication Consortium*(C2C-CC) [6] founded by six European car manufacturers. Currently, the members are delegates from Audi, BMW, Daimler Chrysler, Ford, Honda, Opel Peugeot, Renault, Citroen, Volkswagen and others.

In the V2V communication, the messages transmitted between messages can be cyclically repeated or a message is sent only based on a specific event. The formats of messages depend on the application used.

The highest security degree is required by applications focusing on safety. Currently, there are many categories or classes of automobile safety focused applications. The outputs of the SeVeCom project [5] provide a specification of the most critical safety relevant applications, which can be summarised as follows:

- Pre-Crash Sensing,
- Cooperative Forward Collision Warning,
- Electronic Brake Lights,
- Blind-stop and Lane Change Warning.

Systems of passive and active safety include technical means to actively help prevent accident or allow mitigating its consequences. Many car manufacturers developing their own passenger protection systems, as well as cars and these assets may be available as standard or optional equipment. For data capture and further evaluation of data in the area of transport many types of sensors are being used like radars [7], lidars [8], CCTV systems [9] or the sensor fusion [10].

Currently, the research in vehicular networks is primarily focusing on routing protocols, antennas performance, decrease of error rate, mobility control, but also on communication security with the use of modern cryptographic schemes and constructions, mainly based on *Public Key Infrastructure*(PKI) or hybrid schemes, respectively. Although many works have been published regarding security of vehicular networks and several solution have been proposed, it is still a very recent topic requiring continuous analysis. The design of new or modified security solutions is implied by a detailed analysis of network attacks, which variety continues to rise. The design of effective solutions is often a result of compromises between the chosen security degree and the required message processing speed in vehicle, the required delay between messages and other important application parameters requiring message verification and reaction in real-time.

2   Basic Scenario for Maintaining the Transmitted Messages Trustworthy

The digital signature technique based on asymmetric cryptography using PKI is established within authorised communication between vehicles. The development of authentication cryptographic schemes based on digital signatures is conditioned by the fact, that strong cryptographic are involved satisfying all security requirements in VANETs (authorisation of messages transmitted between vehicles, confidentiality, integrity and nonrepundation).The authentication protocols emerge from the premise of existence of Certification Authorities (CA). Each CA is responsible for its associated region in road infrastructure and manages the identification of all mobile nodes (vehicles) registered within. In order to grant communication between nodes from different regions, the CA has to provide certificates (*Cert*) for other CAs, too. The certificates are issued by the CA after node registration. The certificate contains a list of node parameters and certificate duration. From the perspective of message authorisation service, it is necessary to consider authorisation of moving group of nodes (vehicles) and the same safety relevant message can be transmitted to a group of vehicles. That means, that often in the same moment multiple authorisations occur.

It is obvious, that a secured vehicle network communication has some specific characteristics and its security properties have to be modelled using mobile models involving parameters like geographic data about nodes position, velocity, direction etc. Well known models are the Manhattan Grid Model [11] or the Random Waypoint Model [12]. The car manufacturer issues a unique identifier *Long Term Identity* (LTI) for each intelligent vehicle, which is associated with a pair of cryptographic keys – a *long term public key* and a *long term private key,* which are certified in "offline mode" during the initial registration of the node by the corresponding regional CA. The keys are stored in the vehicle in a *Hardware Security Module*(HSM), which also provides a secure time-base for generating digital signatures timestamps. Another purpose of the HSM is to manage all cryptographic operations involving private keys. In case of threatening these sensitive information, these should be deleted from the HSM. Using the LTI the anonymous key pair is derived (*short term public key*) and (*long term private key)*for a so called *Short Term Identity* (STI), which is of shorter validity. The anonymity of vehicle user is based on a frequent change of public part of the key by generating pseudonyms *Pseud* as follows: to obtain a pseudonym the vehicle V_i generates a set of short term key pairs $\{SK_{1v}, PK_{1v}\},..., \{SK_{nv}, PK_{nv}\}$. The public keys are sent to a corresponding CA via a secure communication channel. Consequently, the certification authority signs each of the public keys *cert* $(PK_{iv})$and generates a set of pseudonyms $\{Pseud_1, Pseud_2,..., Pseud_n\}$ for the vehicle V_i. Each pseudonym contains a CA identifier, pseudonym lifetime, public key, and CA signature. So no information on vehicle is provided. The management of pseudonyms is based on limited lifetime of each pseudonym used. The frequency of pseudonyms change depends on vehicle protection degree, input parameters (position, velocity) and system settings. To provide other pseudonyms a so called pseudonyms sets are being utilised. These pseudonyms are periodically complemented from the CA. As soon as a node moves from the pseudonym set 1 to pseudonym set 2, it is no longer permitted to utilise a pseudonym from set 1.

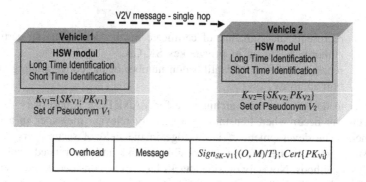

Fig. 1. Security scenario of beacon type authorised V2V message transmission [own study]

The message authorisation security scenario between mobile nodes is shown in Fig. 1 for the communication between vehicles V_1 and V_2 via V2V type messages in a one-directional simplex communication (*direct communication*) in *single hope* mode. Before sending a security relevant message (a *beacon packet* in our application), the security unit of vehicle V_1 generates a digital signature using its short-term private key SK_{V1}, which is a function of message M and over head O, as in principle depicted in Fig. 1. This way generated cryptographic number is attached to the message together with the certificate *Cert* which is coupled on the V_1 sender's public key. First, on the V_2 vehicle side, the certificate received is verified (if not done before) and the digital signature received is verified using vehicle's public key PK_{V1}. At the same time, the *geo stamp* information from overhead O (coupled on geographic data and GPS coordinates) is verified. After these procedures the security relevant message is accepted or not.

The process of digital signature generation by vehicle V_1 can be mathematically expressed as follows:

$$V1 \rightarrow * : M, O, Sign_{SK_{V1}}[(M, O)|T], Cert_{PKVi}. \tag{1}$$

Where:

M represents the transmitted security relevant message,

O represents message overhead,

SK_{V1} is private(*secret*) key of vehicle V_1,

PK_{V1} is public (*public*) key of vehicle V_1,

T is timestamp,

Cert is certificate valid for vehicle V_1 (signed by anonymous public key PK_{Vi}),

$*$ represents the number of receivers (in case the message is transmitted to multiple vehicles).

The current certificate of vehicle V_1 signed in the i-th moment by the anonymous public key of vehicle V_1 (PK_i) contains:

$$Cert_{V1}[PK_i] = PK_i|Sign_{SK-CA}[PK_{Vi}|ID_{CA}]. \tag{2}$$

Where:

$Sign_{SK-CA}$ represents the signature of certificate by the corresponding certification authority based on its private key SK-CA,

ID_{CA} represents a unique identification number of the corresponding certification authority.

In order to design a security architecture for VANETs, it is necessary to analyse risks which can occur when transmitting a security relevant messages in a wireless environment. The development of knowledge in the field of secured cryptographic transmission increases the number of possible attacks and the related sophisticated cryptanalysis methods. Not only outside attacks have to be considered, but also attacks based on manipulation of data in the OBU (inside attacks).Many attacks are very sophisticated and often performed by several coordinated mobile nodes (dependent, prearranged attacks).

To name a few of them [13]: DoS (*Denial of Service*), sensors manipulation, messages manipulation, eavesdropping, masking and Sybil attack, discovery of secret keys, Man in the Middle attack, GNSS (*Global Navigation Satellite System*) attack etc.

3   Experimental Part

When analysing transmission of SR messages between mobile nodes in a VANET it is necessary to focus on various traffic scenarios with relation on the applications implemented in an intelligent vehicle. In [14] two scenarios are primarily considered:

- transmission of SR messages in fluent traffic, highway, for example – in a single drive lane or in several drive lanes,
- transmission of SR messages in congested traffic, rush hour or congestion, for example.

A SR message contains, besides payload P carrying information for driver, an overhead *O*, in most formats containing the MAC address, message type and geographic data header. The last field, which is an obligatory part of message format, is the *Secure overhead (S)*, containing the generated digital signature together with the certificate. Figure 2 shows, that the field *P* is of variable length (its size depends on the SR application). However, the overall message size also depends on the cryptographic security field *S*, which is also of variable length and its size depends on the chosen digital signature scheme.

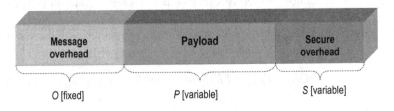

Fig. 2. Message format [own study]

When deeply analysing V2V transmission, following application parameters have to be taken into account:

- M (*message*) size of SR message bearing information for drivers [bytes],
- S (*security*) size of security field [bytes],
- O (*overhead*) size of cryptographic header [bytes],
- T (*throughput*) throughput [bits/sec],
- n (*number*) number of mobile nodes,
- R (*rate*) number of messages transmitted per second [beacon/sec relative to 1 vehicle],
- l (*latency*) maximum allowed delay of messages between nodes.

For various traffic scenarios, threshold values of parameters have to be determined or modelled (worst case), to achieve the required security degree, network throughput and delay. Obviously, the security degree of SR message impacts the size of security field in message format in Fig. 2 as well as the size of cryptographic header, which prolongs the time of processing SR message (messages)in vehicle's receiver.

Therefore, when choosing authorisation protocols for VANETs, it is of high importance to focus on effective digital signatures schemes achieving the shortest possible processing time within the process of signature generation and verification, while respecting the required security level. Considering that the receiver in vehicle can in a short moment receive more messages than it is transmitting by itself, it is necessary to target digital signature schemes with shortest verification times.

In the experimental part of this paper we focused on two traffic scenarios for V2V communication, which have been analysed for traffic data acquired from the D1 highway [15]. The D1 highway is Slovakia's most important and longest highway. The line of highway starts in Bratislava in the Pečňa crossing (where it crosses the D2 highway) and continues north-eastward via Trnava, Trenčín, Žilina, Martin, Ružomberok, Poprad, Prešov, Košice, Michalovce and after finishing, it should end on the state border with Ukraine on the border crossing Vyšné Nemecké – Užhorod. The overall length of the highway is 516 419 m, from which 312 039 m is in operation, 46 170 m under construction and 150 m in preparing. The construction of the highway started in 1972 and finalising is planned on 2019.

Data from the D1 highway have been acquired in one driving direction for both lanes during March, April and May in 2013. Following traffic parameters have been monitored within 1 min interval for two driving lanes: intensity (number of vehicles per minute), velocity (km/h) and density (%).

For our needs, we focused the traffic density parameter from data acquired.

The analysis was performed for two traffic scenarios:

(a) traffic beside traffic peak (average of data within one week in March 2013) at 1:00.
(b) traffic during traffic peak (average of data within one week in March 2013) at 8:00.

Table 1 contains calculation of average number of vehicles passing the D1 highway beside traffic peak and during traffic peak within one hour.

Let us assume that for both scenarios a 60 km section is analysed. Another initial parameters used for considerations are the following:

Table 1. Number of vehicles passed along per hour on traffic peak and beside traffic peak [own study]

Weekday	Number of vehicles	
	Scenario a Beside traffic peak 1:00	Scenario b Traffic peak 8:00
Monday	160	879
Tuesday	173	1089
Wednesday	202	1153
Thursday	229	1150
Friday	235	892
Saturday	260	512
Sunday	112	160
Average	n_a = 196 vehicles	n_b = 834 vehicles

- All vehicles dispose of OBUs and are able to communicate via V2V messages.
- The velocity of moving vehicles is constant on the section monitored (v_t = 110 km/h).
- The analysis is conducted for vehicle V_i located in the middle of the section monitored, which is the worst case scenario when considering the number of messages received by vehicle V_i in range.
- The communication range is considered to be 300 m.

Figure 3 shows the analysed scenario at 1:00 AM. If we divide the 60 km section in Fig. 3 equally according to the calculated average number of vehicles from D1 for the first scenario (n_a = 196 vehicles), then the distance between vehicles is 306 m,

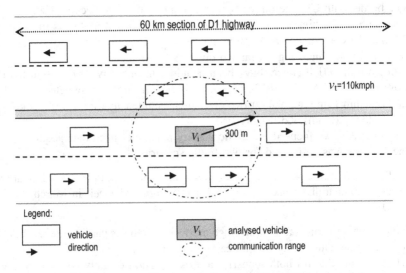

Fig. 3. The worst traffic scenario (beside traffic peak) [own study]

i.e. vehicle V_i can receive two V2V messages from one driving direction and four V2V messages from two driving directions. Analogically, for the second scenario ($n_b = 834$ vehicles) the distance between vehicles is 72 m, i.e. vehicle V_i can receive seven V2V messages from one driving direction and fourteen V2V messages from two driving directions.

Before the vehicle V_i wants to send a SR message, it has to process (verify) all SR messages received with a defined latency l. For SR messages transmission, the maximum value of l is within the range 100–300 ms. Let each message from the scenarios analysed be delayed by $l = 100$ ms. Next, let the number of messages sent per second by a single vehicle be $R = 10$, then for the scenario:

(a) V_i has to evaluate 20 messages within 1000 ms (for one driving direction),
(b) V_i has to evaluate 70 messages within 1000 ms (for one driving direction).

For both traffic scenarios, we focused on the network throughput application parameter. The throughput T of VANET depends on number of communicating nodes n, size of the message transmitted M and number of messages transmitted by a single vehicle per second R (*Rate*), as expressed by the following relation

$$T = \frac{n.R.M.8}{1024.1024} \quad [Mb/s] \tag{3}$$

As results from Fig. 2, the size of message depends on the sizes of O, P and S fields. The size of payload P ranges in SR applications from 100 to 280 B. The size of cryptographic header S is determined by the selection of digital signature scheme. Currently, the mostly utilised schemes are: deterministic RSA (*Rivest Shamir Adleman*) scheme and stochastic ECDSA (*Elliptic Curve Digital Signature Algorithms*) scheme, respectively. For the recommended key-sizes the size of field S can vary from 75 (ECDSA-192) to 500 (RSA 2048) bytes. Then the overall size of message M can be within 200 and 800B [16].

It is obvious, that increasing size of message M increases the network load. The network throughput calculated for the analysed traffic scenarios from the D1 highway is summarised in Table 2. Graphical dependencies of throughput T on message size M are shown in Fig. 4.

Table 2. VANET throughput for the analysed traffic scenarios from D1 [own study]

M (message length) [Bytes]	100	200	300	400	500	600	700	800
Throughput (Mbps) for 4 vehicles	0,03	0,06	0,09	0,12	0,15	0,18	0,21	0,24
Throughput (Mbps) for 14 vehicles	0,11	0,21	0,32	0,43	0,53	0,64	0,75	0,85

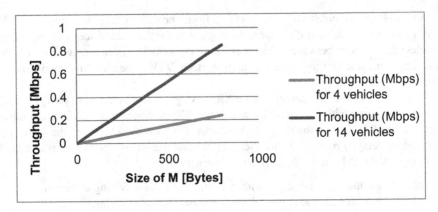

Fig. 4. Message size vs. system throughput [own study]

4   Conclusion

When developing safety critical applications in C-ITS, the authentication of messages transmitted between vehicles play a significant role. One of important parameters in on-line message authentication is the length of cryptographic header and the related limits for the overall message length and receiver processing time when receiving messages from multiple vehicles in range. The authors considered securing using the ECDSA-192 signature scheme. In the practical part, based on actual data acquired from the D1 highway, the authors analysed two scenarios (beside traffic peak 1:00 and traffic peak 8:00), while two limit instances were focused from the perspective of the position of analysed vehicle Vi.

The results are evaluated in dependence on the required application parameters of chosen C-ITS safety critical applications, like the maximum length of message transmitted, the maximum size of security field in line with the required security as well as throughput of VANET (on number of communicating nodes) and the maximum allowed network delay.

Acknowledgement.   This work has been supported by the Educational Grant Agency of the Slovak Republic (KEGA) Number: 008ŽU-4/2015: Innovation of HW and SW tools and methods of laboratory education focused on safety aspects of ICT within safety critical applications of processes control.

References

1. Mikulski, J.: Telematic technologies in transportation. In: Janecki, R., Sierpiński, G. (eds.) Contemporary Transportation Systems. Selected Theoretical and Practical Problems. New Culture of mobility, pp. 131–143. Publishing House of the Silesian University of Technology. Monograph no. 324, Gliwice (2011)

2. http://www.etsi.org/technologies-clusters/technologies/intelligent-transport/dsrc.   Accessed from 5 January 2015
3. VANET SeVeCom. http://www.sevecom.org. Accessed from 14 January 2015
4. CARLINK: Wireless Traffic Service Platform for Linking Cars. http://carlink.lcc.uma.es. Accessed from 29 January 2015
5. SeVeCom. Secure Vehicular Communications: Security Architecture and Mechanisms for V2V/V2I, Deliverable 2.1, 2007–2008. http://www.sevecom.org. Accessed from 16 January 2015
6. Car2Car Communication Consortium. http://www.car-2-car.org/. Accessed from 16 January 2015
7. Hofman, U., Rieder, A., Dickmanns, E.: Radar vision data function for hybrid adaptive cruise control on highways. Mach. Vis. Appl. 14(1), 42–49 (2003)
8. Huang, A.S., et al.: Finding multiple lanes in urban road networks with vision and lidar. Auton. Robots 26(2), 103–122 (2009)
9. Bubeníková, E., Franeková, M., Holečko, P.: Security increasing trends in intelligent transportation systems utilising modern image processing methods. In: Mikulski, J. (ed.) Telematics in the Transport Environment, Springer, Heidelberg, CCIS 395, pp. 353–360 (2013)
10. Hruboš, M., Janota, A.: Algorithm for surface creation from a cloud of points. In: Mikulski, J. (ed.) TST 2013. CCIS, vol. 395, pp. 42–49. Springer, Heidelberg (2013)
11. Oo, M.Z., Lumpur, K., Othman, M.: Analysis of single-path and multi-path AODVs over Manhattan Grid mobility model for mobile Ad hoc networks. In: International Conference Electronics and Information Engineering (ICEIE), ISBN: 978-1-4244-7679-4 (2010)
12. Roy, R.R.: Handbook of Mobile Ad Hoc Networks for Mobility Models. Springer, London (2011). ISBN 978-1-4419-6048-1
13. Mardberg, L.: Security in Cooperative Systems within intelligent Transport Systems. Master of Science Thesis. Chalmers of University of Technology, Göteborg, Sweden (2011)
14. Raya, M., Hubaux, J.P.: Securing vehicular ad hoc networks. J. Comput. Secur. Spec. Issue Secur. Ad Hoc Sensor Netw. 15(1), 39–68 (2007)
15. Intelligent Transport Systems & Services SDT: http://www.sdt.cz/. Accessed from January 10, 2015
16. Franeková, Mária, Lüley, Peter: Security of digital signature schemes for Car-to-Car communications within intelligent transportation systems. In: Mikulski, Jerzy (ed.) TST 2013. CCIS, vol. 395, pp. 258–267. Springer, Heidelberg (2013)

Improvement of Public Transportation as an Instrument of Transport Policy in Cities of Agglomeration

Ryszard Janecki[✉]

University of Economics in Katowice, 1 Maja 50, 40-287 Katowice, Poland
ryszard.janecki@ue.katowice.pl

Abstract. This paper presents implementation of transportation policy in cities of agglomeration in the field of public transportation. The activities in this area should be regarded as one of the principal tools in public policies of cities included in urban agglomeration, which particular focus on its central municipality or municipalities. The starting point for this type of activities that include e.g. modernizations and investments in the transport system of the city, application of "clear" traction and propagation of solutions that minimize environmental conflicts, elimination of exclusion (also exclusion of the disabled) and optimization of the transportation offer is the evaluation of the level of adjustment of communication lines to identified needs of the inhabitants. With regard to this context, the paper discusses the method of evaluation developed for the purposes of the city of Rybnik, Poland, which is a central municipality of the Rybnik agglomeration and western sub-region of the Silesian Voivodeship.

Keywords: Urban transportation policy · Policy instrument · Public transportation

1 Introduction

One of the important tools of transportation policy in cities that form agglomeration are initiatives in the field of public transportation in their area. This results from implementation, by local governments, of a function of organizer of public transportation that allows for effective performance of statutory tasks connected with these areas of city functioning.

Creation and implementation of urban transportation policy necessitates suitable information. This includes, among other things, two principal information sets:

- set of information concerning transportation needs and communication preferences of urban transportation users,
- set of information in terms of operation of the urban public transportation system.

They represent a necessary element in the process of creation of resources of knowledge about urban transportation system, which are used for building a program of urban transportation policy and consequently, its implementation and realization.

© Springer International Publishing Switzerland 2015
J. Mikulski (Ed.): TST 2015, CCIS 531, pp. 230–243, 2015.
DOI: 10.1007/978-3-319-24577-5_23

Various methods to approach the problems connected with instrumental utilization of urban public transportation in transportation policies of cities are observed in practice. This paper presents one of them. The data collected in the system of managing public transportation in the area of activity of the Board of Public Transport in Rybnik, originating from various sources, including the ITS modules, can be used in specific procedures of evaluation of dedicated public transportation systems. The results of these analyses represent the basis for identification of problems and presentation of proposals for solving them, which allows for using them within the program for urban transportation policy.

2 Transportation Policy in Cities of Agglomeration: Goals and Instruments for Implementation

Due to variation of the function of transportation, noticeable in the area of the cities that form agglomeration, creation of transportation policies represent an activity of local governments oriented at searching for effective solutions in such areas as:

– internal urban transportation availability and external availability of a specific city,
– model of mobility of inhabitants that determines division of transportation tasks in the city between public transportation and individual transportation,
– transportation as an area of economic activity, thus one of the domains of economy, from local to global: this area of urban transportation policy includes problems connected with financing of transportation, comprehensive transportation needs, transportation infrastructure, traffic organization and management of urban transportation.

Compared to current financial situation and economic opportunities of a specific city and the developmental goals of other cities in the agglomeration as well as in the national and European dimension, the aspects of transportation policy provide the basis for formulation of the aims of transportation policy of this city. It can be approached using two standpoints: general and detailed, with the latter including hierarchization of goals.

The general purposes of urban transportation policy include [1]:

– limitation of transportation needs in the area of the city in a long-term perspective,
– having a nature of a continuous process, formation of public transportation services, oriented at improved adjustment to the needs and expectation of transportation users,
– creation of the expected communicational behaviour of city inhabitants.

With regard to the detailed approach, the basic aims of transportation policy are [1, 2]:

– achievement of the accepted level of availability of principal locations in the city that absorb traffic and generate transportation needs, such as housing and industrial districts, other workplaces, places for learning, services, recreation and relax for all social groups, including the elderly and the disabled,
– creation of material and social conditions for economic development of the city,

- implementation of the principles of sustainable mobility that leads to rational demand for alternative means of transportation with respect to personal cars,
- improved transportation safety in the areas of the city,
- limitation of the unfavourable effect of transportation on natural environment,
- continuous activity aimed at reduction of travel costs incurred by urban public transportation systems.

It is necessary for these goals of urban transportation policy, which are consistent with the strategy of sustainable development, to utilize effective tools for implementation. Differentiation of the goals of policy also affects the differentiation of the set of instruments for its realization. These include [1, 2]:

- tools dedicated to real area of management processes in urban transportation,
- tools that affect the regulatory area of the management processes.

The instruments connected with the real areas include:

- programs for improvement and development of public transportation that increase its importance in transportation services in the area of the cities in urban agglomerations; the initiatives concerning regulation of prices for public transportation, financing public transportation from public resources that prefers urban transportation, division of transportation tasks and functional solutions for the system of communication lines adjusted to the inhabitants' needs are especially important in this area,
- modernization and investment programs in terms of individual transportation, its motorized and non-motorized part,
- education and training programmes.

The regulatory area involves such tools as:

- studies of conditions and directions for urban land development and local land development plans,
- legal regulations that set the principles for operation and development of urban transportation.

The framework of instruments of transportation policy of the cities in agglomeration (Fig. 1) meets wide spectrum of activity and partial tools used for implementation of this policy.

The inclusion of the initiatives in the area of both subsystem of urban public transportation in the instruments of urban transportation policy, thus both public and individual transportation, should be, on the one hand, regarded as a result of all the goals of policy adopted and acceptance of the strategy of sustainable development and sustainable mobility. On the other hand, this approach represents a realistic proposal that takes into consideration current legal regulations and financial opportunities of the cities in agglomeration. The mechanism of creation of their transportation policy allows considering this type of approach and the instruments used not only as available but also as the most frequently used.

The activities taken in urban public transportation are especially important. Their basis, opportunities and effects are the topic of investigations of the further part of this paper.

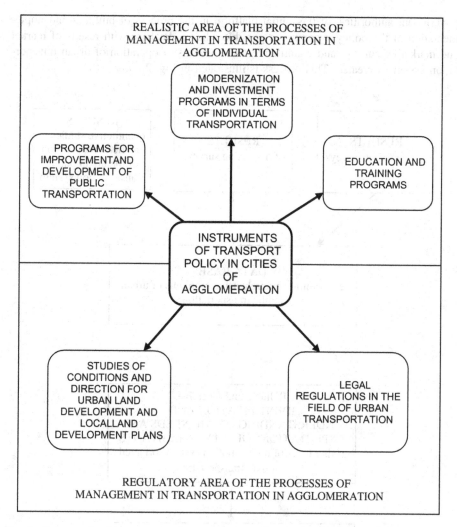

Fig. 1. Framework of instruments of transportation policy in the cities of agglomeration [own study]

3   Information Basis for Activities Programmed in Public Transportation that Represent an Instrument of Transportation Policy in the Cities of Agglomeration

In the process of construction of transportation policy of a particular city in urban agglomeration, utilization of activities in the field of public transportation, facilitation of its operation and making transportation services more attractive requires a reliable and objective knowledge of the needs and expectations of inhabitants, connected with urban transportation system, including the quality of services. Creation, by the local

government authorities, of this initial platform in the process of building and implementation of the policy programs is possible when a database with results of market
and marketing surveys and quantitative tests in terms of operation of urban transportation system is created. This process is illustrated in Fig. 2.

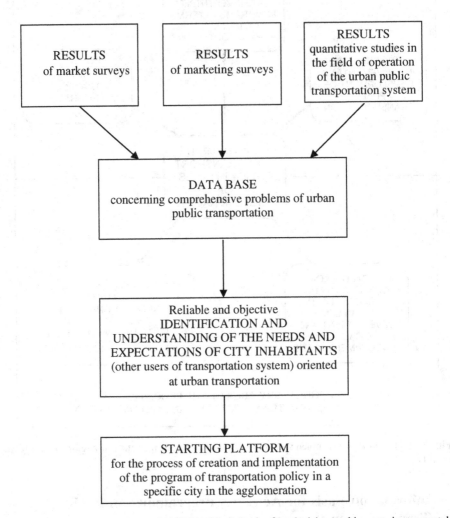

Fig. 2. Activities that represent informational basis for decision-making at instrumental
utilization of public transportation in transportation policy of cities in the agglomeration [own
study]

The focus of market and marketing surveys is on:

– transportation needs and demand for urban transportation services,
– behaviours and communication preferences of population,
– quality of urban public transportation services.

Furthermore, the investigations of the urban transportation system allow for collection of the data concerning:

- external conditions of its functioning in a specific city in the agglomeration, thus the supply side of the market of urban transportation services,
- internal conditions of operation, including in particular all the technical and technological aspects of the process of providing transportation services and resources which should be used by the entities present in the market.

The data collected in the above studies are not processed. The information collected in this way in the process of diagnosis of the current status of urban transportation system are used to create knowledge about the system. It is resources combined with information that are used in the process of construction and implementation of transportation policy in individual cities of agglomerations.

This approach was used in the urban public transportation system in the area of Rybnik agglomeration in Poland, which is the area of activity of the Board of Public Transport (ZTZ). The board organizes public transportation in the area of this agglomeration. The next part of this paper presents practical aspects of the discussed method of forming informational basis for program decisions within urban transportation policy in the central city of the agglomeration of Rybnik.

4 Urban Public Transportation Organized by ZTZ in Rybnik as an Instrument of Urban Transportation Policy

Creation of the information basis for the decision process, which formulates the proposals in terms of the urban transportation policy in the city of Rybnik concerning public transportation was performed according to the procedure presented in Fig. 3. Three basic stages in this process should be emphasized [3]:

- identification of the current status of the system of public transportation organized by ZTZ in Rybnik
- evaluation of the current status of the system,
- formulation of principal directions of changes in urban transportation policy in Rybnik

The starting point for the diagnosed transportation system organized by ZTZ in Rybnik is results of its identification. It includes the following elements of the ZTZ's transportation system:

- system of bus lines,
- scope and level of the operational work, thus supply of transportation services,
- demand, which is a response of transportation users to the market supply.

The scope of identification was firstly expected to collect all the necessary information for creation of the most credible view of transportation reality in this part of the western sub-region of the Silesian Voivodeship, which is the area of activity of ZTZ in Rybnik.

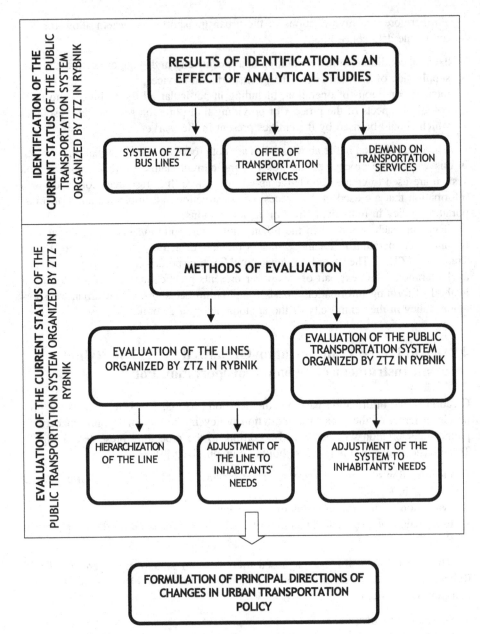

Fig. 3. Procedure for instrumental utilization of public transportation organized by ZTZ in Rybnik [3]

The database prepared during analytical work aimed at identification of the public transportation system organized by ZTZ oriented the area of tools for evaluation towards the use of the point-based method. Using this method required:

- formulation of the goals of the diagnostic surveys,
- development of the list of criteria to differentiate between the object of evaluation, i.e. individual ZTZ bus lines, and the whole public transportation system of the organizer; selection of criteria depends on the goals achieved using the results of the evaluation,
- determination of weights for criteria because they are not equally important for evaluation of a line or system; differentiation of weights can be achieved directly, through adoption of various values or indirectly, through hierarchization of the object of evaluation according to a specific criterion,
- determination of a suitable scale for evaluation of meeting a specific criterion by the evaluated item (a bus line or the ZTZ transportation system).

In the point-based method, the total weighted value is calculated: it represents the total of partial weighted values that correspond to individual criteria. An average value can also be computed through division of the total weighted value by the sum of weights.

Three goals of the evaluation activities were adopted:

- evaluation of the line that is the basis for hierarchization,
- evaluation of the line aimed at determination of the level of adjustment of the line to identified needs of inhabitants,
- evaluation of the system of public transportation in terms of its adjustment to the inhabitant's needs and contemporary requirements.

It should be emphasized that the evaluation of the current system of ZTZ transportation represents the main information basis necessary for making rational decisions connected with current facilitation and further development. Utilization of its results allows for e.g. [4]:

- orientation of activities so that the necessary social acceptance is achieved,
- marketing activities,
- promotion of the use of public transportation as a demanded communicational and social behaviour.

The aim of the first of the evaluations of the ZTZ's bus lines in Rybnik is to collect the data that allow for hierarchization of the lines that operate within the ZTZ transportation system. Hierarchization of lines is understood as ranking according to their importance and position in the current system of ZTZ bus lines in Rybnik.

The adopted evaluation criteria were:

- level of operational work in the line on a working day in vehicle-kilometres,
- number of courses on a working day,
- number of passengers transported in a line on a working day,
- line productivity in passengers/vehicle-kilometres,
- line profitability expressed in the level of subsidies to 1 vehicle-kilometre in %.

The criteria adopted point to the quantitative character of the evaluation.

Further, the corresponding weights were determined for the criteria adopted and the bus lines were evaluated using a scale of 0.1 to 4.0. Weighted values for the bus lines analysed ranged from 42.60 (maximum value) to 4.30 (minimal value).

The values obtained for bus lines allowed for distinguishing between the three types of lines: main lines, basic lines and supplementary lines.

The first group of lines (7 lines among 40 lines in total) are bus connections in the urban public transportation that are characterized by the broadest scale of offer in the ZTZ transportation system.

Also with respect to the spatial factor, it is noticeable that these lines cover the greatest divisions of the city and areas that generate much traffic (such divisions as Śródmieście, Maroko Nowiny, Niedobczyce, Boguszowice and Północ; region of high-area commercial centres, hospitals and large business entities).

The importance and position of the main lines in the public transportation system organized by ZTZ in Rybnik should require that the activities included in the urban transportation system that are aimed at further improvement in urban public transportation should take into consideration the network of these lines. Their system exists in the north-city centre-south corridor, which is important for operation of public transportation in Rybnik.

The second group of ZTZ lines distinguished using the evaluation was termed basic lines (9 bus lines), whereas the third was termed supplementary lines (24 lines). The basic lines perform mainly services for surrounding districts of the city. In some cases, they are the only connections for these districts with the city centre and other urban and external areas.

Qualitative aspects of operation of public transportation might be evaluated with regards to at least four entities: passenger, operator or carrier, organizer of public transportation and local government authorities. The most important evaluation is evaluation of passenger since it has an effect on the level of pricing in transport organizers. It should be reflected by the evaluation carried out by local government authorities, while the critical comments from the inhabitants should represent, if justified and rational, the subject of effective facilitation activities in the system. These reasons were the basis for evaluation of current lines in terms of adjustment to the needs of the inhabitants.

Criteria of evaluation of the level of adjustment of ZTZ bus lines in Rybnik to identified needs of inhabitants included the following set of factors:

- days of operation of the line (weekdays, Saturday, Sunday or holidays)
- time of operation of lines (in hours),
- important traffic generators used in the line,
- average number of places on weekdays available in the periods of rush hours in buses per 1 passenger,
- communication speed of a line on a weekday,
- mean frequency of line operation in rush hours on a working day,
- mean frequency of line operation at midday (10:00am – 01:00 pm),
- mean frequency of line operation in the afternoon (02:00 pm – 05:00 pm) on Sundays or holidays.

Specific weights were determined for the above criteria. They were determined based on the proposals of the author's team that implemented the project presented.

ZTZ bus lines were evaluated on a scale of 1 to 5. The method of evaluation uses comparison, for each line evaluated, of the value of a specific criterion with the model

Table 1. Model of bus line adjusted to inhabitants' needs in the transportation system of ZTZ in Rybnik [3]

Name of criterion for evaluation of the ZTZ bus line	Model values for criterion and (evaluation)
1	2
Days of line operation in a week	– **line operates on weekdays, Saturdays and Sundays or holidays (5)** – line operates on weekdays and Saturdays (4) – line operates on weekdays and Sundays or holidays (3) – line operates on holidays (2) – line operates only on weekdays (1)
time of operation of lines in hours	– **> 17 hours and after 10:30 pm (5)** – 15-17 hours and min. to 10:30 pm (4) – 15-17 hours (3) – 12-14 hours (2) – > 11 hours (1)
Services for important traffic generators	– **services by the line of the area that generates substantial and continuous transportation needs (5)** – connections to / from industrial districts (4) – services for outskirt districts (3) – internal lines outside Rybnik (2)
Average number of places on weekdays available in the periods of rush hours in buses per 1 passenger	– **≥ 3,00 [places / 1 pass.] (5)** – ≥ 2,50 [places / 1 pass.] (3) – ≤ 2,00 [places / 1 pass.] (1)
Communication speed of a line on a weekday according to timetable in [km/h]	– **≥ 27 (5)** – ≥ 25 (3) – < 23 (1)
Mean frequency of courses over a line in rush hours during a weekday according to timetable in minutes	– **≤ 30 (5)** – ≤ 60 (3) – ≥ 90 (1)
Mean frequency of courses over a line in the afternoon on Saturdays according to timetable in minutes	– **≤ 45 (5)** – ≤ 90 (3) – ≥ 120 (1)
Mean frequency of courses over a line in the afternoon on Saturdays or holidays according to timetable in minutes	– **≤ 45 (5)** – ≤ 90 (3) – ≥ 120 (1)

of the bus line adjusted to the inhabitant's needs which is presented in Table 1. The results of the evaluation are presented in Fig. 4.

Maximum value of evaluation of the level of adjustment of ZTZ bus lines in Rybnik to inhabitants' needs according to the criteria adopted is 5.00. 75 % of this value (weighted value of 3.75) was reached by 12 lines, including 6 of 7 main lines and 2 of 9 basic lines.

The results presented indicate the necessity of taking actions to better adjust lines to expectations of transportation system users. One of the problems observed in the current transportation system is low frequency of transportation and thus long intervals between the courses. Particularly little attractive services are provided on Saturdays, Sundays and holidays. Using the adopted set of criteria, 11 lines should be evaluated negatively since the weighted value for these lines did not exceed 60 % of maximum weighted value. Over 30 % of the lines evaluated in this manner provide services for

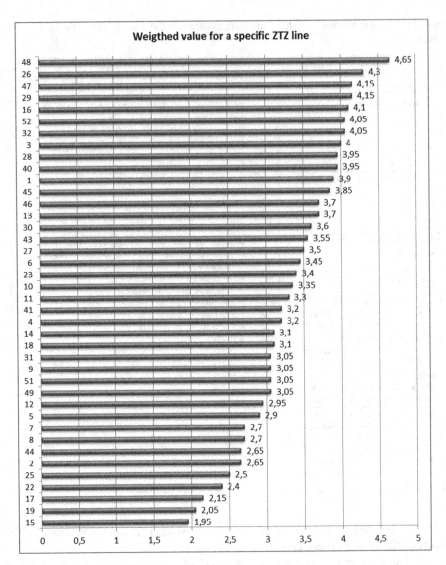

Fig. 4. Hierarchical system of ZTZ's bus lined in Rybnik according to the level of adjustment to inhabitants' needs: results of evaluation [3]

Niedobczyce, one of the biggest districts in the city in terms of inhabitants and number of workplaces offered.

The evaluation of public transportation system was also carried out in the analytical and comparative aspect, approaching the system holistically. This evaluation analysed:

– spatial aspects of evaluation,
– supply-based aspect of evaluation,
– comparison of the recommended standards of services with the values of analysed systematic parameters achieved in ZTZ transportation system.

The most important conclusions that result from the examinations of the ZTZ transportation system approached holistically are:

- local government authorities in the city start varied initiatives that form, under conditions of budgetary limitations and infrastructural and traffic conditions, the transportation system that meets the needs of Rybnik's inhabitants to highest possible degree,
- as a central municipality in the Rybnik agglomeration, the city is also the main entity of the ZTZ transportation system. This role is manifested in the size of bus line network in the city and level of supply of transportation services in the system organized by ZTZ dedicated to city inhabitants and realistic level of demand,
- lack of the approach to organization of local transportation similar to the approach presented in Rybnik can be observed in the communes that concluded an agreement with Rybnik commune and entrusted organization of public transportation in their area; the principal determiner of organization of public transportation in these local government entities is connection with Rybnik and the level of services adjusted to often insufficient budgets of communes rather than actual needs of inhabitants. Furthermore, the communes which are members of MZK Jastrzębie- Zdrój (Inter-commune Transportation Association), used lines organized by ZTZ in Rybnik and participated in costs of operation of these lines to ensure connections with the main city in the urban complex; there is only 4 such lines in the offer of the Association for 11 member communes,
- comparison of selected parameters of ZTZ transportation system in Rybnik with standard values is relatively favourable for the system.

5 Conclusion

The results of the analytical studies carried out during identification of current status of ZTZ transportation system in Rybnik and evaluation of the lines organized by ZTZ and the transportation system created by this entity allow for indication of the directions of changes in the public transportation system that provides services for Rybnik and 11 other communes, with particular focus on Rybnik agglomeration and its direct func-tional environment.

The activities programmed in the system of public transportation organized by ZTZ in Rybnik concern:

- system of ZTZ bus lines,
- supply of transportation services that reflects the transportation offer and its quantitative character,
- demand for transportation services in the market expressed by inhabitants and guests from the area of ZTZ operation which have varied needs.

The most important needs are:

- in terms of the network of bus lines in Rybnik:

1. Transportation services organized by ZTZ in Rybnik for previous areas of the city which do not have connections (elimination of "white spots").
2. Building of transfer nodes, including "park and ride".
3. Improvement in availability of public transportation through elimination of substantial differences (if justified) between the scale of direct connections from individual city districts.
4. Correcting routes of certain bus lines so that they are relatively straight over the whole course, including the city centre in Rybnik.
5. Reduction in mean distance between bus stops at certain routes of a line.
6. Introduction of the lines that ensure shorter time of transportation (fast lines with reduced number of stops).
7. Using realistic timetables so that planned arrival and departure times are adjusted to the conditions of traffic in characteristic times of a day.
8. Introduction, at selected intersections, of traffic lights that ensure preferential traffic for buses moving to the order of ZTZ in Rybnik and other solutions that ensure priority for means of urban public transportation.

– in terms of the supply of transportation services:

1. Increasing frequency of services so that minimal frequencies are adjusted to the needs of inhabitants and guests of the agglomeration and generally accepted standards; it is also remarkable that substantial improvement can be achieved by shortening of long intervals rather than the shorter ones.
2. Better adjustment of departure times to the inhabitants' needs in order to ensure convenient conditions for changes (integration of the systems of public transportation over the agglomeration; more about this problem [5, 6]).
3. Designing of timetables which are easy to remember (e.g. departure time should be at specific minutes of an hour of line operation).
4. Increasing the number of connections on holidays and at night.

– in terms of demand for transportation services:

• Taking demand-driven activities in the city districts with the lowest number of passengers, where the stream of people getting on buses at ZTZ stops does not exceed 10 % of the number of inhabitants in these districts.
• Introduction of small passenger streams of flexible transportation technologies ("hail and ride") that ensure better adjustment of the services to the level needs.

Varied range of proposed activities indicated that they represent an effective tool for achievement of the goals of transportation policy in the city, representing generally accepted type of instruments. One of many possible methods to stimulate these activities was practically verified through application in the process of definition of changes in the transportation policy of the city in essential part that relates to the system of public transportation organized by ZTZ in Rybnik. It should also be emphasized that application of the methodology presented in the study was possible because it was used in the transportation environment that employs ITS technology. In the case of the ZTZ transportation system, this means solutions in the field of electronic toll collection and dynamic passenger information.

References

1. Bogusławski, J., Wołek, M.: Polityka transportowa miasta. In: Wyszomirski, O. (ed.) Transport miejski. Ekonomika i organizacja, pp. 269–271, Wydawnictwo Uniwersytetu Gdańskiego, Gdańsk (2008)
2. Tomanek, R.: Funkcjonowanie transportu, pp. 134–141, Wydawnictwo Akademii Ekonomicznej w Katowicach, Katowice (2004)
3. Janecki, R., et al.: Ocena stanu istniejącego układu linii publicznego transportu ZTZ w Rybniku i rozwiązania funkcjonalne linii dostosowane do potrzeb mieszkańców, pp. 193–216, BUI CONCEPT, Katowice – Rybnik (2013)
4. Rudnicki, A.: Jakość komunikacji miejskiej. Zeszyty Naukowo-Techniczne Oddziału SITK w Krakowie, Seria: Monografie 71(5), 19 (1999)
5. Janecki, R.: Rozwój systemu kolejowych przewozów regionalnych w aglomeracji górnośląskiej poprzez integrację międzygałęziową. Transport Miejski i Regionalny 11, 2–10 (2011)
6. Starowicz, W., Janecki, R.: Integracja regionalnego transportu zbiorowego. Transport Miejski i Regionalny 3, 4–10 (2004)
7. Karoń, G., Mikulski, J.: Problems of its architecture development and ITS implementation in Upper-Silesian Conurbation in Poland. In: Mikulski, J. (ed.) TST 2012. CCIS, vol. 329, pp. 183–198. Springer, Heidelberg (2012)

Comparison of Efficiency of Vehicle Detection and Classification System on Multilane Road

Artur Ryguła[1(✉)], Andrzej Maczyński[1], and Paweł Piwowarczyk[2]

[1] University of Bielsko-Biala, 43-309 Bielsko-Biała, Poland
{arygula, amaczynski}@ath.eu
[2] APM PRO, 43-309 Bielsko-Biała, Poland
pawel.piwowarczyk@apm.pl

Abstract. This article presents the assumptions and results of research aimed at comparing the radar systems and video detection devices. The experiment was conducted on a multilane road section, outside the built-up area. The paper compares the effectiveness of traffic volume detection and vehicle classification. Presented analyses describe the variability in terms of vehicle intensity and as a function of weather conditions.

Keywords: Vehicle detection · Radar systems · Video detection · Traffic analysis

1 Introduction

Vehicle detection devices are an elementary part of traffic management systems. The performance and effectiveness of the motion sensors determine the efficiency of control systems, which use the information containing traffic structure and volume. Currently, on the market, there is a wide range of automatic vehicle detection technologies. Starting from conventional solutions in the form of induction loops [1] and ending with solutions based on Wi-Fi/Bluetooth systems [2]. The important role, due to the non-invasive and relatively high efficiency, is played by radar and video detection systems.

Video detection solutions use extended image processing techniques in order to detect the object in the streams of images. Video technology allows to determine the traffic volume and also provide vehicles identification (number plate recognition). Currently, these techniques also allow to determine the speed (change in position of an object on particular video frames) and more often classify vehicles on the basis of the length of the object [3].

Radar techniques use the Doppler effect, which is based on changing the frequency of radar beam due to reflection from a moving object. Radar techniques enable the vehicle detection, speed measurement, determination of the length of the object (the time representation of the vehicle presence for a certain speed) and at the same time classification.

© Springer International Publishing Switzerland 2015
J. Mikulski (Ed.): TST 2015, CCIS 531, pp. 244–252, 2015.
DOI: 10.1007/978-3-319-24577-5_24

2 Measurement Systems

Measurement system consists of Autoscope RTMS radar and AtalayaImagsa ANPR (automatic number plate) video camera. The subject of analysis was the comparison of traffic volume and structure determination. Basic technical parameters of devices are presented in Table 1.

Manufacturers of ANPR and RTMS systems determine the accuracy of vehicle classification at 90 % and traffic volume detection at even 95 %. In case of the ANPR camera, effectiveness can be decreased by adverse weather conditions (snow, rain, fog) or sunlight directly illuminating optics systems. RTMS radar performance is mainly dependent on the traffic congestions, an obstruction by barriers or high fences [4]. In case of RTMS system in operating manual, detailed guidance about device settings and installation recommendations (distance from lanes, height and beam angles) are provided. In case of side-fired configuration RTMS radar is able to observe even 12 traffic lanes. The Atalaya ANPR camera is designed for 2 lanes.

In RTMS radar, user can define up to 6 vehicle classes. The particular classes are specified by the vehicle length in meters. The default settings, which were used in analysis, are presented in Table 2. For APNR camera, the manufacturer defined four classes: light, heavy, moto and others.

Table 1. ANPR camera/RTMS technical parameters [4, 5]

Feature	RTMS	ANPR
Max detection lanes	12	2
No of vehicle class	6	3 + 1
Mounting	Side-fired, Or forward-Looking	Over lane, back looking
Volume accuracy per lane	95 %	95 %
Classification accuracy	90 %	90 %
Max vehicle speed	160 km/h	250 km/h
Range	2–75 m	not available

Table 2. RTMS Vehicle classes [4]

Class	LIGHT	Vehicle length [m]
1	SMALL	<5
2	REG	$(5 \div 7)$
3	MED	$(7 \div 10)$
4	LARGE	$(10 \div 15)$
5	TRUCK	$(15 \div 20)$
6	XLARGE	>20

3 Location

The detection systems were installed on voivodeship road no 902 in Chorzów. At measurement point the road is a dual carriageway with 4 lanes in each direction (3 straight and one exit lane) The average daily traffic (in two directions) is about 60 thousand vehicles per day. The data was recorded for time period from midnight 18th February till one p.m. on 20th February. During the recording time, the weather conditions where relatively constant without any precipitations and visibility reductions.

RTMS radar was mounted in side-fired position. Due to the availability of mounting construction, power supply and communication network, the radar was installed on the variable message sing gantry using the dedicated arm. Referring to the operating manual, in order to decrease the possibility of signal reflection from bridge structure, the beam angle was set to record vehicles only on 4 lanes on one roadway (Fig. 1).

ANPR cameras are the part of traffic management system described in work [6]. The units are installed on overpass between external and internal lanes. Each camera covers two lanes. The units are capturing the rear-image in order to provide vehicle classification.

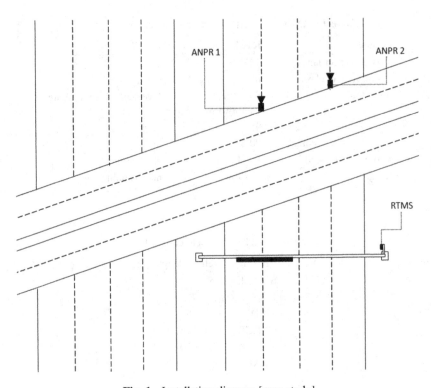

Fig. 1. Installation diagram [own study]

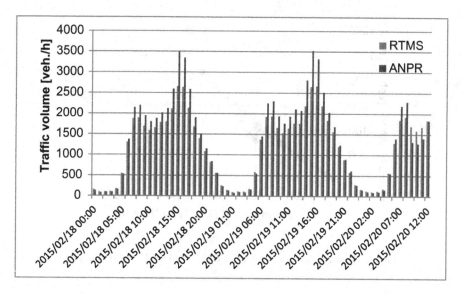

Fig. 2. Traffic volume registered by RTMS and ANPR [own study]

4 Vehicle Detection

The first part of analysis was the evaluation of the vehicle detection rate for RTMS radar system and ANPR cameras.

The results presented in Table 3, indicate a slight discrepancy between the volume data. In daily term, the difference between total number of vehicle on 4 lanes for 18th and 19th February was about 14 %. For 20th February, the difference was only 2 %. It is worth noticing that the data at last day were recorded only till midday.

In Fig. 2 the distribution of the hourly traffic intensity was presented. Analysis of the data clearly show an increased data flow divergence over the level of 1.5 thousand vehicles per hour. For most cases greater amount of ANPR detection was registered.

In order to illustrate the vehicle detection rate, the data were presented in the form of ANPR volume in functions of RTMS detection chart (Fig. 3). The results confirm the mentioned dependency. Up to the level of about 400 vehicles per 15 min, the dependence is linear. Above this level, there is a significant increase of ANPR

Table 3. Traffic volume [own study]

Date	RTMS volume [veh.]	ANPR 1 volume [veh.]	ANPR 2 volume [veh.]
2015-02-18	30 114	15 059	19 705
2015-02-19	30 793	15 705	20 060
2015-02-20	13 112	4 868	7 986

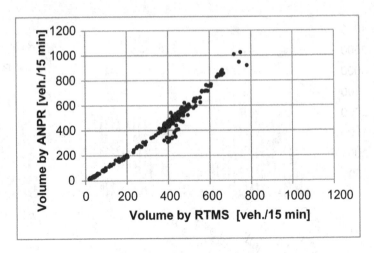

Fig. 3. Traffic volume registered by RTMS and ANPR [own study]

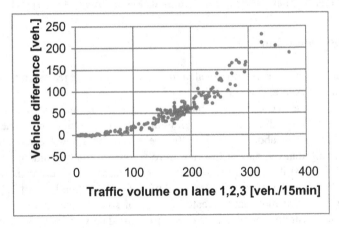

Fig. 4. Influence of traffic on lane 1–3 on the detection rate on 4th lane [own study]

detection. The possible cause of this is the traffic situation on 4th lane, which is being used by drivers in case when total traffic level is over 1600 vehicle per hour.

Figure 4 presented the dependency of the detection difference between ANPR and RTMS system for 4th lane in relation to the traffic volume on lanes 1, 2 and 3. As it can be seen, the dependency has an exponential distribution. For a number of 300 vehicles on lanes 1–3 the difference in detection on lane 4 is even 150 vehicle per 15 min.

The next step of analysis was the determination of traffic directional distribution with the investigation of percentage participation of vehicle on each lane.

The data shown in Fig. 5 indicate a dominance of traffic for lanes 2 and 3 (about 80 % of vehicles). The distribution also shows the differences in the detection for

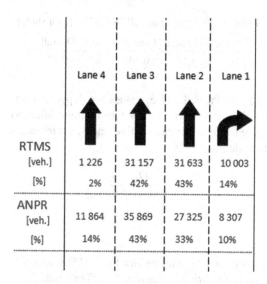

Fig. 5. Traffic volume per lane [own study]

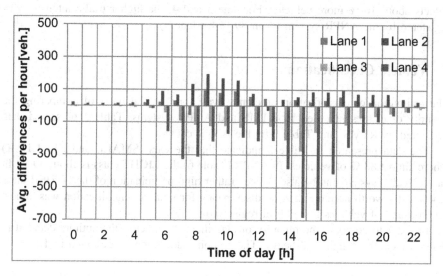

Fig. 6. Average number of vehicle per hour [own study]

particular systems. For lanes 1, 2, 3 the detection rate is at a similar level. For 4th lane, traffic level varies from 2 to 14 % and is probably caused by shadowing other vehicles.

An important part of work was also the comparison of detection related to particular lanes and the hour of the day. Figure 6 presented the average hourly difference in traffic volume. For lane 1 and 2 the largest differences were recorded from 9 a.m., which is probably correlated with the sunlight illuminating the cameras. The phenomena was

Table 4. Detection rate ARTR/RTMS [own study]

Lane 1	Lane 2	Lane 3	Lane 4	Overall
0,16	0,13	−0,13	−0,89	−0,12

described in work [6]. For lanes 4 and 5, values are dependent on the traffic volumes and clearly indicated the local maximum for morning and afternoon rush hours.

In order to compare the total number of differences, a reference detection rate factor for particulate lanes is defined:

$$D_i = \frac{Q_{Ri} - Q_{Ai}}{\max(Q_{Ai}, Q_{Ri})} \tag{1}$$

where:

Q_{Ai} – traffic intensity for *i-th* lane register by ANPR camera,
Q_{Ri} – traffic intensity for *i-th* lane register by RTMS radar.

The indicator values were shown in Table 4. For lane 1 and 2 the RTMS radar detects about 16 % more vehicles. For lane 3 and 4, the higher traffic intensity was registered by the ANPR system (even 89 % for lane 4).

5   Vehicle Classification

The estimation of classification efficiency was done on the basis of comparing the quantity of classes recorded by RTMS and ANPR systems. Table 5 presented data registered by RTMS, and Table 6 by the ANPR camera.

The data presented in Table 5 indicate that the cars (SMALL and REGULAR) where almost 88 % of vehicles. In ANPR (Table 6) the LIGHT class is about 60 %. In case of video system can be also noticed rather high participation of the OTHER class (24 %). It's worth noticing that the discrepancy for total car classification was almost 10 thousand of vehicles for 60 h of registration.

In order to compare the quantity of classification directly, the authors decided to define two classes: light and heavy. The mapping definition is presented in Table 7.

Table 5. Classification RTMS [own study]

Lane	SMALL	REG.	MED.	LARGE	TRUCK	XL.
1	7074	1166	471	453	417	428
2	22643	4178	1739	1321	1135	629
3	26831	2621	721	464	270	268
4	1148	37	14	17	26	8
Overall	57686	7992	2935	2245	1838	1323

Table 6. Classification ANPR [own study]

Lane	LIGHT	HEAVY	MOTO	OTHER
1	1935	1106	1	5266
2	8864	5754	2	12707
3	29177	5027	533	1135
4	9818	1485	81	484
Overall	49784	13362	607	20245

Table 7. RTMS/ANPR classes

Class	RTMS class	ANPR class
Light	SMALL	LIGHT
	REG.	MOTO
Heavy	MED.	HEAVY
	LARGE	
	TRUCK	
	XLARGE	

Data concerning the average number of light vehicles, detected in hour distribution, were shown in Fig. 7. Due to significant differences in the volumes of external lanes, analysis were made only for lane 2 and 3.

As it can be seen in Fig. 7 the amount of detection is of the similar level, with the difference of only several percent. The important difference occurs for lane 2, for the afternoon rush hour (even 100 %).

In the analysis of heavy class vehicles (Fig. 8), significant differences in detection number for almost whole analysis period were observed. On lane 2, RTMS radar detected more heavy vehicles in the period between morning and afternoon rush hours. In case of ANPR, the high detection on lane 2 occurred after 4 p.m. For lane 3 the detection of ANPR system was almost 3-times higher..

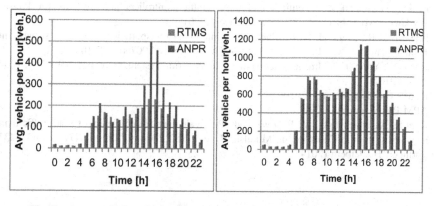

Fig. 7. Average light vehicle class detection for 2nd and 3rd lane [own study]

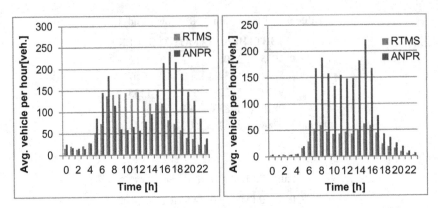

Fig. 8. Average heavy vehicle class detection for 2nd and 3rd lane [own study]

6   Conclusion

The aim of the analysis presented in the paper, was comparison of data recorded by the radar and video vehicle detection systems. In case of determining the traffic volume, recorded data were comparable for middle and external lanes. In case of internal lane (high-speed), the values of RTMS were clearly underestimated. With regards to classification, on lane 3, ANPR detected probably too many of the heavy classes.

The results, particularly, the observed differences indicate the need to do further research using some additional reference method. This method can be laser sensors mounted over the lane or video recording system. Future research should also take into account the relocation of the RTMS unit in order to eliminate possible interference from the reflection of bridge structure.

References

1. Leśko, M., Guzik, J.: Traffic controlling. Traffic controllers and systems [in Polish]. Wydawnictwo Politechniki Śląskiej, Gliwice (2000)
2. Friesen, M.R., McLeod, R.D.: Bluetooth in intelligent transportation systems: a survey. Int. J. Intell. Transp. Syst. Res. 01/2014, **13**(3) (2014). doi:10.1007/s13177-014-0092-1
3. Ng, J. Y., Yong, H.T.: Image-based vehicle classification system. arXiv preprint arXiv: 1204. 2114 (2012)
4. RTMS G4 User Manual (2010)
5. APM Pro Materials
6. Ryguła, A., Maczyński, A., Piwowarczyk, P.: Evaluating the efficiency of road traffic management system in Chorzow. In: Mikulski, J. (ed.) TST 2014. CCIS, vol. 471, pp. 424–433. Springer, Heidelberg (2014)

Analysis of the Problem of Interference
of the Public Network Operators to GSM-R

Marek Sumiła[1]([⊠]) and Andrzej Miszkiewicz[2]

[1] Warsaw University of Technology, 00-662 Warsaw, Poland
sumila@wt.pw.edu.pl
[2] Institute of Railway, 04-275 Warsaw, Poland
amiszkiewicz@ikolej.pl

Abstract. The article presents current state of knowledge of the impact of public mobile networks in the 900 MHz band to GSM-R communication. At the beginning we will present the main problem of interfering networks and the effects of this impact on the receivers GSM-R. In the next paragraph will be introduced an analysis of recorded cases of interference on the GSM-R in the EU and case study of blocking due to Polish case.

Keywords: GSM-R · Safety · Network interference

1 Introduction

GSM-R, Global System for Mobile Communications – Railway or GSM-Railway is an international wireless communications standard for railway communication and applications. The system was developed to standardize radio communications systems for railways in the EU, though today it is successfully used in other countries around the world (e.g. Australia, China and some countries of South Africa). The system is based on GSM and EIRENE – MORANE specifications which guarantee performance at speeds up to 500 km/h, without any communication loss. From the beginning GSM-R was created as a sub-system of European Rail Traffic Management System (ERTMS) and it is used for communication between train and railway regulation control centres.

The GSM operates in two frequency bands. These are 876 MHz–915 MHz (uplink) and 921 MHz-960 MHz (downlink). It should be noted that these bands are adjacent to uplink and downlink bands allocated for public communications networks. The Fig. 1 shows the band width allocation for GSM-R and public networks operating in the 900 MHz band. It can be seen that the band width allocated to the railway communication is directly adjacent to the band allocated to the public means of communication. GSM-R system places much higher demands on quality of service than conventional GSM network. It was confirmed in the works [29–32].This applies to the transmission medium intended for control and signalling system ETCS *(European Train Control System)*. This applies also to transmission on rail tracks. Both of these areas have an impact on the safety of operations. The functional and performance requirements for GSM-R are defined in the EIRENE SRS [19]. Essentially, ETSI TS 100 910 [20] defines the technical and performance specifications for the GSM-R radio

© Springer International Publishing Switzerland 2015
J. Mikulski (Ed.): TST 2015, CCIS 531, pp. 253–263, 2015.
DOI: 10.1007/978-3-319-24577-5_25

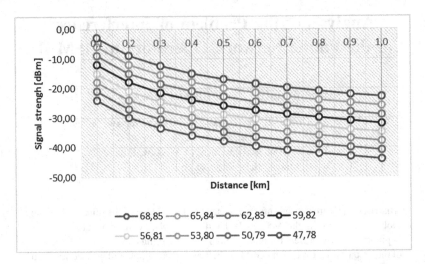

Fig. 1. Decrease in signal strength in dBm according to distance (*f*– const. 925.1 MHz) [own study]

interface. Additionally, Quality of Service (QoS) requirements specific for ETCS data communication have been defined in the UNISIG Subset 093 [21].

In Commission Decision 2012/88/EU [25] "the availability of the GSM-R frequencies is essential for safe and interoperable operations". Lack of availability has an operational and commercial consequences, such as: bad economic and commercial effects, impossible to make voice communication – especially Railway Emergency Calls - can lead to dangerous situations, jammed traffic – major delays, performances of line and rail network is badly affected. Furthermore, based on the railway operational needs, critical zones can be identified on a national basis. The degradation of GSM-R availability or QoS due to interferences is not acceptable [12].

The draft of the report ECC 229 [8] lists the following critical zones: locations where trains start their trip or continue it after a stop, for example: stations, signals, shunting yards and locations where trains can encounter a dangerous situation, for example junctions, rail/road crossings, tunnels and bridges. There are included areas with ETCS L2/3 where continuous data communication is required e.g. ETCS L2/3 entry zones, complete stretch of the ETCS L2/3 lines (including stations, tunnels, bridges, entrance to shunting yards, etc.).

Note that special attention has to be paid to the possible stopping points in the lines equipped with ETCS L2/3, including Radio Block Centre (RBC) handover areas. Preventing interferences in these critical zones and situations should have the highest priority in the coordination process.

The problem of the impact of public mobile network on GSM-R has been investigated since 2007. At present the problem of network impact assessment is investigated by many international institutes and research centers. As a result, the test methods, philosophy and test limits for the black-box-radio are the same as those defined in chapter 14 of the ETSI TS 100 607-1 [22] and paragraph 8.2 of the ETSI TS 100 911 [23].

Direct adhesion of bands is a possibility of mutual interference between coexistence networks. In Directive 87/372/EEC [9] with the amendments introduced by Directive 2009/114/EC [16] on the allocation of radio frequencies allocated for the terrestrial mobile networks, which is referred to the possibility of the coexistence of different mobile networks in the frequency bands 880-915 MHz and 925-960 MHz. The document is the executive of the Directive of the European Commission Decision 2009/766/EC [17] as amended in 2011/251/EU [15] on the harmonization of the frequency bands of 900 MHz and 1800 MHz terrestrial systems designed for public radio. The document indicates the following requirements:

- separation between the nearest edge of the channel and adjacent GSM LTE (*Long-Term Evolution*) network should be at least 200 kHz,
- the frequency separation between two adjacent blocks, UMTS operators should be at least 5 MHz,
- separation between the nearest GSM and UMTS frequency block should be at least 2.8 MHz,
- separation between the edge of the nearest GSM channel and adjacent WiMAX network should be at least 200 kHz.

Among the public networks have been taken into consideration the GSM 900 MHz (SC BTS (Single Carrier Base Transceiver Station) and MCBTS (Multi Carrier Base Transceiver Station)), UMTS (UTRA-FFD (Universal Terrestrial Radio Access - Frequency Division Duplex)), LTE (E-UTRA-FDD (Evolved Universal Terrestrial Radio Access-FDD)) and WiMAX networks.

2   Impact of Public Networks to GSM-R

Evolution of public mobile networks causes that in a radio environment of GSM-R can operate one or multiple mobile networks. Neighbour of GSM, UMTS or LTE network's signals will increase the level of interference on GSM-R receivers. The networks use three different technologies:

- GSM – narrowband 200 kHz channels,
- UMTS – blocks of 5 MHz bands,
- LTE – block of 5 MHz and 10 MHz.

In general, the public network can cause interference affecting the operation of the systems, including: GSM-R base stations, base stations of public network, GSM-R mobile stations, mobile stations of public networks. Detailed analysis of factors affecting on GSM-R network shows that the direct victims are GSM-R mobile stations. In the first half of 2014 the UIC database contains more than 660 interference cases of influence of public networks to GSM-R [12]. The analysis was conducted on 194 cases, due to GSM carriers, as only for this subset sufficient details were available. The number of UMTS900 interference cases is increasing but these are not sufficient to allow a statistical analysis.

European Commission, DG Communications Networks Content & Technology issued in 2013 a working document [11] reported the issues of registered GSM-R networks' interferences and actions taken into account to correct the problem. Also UIC report O-8736-2.0 [12] lists some registered cases of interference. Gathered data are given in Table 1.

Analyzing the number of registered cases of interference to the GSM-R network in each country allows to evaluate the scale of the problem. An unusual high number of cases in Germany and the Netherlands may not only be related to the length of the line working with GSM-R. In the case of the Netherlands it can be due to other reasons. Instatements of the representatives of the Dutch delegation made to the Commission they suggests emerging UMTS and LTE networks operating in the 900 MHz band in their country. In documents [12, 13] indicate broadband networks as a source of many new interferences.

3 Analysis of the Types of Interference on GSM-R

In general, the classification of causes of radio interference in adjacent networks can be classified according to:

- quality of the devices used radio-broadcasting, including:
  - effectiveness of filtration spurious emission,
  - antennas propagation characteristics of transmission,
- power of transmitters,
- geographic location of base stations interfering network,
- size of the separation between the interfering channels,
- levels of the interfering signal at the edge of cells (the quality of the radio coverage).

Referring to the research presented in the reports CEPTECC096 [4], ECC146 [6] and ECC162 [7], it can be seen that the most common occurrences of negative impact on public networks consist of GSM-R blocking and inter modulation occurring in parts of the receiving terminals GSM-R. In some cases, interference phenomenon also appears in the form of other effects, such as wide-band noise. These interference were observed during reception of low rather than high power of signal. As a result of the secauses, the receiver may have reduced sensitivity, blocking signals and overload. Transmitters of public mobile networks can cause such unwanted phenomena as unwanted emissions, inter modulation products, blocking effects [7, 8].

3.1 Out of Band Emission

Out-of-band (OOB) emissions are unwanted emissions that come outside channel bandwidth as a result of modulation process and non-linearity in the transmitter (excluding spurious emissions). OOB emissions are defined in ETSI TS 137 104 in Sect. 6.6 [10]. In the case discussed here, there is an unwanted emission at the interface of adjacent bands.

Table 1. Comparison of the number of registered cases of interference depending on the selected EU countries [own study]

Country	Total Rail lines 2012	GSM-R in operation[a]		Per cent of total network	Per cent of implementation	Number of cases	Analyzed cases (UIC)
		2012	Total planned				
Austria	9740	2125	3500	21,82 %	60,71 %	25	0
Belgium	3575	3000	unknown	83,92 %	unknown	43[b]	0
Finland	5919	5000	5000	84,47 %	100,00 %	≥9	9
France	29213	3500	16000	11,98 %	21,88 %	17[c]	7
Germany	41315	27597	32500	66,80 %	84,91 %	271[d]	132
Great Britain	15753	6000	15000	38,09 %	40,00 %	≥16	16
Netherlands	3061	3000	3000	98,01 %	100,00 %	200[e]	23
Norway	4087	3800	unknown	92,98 %	unknown	7	0
Spain	16026	2000	13000	12,48 %	15,38 %	≥3	3
Sweden	12821	10000	10300	78,00 %	97,09 %	0	0
Switzerland	3652	2050	2500	56,13 %	82,00 %	≥4	4

[a]FM54(15)07_ New Annex to inform about the questionnaire to CEPT Administrations on Interference into GSM-R.doc (http://www.cept.org/ecc/groups/ecc/wg-fm/fm-54/client/meeting-documents)

[b]Infrabel – SNCB DG Move ERA meeting Lille 5th November 2012. http://www.era.europa.eu/Document-Register/Pages/Presentation-workshop-5.11.2012.aspx

[c]ERA – Frequency workshop Lille – 5th November 2012 RFF interference status. http://www.era.europa.eu/Document-Register/Pages/Presentation-workshop-5.11.2012.aspx

[d]INTERFERENCE INTO GSM-R Country-Case Germany. Lille, 05.11.2012 http://www.era.europa.eu/Document-Register/Pages/Presentation-workshop-5.11.2012.aspx

[e]ProRail Interferences on GSM-R. 7a_Prorail1_Interference Workshop.pdf http://www.era.europa.eu/Document-Register/Pages/Presentation-workshop-5.11.2012.aspx

3.2 Receiver Blocking Due to High Input Powers

Receiver blocking is caused by a very strong signal out of channel appearing at the input of the receiver. The effect arises because the front end amplifiers run into compression as a result of the off channel signal. This often arises when a receiver and transmitter are run from the same site and the transmitter signal is exceedingly strong. When this occurs it has the effect of suppressing all other signals trying to pass through the amplifier, giving the effect of a reduction in gain.

It is difficult to estimate the blocking behaviour of a receiver because specified blocking values are aimed for CW signals as a blocker and serving cell signal is static. In practice, it was noticed that GSM-R mobile station starts to suffer from blocking when the public network signal level exceeds -40 dBm [7] or -35 dBm as it was concluded in the latest work [13]. It is therefore suggested to use the value of -40 dBm to describe blocking threshold value from GSM BTS interference to GSM-R mobile station. This means that GSM-R devices, despite the fact that they are consistent with the TSI and EIRENE requirements still can be exposed to interferences.

3.3 Intermodulation

Intermodulation (IM) is the amplitude modulation of signals containing two or more different frequencies in a system with nonlinearities. The intermodulation between each frequency component will form additional signals at frequencies that are not just at harmonic frequencies (integer multiples) of either, but also at the summed and frequencies and at the differences between them, of the original frequencies and at multiples of those summed frequencies and at differences between them. Intermodulation is caused by non-linear behaviour of the signal processing (physical equipment or even algorithms) being used.

In the case of the coexistence of GSM-R and public GSM network the two or more narrowband signals intermodulation cases occur for the GSM 900 network. The receiver, listening to a channel whose frequency is f_0, is interfered by intermodulation products when the following conditions are met: $f_0 = 2f_1 - f_2$ and $f_0 = 2f_2 - f_1$ and the strength of the signals f_1 and f_2 is above a given threshold.

In case of more than two adjacent GSM signals the order of IM products are the sum of the absolute values of the coefficients. In typical GSM site the order of IM is three. In such case we have

$$f_0 = f_1 + f_2 - f_3 \text{ and } f_0 = f_1 + f_3 - f_2 \text{ and } f_0 = f_2 + f_3 - f_1 \text{ and}$$
$$f_0 = 2f_1 - f_2 \text{ and } f_0 = 2f_1 - f_3 \text{ and } f_0 = 2f_2 - f_1 \text{ and}$$
$$f_0 = 2f_2 - f_3 \text{ and } f_0 = 2f_3 - f_1 \text{ and } f_0 = 2f_3 - f_2$$

Unfortunately, intermodulation products may interfere to form another band interference frequencies.

For the wideband networks such as UMTS, LTE or WiMax intermodulation products are a normal situation and a receiver generates it by mixing different spectral components corresponding to multiple GSM channels of 200 kHz.In practice, the vast majority of intermodulation cases are seen when the public BTS is closer than 250 m from the rail tracks.

4 Case Study

Considering the negative impact of the BTS signal GSM-R signal level should be assessed in the railway. The following case study considers a problem blocking GSM-R receiver. For this purpose, we can use the formulas for the attenuation of the signal in free space [24]. This assumption can be accepted without significant error in most of the cases for Cab-Radio and EDOR (ETCS Data Only Radio), because antennas of these devices are mounted at a height of 4 m. To calculate the free-space attenuation between isotropic antennas, the free-space basic transmission loss it can be used:

$$L_{bf} = 20\log\left(\frac{4\pi d}{\lambda}\right) \quad [dB]$$

where:

- L_{bf} – free-space basic transmission loss (dB),
- λ – wavelengt,
- d – distance from the BTS to the point of a railway track (λ and d are expressed in the same unit).

The equation can be converted to use more practical units of the frequency instead of the wavelength. Then we obtain

$$L_{bf} = 32.4 + 20\log f + 20\log d \quad [dB]$$

where:

- f – frequency (MHz),
- d – distance from the BTS to the point of a railway track (km).

The table shows the evaluation of the level of attenuation in free-space depending on the frequency and the distance. The calculation has been done for the initial channel in each frequency range.

In Table 2 it can be seen that for the smallest attenuation is the lowest frequency channel and a shorter distance. When both distance and frequency are increasing. For our calculations the attenuation reaches the value approximately 90 dB.

Public network operators, in order to offer a high quality of service, put their BTS in close proximity to the railroad tracks, or increase the transmission power. As a result, the signal level near the railroad tracks is high, and at the same time does not exceed in Polish conditions, the value of 7 V/m.

Table 2. The effect of distance on the growth attenuation in free-space for initial channel of each band [own study]

| Operator | Network | Band - DL [MHz] | | Distance to a railway track [km] | | | | | | | |
		from	to	0.1	0.2	0.3	0.4	0.5	0.6	0.7	0.8
P4	GSM900, UMTS900	925.1	930.1	71.72	77.74	81.27	83.76	85.70	87.29	88.63	89.79
Aero2	UMTS900	930.1	935.1	71.77	77.79	81.31	83.81	85.75	87.33	88.67	89.83
Polkomtel	GSM900	935.1	937.9	71.82	77.84	81.36	83.86	85.80	87.38	88.72	89.88
T-Mobile Polska	GSM900	937.9	942.3	71.84	77.86	81.39	83.88	85.82	87.41	88.75	89.90
Polkomtel	GSM900	942.3	948.5	71.88	77.90	81.43	83.92	85.86	87.45	88.79	89.95
T-Mobile Polska	GSM900, UMTS900	948.5	953.1	71.94	77.96	81.48	83.98	85.92	87.50	88.84	90.00
Orange	GSM900, UMTS900	953.1	959.9	71.98	78.00	81.53	84.02	85.96	87.55	88.88	90.04

The Fig. 1 shows the results of calculations of the signal's strength from public BTS for the closest GSM frequency (925.1 MHz) depending on the distance from the BTS and transmitted power (e.i.r.p.).

Following the guidelines indicated in the EIRENE SRS [19] the values concerning coverage and speed-limitations. The minimum values of the coverage probability of 95 % are based on a coverage level of 38.5 dBuV/m (−98 dBm) for voice and non-safety critical data. The coverage probability of 95 % are based on a coverage level between 41.5 dBuV/m and 44.5 dBuV/m (−95 dBm and −92 dBm) on lines with ETCS levels 2/3 for speeds above 220 km/h and lower than or equal to 280 km/h. The EIRENE minimum coverage includes 3 dB margin for cable loss, plus 3 dB margin for other effects, e.g. aging, and additional losses for splitters or filters. The value 6 dB is defined in order to ensure that the level at the input of the receiver will never be lower than the reference sensitivity level of the receiver.

As a result of the requirements set for area coverage, it can be seen that, for example, if the power emitted by the BTS's transmitter is equal 60 dBm and the channel is close to GSM-R band (e.g. 925.1 MHz in Table 3), the signal level on a railway track which is at a distance of 500 mequals-25.7 dBm. The value is higher by 72.3 dB than the expected level of GSM-R signal (e.g. −98 dBm). This value can lead to the blockage of the receiver of GSM-R.

5 Conclusion

The article presents the problem of interfering the public mobile network to GSM-R network. The relatively small distance between BTS location and high transmission power increases the likelihood of interference to GSM-R network. On the other hand, public operators do not exceed the rules on transmission powers, the refore public operators could not be obligated to the reorganization of the network near the railroad or for reduction of the transmission power of their transmitters, even if it leads to a loss of communication of passengers traveling by train.

The study of works [12] and [28] indicate that the newer radio GSM-R modems using improved filtration systems due to ETSI specification TS 102 933-1 [26] and TS 102 933-2 [27] at least version 1.2.1 are more resistant to the effects of blocking and intermodulation than the existing solutions. The use of new modems GSM-R allow to increase resistance by approx. 10 dB. The collected documentation contained in the References to this article mentions a number of actions that could mitigate the impact of public networks for GSM-R. These are filters in public operators' BTS, improved GSM-R coverage, fine tuning on engineering parameters, frequency band management, usage of ER-GSM band (restricted to some applications).

Finally, the solution to the problem of interfering with the network can be achieved only with effort on both sides.

References

1. SM.329-10 Unwanted emissions in the spurious domain. Recommendation ITU-R Geneva (2010)
2. Lille. http://www.era.europa.eu/Document-Register/Pages/Presentations-2ndWorkshop-11.11.2013.aspx. Accessed on 11 November 2013
3. CEPT Report 41 Compatibility between LTE and WiMAX operating within the bands 880-915 MHz/925-960 MHz and 1710-1785 MHz/1805-1880 MHz (900/1800 MHz bands) and systems operating in adjacent bands
4. CEPT ECC Report 096. Compatibility between UMTS 900/1800 and systems operating in adjacent bands. Krakow March 2007
5. CEPT ECC Report 127: The impact of receiver standards on spectrum management. Cordoba October 2008
6. CEPT ECC Report 146: Compatibility between GSM MCBTS and other services operating in the 900 and 1800 MHz frequency bands June 2010
7. CEPT ECC Report 162: Practical mechanism to improve the compatibility between GSM-R and public mobile networks and guidance on practical coordination May 2011
8. CEPT ECC Report 229: Guidance for improving coexistence between GSM-R and MFCN. Working Document CEPT 15 December 2014
9. Council Directive 87/372/EEC of 25 June 1987 on the frequency bands to be reserved for the coordinated introduction of public pan-European cellular digital land-based mobile communications in the Community
10. ETSI: TS 137 104: E-UTRA. UTRA and GSM/EDGE; Multi-Standard Radio (MSR) Base Station (BS) radio transmission and reception
11. RADIO SPECTRUM COMMITTEE: GSM-R Interferences – Contributions from delegations and ERA on issues. Statistics and best practices as a follow-up to the discussion in RSC#42. Working Document. European Commission. DG Communications Networks Content & Technology. Brussels, 26 February 2013
12. UIC O-8740: Report on the UIC interference field test activities in UK. September 2013
13. UIC O-8736-2.0: UIC Assessment report on GSM-R current and future radio environment; version of July 2014
14. Response to Information Notice 10/84. Licensing Regime for GSM for Railway Operations. Commission for Communications Regulation. Dublin 29 November 2011
15. 2011/251/EU: Commission Implementing Decision of 18 April 2011 amending Decision 2009/766/EC on the harmonization of the 900 MHz and 1800 MHz frequency bands for terrestrial systems capable of providing pan-European electronic communications services in the Community (notified under document C(2011) 2633) Text with EEA relevance
16. Directive 2009/114/EC of the European Parliament and of the Council of 16 September 2009 amending Council Directive 87/372/EEC on the frequency bands to be reserved for the coordinated introduction of public pan-European cellular digital land-based mobile communications in the Community (Text with EEA relevance)
17. 2009/766/EC: Commission Decision of 16 October 2009 on the harmonization of the 900 MHz and 1800 MHz frequency bands for terrestrial systems capable of providing pan-European electronic communications services in the Community (notified under document C(2009) 7801
18. Directive 2008/57/EC of the European Parliament and of the Council Of 17 June 2008 on the interoperability of the rail system within the Community

19. EIRENE: System Requirements Specification. European Integrated Railway Radio Enhanced Network. GSM-R Operators Group. UIC CODE 951. Version 15.3.0. Paris March 2012

20. ETSI: TS 100 910: Technical Specification. Digital cellular telecommunications system (Phase 2 +). Radio Transmission and Reception (3GPP TS 05.05 version 8.20.0 Release 1999) European Telecommunications Standards Institute (2005–2011)

21. SUBSET-093: ERTMS/ETCS – Class 1. GSM-R Interfaces. Class 1 Requirements. ISSUE: 2.3.0. 10 October 2005

22. ETSI: TS 100 607-1: Technical Specification. Digital cellular telecommunications system (Phase 2 +). Mobile Station (MS) conformance specification. Part 1: Conformance specification. (GSM 11.10-1 version 8.3.0) European Telecommunications Standards Institute (2001-2009)

23. ETSI: TS 100 911: Technical Specification. Digital cellular telecommunications system (Phase 2 +). Radio subsystem link control. (3GPP TS 05.08 version 8.23.0 Release 1999) European Telecommunications Standards Institute (2005–2011)

24. ITU-R P.525-2 ITU-R Recommendation. Calculation of free-space attenuation (1994)

25. 2012/88/EU Commission Decision of 25 January 2012 on the technical specification for interoperability relating to the control-command and signalling subsystems of the trans-European rail system (notified under document C(2012) 172)

26. ETSI TS 102 933-1 Railway Telecommunications. GSM-R improved receiver parameters. Part 1: Requirements for radio reception

27. ETSI TS 102 933-2: Railway Telecommunications (RT).GSM-R improved receiver parameters. Part 2: Radio conformance testing. V1.3.1 (2014-08)

28. CG-GSM-R(13)035 Bundesnetzagentur; Coordination between UMTS and GSM-R

29. Lewiński, A., Toruń, A., Perzyński, T.: Risk analysis as a basic method of safety transmission system certification. In: Mikulski, J. (ed.) TST 2011. CCIS, vol. 239, pp. 47–53. Springer, Heidelberg (2011)

30. Lewiński, A., Perzyński, T., Toruń, A.: The analysis of open transmission standards in railway control and management. In: Mikulski, J. (ed.) TST 2012. CCIS, vol. 329, pp. 10–17. Springer, Heidelberg (2012)

31. Siergiejczyk, M., Krzykowska, K., Rosiński, A.: Reliability assessment of cooperation and replacement of surveillance systems in air traffic. In: Zamojski, W., Mazurkiewicz, J., Sugier, J., Walkowiak, T., Kacprzyk, J. (eds.) Proceedings of the Ninth International Conference on DepCoS-RELCOMEX. AISC, vol. 286, pp. 403–412. Springer, Heidelberg (2014)

32. Siergiejczyk, M., Pawlik, M., Gago, S.: Safety of the new control command European System. In: Nowakowski, T., Młyńczak, M., Jodejko-Pietruczuk, A., Werbińska-Wojciechowska, S. (eds.) The Monograph Safety and Reliability: Methodology and Applications - Proceedings of the European Safety and Reliability Conference ESREL 2014, pp. 635–642. CRC Press/Balkema, London (2015)

33. Gorczyca, P., Mikulski, J., Białoń, A.: Wirelles local network to record the railway traffic control equipment data. Adv. Electr. Electron. Eng 5(1–2), 128–131 (2011)

Rail Traffic Remote Control Systems Within the Areas Affected by the Occurrence of Mining Damage and Railway Safety

Beata Grabowska–Bujna[1(✉)], Sonia Wieczorek[1], and Jerzy Mikulski[2]

[1] Jastrzębska Spółka Kolejowa sp.z o.o., 40-335 Jastrzębie Zdrój, Poland
{bbujna, swieczorek}@jsk.pl
[2] University of Economics in Katowice, 40-287 Katowice, Poland
jerzy.mikulski@ue.katowice.pl

Abstract. Current railway with the use of the whole automation industry news should primarily be safe. This rule applies mainly to those systems which are directly related to the management of railway traffic. The difficulty of selecting appropriate rail traffic control systems occurs when the railway infrastructure is located within the areas affected by mining operations. From the point of view of railway safety in general, Railway Board identifies the results of the mining damage and its impact on railway infrastructure as a potential risk, which can lead to the accident. The aim of this article is to indicate the methods of identification, analysis and risk assessment of rail traffic remote control systems installation process in areas affected by the occurrence of mining damage in terms of safety improvement.

Keywords: Railway traffic control · Mining damages · Safety · Risk assessment

1 Introduction

Modern railways, using innovative solutions of the automation, should be primarily safe. Despite numerous other premises, which indicate the legitimacy of implementing modern transport systems, the safety should always rank the first. This rule applies in particular to those systems, which are directly related to the railway traffic management. A difficulty to select an appropriate railway traffic control system appears, when an entrepreneur invests in the areas subject to mining damage occurrence. The railway infrastructure situated in areas of mines operation, frequently a few decades old, not modernized for years, is many times exposed additionally to the influence of mining damage. From generally understood railway safety point of view, the effects of mining damage occurrence and its influence on the railway infrastructure are identified by a railway manager as a potential hazard, which can result in an accident.

The basic objective of the paper consists of showing the methods of identification, analysis and assessment of the risk related to the process of computer railway traffic control system installation in the areas of mining damage occurrence from the safety point of view.

J. Mikulski (Ed.): TST 2015, CCIS 531, pp. 264–273, 2015.
DOI: 10.1007/978-3-319-24577-5_26

2 Mining Damage to the Railway Infrastructure as a Potential Hazard (Risk)

Field observations and measurements, which have been carried out by railway managers for many years, show that the failure frequency of all elements of superstructure and substructure in the areas subject to the mining damage influence is 3 times higher than the number of failures in other areas of the network with comparable load and design parameters. It is obviously related to incurring additional expenditure on the infrastructure, but primarily results in the lack of maintaining an acceptable safety level of services rendered by railway entrepreneurs, both carriers and managers.

Under the influence of mining damage (continuous, discontinuous deformations and para-seismic influences) the entire railway infrastructure gets damaged. Typical types of damage for individual groups of railway structures are presented below:

(a) railway superstructure - lateral buckling of the track, uplifts, tightening and breaking of rail butt joints, degradation of sleepers, base plates and rail bonds, buckling of points and crossings geometry,

(b) buildings (signal boxes) - mainly fractures - skew, horizontal in ceilings, side walls, depression cones under the building,

(c) other structures (bridges, flyovers, culverts, embankments, power supply equipment and also traffic protection and control equipment) - above-standard and non-uniform declines, origination of cones under culverts, opening of expansion joints, flooded end walls, displacements of bearing parts, stresses of midpoint anchoring ropes, fractured foundation heads, inclinations of signals, catenary supports, overhead transmission lines, displacement of supports, breaking cable and communication routes by excessive stressing of conductors.

Expenditures on removing effects of mining damage to the railway infrastructure for the selected area subject to the greatest influence of mining operations in the Jastrzębska Spółka Kolejowa Sp. z o.o./Jastrzębie Railway Company, Ltd./(JSK) comprising 120 km of tracks are presented in Fig. 1.

The data presented in Fig. 1 reflect only and exclusively the expenditures actually incurred during the works for mining damage effects removal in the specified JSK railway infrastructure together with buying out land and preparing the necessary documentation. It should be remembered that the same infrastructure is also subject to the current maintenance in accordance with provisions of relevant instructions and is modernised, repaired and replaced according to plans resulting from annual and periodic inspections.

Figure 2 presents a comparison of individual cost types calculated per 1 km of track (including points and crossings) for 120 km. The graph shows that the expenditures on mining damage effects removing in the studied area of JSK have the highest share in the group of costs related to the technical condition of the railway infrastructure.

However, these are not all costs incurred by the infrastructure manager. Because of poor technical condition of the railway line permanent speed restrictions for train driving are introduced, even to 10 km/h, cable routes are frequently broken,

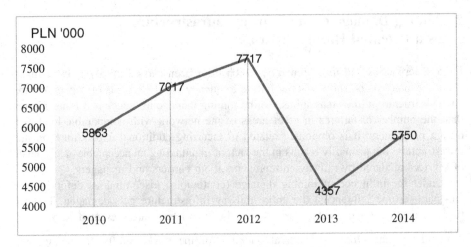

Fig. 1. The amount of expenditure incurred due to removing mining damage effects in the years 2010–2014 in the Jastrzębska Spółka Kolejowa for the area subject to the largest influences of mining operations, comprising around 120 km of tracks [own study].

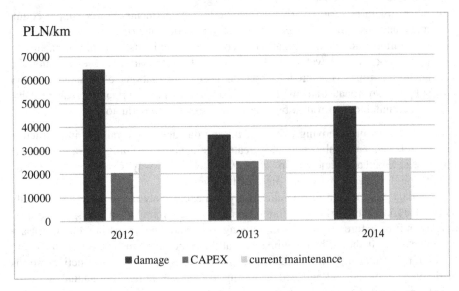

Fig. 2. Comparison of expenditures for various cost types related to the poor technical condition of infrastructure in the Jastrzębska Spółka Kolejowa. incurred in the years 2012–2014 for the area subject to the largest effects of mining operations, comprising approx. 120 km of tracks, calculated per 1 km (including points and crossings) [own study].

which results in the lack of communication and in the fact that the train traffic is carried out with so-called special instructions. The infrastructure exposed to the mining damage requires a larger number of inspections, which prevent potential hazards in the train traffic.

Additional difficulties occur also during performance of repairs related to removal of damage to the infrastructure. Such works reduce the line capacity, make a timely arrival of the rolling stock to loading stations difficult. In places with a high inclination per mille defects in the head of rail frequently occur due to high contact stresses, the friction between wheels and the rail and also to wheels spinning. Most frequent of them include cracks, lamellar scaling, fractures and local pits of the rail surface and spinned out places.

All these factors generate additional costs both for the railway manager (extended working time in control sections and signal boxes, above-standard inspections) and for railway carriers (additional pushing engines for heavy-weight trains). Costs are one of a few aspects of mining damage effects occurrence. There are already methods in place, which allow estimating them, e.g. the method for forecasting costs of damage caused by mining (PKSE) [1]. This method utilizes:

- statistics of carried out repairs and applied preventive measures against damage as well as costs with arrears,
- geological-mining data on carried out and planned mining as well as results of caused by it surface deformations measurements and calculations,
- characteristic of surface development and the assessment of resistance to deformation.

The influence on safety is another aspect of mining damage to railway infra- structure occurrence. That forces carrying out specific actions to improve safety.

The mining damage occurrence and its influence on the railway infrastructure may be identified by a railway manager as a potential hazard, which can result in an accident.

A hazard defined in such a way will be only one of many elements of the hazards or events list (hazards register), which are the input for the manager to carry out a risk analysis taking into account all aspects of company operation (organizational, eco- nomic, technical).

A railway manager keeps the mandatory hazards register in accordance with the Safety Management System (SMS) and this is a document (database) comprising information on identified potential hazards, sources of those hazards and safety mea- sures related to those hazards. Table 1 presents an example of the hazards register.

The manager, within its structures, shall appoint a team, which evaluates individual hazards by means of the FMEA method (*Failure Mode and Effects Analysis*) using three parameters [2]:

- W - probability of occurrence,
- Z - ease of detection,
- S - effect of hazard.

In Poland tables have been prepared for each of parameters, assigning values ranging from 1 to 10 - Table 2.

Table 1. Hazards register [own study]

Hazard type	Source/hazard reason	Risk valuation method	Influence on the system (safety level)	Measures/actions eliminating or mitigating the risk	Responsible for risk management and supervision
Mining damage	Mining plants operation	FMEA	Large	- Increased monitoring of areas subject to damage (additional inspections) - Speed restrictions - Obtaining from mining plants the information on the ground subsidence forecast in periods not shorter than 3 months - Preparing the action plan in case of damage occurrence - Introduction of transport systems eliminating the amount of railway equipment, buildings and structures exposed to the mining damage	Technical department manager, traffic engineering manager

Table 2. Parameters used to estimate the risk (hazard) in Jastrzębska Spółka Kolejowa [own study]

Occurrence probability - W	Frequency (1 case/travelled train-kilometres)*	Score
Low probability of hazard occurrence. The danger of hazard occurrence is practically excluded	1/220,000	1
Small probability of hazard occurrence. Hazard reasons occur very seldom	1/195 000 1/170 000	2 3
Probability of hazard occurrence is medium or high. Hazard reasons occur occasionally and do not affect the process	1/145,000 1/120,000 1/95,000	4 5 6
Possibility of hazard occurrence is high. Hazard reasons occur regularly	1/75,000 1/55,000	7 8
Possibility of hazard occurrence is very high. It is almost certain, that a given hazard will occur	1/35,000 1/15,000	9, 10

(*Continued*)

Table 2. (*Continued*)

Occurrence probability - W	Frequency (1 case/travelled train-kilometres)*	Score
Ease of detection - Z		**Score**
Very high probability of hazard detection. Determination of error cause is certain		1
High probability of hazard detection. The error cause is determined based on known factors		2, 3
Normal probability of hazard detection. Determination of error cause is based on measurable characteristics		4, 5, 6
Small probability of hazard detection. Determination of error cause is very difficult		7, 8
Very small probability of hazard detection. Detection of error cause is impossible		9, 10
Effect of hazard - S		**Score**
Effects of hazard occurrence are immaterial for the safety level and are not related to costs		1
Effects of hazard occurrence may be small and result only in insignificant lowering of the safety level and in costs: under item 2 to EUR 10,000 and under item 3 to EUR 50,000		2, 3
Effects of hazard occurrence may be pretty significant and result in lowering of the safety level and in costs: under item 4 to EUR 100,000, under item 5 to EUR 250,000 and under item 6 to EUR 500,000		4, 5, 6
Effects of hazard occurrence may be serious and result in significant lowering of the safety level and in costs: under item 7 to EUR 750,000 and under item 8 to EUR 1,000,000		7, 8
Effects of hazard occurrence may be very serious and result in drastic lowering of the safety level and in costs: under item 9 to EUR 2,000,000 and under item 10 to more than EUR 2,000,000		9, 10

* "Frequency" ranges refer to the transport work (amount of train-kilometers) performed by carriers on railway lines of Jastrzębska Spółka Kolejowa

For an identified hazard the values should be assigned from the above table and the risk level calculated acc. to the formula:

$$R = W * Z * S$$

The risk level is assessed based on the risk matrix – Table 3.

Table 3. Risk matrix – the level of risk acceptability [3]

Risk class	Risk – R	Risk level
1	R ≤ 120	ACCEPTABLE
2	120 < R ≤ 150	TOLERATED
3	R > 150	NOT ACCEPTABLE

Table 4 presents the risk estimation for the mining damage occurrence in a defined railway area of JSK for around 120 km (including points and crossings).

Table 4. Risk estimation in the Jastrzębska Spółka Kolejowa. by means of FMEA method for the hazard (risk) – mining damage occurrence [own study].

Hazard type	Occurrence probability W	Ease of detection Z	Effect of hazard S	Risk level - R	Recommended actions	Actions taken	W	Z	S	R
Mining damage occurrence	7	6	8	336						

As it results from Table 4 the risk of mining damage occurrence acc. to the JSK assessment for specific area is not acceptable. The company must define the scenario of proceeding to reduce the risk level and after starting the actions – to redetermine its level. In the case of obtaining again an unsatisfactory risk level, the company must undertake additional actions. If a satisfactory risk level is achieved, the procedure will be finished.

3   Safety of Modern Railway Traffic Control Systems

When analyzing modern railway traffic control systems from the safety point of view, it is necessary to start from absolutely observed *"fail-safe"* rule, i.e. a failure in a safe direction. This means that the system after a failure automatically switches to a safe state and causes a limitation of accessibility. Each system failure is detectable and does not cause dangerous states. For remote systems of railway traffic control this rule applies both to hardware and software [4].

Safety levels for the above systems are determined based on the failure intensity, so-called SIL (*Safety Integrity Level*).

There are five safety levels:

– Level 4 - very high (*fail safe*),
– Level 3 - high (*high integrity*),
– Level 2 - medium (*safety involved*),
– Level 1 - low (*low integrity*),
– Level 0 - *non safety related.*

The railway traffic control equipment should meet level 4 and the reliability parameters have been defined in standard EN 50129. All standards binding in Poland for control systems (equipment) and adapted to the EU standards are:

- PN-EN 50126 – Specification and demonstration of Reliability, Availability, Maintainability, Safety [5],
- PN-EN 50128 - Software for railway control and protection systems; the standard applies to the acceptance of sub-systems, which may operate within the control and protection system,
- PN-EN 50129 - Safety related electronic systems for signalling; the document defines requirements related to the acceptance and approval of safe electronic systems (including sub-systems and equipment) in the field of railway traffic control,
- EN 50159-1 - Safety related communication in closed transmission systems,
- EN 50159-2 - Safety related communication in open transmission systems,
- EN 50125-3 - Environmental conditions for equipment. Equipment for signalling and telecommunications (Part 3) [6].

The railway traffic control equipment and systems in the field of safety and reliability should feature as small as possible number of failures, and in the case of their occurrence the state of system and equipment should be safe. In addition, the most frequently used index for railway traffic control equipment and systems is the mean time between failures (MTBF), the mean time to the first failure (MTTF), the mean repair time (MRT) and the technical readiness coefficient.

From the railway system safety point of view, in the case of analysis of specific equipment, structures, materials, products or IT systems used and operated in the railway infrastructure, there are numerous provisions and legal regulations in place, which determine activities of manufacturers, suppliers and maintenance companies.

Possession by the manufacturer of an indefinite certificate of approval for type operation for the given product is a condition, which must be absolutely met. Strict procedures are in place to be followed to obtain the certificate in question [7]. Based on the regulations in question, to obtain an indefinite certificate of approval for type operation for the remote railway traffic control, which is a component of the structural control sub-system and is the first piece of a new type equipment for one manufacturer, it is necessary to:

- obtain from the authorized body (indicated by the President of the Office of Rail Transport in the Public Information Bulletin) a certificate of conformity with type, which confirms a positive result of technical tests carried out for the system by the authorized body,
- file an application to the President of the Office of Rail Transport to issue *a certificate of approval for type operation for a specific period of time*, to carry out operational tests of the system; the application should contain the name and registered office of the company, the place and date of application preparation, the kind and type of equipment (structure), the signature of person authorized to represent the company; the certificate of conformity with type shall be attached to the application,
- having obtained the certificate of approval for type operation for a specific period of time, to sign an agreement with the entity, on whose site operational tests will take place, carried out by the authorized body in accordance with the schedule,

- having carried out operational tests, to obtain from the entity, on whose site the tests were carried out, *an operational opinion for specific type of equipment (structure)*; the operational opinion is indispensable for the authorized body to give *a technical opinion* and ultimately to issue again *the certificate of conformity with type*,
- file an application to the President of the Office of Rail Transport to issue *an indefinite certificate of approval for type operation*.
- Other procedures have been specified for structures or equipment, for which certificates of approval for operation have been issued before 31 March 2014. In each case, the obtained document guarantees to the user that the system meets all necessary safety requirements, stipulated in the Act on Rail Transport and in other regulations.

The manager, undertaking actions consisting in modernization of railway traffic protection and control equipment in the areas of mining damage occurrence, expects an improvement to safety and a reduction of the risk level in various areas of his activity. The equipment related to the railway traffic management will be replaced by the manager with a modern computer system for railway traffic control. However, it is necessary to remember, that neither the fail-safe rule nor a high SIL level necessary for remote railway traffic control systems guarantee a full safety and ensure total elimination of accidents and incidents.

The railway manager, according to the needs, technical conditions and financial capabilities, must analyze the importance of the "process change", consisting in implementing and commissioning a modern railway traffic control system in areas of mining damage occurrence. After a preliminary assessment of the aforementioned change and determination, whether it affects safety, the railway manager has a duty to analyze the change importance through:

(a) defining the change (change description),
(b) justification of the opinion on classification of the change importance based on the following criteria [8]:

- effects of system failure: a reliable worst-case scenario in the case of assessed system failure, taking into account the existence of protective barriers outside the system,
- innovation used at the change introduction: the criterion includes innovations related both to the whole railway sector and only to the organization introducing the change,
- complexity of the change,
- monitoring: incapability to monitor the introduced change throughout the whole system life and to make appropriate interventions,
- reversibility of the change: incapability to return to the system prior to the change,
- additionally, the assessment of change importance taking into account all recently made changes of the assessed system, which were safety related and were not assessed as significant,

(c) description of the organization, definition, scope, functions and interfaces of the analyzed system,

(d) carrying out the risk analysis acc. to a specific method,
(e) determination of safety measures, i.e. preventive and adjusting actions to identify
      hazards.

As it may be noticed, the analysis of risk, which is e.g. effects of mining damage occurrence, is only one of numerous elements of assessment of potential change impact on the railway system safety.

4   Conclusion

Safety is the priority on modern railways. Regulations in force in this field are a tool for railway market participants in the risk management process. This process is subject to continuous modifications and adaptations to the legislation in force, therefore a great involvement in the process of management and staff is required.

The investor-manager, operating under unstable market conditions, taking into account an area difficult in terms of geology, in which an investment is to be implemented, must obtain optimum benefits at an acceptable risk level. The available methods for risk identification, analysis and assessment allow effectively to adapt the corrective actions to identified hazards and to determine properly the change importance in a specific process. The infrastructure manager using the risk management has a possibility to reconcile two frequently divergent objectives, i.e. the safety improvement and the reduction of operational costs.

References

1. Gruchalik, P., Kowalski, A.: Metodyka identyfikacji i szacowania potencjalnych szkód ekologicznych na terenach górniczych dla potrzeb wspomagania zarządzania terenami przekształconymi antropologicznie, No. 62, pp. 31–36. Zeszyty Naukowe Politechniki Śląskiej, Gliwice (2012)
2. Analiza znaczenia zmiany wraz z analizą ryzyka. Training materials for the company Jastrzębska Spółka Kolejowa Sp. z o.o., p. 27. Jastrzębie Zdrój (2014)
3. Chruzik, K., Drzewiecki, A., Wachnik, R.: Wykorzystanie metody FMEA do oceny ryzyka w MMS. Zeszyty Naukowe Politechniki Śląskiej, Seria: Transport, no. 81, p. 21, Gliwice (2013)
4. http://www.wikipedia.pl. Accessed 15 January 2015
5. PN-EN 50126:2002 (U) Railway Applications. Specification and demonstration of Reliability, Availability, Maintainability, Safety (RAMS). Part 1: Basic requirements and general purpose processes (2002)
6. Leksykon Terminów Kolejowych, p. 27. Wydawnictwo KOW media&marketing, Warszawa (2011)
7. The Act of 28 March 2003 on the Rail Transport (2003), EC (European Community): Directive 2008/57/EC of the European Parliament and of the Council (2008) and 2004/49/EC of the European Parliament and of the Council (2004)
8. Commission Regulation (EC) 352/2009 on the adoption of a common safety method on risk evaluation and assessment as referred to in Article 6(3)(a) of Directive 2004/49/EC of the European Parliament and of the Council, L 108/4 (2009)

Problems of Maritime Radio Systems Integration with E-navigation

Karol Korcz[✉]

Gdynia Maritime University, 81-225 Gdynia, Poland
korcz@am.gdynia.pl

Abstract. One of the fundamental elements of e-navigation will be a data communication network based on the maritime radio communication infrastructure. The article presents the identified needs of the future maritime users of e-navigation, the current capabilities for achieving these needs within the GMDSS and discusses correlated key elements of the modernization of the GMDSS.

Keywords: E-navigation · GMDSS · Maritime radio communication

1 Introduction

The Maritime Safety Committee (MSC), the technical committee of the International Maritime Organization (IMO), in 2006 decided to include in the work programmes of the Safety of Navigation (NAV) and Radio communications and Search and Rescue (COMSAR) Sub-Committees of the IMO, a high priority item on "Development of an E-navigation Strategy". It needs to be noted that the development of e-navigation is an ongoing process and that the "Development of an E-navigation Strategy Implementation Plan", as a next step of the project, was included in the work programmes of the COMSAR, NAV and Standards of Training and Watchkeeping (STW) Sub-Committees by MSC in 2008.

Without a doubt, one of the fundamental elements of e-navigation will be a data communication network based on the maritime radio communication infrastructure. Taking into account the above, in 2009 the MSC Committee agreed to include in the COMSAR Sub-Committee work programme an item on "Scoping Exercise to Establish the Need for a Review of the Elements and Procedures of the Global Maritime Distress and Safety Systems(GMDSS)".

In the aftermath of this work in 2012 MSC agreed to include in agenda of the COMSAR, NAV and STW Sub-Committees a high priority item on "Review and Modernization of the Global Maritime Distress and Safety System (GMDSS)", with a target completion year of 2017, assigning the COMSAR Sub-Committee as the coordinating organ.

After the changes in the organization of the work of IMO subcommittees at the end of 2013, the issue of "Review and Modernization of the Global Maritime Distress and Safety System" is, just as the issue of "Development of an E-navigation Strategy Implementation Plan", the competence of the new IMO Sub-Committee on Safety of Navigation,

© Springer International Publishing Switzerland 2015
J. Mikulski (Ed.): TST 2015, CCIS 531, pp. 274–283, 2015.
DOI: 10.1007/978-3-319-24577-5_27

Communication and Search and Rescue (NCSR), resulting from connections of the NAV and COMSAR Sub-Committees. So, at present the problems of proper integration of the maritime radio communication systems with the e-navigation is the matter of the same subcommittee of the IMO.

2 Global Maritime Distress and Safety System

In 1988, the Conference of Contracting Governments to the Safety of Life at Sea (SOLAS) Convention on the Global Maritime Distress and Safety System (GMDSS), adopted amendments to the SOLAS Convention concerning radio communications for the GMDSS. These amendments entered into force on 1 February 1992. On 1 February 1999 the GMDSS has become fully implemented for all SOLAS ships.

2.1 GMDSS Fundamentals

The original concept of the GMDSS is that search and rescue authorities ashore, as well as shipping in the immediate vicinity of the ship in distress, will be rapidly alerted to a distress incident so they can assist in a coordinated search and rescue operation (SAR operation) with the minimum delay. The system also provides for urgency and safety communications and the promulgation of maritime safety information (MSI).

Functional Requirements. The GMDSS lays down nine principal communications functions which all ships, while at sea, need to be able to perform [1]:

– transmitting ship-to-shore distress alerts by at least two separate and independent means, each using a different radio communication service;
– receiving shore-to-ship distress alerts;
– transmitting and receiving ship-to-ship distress alerts;
– transmitting and receiving search and rescue co-ordinating communication;
– transmitting and receiving on-scene communication;
– transmitting and receiving signals for locating;
– transmitting and receiving maritime safety information;
– transmitting and receiving general radio communication to/from shore based radio systems or networks;
– transmitting and receiving bridge-to-bridge communication.

   Distress alerting is the rapid and successful reporting of a distress incident to a unit which can provide or co-ordinate assistance. This would be a rescue co-ordination centre (RCC) or another ship in the vicinity. When an alert is received by an RCC, normally via a coast station or a land earth station, the RCC will relay the alert to SAR units and to ships in the vicinity of the distress incident.

   Search and rescue (SAR) co-ordinating communications are the communications necessary for the co-ordination of ships and aircraft participating in a search and rescue operation following a distress alert, and include communications between RCCs and any on-scene co-ordinator (OSC) in the area of the distress incident.

   On-scene communications are the communications between the ship in distress and assisting units relate to the provision of assistance to the ship or the rescue of survivors.

Locating is the finding of a ship/aircraft in distress or its survival craft or survivors.

Ships need to be provided with up-to-date navigational warnings and meteorological warnings and forecasts and other urgent maritime safety information (MSI). MSI is made available by *Promulgation of MSI* by the responsible administration means.

General radio communications in the GMDSS are those communications between ship stations and shore-based communication networks which concern the management and operation of the ship and may have an impact on its safety.

Bridge-to-bridge communications are inter-ship safety communications conducted from the position from which the ship is normally navigated.

GMDSS Sea Areas. Radio communication services incorporated in the GMDSS system have individual limitations with respect to the geographical coverage and services provided. The range of communication equipment carried on board the ship is determined not by the size of the ship or she's type but by the area in which she operates.

Four sea areas for communications within the GMDSS have been specified by the IMO. These areas are designated as follows [1] – see Fig. 1:

- sea area A1 – an area within the radiotelephone coverage of at least one VHF coast station in which continuous DSC alerting is available;
- sea area A2 – an area, excluding sea area A1, within the radiotelephone coverage of at least one MF coast station in which continuous DSC alerting is available;
- sea area A3 – an area, excluding sea areas A1 and A2, within the coverage of an Inmarsat geostationary satellite in which continuous alerting is available;
- sea area A4 – an area outside sea areas A1, A2 and A3 (that is the polar regions north and south of 70° latitude, outside the Inmarsat satellite coverage area).

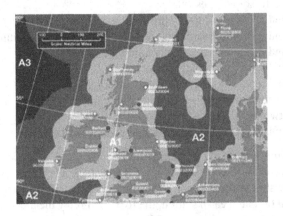

Fig. 1. Sample the limits of sea areas [1]

Equipment Carriage Requirements. In accordance with SOLAS Convention every ship shall be provided with radio installations capable of complying with the functional requirements (see above) throughout its intended voyage. The type of radio equipment required to be carried by a ship is determined by the sea areas (see above) through which a ship travels on its voyage.

Order of Communications Priority. All stations in the maritime mobile service and the maritime mobile-satellite service shall be capable of offering four levels of priority in the following order [2]:

(1) distress communications,
(2) urgency communications,
(3) safety communications,
(4) other communications.

The transmission of *a distress call* indicates that a mobile unit or person is threatened by grave and imminent danger and requires immediate assistance.

The urgency call indicates that the calling station has a very urgent message to transmit concerning the safety of a mobile unit or a person (for example medical advice or medical assistance).

The safety call indicates that the calling station has an important navigational or meteorological warning to transmit.

The other communication means any communication beyond distress, urgency and safety communications, for example *public correspondence* (any telecommunication which the offices and stations must, by reason of their being at the disposal of the public, accept for transmission).

2.2 Current Status of the GMDSS

Since implementation of the Global Maritime Distress and Safety System (GMDSS) in 1999 some technical changes have occurred. One of the most important changes has concerned the maritime satellite system Inmarsat. In 1999, Inmarsat became the first intergovernmental organization to be transformed into a private company. It caused that at present Inmarsat is recognised as a leader in global mobile satellite communication field.

In 2007, the new Geostationary Search and Rescue System (GEOSAR) has been introduced by Cospas-Sarsat organization as completion of the Low-altitude Earth Orbit System (LEOSAR). These two Cospas-Sarsat systems (GEOSAR and LEOSAR) create the complementary systems assisting search and rescue (SAR) operations.

It is also worth to note that in 2010 Automatic Identification System-Search and Rescue Transmitter (AIS-SART) was introduced. So, shipboard GMDSS installations include one or more Search and Rescue Locating Devices (SARLD) supporting SAR operations. These devices may be either an AIS-SART or a SART (Search and Rescue Transponder).

And at the end, as the result of the hard work of International Maritime Organization (IMO) and other bodies, two new systems have been introduced:

– Ship Security Alert System – SSAS (in 2004),
– Long-Range Identification and Tracking of ships – LRIT (in 2009).

Although the SSAS and LRIT systems are not a part of the GMDSS, in the direct way they use its communication means.

Taking into account the all changes, up to date equipment and systems used in the GMDSS is showed in Fig. 2 [4]. Used in Fig. 2 devices and systems abbreviations mean:

- MES –Inmarsat Mobile Earth Station;
- LES - Inmarsat Land Earth Station;
- EPIRB - Emergency Position Indicating Radio-Beacon;
- LUT - COSPAS/SARSAT Local User Terminal;
- DSC - Digital Selective Calling;
- NBDP - Narrow Band Direct Printing;
- RTF - Radiotelephony;
- GNSS - Global Navigation Satellite System - for support (mainly GPS- Global Positioning System);
- SARLD - Search and Rescue Locating Device;
- NAVTEX System;
- RCC - Rescue Coordination Centre;
- SAR – Search and Rescue Service.

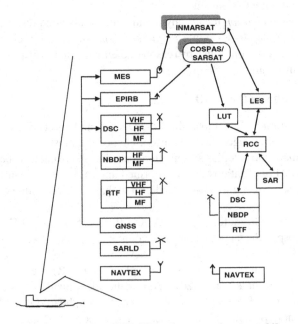

Fig. 2. Up to date GMDSS equipment and systems [4]

From the Radio communication point of view, the most important regulatory change was adoption in 2007 by IMO Assembly of Resolution A.1001(25) on Criteria for the Provision of Mobile Satellite Communication Systems in the GMDSS, allowing to be the GMDSS operator by any satellite operator which fits the above criteria [3].

3   The Radio Communication Aspects of E-navigation

For realizing the full potential of e-navigation, the following three fundamental elements should be present [5]:

- Electronic Navigation Chart (ENC) coverage of all navigational areas,
- a robust electronic position-fixing system (with redundancy), and
- an agreed infrastructure of communications to link ships and shore.

Any communications systems used for e-navigation must be able to:

- deliver appropriate electronic information to and from ships and shore and between ships and between shore;
- in a harmonised and structured way using the agreed IHO S-100 data structure and the approved overarching e-navigation architecture wherever possible.

For e-navigation purposes, the implications of developing a common information data source, delivering resilient communications, data provision and integrity, based on the requirements and the general conclusions from the preliminary user needs analysis have been considered [6].

One of the main tasks referring to the development of e-navigation system is to identify and draft guidelines on seamless integration of all the currently available communications infrastructure and how they can be used (range bandwidth etc.) and what systems are being developed (for example, maritime cloud) and will be in use when e-navigation is live.

Because the e-navigation Strategy Implementation Plan (SIP) was just completed, the work on the detailed technical aspects of communications supporting e-navigation is still in its infancy [7]. However before detailed consideration some basic assumptions should be made:

- it should concern data communications; voice communications would also form a part of e-navigation, but the present emphasis was primarily on data transfer,
- there would be different requirements for data availability depending upon the nature of the information being transmitted; for instance, information that was time and safety critical needed to be transmitted and received by the affected users quickly and reliably, whilst less time critical information would have a lower priority,
- the ship would receive a lot of information and it was important for the crew to be able to manage these data effectively,
- e-navigation should not be seen as limited to safety and security at sea and protection of the marine environment functions only, as efficiency was an important potential benefit for ships and their crews, and
- data communications via satellite, as well as over terrestrial links, e.g., Medium Frequency (MF), High Frequency (HF), and Very High Frequency (VHF) would be used.

Based on the above mentioned assumptions the following three main recommendations could be given.

Existing International Regulations and Standards. There are about 130 performance standards and test standards related to GMDSS equipment mandatory or not mandatory according to SOLAS. As of today, taking into account present development of the marine electronics systems, about 10 of them should be modified or suppressed and about 40 should be definitely suppressed as obsolete. But it is difficult to identify in details which existing regulations and standards would need to be further developed or revised.

Existing Technical Constraints. E-navigation should not be limited to communications using existing equipment, but the first phase should be to make better use of existing technology. Other technologies could come later. It had to be recognized that there were limitations on spectrum availability and that other types of technology might have to be used. It is also recognized that the current systems were not adequate for expected types of high rate data (for example Inmarsat C had a data rate of 600 bps). There are no mandated requirement for a higher data rate but other satellite systems are available and can possibly be used for transfer of e-navigation data.

There is a need to have a common data structure and management so that the information would be available on board and could be used by different systems without the need to have to continually re-enter data. This would reduce the administrative load on ship crew as various reporting requirements could be extracted through filters automatically.

E-navigation Scalability. The question of e-navigation being scalable across small and large vessels alike is of relevance when small vessels and SOLAS ships needed to access e-navigation data. National maritime administrations would need to include smaller vessels in the e-navigation system. However, small vessels might have other means in addition to mandatory communications equipment such as VHF, of obtaining e-navigation information such as mobile phones. Smaller vessels might also have power limitations and smaller presentation displays.

4   Status of GMDSS Modernization

As a result of the work on "Scoping Exercise to establish the need for a review of the elements and procedures of the GMDSS", IMO in 2012 decided to start work on "The review and modernization of the Global Maritime Distress and Safety System (GMDSS)". The modernization programme should implement more modern and efficient communications technologies in the GMDSS, and support the communications needs of the e-navigation.

At the beginning of the GMDSS modernization process a lot of issues are considered but the most important considerations are concerning the key issues presented in Sect. 2.1.

4.1   Functional Requirements

In considering the nine functional requirements (see Sect. 2.1), the following over-arching issues is considered [7]:

- the possible need for inclusion of "security-related communications" in the GMDSS, and
- the possible need to develop a clearer definition of "general communications".

A new definition of "security-related communications" is proposed as follows [7]:

"Security-related communications means communications associated with the update of security levels, security incidents or threat thereof and security-related information prior to the entry of a ship into a port."

Operational communications is now covered under the definition of urgency and safety communications. It is proposed, therefore, to redefine the term "general communications" by aligning it with the Radio Regulations. The new definition proposed is:

"General communications means operational communications, other than distress conducted by radio".

So, the proposed new text of functional requirements for the modernized GMDSS is following (see also Sect. 2.1) [7]:

1. performing the GMDSS functions as follows:
   a. transmitting ship-to-shore distress alerts by at least two separate and independent means, each using a different radio communication service,
   b. receiving shore-to-ship distress alert relays,
   c. transmitting and receiving ship-to-ship distress alerts,
   d. transmitting and receiving search and rescue coordinating communications,
   e. transmitting and receiving on-scene communications,
   f. transmitting and receiving signals for locating,
   g. transmitting and receiving safety-related information,
   h. receiving Maritime Safety Information (MSI),
   i. transmitting and receiving general communications, and
   j. transmitting and receiving bridge-to-bridge communications,
2. transmitting and receiving security-related communications, in accordance with the requirements of the International Ship and Port Facility Security Code, and
3. transmitting and receiving other communications to and from shore-based systems or networks.

4.2 GMDSS Sea Areas

Four sea areas have been defined according to the coverage of VHF, HF and MF Coast Radio Services and Inmarsat Services as given in Sect. 2.1. During the review it was noted that extensive use was made of VHF communications and, therefore, sea area A1 should be retained. Because of considerable use of MF voice communications, it was finally concluded that sea area A2 should be retained as a separate sea area as well [7].

The definition of the boundary between sea area A3 and A4 is currently defined by Inmarsat coverage, but Inmarsat might not always be the only GMDSS satellite provider. In future, the IMO might recognize regional or global satellite systems to provide GMDSS services in an A3 sea area, each of them providing coverage different to the current A3 sea area. Recognizing some options for the definition of sea areas A3 and A4, at this time the following definition of sea areas A3 and A4 were identified:

- *sea area A3* means an area, excluding sea areas A1 and A2, within the coverage of a recognized mobile-satellite communication service supported by the ship earth station carried on board in which continuous alerting is available,
- *sea area A4* means an area outside of sea areas A1, A2 and A3.

Sea Area A4 would now refer to an area where the "HF option" applies to the ship. So, a ship not using a GMDSS satellite service provider would not have an A3 area.

4.3 Ship Requirements

In future, if other satellite service providers are recognized by the IMO, the safety radio certificates of the ship should be required to define the geographic area in which the ship is permitted to operate. Taking into account the changes of the functional requirements (see Sect. 3.1) and GMDSS sea areas (see Sect. 3.2) also there will be the necessary changes in the basic equipment of ships (see Sect. 2.1).

4.4 Order of Priority of Communications

The Radio Regulations provide the existing order of four levels of priority (see Sect. 2.1). The four priorities are needed for communications and operational use in general. It is concluded, therefore, that the four levels of priority should be retained, and apply to voice, text, and data messages and that there is no need to revise Radio Regulations in this respect. But automated systems should give priority to category distress and should also give priority to categories urgency and safety (ahead of category other communications - see Sect. 2.1).

5 Conclusion

One of the three main elements of e-navigation is communications. Taking into account the earlier consideration, doubtlessly the communications media for e-navigation should include both terrestrial and satellite communications.

The GMDSS equipment can be an effective way to increase the reliability of e-navigation data communication network but must be improved. There are many data communications technologies that are likely to play a role in e-navigation. The selection of the particular technologies used to provide services must be made carefully and should depend on the specific task to be undertaken. It is worth noting that a target completion year for IMO work on "Review and modernization of the Global Maritime Distress and Safety System (GMDSS)" is 2017.

Furthermore, the continuous and open process is needed to ensure maritime radio systems remain modern and fully responsive to changes in requirements and evolutions of technology and they will meet the expected e-navigation requirements.

During work on the integration the maritime radio systems with e-navigation it is necessary first to identify real user needs and secondly to realize that the modernization of the maritime radio communication should not be driven only by technical requirements.

In this approach to development of the GMDSS it is very important that the integrity of GMDSS, for safety purposes, must not be jeopardized.

And finally it should be noted that a key to the success of the integration process the maritime radio systems with e-navigation is not only that the work is completed on time, but also that it has the flexibility to implement changes ahead of schedule.

References

1. International Maritime Organization (IMO): International Convention for the Safety of Life at Sea (SOLAS), London (2014)
2. International Telecommunication Union (ITU): Radio Regulations (RR), Geneva (2012)
3. Korcz, K.: Some radiocommunication aspects of e-navigation. In: 8th International Navigational Symposium on Marine Navigation and Safety of Sea Transportation, TRANS-NAV, Gdynia, pp. 291–295 (2009)
4. Korcz, K.: Modernization of the GMDSS. In: 10th International Symposium on Marine Navigation and Safety of Sea Transportation, TRANS-NAV, Gdynia, pp. 305—312 (2013)
5. Korcz, K.: Strategia e-nawigacji w żegludze morskiej. Przegląd Telekomuni kacyjny + Wiadomości Telekomunikacyjne, nr 5, pp. 172–175, Warszawa (2009)
6. International Maritime Organization (IMO): COMSAR 16/17 Report to the Maritime Safety Committee (MSC), London (2009)
7. International Maritime Organization (IMO): NCSR 2/9 Report of the Correspondence Group on the Review of the GMDSS, London (2014)

Hazardous Failure Rate of the Safety Function

Karol Rástočný[✉] and Juraj Ždánsky

Faculty of Electrical Engineering, Department of Information
and Control Systems, University of Žilina, Univerzitná 1, 01026 Žilina, Slovakia
{karol.rastocny,juraj.zdansky}@fel.uniza.sk

Abstract. Quantitative assessment of safety function integrity against random failures is necessary assumption for railway signalling system acceptance and its implementation into operation. The railway signalling system can be modelled as continuous mode system and therefore the criterion for quantitative assessment safety integrity of safety function is hazardous failure rate. Most of commonly available software tools for evaluation of the RAMS parameters offer calculation of safety function failure probability, but don't offer direct calculation of safety function failure rate. The paper is focused on some of problems associated with comparing the exact analytical solution and approximate calculation of safety function failure rate due to presence of random failures. This approach can be successfully applied to "manual" calculation of also complex analytical terms. The proposed method is based on the generally accepted assumption that occurrence of random failures of electronic systems corresponds to an exponential distribution law.

Keywords: Failure rate · Exponential distribution · Safety function · Signalling system

1 Introduction

Electronic railway signaling systems belong to control systems which realize, in addition to standard functions, the so-called safety functions. The safety function is a function that is intended to ensure a safe state of controlled traffic process given the specific danger [1].

Depending on the usage method of the safety function, [2] distinguishes two operation modes - mode with demand (low or high) and continuous operation mode. In case of the operation mode with low demand, the safety integrity against random failures of safety function is evaluated as average probability of dangerous failure on demand of the safety function. In case of the operation mode with high demand or the continuous operation mode, the safety integrity against random failures of the safety function is evaluated as average frequency of dangerous failure of the safety function. According to [3] is necessary to evaluate all safety functions of railway signalling system given the continuous operation mode.

There are several software tools that can be used to analyze RAMS parameters of railway signalling system. These tools generally allow to calculate the probability of the safety function dangerous failure, but don't allow to calculate the safety function failure rate. Moreover, these tools generally don't provide an analytical relation for

© Springer International Publishing Switzerland 2015
J. Mikulski (Ed.): TST 2015, CCIS 531, pp. 284–291, 2015.
DOI: 10.1007/978-3-319-24577-5_28

calculation of observed variable, but only the point values of observed variable for specific values of certain parameter (e.g. time). In many cases it's necessary to combine more software tools, for example, one tool can be used for the qualitative part of the analysis (creation of model which describes impact of RAM parameters of railway signalling system on the safety properties of the analyzed safety function) and second tool can be used to support the mathematical calculations. The authors of this paper have positive experiences with using of combination of software tools [4] and [5] for evaluation of the safety integrity against random failures of the safety functions. This paper builds on [6], which deals with the calculation problem of the dangerous failure occurrence rate of the safety function realized by several channels, which are differently by hardware.

2 Using of the FTA for Evaluation of Safety Integrity Against Random Failures

One of the most frequently used methods for analysis of integrity against random failures is Fault Tree Analysis (FTA). This traditional method of analysis can be used in several stages of the life cycle of railway signaling system. Whether in the phase of risk analysis in hazard identification [7] or in the design phase in connection with methods supporting object-oriented system development [8, 9], but mainly in the system safety evaluation [10, 11]. It's a deductive analytical method which takes into account the influence of failures on the system safety, regardless of their occurrence order. From perspective of this analysis, the system can be only in two states - functional or dysfunctional, resp. safe or unsafe. FTA is focused to determine the cause or combination of causes (basic events) that may lead to the defined top event. The top event is undesirable event - in case of the safety analysis it's a dangerous failure of the safety function. The basic events are generally failures of railway signalling system elements. The tree of failure states can be described by the logical function

$$D = \sum_{i=1}^{n} C_i, \tag{1}$$

where D is the top event and C_i is i-th minimum cut.
The top event probability $Pr_D(t)$ can be calculated according to equation

$$Pr_D(t) = \sum_{i=1}^{n} Pr(C_i) - \sum_{i=1}^{n=1} \sum_{j=i+1}^{n} Pr(C_i \cap C_j) + \dots \tag{2}$$

Because the tree of failure states has only one top function, it can be concluded that the function $Pr_D(t)$ has the properties of the distribution function of a random variable, which means that all following conditions are fulfilled:

- is left continuous, $\lim_{t \to \alpha^+} Pr_D(t) = Pr_D(\alpha)$;
- is non-decreasing, $\forall \alpha < \beta \quad Pr_D(\alpha) < Pr_D(\beta)$;

- has asymptotic properties $\lim\limits_{t\to 0} Pr_D(t) = 0$ and $\lim\limits_{t\to\infty} Pr_D(t) = 1$;
- $\forall \alpha < \beta$ is probability $Pr_D[\alpha < t \le \beta] = Pr_D(\beta) - Pr_D(\alpha)$.

Then the top event occurrence rate D can be calculated according to equation

$$\lambda_D(t) = \frac{\frac{dPr_D(t)}{dt}}{1 - Pr_D(t)}. \tag{3}$$

If the logic function (1) has more minimum cuts with more basic events, so the calculation of the top even rate by the Eq. (3) is problematic and highly difficult in manual (hand) calculation. Is desirable to have a computationally undemanding method which would allow to realize the checksum calculations of the top event rate with sufficient (satisfactory) accuracy, especially during the design of railway signalling system.

The logic function (1) can be modified to shape

$$D = \sum_{i=0}^{j} C_i^1 + \sum_{i=0}^{k} C_i^2 + \sum_{i=0}^{l} C_i^3 + \ldots + \sum_{i=0}^{m} C_i^x, \tag{4}$$

where D is top event, C_i^x is minimum cut containing x basic events ($x = 1, 2, 3, \ldots$) and i is number of minimum cuts containing x basic events.

For real railway signaling systems is important to consider only the minimum cuts which contain less than four basic events, i.e. $x \le 3$ (the probability that top event occurs due to simultaneous occurrence of four or more basic events is practically negligible).

Let's assume that occurrence of basic events corresponds to an exponential distribution law and is valid

$$\lambda.t \ll 1, \text{ then } \left(1 - e^{-\lambda t}\right) \approx \lambda.t. \tag{5}$$

If the logic function (1) has shape (Fig. 1a)

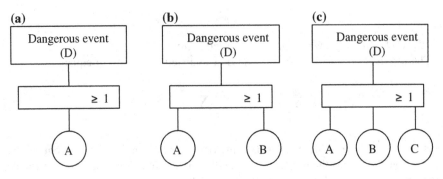

Fig. 1. The failure states tree [own study]

$$D = C_1^1 = A, \tag{6}$$

then

$$Pr_D(t) = \left(1 - e^{-\lambda_A t}\right),$$
$$\lambda_D = \lambda_A. \tag{7}$$

If the logic function (1) has shape (Fig. 1b)

$$D = C_2^1 = A.B, \tag{8}$$

then

$$Pr_D(t) = \left(1 - e^{-\lambda_A t}\right).\left(1 - e^{-\lambda_B t}\right),$$
$$\lambda_D(t) < 2.\lambda_A.\lambda_B.t, \tag{9}$$

if is valid (5).
If the logic function (1) has shape (Fig. 1c)

$$D = C_3^1 = A.B.C, \tag{10}$$

then

$$Pr_T(t) = \left(1 - e^{-\lambda_A t}\right).\left(1 - e^{-\lambda_B t}\right),$$
$$\lambda_T(t) < 3.\lambda_A.\lambda_B.\lambda_C.t^2, \tag{11}$$

if is valid (5).
In general it can be concluded that if the minimum cuts are independent of each other, so

$$\lambda_D(t) = \sum_{i=0}^{n} \lambda_{Ci}(t), \tag{12}$$

where rates of individual minimum cuts $\lambda_{Ci}(t)$ can be expressed according to (7), (9) and (11).

The logic function (1) can contain (and generally contains) minimum cuts, which are independent of each other. Then is questionable whether for calculation of the top event rate can be used the Eq. (12).

If the logic function (1) contains two minimum cuts, which are independent of each other

$$D = A.B + A.C.\tag{13}$$

The top event probability

$$Pr_D(t) = Pr(A).Pr(B) + Pr(A).Pr(C) - Pr(A).Pr(B).Pr(C)\tag{14}$$

and the top event rate, if the occurrence of the basic events corresponds to an exponential law, is

$$\lambda_D(t) = \frac{(\lambda_B + \lambda_C).\left(1 - e^{-\lambda_A t}\right).e^{-(\lambda_B + \lambda_C)t} + \lambda_A.\left(1 - e^{-(\lambda_B + \lambda_C)t}\right).e^{-\lambda_A t}}{1 - (1 - e^{-\lambda_A t}).(1 - e^{-(\lambda_B + \lambda_C)t})}.\tag{15}$$

If $\lambda.t < 0, 1$, then can be the Eq. (14) simplified (without a negative influence on safety)

$$Pr_D(t) < Pr(A).Pr(B) + Pr(A).Pr(C).\tag{16}$$

In accordance with (9) is valid

$$\lambda_D(t) < \lambda_D^{AP} = 2.\lambda_A.\lambda_B.t + 2.\lambda_A.\lambda_C.t.\tag{17}$$

As can be seen also in the simple tree of failure states (13) the solution is relatively difficult (15). There are in Fig. 2 graphics waveforms $\lambda_D(t)$ (Eq. (15)) and λ_D^{AP} (Eq. (17)) for specific values $\lambda_A = 1.10^{-4}\,\mathrm{h}^{-1}$, $\lambda_B = 5.10^{-4}\,\mathrm{h}^{-1}$, $\lambda_C = 1.10^{-5}\,\mathrm{h}^{-1}$.

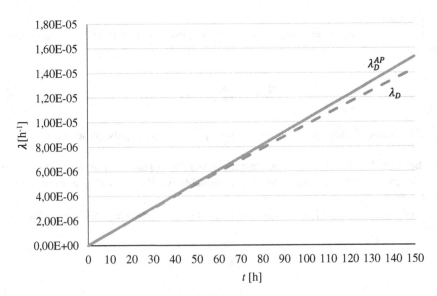

Fig. 2. The graph of the top event rate [own study]

Based on the above considerations, it can be concluded that for calculation of the top event rate can be used Eq. (12), while the calculated top event rate won't be less than the real value.

3 Approximation of the Top Event Probability

Another approach for evaluating of the random failures influence on safety integrity level of the safety function can be based on the assumption that

$$Pr_D(t) \leq Pr_D^A(t), for \; t \in \langle 0, T \rangle, \tag{18}$$

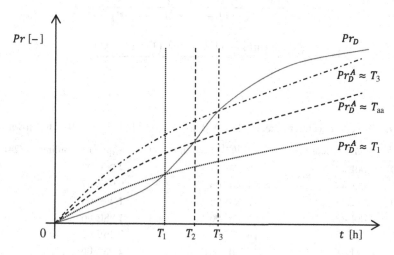

Fig. 3. Approximation of the dangerous failure probability of the safety function by an exponential function [own study]

where $Pr_D^A(t)$ is the tolerable probability of dangerous failure of the safety function. Basically it's an approximation of the top event probability. Because according to [2] the tolerable dangerous failure rate of the safety function is constant, approximation can be done by an exponential function (Fig. 3).

$$\left(1 - e^{-\lambda_D^A \cdot t}\right) \geq Pr_D(t), for \; t \in \langle 0, T \rangle, \tag{19}$$

if is valid (5), then

$$\lambda_D^A \geq \frac{Pr_T(t)}{T} = \lambda_{Tavg}, for \; t \in \langle 0, T \rangle, \tag{20}$$

where λ_{Tavg} is average value of instantaneous value of the top event rate.

$$\lambda_{Tavg} = \frac{1}{T} \int_0^T \lambda_T(t) dt. \tag{21}$$

Let's assume, that the safety function is realized by two elements (element A, element B) and the safety function dangerous failure occurs during the failure of both elements (element A and element B). The logic function (1), which describes the safety function dangerous failure, contains one minimum cut, i.e. $D = A.B$. Then

$$\left(1 - e^{-\lambda_D^A . t}\right) \geq \left(1 - e^{-\lambda_A t}\right).\left(1 - e^{-\lambda_B t}\right), \text{for } t \in \langle 0, T \rangle, \tag{22}$$

$$\lambda_D(t) = \frac{\lambda_A . e^{-\lambda_A t} + \lambda_B . e^{-\lambda_B t} - (\lambda_A + \lambda_B).e^{-(\lambda_A + \lambda_B)t}}{1 - \left(1 - e^{-\lambda_A t}\right).\left(1 - e^{-\lambda_B t}\right)}, \tag{23}$$

$$\lambda_D^A \geq -\frac{\left(\ln\left(1 - \left(1 - e^{-\lambda_A t}\right).\left(1 - e^{-\lambda_B t}\right)\right)\right)}{t}, \tag{24}$$

Table 1. Top event occurrence rate, if $D = A.B$, $\lambda_A = 1.10^{-4} \, h^{-1}$, $\lambda_B = 5.10^{-4} \, h^{-1}$ [own study]

$T[h]$	$\lambda_D[h^{-1}]$ according to (9)	$\lambda_D[h^{-1}]$ according to (23)	$\lambda_D^A[h^{-1}]$ according to (24)
10	1.00E-06	9.96E-07	4.99E-07
20	2.00E-06	1.98E-06	9.94E-07
30	3.00E-06	2.96E-06	1.49E-06
40	4.00E-06	3.93E-06	1.98E-06
50	5.00E-06	4.89E-06	2.46E-06
60	6.00E-06	5.84E-06	2.95E-06
70	7.00E-06	6.78E-06	3.43E-06
80	8.00E-06	7.72E-06	3.91E-06
90	9.00E-06	8.65E-06	4.38E-06
100	1.00E-05	9.57E-06	4.85E-06

$$\lambda_{Davg} = \frac{1}{T} \int_0^T \lambda_D(t) dt = \frac{1}{T} \int_0^T (2.\lambda_A.\lambda_B.t) dt = \lambda_A.\lambda_B.T \tag{25}$$

The results of the analysis are shown in Table 1.

4 Conclusion

Although the FTA is in practice very often used method for safety analysis, but has its limitations. These limitations are related to the fact that FTA doesn't allow the analysis of simultaneous influence of several factors (diagnostic cover, recovery, change of architecture, ...) on the safety integrity of the safety function. The influence of several factors on the safety integrity of the safety function can be successfully modeled using the Markov analysis [7, 12].

Acknowledgement. This work has been supported by the scientific grant agency VEGA, grant No. VEGA-1/0035/15 "Analysis of operator – control system interaction effect on the controlled process' safety" (50 %) and also by the project of the Educational Grant Agency of the Slovak Republic (KEGA) Number: 005ŽU-4/2015: Modernization of technologies and methods of education with a focus on control systems with safety PLC (50 %).

References

1. Rástočný, K., Pekár, L., Ždánsky, J.: Safety of signalling systems - opinions and reality. In: Mikulski, J. (ed.) TST 2013. CCIS, vol. 395, pp. 155–162. Springer, Heidelberg (2013)
2. EN IEC 61508: Functional safety of electrical/electronic/programmable electronic safety-related systems (2010)
3. EN 50 129: Railway applications – communication, signalling and processing systems – safety-related electronic systems for signaling (2003)
4. http://www.wolfram.com/mathematica/?source=nav. Accessed 12 February 2015
5. http://www.ptc.com/product/windchill. Accessed 12 February 2015
6. Binti Abdullah, A., Shaoying, L.: Hazard analysis for safety-critical systems using SOFL. In: Proceedings of international conference Computational Intelligence for Engineering Solutions (CIES), pp. 133–140 (2013). ISBN 978-1-4673-5851-4
7. Rástočný, K., Ilavský, J.: What is concealed behind the hazardous failure rate of a system? In: Mikulski, J. (ed.) TST 2011. CCIS, vol. 239, pp. 372–381. Springer, Heidelberg (2011)
8. Briones, J.F., de Miguel, M., Silva, J.P., Alonso, A.: Integration of safety analysis and software development methods. In: Proceedings of International Conference System Safety, pp. 275–284 (2006). ISBN 0 86341 646
9. Mhenni, F., Nga, N., Choley, J.-Y.: Automatic fault tree generation from SysML system models. In: Proceedings of international conference Advanced Intelligent Mechatronics, pp. 715–720 (2014)
10. Pan, H., Tu, J., Zhang, X., Dong, D.: The FTA based safety analysis method for urban transit signal system. In: Proceedings of International Conference Reliability, Maintainability and Safety (ICRMS), pp. 527–532 (2011). ISBN 978-1-61284-664-4
11. Mikulski, J.: Malfunctions of railway traffic control systems - failure rate analysis. In: Proceedings of International Conference on Computer Simulation in Risk Analysis and Hazard Mitigation, pp. 141–147 (2002). ISBN 1-85312-915-1
12. Mechri, W., Simon, C., Bicking, F., Ben Othman, K.: Probability of failure on demand of safety systems by multiphase Markov chains. In: Proceedings of International Conference Control and Fault-Tolerant Systems, pp. 98–103 (2013). ISBN 978-1-4799-2855-2

Telematics Applications, an Important Basis for Improving the Road Safety

Alica Kalašová[1(✉)], Peter Faith[1], and Jerzy Mikulski[2]

[1] The Faculty of Operation and Economics of Transport and Communications, Department Univerzitná 1, University of Žilina, 01026 Žilina, Slovakia
{alica.kalasova,peter.faith}@fpedas.uniza.sk
[2] University of Economics in Katowice, ul. 1 Maja 50, 40-287 Katowice, Poland
jerzy.mikulski@polsl.pl

Abstract. An accompanying sign of development in Slovakia, as in the developed countries, is intensification of traffic which manifests itself not only as a contribution to mobility, but also with its negative impacts on the environment, increasingly worse throughput of road infrastructure, increase of number of traffic accidents and road traffic inefficiency. Currently, the EU major challenge is to increase the road safety. Safety is the relevance from accidents and losses of human lives. It also deals with property protection, regulation, management and transport technology development. The analysis of accidents indicates that 95 % of transport accidents are caused by human factor failure (wrong determination of situation, participant's skills/abilities etc.) One of the most frequent errors of drivers is a wrong decision in a critical situation. The decision process is very complicated since the driver has to evaluate the arisen situation correctly within fractions of a second. The implementation of telematics systems into vehicle equipment reduces the energetic intensity, reduces environmental impacts, increases safety etc. Reduction of total operating costs of road vehicles, simplification of vehicle control to maximum extent and reduction of driver's informational overload is largely stressed. In this paper we evaluate traffic accidents in the EU and the possibilities to increase road safety in Slovakia and Poland. In conclusion, we identify possibilities to reduce the accident rate by means of telematics applications, which constitute an important part of transport issues and aim at safer and more efficient transport with less congestion, lower economic burden on the environment and higher safety.

Keywords: Transport safety · Telematics applications · Traffic accidents

1 Introduction

In the recent decades humans started to realize that unregulated development and growth set in an environment of limited resources of our planet is unsustainable in the long term.

In 1987, the United Nations General Assembly adopted the report "Our common future", in which sustainable development was defined as a development, which is able to meet the needs of current generations without jeopardizing the ability of future generations to meet their own needs.

© Springer International Publishing Switzerland 2015
J. Mikulski (Ed.): TST 2015, CCIS 531, pp. 292–299, 2015.
DOI: 10.1007/978-3-319-24577-5_29

This definition mainly includes the fundamental principle of sustainability, some kind of ethical issue, namely the principle of responsibility towards future generations. We talk about sustainable development whenever the connection between human needs and natural resources is recognized. Sustainable development is a way of searching and finding solutions that benefit people, economy and the environment in the long term horizon.

If we ask the question: Why do we need sustainable development? the answer is obvious. Because the existing one does not work. Sustainable development is for the society rather moral challenge than the scientific solution. It is an answer to the current important need for future development based on a new relation between people and their relationship with the environment they live in. It rejects outdated idea that economical, technical and environmental objectives are opposing each other. Sustainable development is not an abstraction. It is based on the common sense and basic human values, which are combined with modern, everyday life.

Creating negative externalities, road transport is one of the largest violators of sustainable development. Significant externalities are: accidents caused by the operation of transport systems (loss of life; medical care for disabled; etc.), congestion and others (air pollution; emissions damaging environment, health and buildings; climate change; greenhouse gas emissions (CO_2), which have lasting impact on Earth's climate; noise). The largest share of transport related negative externalities is linked to the traffic accidents. Every user risks injury or death when entering the transport network. The amount of this risk is obviously different and varies in place and time. Due to the vehicles speed and the condition of infrastructure, traffic accidents are becoming a serious problem. Traffic congestions cause huge losses in terms of lost time, impact on the environment and they limit the zone availability. This can be reduced by increasing car occupancy and by the use of alternative transport modes. By estimate, 10 % of the road network currently faces congestion problem. Predictions for next 10 years are alarming. It is important for the European Community to solve the congestion problem, because otherwise it will multiply and reach 80 billion/year, what will account for 1 % of EU GDP by 2020.

The application of intelligent transport systems is essential for sustainable development and road safety improvement. A whole set of measures and technologies using ITS, based on the collection, processing, evaluation and distribution of information is introduced in developed countries. It is possible to decrease the number of road accidents by sufficient awareness of drivers and other road users. The most common cause of traffic accidents is a lack of information that drivers receive about the traffic situation in front of them. They are not able to respond properly and in time to the unexpected situation what leads to a traffic accident.

2 Traffic Accidents in Europe

Accident rate as a manifestation of imperfection of movement of citizens and goods transportation has been for several decades one of the most serious social problem. Each traffic accident ends with material damage or harm to human health. It is necessary to pay attention to factors that affect the level of risk and consequences of traffic accidents.

Different actions to improve road safety are organized in each country. International projects are solved within cooperation of research and scientific teams that are dealing with complex problems of traffic accidents. Different campaigns aimed at safer behavior of road users have been implemented.

Based on experience from introduction of some measures in practice, in order to increase the road safety, challenges and measures are formulated in national strategies. Security can be defined as preventing the risk of injury.

Factors influencing the level of risk include, e.g. [8]:

− Protection of human body injury of the accident participant;
− Characteristics of the vehicle - car, motorcycle, bicycle;
− Planning of roads which contribute to the safety of all road users;
− Increasing the application of intelligent transport systems in vehicles on roads.

Accident data in different European countries indicates that traffic safety still represents a serious problem that requires an effective solution (Fig. 1 and Table 1).

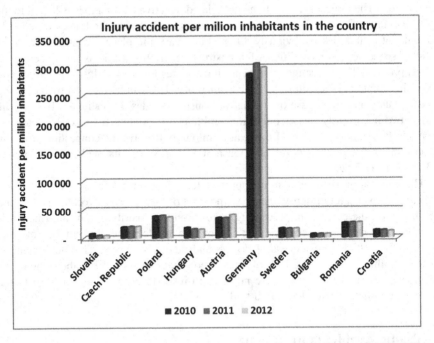

Fig. 1. Injury accident per milion inhabitants in the country (in 2012) [Source: CARE (EU road accidents database]

Table 1. Fatalities in the country

Fatalities			
Country	2010	2011	2012
Slovakia	371	324	298
Czech Republic	802	772	742
Poland	3 908	4 189	3 571
Hungary	740	638	606
Austria	552	523	531
Germany	3 648	4 009	3 600
Sweden	266	319	285
Bulgaria	776	657	602
Romania	2 377	2 018	2 042
Croatia	426	418	390

Source: CARE (EU road accidents database)

3 Intelligent Transport Services

Transport of people and goods and its impact on the quality of life in a society is one of the essential elements for assessing the standard of living around the world. At the beginning of the 21st century, the society cannot avoid the effects of the trends in development of information and communication technologies, which have a very significant impact on the transport processes. The use of new technologies is an essential condition for the implementation of advanced services designed to meet today's challenges and for the reduction of negative externalities produced by the transport sector. Intelligent transport systems (telematics) are sophisticated multimodal interdisciplinary tools integrating advanced technologies from different fields that are applied in transport and traffic in order to develop solutions to significantly improve the quality of life. The main objective of transport telematics is to provide the users with intelligent transport services, which are monitored at several levels as the services for [1]:

- Passengers and drivers (users);
- Infrastructure managers (managers of transport network, managers of traffic terminals);
- Transport operators (carriers);
- Public administration;
- Safety and rescue system;
- Financial and control institutions;

Transport telematics is a comprehensive department, where telecommunication and information technologies are only a small part of the whole issue. This includes legislation (for example tolls), big part consists of the transport knowledge - traffic flow modelling and if we want to use information and telecommunication technologies in order to optimize the transport system, we have to understand this system. We must have alternative routes, destination which we want to reach and then make use of these technologies in order to achieve the objective given. It is the combination of several disciplines such as: transport engineering, the above mentioned information and tele-communication technologies, legislation, economics, and possibly others. It is a comprehensive (synthetic) department. The information superstructure in transport is the result of the conceptual connection between the subsystems of transport telematics. This superstructure allows us to implement the same management tools for this net-work industry as it is, for example, in today's management of manufacturing enter-prises (costs monitoring, creation of separate cost centers). Directive 2010/40 /EU of the European Parliament and the Council from 7th July 2010 is about the framework for the deployment of intelligent transport systems in the field of road transport and for interfaces with other modes of transport. It provides a framework for the support of coordinated and continuous deployment and use of intelligent transport systems within the European Union and lays down the general conditions necessary for this purpose.

The priority areas of this directive are:

- Optimal use of road, traffic and travel data;
- Continual management of ITS services in road and freight transport;
- ITS applications for road traffic safety;
- Connection of vehicles with transport infrastructure.

The following priority actions necessary for the development and use of specifi-cations and standards within the priority areas are further defined:

- Provide multi-modal travel information across the EU;
- Provide real-time traffic information throughout the EU;
- Data and procedures to provide free traffic information concerning safety of road users;
- Reconciliation of providing e-Call service across the EU;
- Provide information services on safe and secure parking places for trucks and commercial vehicles;
- Ensure safe and secure parking places for trucks and commercial vehicles;

Every member state has to take the necessary measures to achieve these actions. Slovak republic adopted the above mentioned directive into its legislation. Therefore, they are obliged to fulfill the terms of implementation and application of intelligent transport systems. The Act No. 317/2012 Coll. on intelligent transport systems in road transport and on the amendment and completion of certain acts was adopted [2].

4 ITS Deployment in Slovakia and Abroad

An example of the above mentioned act application in the Slovak Republic in the previous period of time, was the project of implementing pilot solutions- National traffic information centre and ITS in Trnava. It is a system that uses traffic data from its own telematics devices, which is also capable of receiving traffic information from integrated as well as surrounding transport systems.

As a part of the project, a nodal-linear model of the crucial city transport network with detail on the individual lanes was created. This model is adjusted to the road network database. Strategic traffic detectors were placed into this network. They are located between intersections. Their task is to acquire basic characteristics of the traffic flow and send time indications of transit, speed and vehicle length to the central application. Thanks to the location of detectors, a failure of the traffic flow in the given section of the network can be indicated from obtained characteristics.

The system can determine the degree of traffic and is also able to predict the traffic based on the obtained traffic and traffic related data. From the information used, it is worth to mention that the system takes on-line information about the current weather conditions from the nearest meteorological stations. Based on the information of the entire transport network, the system is able to generate instructions for the strategic management by informing, navigating or directly stopping the vehicles.

The important thing is the use of system outputs in long term aspect. Except an immediate use of the system outputs in the form of traffic information and instructions related to the strategic management in the specific situations, the system provides valuable outputs from the continual areal traffic survey. Those are interesting for assessing the actual road infrastructure volume of the city in time and place. In the wider context, it is possible to monitor local failures of the traffic flow in individual, cordon or areal manner. It can be also done in daily, weekly, monthly or annual traffic variations and other important indicators can be monitored.

All these outputs are valuable for making decisions about the implementation of other telematics applications in the transport infrastructure of the city and its surroundings. With their help it is possible to:

- Review the traffic volume of transport infrastructure in space and time;
- Objectively search and sort problematic places in transport infrastructure by severity;
- Assess various points with surroundings by providing alternative detours and their traffic volumes;
- Process quality simulations based on real, long-term monitored entries;
- Quantify the benefits of intended transport telematics implementations;

This project tried to create realistic outputs and test modern approaches with emphasis on the EU trends. Either from the central point of view of the NDIC or from a local perspective of IDS Trnava, there was no ambition to create a final solution, but to show approaches that could be followed [3].

The Czech Republic as a member state of the European Union adopted Directive 2010/40/EU into their binding regulations as Act No. 361/2000 Coll., on traffic on the road network and changing certain acts, as amended, on 14th September 2000.

According to this act, ministry or its representative ensures public awareness of traffic situation on the road network, which affect the safety and free flow of traffic on the road network. For this purpose, police, municipality police, road administrative authorities, road network administrators and fire department are obliged to provide the ministry with current information affecting the safety and continuity of the traffic. The legislation will define the type of information that affect the safety and fluency of the traffic, the way of providing information, data collection method and the way of publishing information for public use [4, 5].

5 Conclusion

An important application of ITS is in transport information system, which when combined with the navigation system in the vehicle, is capable of providing comprehensive information about the number of vehicles on individual sections of the network, congestions, parking, etc. Thanks to the actual information, the system can also perform the optimization of the traffic that comes from the need to capture the current lengths of congestions on the shoulders of individual intersections, which cannot always be accurately measured by detectors. The strategy to minimize the total vehicle delay on the communication network can be solved by knowing the real number of vehicles in the network [6, 7].

In public passenger transport, the ability to plan multimodal trip is an important factor for the preference of public transport over individual. It is a journey, which from its beginning until the end involves more than one mode of transport (bus, tram, underground, train, etc.). Another important application is the preference on light-controlled intersections.

In the area of commercial vehicles, we can generally say that ITS is focused on the following improvements:

- Fewer empty kilometers;
- Less detours, what inevitably leads to a reduction in fuel consumption;
- Shorter planning time;
- Better customer services leading to a higher customer satisfaction and similar;

The proper implementation of ITS must be necessarily based on a detailed analysis of the current traffic situation and clearly defined solution objective. As stated in [6] ITS system cannot be bought, but the system can be purposefully build.

Acknowledgement. This contribution is the result of the project implementation:

The quality of education and development of the human resources as pillars of the knowledge society at the Faculty PEDAS", ITMS project code 26110230083, University of Žilina.

VEGA Project no. 1/0159/13 – KALAŠOVÁ, A. and collective: Basic Research of Telematic Systems, Conditions of Their Development and Necessity of Long-term Strategy. University of Žilina in Žilina, The Faculty of Operation and Economics of Transport and Communications, 2013–2015.

References

1. www.mdcr.cz
2. Inteligentný dopravný systém v Trnave. [elektronický časopis], [júl 2014], dostupné na: http://www.asb.sk/inzinierske-stavby/doprava/inteligentny-dopravny-system-v-trnave
3. Zákon z 18. septembra 2012 o inteligentných dopravných systémoch v cestnej doprave a o zmene a doplnení niektorých zákonov [január 2014], dostupné na: www.telecom.gov.sk/index/open_file.php?file=doprava/cesta/

4. Zákon č. 361/2000 Sb., ze dne 14. září 2000, o provozu na pozemních komunikacích a o změnách některých zákonů ve znění pozdejších zákonů. [elektronický zdroj], [júl 2014], dostupné na: http://www.zakonyprolidi.cz/cs/2000-361
5. Kubíková, S.: Systems for intelligent transport management. In: Conference proceeding, 3rd International scientific conference Logistika-Ekonomika-Prax 2014, Žilina (20 november 2014). ISSN 1336-5851
6. Přibyl, P., Svítek, M.: Inteligentní dopravní systémy. Technická literatúra BEN, Praha (2001)
7. Skrúcaný, T., Gnap, J.: Energy intensity and greenhouse gases production of the road and rail Cargo transport using a software in simulate the energy consumption of a train. In: Mikulski, J. (ed.) TST 2012. CCIS, vol. 471, pp. 263–272. Springer, Heidelberg (2012)
8. Majerová, Z., Rievaj, V.: Legislation and road safety. Arch. Transp. Syst. Telematics 6(1), 36–39 (2013). ISSN 1899-8208
9. www.ec.europa.eu

Relation of Social Legislation in Road Transport on Driver's Work Quality

Miloš Poliak[1(✉)] and Adela Poliaková[2]

[1] Fakulta prevádzky a ekonomiky dopravy a spojov, Žilinská univerzita v Žiline,
Univerzitná 8215/1, 010 26 Žilina, Slovakia
milos.poliak@fpedas.uniza.sk
[2] Materiálovotechnologická fakulta v Trnave,
Slovenská technická univerzita v Bratislave,
Botanická 49, 917 08 Trnava, Slovakia
adela.poliakova@stuba.sk

Abstract. This paper analyses a problematics of a social law limitation in road transport on drivers work. It analyses the demands on drivers in road freight transport in European Union and compares them with demands in chosen states (USA, Canada, Australia, New Zealand) and with demands for AETR Agreement Member States. From 2010 the conditions of social right are unified for AETR Agreement Member States, including Russia, Ukraine, Belarus, Serbia and for European Union Member States, but these unified conditions are much stronger comparing to conditions in said analysed countries that are not EU members nor AETR Agreement members. The paper shows on social right limitation influence in road transport on transport economy that is indirectly influencing on safety and quality of driver's work. The paper refers the possible risks of driver's work from the point of view of safety and quality that are caused by road transport social right limitation.

Keywords: Driver · Driver's work · Driving time · Breaks · Rest · Safety · Quality · Social legislation

1 Introduction

Road transport in Europe is currently the most important transportation system in inland transport. In the European Union, approximately 70 % of transport outcomes is carried by road transport [16]. Shipment of goods is one of the significant factors affecting the economic development of the reference area. Territory develops more slowly in comparison with the territory with a good road network if there is not adequate infrastructure limiting the fluidity of shipments [8]. Regulation of the operation of vehicles also negatively affects the economy [5]. If the carrier with a particular vehicle is able to realize lower power due to regulatory action or state public power, the unit realized performance achieves higher costs [1], which are passed into the final price of the shipment transported. The aim of this paper is to highlight the impact of regulation works drivers in road freight transport in the gross domestic product of the monitored area. Moreover, the aim is to highlight the differences in the regulation of the work of drivers in different countries analysed.

© Springer International Publishing Switzerland 2015
J. Mikulski (Ed.): TST 2015, CCIS 531, pp. 300–310, 2015.
DOI: 10.1007/978-3-319-24577-5_30

2 Regulation of the Drivers Work in EU Countries Reparation

Operation of international road transport in the European Union Member states requires compliance with social legislation, particularly with Regulation (EC) No. 561/2006 of the European Parliament and of the Council on the on the harmonization of certain social legislation relating to road transport (Table 1) and amending Council Regulations (EEC) No. 165/2014 on recording equipment in road transport.

There are defined the following maximum marginal times in EU member states:

- maximum continuous time of vehicle driving,
- maximum daily driving,
- maximum week driving,
- maximum two-week driving time,
- maximum number of gangs that may be consecutive.

Table 1. Requirements for operation mode drivers under Regulation Nr. 561/2006 (own study based on [7])

Operation mode	Requirement of Regulation Nr. 561/2006
Maximum continuous time of vehicle driving	4.5 h
Maximum daily driving	9 h, 2-times per week 10 h
Maximum week driving	56 h
Maximum bi-weekly driving time	90 h
Minimum length of break after 4.5 h of driving	45 min (possible distribution into 2 time periods in duration of at least 15 min and subsequently 30 min)
Minimum length of daily rest (within 24 h)	11 h, possibility of reducing in 9 h three times per week. The rest is possible to divided into two part that are drawn within 24 h with duration at least 3 h of a first part and 9 h of a second part.
Minimum length of weekly rest	45 h, possibility of reducing in 24 h, but this reduction is necessary to compensate before the third week end after the reduction. During two consecutive week is possible to reduce maximum one time the week rest.

In the form of minimum times are provided:

- minimum length of rest periods after 4.5 h driving,
- minimum length of daily rest period and the time of its latest termination,
- minimum length of weekly rest period.

In addition, except directly enforceable EU regulations, there are also national regulations that are connected to social issues. Anyway, they are based on EU directives.

National regulations contain especially Directive 2002/15/EC on the organization of the working time of persons performing mobile road transport activities. The purpose of this measure is to ensure the health and safety of mobile workers in road transport, as well as other road users and overall road safety.

According to Article 1 of the Regulation, the main purpose is expressed as: "The purpose of this Directive shall be to establish minimum requirements in relation to the organization of working time in order to improve the health and safety protection of persons performing mobile road transport activities and to improve road safety and align conditions of competition." The main requirements of Directive No. 2002/15/EC are listed in Table 2 and define:

– maximum weekly working time,
– average maximum weekly working time,
– breaks in working time,
– subdivision of breaks,
– maximum daily working time if the night work is performed.

Table 2. Summary of requirements for operating mode drivers under Directive 2002/15/ES (own study based on [7])

Operation mode	Directive 2002/15/ES requirements
Maximum week working time	60 h
Maximum average week working time	48 h
Breaks	Working time over 6 h and less than 9 h – 30 min Working time over 9 h – 45 min
Break subdivision	After 15 min
Maximum day working time whether night work is performed	10 h

3 Regulation of Drivers Work in Selected Countries

Social rules governing the work of drivers in Europe at an international level were defined in 1976, when came into force the European Agreement concerning the Work Crews of Vehicles engaged in International Road Transport – AETR Agreement. AETR is valid in all EU Member States and next in the following countries: Albania, Andorra, Armenia, Azerbaijan, Belarus, Bosnia and Herzegovina, Montenegro, Kazakhstan, Macedonia, Moldova, Russian Federation, Serbia, Turkey and Turkmenistan, Ukraine and Uzbekistan.

Since its original version was AETR several times amended and updated. Various additions have changed the time limits but also introduced gradually recording equipment, what must be in digital format since 2011 newly registered vehicles. Since 20 September 2010 the text of the AETR is fully following the requirements for operation mode driver in accordance with Regulation (EC) No. 561/2006, i.e. the requirements for the work of the driver shown in Table 1 are valid in listed countries.

3.1   The Requirements of Social Legislation in the United States

In the United States the driving times and rest periods are regulated by governed by Federal safety regulations for car carriers. This Regulation lays down conditions for driving times, breaks and rest periods in interstate transportation. Federal safety regulations apply to all vehicles used for road freight and passenger traffic, with the following exceptions [17]:

- in bad weather and poor visibility,
- the driver – seller, whose total driving time does not exceed 40 h in 7 consecutive days,
- for drivers who provide transportation equipment and components in the oil fields,
- when transporting a short distance – 100 miles as the crow flies (160.9344 km),
- for deliveries to retail stores, where the distance does not exceed 100 km,
- when transporting agricultural commodities and economic needs, which are used for agricultural purposes.

Federal social prescriptions specify the following limits:

- Fourteen hour working time - a 14 consecutive hours spent by a driver in the work. It is usually understood as a daily limit, although it does not control a time of 24 h nor the calendar day. Service of driver begins to run when the driver begins to perform any work. After 14 h from the start of work the driver may not drive until he has drawn the 10 consecutive hours of rest, but may perform other work. By the time of driver's work are added all the breaks that he draws - break for lunch and breaks in driving.
- eleven hours driving time - during the fourteen hours of work the driver may drive the vehicle not more than 11 h. Driving time, after which the driver should draw a break is not limited. This means that the driver can drive the 11 h of uninterrupted driving. If the driver has just driven 11 h, he must not ride before the draw 10 consecutive hours of rest. After exhausting the driving time the driver may do yet another work.
- 60/70 h limit - the limit is usually seen as a weekly limit. It is based on the 7 or 8 day period. This period shall begin with the time specified by the carrier as the beginning of a 24 h period. It does not apply to the right week, i.e. from Monday to Sunday, but it is called as "floating period" of 7 or 8 days. Then a calculation of hours is done as follows: when the driver is operating in the 60 h for 7 consecutive days, he counts the number of hours of the current date, it means he sum the number of hours of the actual day and the hours added the last 6 days. Hours driven before 7 and more days ago are no longer incorporated.
- thirty-four hour time of "restart" - a time of continuous rest in duration of 34 h. The driver can "restart" his 60 or 70 h limit by drawing his 34 h rest. After drawing the 34 h of rest, the driver has available full 60 or 70 h in service (depending on working mode). The driver can then count the hours worked from the 34 h of rest drawing and not the hours for a full 7 or 8 days back (including the current).
- ten-hours rest period - a 10 consecutive hours that a driver is absent from the service. After exhausting hours of rest, the driver can drive again (if it meets with

60/7 or 70/8 limits under the mode, which works). During the rest period drawing the driver must have an access to a bed.

The operators operating vehicles in the state of Alaska have an exception from the above rules [6]:

- allowable driving time is 15 h,
- time in service is 20 h,
- modes of operation are as follows:
  - 70 h/7 days for operator that do not operate vehicles every weekday,
  - 80 h/8 days for operator that operates vehicles every weekday.

Another exception is driving in bad weather and poor visibility: in this case, the driver can drive the vehicle 13 h, this time must fall within the 14 h of service. This exemption is applicable only in case when the operator does not have information about bad weather or poor visibility (Table 3).

Table 3. Summary of requirements for operating mode drivers in USA [own study based on [17]]

Operation mode	Requirements valid in USA
Vehicle riding time	11 h, 15 h in Alaska
Daily time in work	14 h, 20 h in Alaska
Rest time	10 h
Number of hours in work during "floating" week:	
– 7 consecutive days	60 h, 70 h in Alaska
– 8 consecutive days	70 h, 80 h in Alaska
"Restart" time	34 h

3.2   Social Regulation Requirements in Canada

Social issues relating to drivers working in road transport in Canada are regulated by national safety regulations for motor vehicles, standard 9. Validity of the legislation is only applied on truck, tractor, trailer or their combination which has a total weight over 4500 kg and a bus, which is designed and manufactured so that it has a capacity of more than 10 persons including the driver.

Social regulation is not valid for [18]:

- two- or three-axle commercial vehicle, which carries the primary products from the farm, forest or sea, if the driver or operator is the manufacturer of this product and also during transporting of the product used to ensure the basic functionality of farms and forests,
- emergency vehicles,
- vehicles helping in case public safety threat,
- commercial vehicle used for personal need under this conditions: the vehicle was unloaded, a trailer disconnected, the driving distance does not exceed 75 km per day, and it may not by the using of driver for business connection with the transporter.

Regulation divides the conditions for the commercial vehicles riding in two categories as follows:

- vehicle driving south of 60° northern latitude,
- vehicle driving north of 60° northern latitude.

During vehicle driving south from 60° northern latitude next rules are valid:

- a driver may not drive after accumulation of 13 h driving during 24 h, which start from the end of daily rest,
- the maximum time that a driver may spend on call is 14 h,
- each driver must be during the day 10 h off duty. It is 8 h minimum daily rest period that a driver must draw on the whole, and the remaining two hours may be distributed freely in blocks lasting at least 30 min. Day is understood as a 24-h period and not as a calendar day,
- drivers have the opportunity to work in two different modes. These modes are called cycles in the Regulation:
  - Cycle 1 is a cycle lasting 7 days. If the driver has accumulated 70 h in service, he must not to drive a motor vehicle more, until the start of a new cycle. For completing one cycle by the driver and for the possibility of new start, he must draw a weekly rest period, entitled "reset" in the regulation. For cycle 1 is this rest period at least 36 consecutive hours.
  - Cycle 2 is the cycle lasting 14 days. In this cycle, there are two possibilities:
    - driver may not drive a vehicle after the accumulation of 120 h in service during 14 days, if the driver has to restore cycle by weekly rest period,
    - driver may not drive the vehicle after accumulation of 70 h in service during 14 days, but in this case the driver does not have the obligation to draw the rest in duration of at least 24 consecutive hours. The weekly rest period (reset) for cycle 2 is at least 72 consecutive hours.

The requirements of social legislation for drivers' work in Canada are listed in Table 4, which sets out the regulatory requirements if the driver performs vehicle driving north of 60° north latitude.

Table 4. Summary of requirements for operating mode drivers in Canada (own study based on [18])

Operation mode	South of 60° northern latitude	North of 60° northern latitude
Maximum vehicle riding time:		
– Daily	13 h	15 h
– Weekly	70 h	80 h
– Bi-weekly	120 h	120 h
Maximum daily time in service	14 h	18 h
Minimum daily time of rest	10 h	8 h
Weekly time of rest:		
Cycle 1	36 h	36 h
Cycle 2	72 h	72 h

3.3   Social Regulation Requirements in New Zealand

In New Zealand, the working mode of drivers is regulated by "The Land Transport Act from 1998 and by regulation "Land Transport Rule: Work Time and Logbooks" from 2007. This regulation was amended in 2011 and changes therein are valid from the first October 2011.

The rules for drivers' working time shall apply in the event that the operation of the vehicle meets the following conditions [19]:

– vehicles with a gross weight over 4.5 tons,
– if the vehicle is operated under carrier license,
– if the vehicle is used for transport of goods for external needs.

The regulations do not apply for vehicles with a gross weight of 6 tons if the vehicle operation is performed in a 50 km radius from the operation place and if the vehicle is not used to carry goods for external purposes.

Under current rules is valid that the driver has to draw a break in duration at least 30 min after a 5.5 h working time, regardless of what work he has carried out.

Maximum time of working hours during the day is 13 h. Working day is a time in which the driver performs work and:

– is not exceeding 24 h,
– begin to run after the daily rest.

Daily rest period must last for at least 10 consecutive hours. After cumulating 70 h of working time, the driver is required to draw rest period in duration at least 24 consecutive hours. Time of working hours may start at the end of 24 h of rest, or at noon or midnight. Operator may itself determine the method of working time calculating.

Break is defined as the time when the driver does not perform the work, it is at least 30 min and the driver must not spend in a moving vehicle.

If the driver is not able to complete the trip within his working time because of unavoidable delays, he may exceed the limited working time, but he must note this duly in the logbook. The unavoidable delay means circumstances that could not be foreseen or special events. Summary of the working mode driver rules in New Zealand is shown in Table 5.

Table 5. Summary of requirements for operating mode drivers in New Zealand (own study based on [19])

Operation mode	Requirements valid in New Zealand
Maximum continuous time of vehicle driving	5.5 h
Minimum break time	30 min
Maximum daily working time	13 h
Minimum daily rest period	10 h
Maximum accumulated working time	70 h
Minimum rest time after accumulating of hours	24 h

4   The Impact of Social Regulation in Road Transport on Safety and Quality of Driver's Work

Based on processed analysis, Table 6 is showing processed comparison of driver's work restrictions in road freight transport in the analysed countries. The analysis shows that when the vehicle is operating in the EU and the contracting states of AETR agreement, it is possible to implement the lowest performance for a week and for two consecutive weeks. In the EU, a driver is allowed to drive maximum of 90 h during two weeks, in other states it is not less than 120 h, in the US even 140 h when restarting the week and in New Zealand even 166 h.

Table 6. Summary of maximum driving times and minimum rest periods [own study]

Requirement	EU	USA	Canada	Australia	New Zealand
Continuous driving	4.5 h	8 h	13/15 h	5.25 h	5.5 h
Break	45 min	30 min	–	15 min	30 min
Daily driving time	9 h	11 h	13/15 h	12 h	13 h
Daily rest period	11 h	10 h	10/8 h	7 h	10 h
Weekly driving time	56 h	60/70 h	70/80 h	72 h	70 h
Weekly rest period	45 h	34 h	36 h	24 h	24 h
Bi-weekly driving time	90 h	120/148 h	147 h	144 h	166 h

Based on the foregoing, two facts can be stated:

- in other analysed countries higher driving performance can be implemented than in the EU in comparable period,
- greater driving performance in comparable period reduces the cost of transport.

Due to the competitiveness of EU production with goods imported from other countries it is necessary to reduce costs, including the cost of logistics. These costs are involved in the final price of the product in the range of 10–20 %. Where is limited in particular monitored time interval of vehicle driving, such regulation affects the amount of fixed costs (e.g. Depreciation of vehicles, car insurance), entering the final shipping costs as well as the final price of the transported shipment [9, 10].

Impact on the unit fixed costs is shown in Table 7. The comparison is processed assuming an average speed of a vehicle is 50 km/h and the total fixed costs per year are €70,200 [4].

If we assume the same variable costs, that are dependent on travelled distance, regime of drives in the EU causes that the price of delivery is increased by almost 100 % higher ratio of fixed costs per kilometre.

That raises the requirement of employment more drivers, or creates a pressure on the driver that he should realize maximum driving performance in legislation regulated time; it means drive the greatest distance with the vehicle. This argument is supported by the explanatory memorandum to the adoption of Regulation (EC) No. 165/2014, according to which in every moment the laws of social rights is violated by 45 000 vehicles in EU [20].

Table 7. Impact of the change in driving performance on the unit fixed costs [own study]

Country	Maximal amount of driven hours in two consecutive weeks	Ratio of fixed costs per one kilometre
European Union, countries of AETR	90	0.600 €/km
USA	148	0.365 €/km
Canada	147	0.367 €/km
Australia	144	0.375 €/km
New Zealand	166	0.325 €/km

But the support for increasing the vehicles speed adversely affects the quality and mainly the safety of driver's work. Road safety and the safety of the driver's work is given to many authors.

Road safety is influenced by three groups of factors [11]:

- The quality and characteristics of transport infrastructure,
- Characteristics and performance of the vehicle,
- Driver's behavior and performance.

The behavior and condition of the driver is defines as the most important factor in road safety [13]. Term landing with severe restrictions on driving time puts pressure on the driver, who is forced to drive in a higher speed and under stress of a possible infringement. Many authors were interested in relation between the speed of the move and the probability of death of the driver in a traffic accident [e.g. 14]. In this study confirmed that there is a high correlation between vehicle speed of travel and the driver's probability of death due to an accident.

The risk of death is increasing in the case of increasing the ratio of vehicles on the road and in particular when increasing the weight difference of vehicles using the road [12]. Assuming that the road freight vehicle is definitely harder than two cars, then, according to [12], the risk of driver's death in a lighter vehicle is 12 times higher as compared to the heavier vehicle driver. Results from research point to the fact that the performance of the driver and his behavior are the biggest challenges to improve road safety [15]. In particular, the factors such as speed, impaired and distracted driving and non-use of protective equipment are most important.

5   Conclusion

Based on the analysis of legislation regulating the work of drivers, it is necessary to claim, that in the EU are the most stringent working conditions of drivers, which are giving enough time to regenerate at a reasonable time of vehicle driving to the driver at first sight, on the other hand, those conditions motivate drivers to drive more quickly. In the EU, on the basis of the study it was shown that comes to the significant violations of social rights, which not only deform the market, because the operator who violates social law, can provide a lower price of transport but also reduces road safety.

Restrictions of social rights motivate the driver to realize the transport by higher speed, which is associated with a higher risk of a traffic accident or a higher risk of death of the driver. Also, such restrictions cause discomfort to the driver during the work, especially when futures contracts with predetermined time of delivery and possible limitations in traffic arise (e.g. road reconstruction). Then is the driver under pressure "or to violate a social lay or accept possible penalization.

It would therefore be appropriate within the EU to simplify social right and adjust the driver's work under conditions in other countries.

Acknowledgement. This contribution was made with the support of the project: VEGA č. 1/0320/14 POLIAK, M.: Road Safety Improvement through Promoting Public Passenger Transport

References

1. Cyprich, O., Konečný, V., Kilianová, K.: Short-term passenger demand forecasting using univariate time series theory. Promet Traffic Transp. Sci. J. Traffic Transp. Res. **25**(6), 533–541 (2013). ISSN 0353-5320
2. Kalasova, A., Cernicky, L., Kubikova, S.: Microscopic Simulation of Coordinated Route in the City of Zilina. In: Communications – Scientific Letters of the University of Zilina, no. 2, pp. 46–50 (2014)
3. Kalašová, A., Kubíková, S.: The European Union's approach to building transport infrastructure In: ARSA 2013 [electronic source]: Proceedings in Advances research in scientific areas : the 2nd virtual Conference, pp. 503–507. University in Žilina, Žilina 2–6 December 2013. ISBN 978-80-554-0825-5. - CD-ROM
4. Konecny, V., Poliak, M., Poliakova, A.: Economic Analysis of a Road Transport Company. University of Zilina, Zilina (2010). (in Slovak)
5. Poliak, M.: Impact of road network charging system on pricing for general cargo transportation. PROMET Traffic Transp. Sci. J. Traffic Transp. Res. **24**(1), 25–33 (2012)
6. Poliak, M.: Social legislation and its impact on pricing in road transport (in Slovak). Perner's Contacts [electronic source] **9**(3), 169–178 2014. http://pernerscontacts.upce.cz/36_2014/Poliak.pdf. Accessed 12 March 2015
7. Poliak, M., Gnap, J.: Práca vodičov nákladných automobilov a autobusov, EDIS. Žilinská univerzita v Žiline, Žilina (2011). ISBN 978-80-554-0333-5
8. Poliak, M., Konečny, V.: Faktory determinujúce rozsah spoplatnenia cestnej infraštruktúry elektronickým mýtom (Factors determining the electronic tolling scope of road network). Ekonomický časopis (J. Econ.) **56**(7), 712–731 (2008). ISSN 0013-3035
9. Poliak, M., Konecny, V.: Factors determining the extent of charging of road infrastructure by using electronic toll. Ekonomicky casopis J. Econ. **56**(7), 712–731 (2008). (in Slovak)
10. Poliakova, A.: Customer satisfaction index with a quality of service in public mass transport. Transp. Commun. **2**, 43–49 (2010)
11. Oster, C.V., John, S.: Strong: analyzing road safety in the United States. Res. Transp. Econ. **43**, 98–111 (2013)
12. Davis, G.A.: Accident reduction factors and causal inference in traffic safety studies: a review. Accid. Anal. Prev. **32**(1), 95–109 (2000)
13. Evans, L.: Traffic Safety. Science Serving Society, Bloomfield Hills (2004)

14. Lave, C., Elias, P.: Did the 65 mph speed limit save lives? Accid. Anal. Prev. **26**(1), 49–62 (1994)
15. Shinar, D.: Traffic Safety and Human Behavior. Emerald Group Publishing, Bingley (2007)
16. http://appsso.eurostat.ec.europa.eu/nui/show.do?dataset=road_go_ta_tott&lang=en. Accessed 11 December 2014
17. https://cms.fmcsa.dot.gov/regulations/hours-service/summary-hours-service-regulations. Accessed 7 January 2015
18. http://laws-lois.justice.gc.ca/eng/regulations/SOR-2005-313/. Access 5 January 2015
19. http://www.nzta.govt.nz/resources/rules/docs/work-time-and-logbooks-2007.pdf. Accessed 14 January 2015
20. http://eur-lex.europa.eu/LexUriServ/LexUriServ.do?uri=OJ:L:2014:060:0001:0033:EN: PDF. Accessed 15 December 2014

Key Challenges and Problems in Conducting Independent Evaluations of the Adequacy of the Risk Management Process in Rail Transport

Adam Jabłoński[✉] and Marek Jabłoński

OTTIMA plus Sp. z o.o., Southern Railway Cluster, 40-594 Katowice, Poland
{adam.jablonski,marek.jablonski}@ottima-plus.com.pl

Abstract. The authors have presented the key legal, technical and organizational assumptions related to conducting independent evaluations of the adequacy of the risk management process in the rail sector. Key problems related to change management in the railway sector have been defined. On the basis of a number of case studies, a few examples of the implementation of technical, organizational and operational changes have been presented. The authors have suggested their own approach to conducting independent evaluations of risk management processes in rail transport. The proposed approach can be applied successfully in other modes of transport.

Keywords: Safety management · Independent assessment · Change management · The process of risk management

1 Introduction

The approach to the safety of rail transport in Poland but also in Europe is being significantly modified. These changes were initiated in 2004 by the provisions of the Railway Safety Directive [2]. The directive started the process of creating a new look at responsibility in rail transport processes, clearly indicating that all operators of railway systems, infrastructure managers and railway undertakings should bear full responsibility for the system safety in their area. Operators should cooperate in implementing risk control measures when it is necessary. The leading actors in rail transport, i.e. in particular railway undertakings, infrastructure managers and entities responsible for the maintenance of freight wagons were obliged to introduce risk management processes to their operational activities. This issue is new for the railway sector and causes a lot of confusion as regards interpretation, in particular due to the fact that it concerns both technical and management sciences. The need for activity of entities assessing the adequacy of the risk management process in rail transport was forced by Commission Regulation (EC) No 352/2009 on the adoption of a common safety method for risk evaluation and assessment and Commission Implementing Regulation (EU) No 402/2013 on a common safety method for risk evaluation and assessment, repealing the Regulation (EC) No 352/2009 [12]. The introduction of the provisions of these Regulations resulted in the need for a systematic approach to risk management processes

© Springer International Publishing Switzerland 2015
J. Mikulski (Ed.): TST 2015, CCIS 531, pp. 311–321, 2015.
DOI: 10.1007/978-3-319-24577-5_31

including risk evaluation and assessment, which applies to any change in the railway system considered significant.

In the paper, the authors try to organize the concepts referring to a modern approach to risk and safety management in rail transport from the point of view of the need to create new players in the rail market. In the near future, they will include bodies assessing the adequacy of using the risk management process in rail transport. The bodies assessing according to the Polish law will have to be accredited[1]. By the Polish standard PN-EN ISO/IEC 17020, which refers to the assessment of conformity with the requirements for the operation of various types of bodies performing inspections [8]. Such a model of maintaining competences by these bodies will introduce a number of new interpretations and lead to a new situation, in which new players taking an active part in the development of safety management systems in rail transport will join the current group.

2   Risk Management in Rail Transport in Terms of Ensuring an Acceptable Level of Safety on the Railways

The concept of risk management is very broad and applies to many areas of business activity. Risk is part of so many scientific disciplines, ranging from insurance, through engineering, to the portfolio theory, that it should not be surprising that it is defined in different ways by each of them. While some definitions focus exclusively on the probability of an event, the more complex definitions reflect both the probability of an event occurring and the consequences of the event. Some definitions of risk focus exclusively on negative scenarios, while others are broader and they consider each variable as risk. In engineering, risk is defined as the product of the probability of the occurrence of an event which is seen as unfavorable and the estimate of the expected losses if the event occurs. Risk in finance is defined in the category of variation of real investment returns rate around the expected rate of return, even if the rate of return is positive [1]. In rail transport, risk has been exposed by provisions resulting from the European and national legislation in the context of the legal requirements for building safety management systems and freight wagons maintenance management. They have now become an integral part of the implementation of key processes in railway undertakings.

Risk management is one of the core elements of the safety management system. Therefore, the system requirements for risk management are that a railway company, an infrastructure manager or a railway undertaking describe in detail the procedures and methods for assessing risk in the company resulting from using the railway infrastructure, equipment used in railway traffic and railway vehicles and identify ways to supervise risk assessment while conducting activities on the existing conditions as well as in the event of introducing change in the existing activity or when a new type of equipment or material giving rise to new risks, which have not occurred so far, is used [16].

As regards risk management processes, infrastructure managers are required to establish procedures related to ensuring [14]:

---

[1] Law on amending the Law on Railway Transport - the choice of the accreditation process as a means of confirming competence of the assessment body (Journal of Laws 2015, item 200).

1. Risk control measures for all risk factors associated with the activity of the infrastructure manager,
2. The control of risk associated with maintenance services and supplied materials,
3. The control of risk associated with the involvement of contractors and control of suppliers,
4. Management of risk resulting from the activities of other parties outside the railway system,
5. The development of procedures and methods for risk assessment and the implementation of risk control measures whenever a change in the operating conditions or introducing new material result in new risk for the infrastructure or conducted activity.

Railway undertakings are required to establish procedures related to ensuring [13]:

1. Risk control measures for all risk factors associated with the activity of a railway company.
2. The control of risk associated with the involvement of contractors and control of suppliers.
3. The control of risk associated with the involvement of contractors and control of suppliers.
4. Management of risk resulting from the activities of other parties outside the railway system.
5. The development of procedures and methods for risk assessment and the implementation of risk control measures whenever a change in the operating conditions or introducing new material result in new risk for the infrastructure or conducted activity.

The requirements for both infrastructure managers and railway undertakings are similar, but their nature is different because of the different specific character of these two groups of railway companies.

The third group of railway companies which are obliged to manage risk is entities responsible for maintaining freight wagons (ECM - Entity in Charge of Maintenance). They are required to have appropriate procedures to [15]:

(a) analyze risk related to the scope of operations, including risk arising from defects and construction non-conformities or irregularities throughout the lifecycle,
(b) assess risk referred to in point (a)
(c) develop and implement risk management measures.

When analyzing these legal requirements, the following three groups of risks can be identified [12]:

1. Technical risk[2].

---

[2] Technical risk is a combination of frequency or probability of occurrence of a dangerous event and the consequences of this event. Risk management is a systematic introduction of the management policy, procedures, practices to the tasks of analyzing, determining and controlling risk. The system is an ordered set of any level of complexity, which includes: staff, procedures, materials, tools, equipment, and software. The elements of the ordered set are used in combination in the expected operating environment or supporting the action to perform a task or achieve a particular purpose. Cf: BS - IEC 300-3-9, reliability management, a guide of uses, analysis of risk in technical systems.

2. The risk associated with the implementation of operational processes by infrastructure managers, railway undertakings or entities responsible for the maintenance of freight wagons (the risk of errors in the processes).
3. Risk evaluation and assessment, which applies to any change in the railway system, which is considered to be significant. Such change may be technical, operational or organizational. As regards organizational change, only the change that may affect the operating conditions is taken into account.

The presented approach to risk management includes all activities taken by railway companies that affect the safety of rail traffic.

3   Change Management in the Context of the Implementation of Rail Transport Processes

The concept of change management in enterprises has a wide dimension. In railway undertakings, in addition to organizational changes, technical and operational changes may occur. As regards organizational changes, only the changes that may affect operating or maintenance processes are taken into account. These changes need to be appropriately documented in the railway system in terms of ensuring an acceptable level of rail transport safety. The following groups are required to comply with regulations related to risk evaluation and assessment in the context of significant changes:

1. Railway undertakings pursuant to Directive 2004/49/EC.
2. Infrastructure managers pursuant to Directive 2004/49/EC.
3. Ordering parties or manufacturer pursuant to Directive 2008/57/EC [4].
4. Applicants for being permitted to operate pursuant to Directive 2008/57/EC.
5. Entities in charge of the maintenance of freight wagons pursuant to Commission Regulation (EU) No 445/2011.

As regards the process when structural subsystems are permitted to operate, if the change is significant, it is necessary to ensure, within the framework of risk management, the safe integration of admitted systems with the existing system. When the proposed change has an impact on safety, the entities, by expert judgment, decide about the significance of the change on the basis of the following criteria:

(a) system failure consequence: a reliable worst-case scenario in the event of the failure of the system under assessment, taking into account the existence of safety barriers outside the system;
(b) innovation used in implementing the change; this criterion includes innovation in both the railway sector, as well as in the organization implementing the change;
(c) the complexity of the change;
(d) monitoring: the inability to monitor the implemented change throughout the system life-cycle and take appropriate interventions;
(e) reversibility: the inability to revert to the system before the change;
(f) additionality: the assessment of change significance taking into account all recent changes in the system under assessment, which were related to safety and not considered as significant.

The applicant keeps relevant documentation which justifies his/her decision [12].

A criterion that causes the most trouble as regards railway traffic safety is innovation. The criterion can be examined very subjectively. Innovation in the rail industry is related to the areas covered by legislation and those which can be shaped freely [5]. In recent years in particular, the creation of innovative solutions based on an open innovation model gives new opportunities for the implementation of these solutions. First of all, innovative solutions must fulfil strict requirements for safety in rail transport [6]. It should be noted that innovations used in implementing change includes innovations in both the railway sector as a whole, as well as the organization implementing the change. Ideas can emerge from the needs for technical progress in the industry as well as new solutions for specific processes or services developed at the level of various players in the sector.

The examples of various changes which the requirements based on the Polish experience may apply to include:

1. Technical changes (the modernization of railway traffic control devices - replacing relay devices with digital ones, the modernization of rolling stock construction, reconstruction of railway lines).
2. Operating changes: (change in service-repair cycles of rolling stock, changing rules of organizing railway traffic).
3. Organizational change (outsourcing of train dispatchers, the acquisition of railway infrastructure maintenance processes by external companies based on their original approach).

Many changes in rail transport can be defined and with an increase in funding for investment, maintenance and modernization of railway infrastructure in Poland, there will be many more. Therefore, the issue needs further scientific research and practical implementations. It also involves the processes of railway traffic safety issues [7].

4 The Role of the Assessment Body in the Risk Management Process

A key role in risk evaluation and assessment in rail transport is played by a body[3] assessing the adequacy of the risk management process and its outcomes in rail transport. It should be noted that according to the definition in the Regulation 352/2009, an "assessment body" means an independent and competent person,

---

[3] To conduct an independent evaluation, the assessment body:

    (a) ensures the full understanding of a significant change based on the documentation provided by the applicant;

    (b) conducts an assessment of safety and quality management processes in designing and implementing the significant change, if these processes are no longer certified by the competent body assessing conformity;

    (c) conducts an assessment of how the processes of safety and quality management in designing and implementing the significant change are applied.

organization or entity[4] that conduct research in order to assess, on the basis of the evidence, the ability of the system to meet safety requirements applicable to it. Both Regulation 352/2009 and Regulation 402/2013 set out the criteria to be met by assessment bodies, and they are different[5]. When Regulation 402/2013 replacing Regulation 352/2009 is in force, requirements for assessment bodies will be higher. Currently, Regulation 352/2009 in Annex II shows the following requirements:

1. An assessment body may not become involved, either directly or as an authorized representative in the design, manufacture, building, launching, operation or maintenance of the system under assessment. This criterion does not exclude the possibility of exchange of technical information between that body and all the involved entities.

2. An assessment body must conduct assessment activities with the highest degree of professional integrity and technical competence and must be free from all pressures and inducements, particularly financial, which might influence their judgment or the results of the assessments, in particular from persons or groups of persons affected by the assessments

3. An assessment body must possess the means required to perform adequately the technical and administrative tasks linked with the assessments. It must also have access to the equipment needed for exceptional assessments.

4. The staff responsible for assessment:

   - must be properly technically and professionally trained,
   - must have sufficient knowledge of the requirements relating to the assessments and sufficient experience in conducting them,
   - must have the ability to prepare reports on safety assessment, which constitute formal conclusions of the assessment.

5. It is necessary to ensure the independence of the staff responsible for independent assessments. An official cannot be remunerated based on the number of assessments carried out or on their results.

6. When an assessment body does not belong to the applicant's organizational structure, the body is required to have liability insurance, unless in accordance with national law, liability lies with the member state or assessments are carried out directly by the member State.

7. When an assessment body does not belong to the applicant's organizational structure, personnel of the body is obliged to observe professional secrecy with regard to all information obtained during the performance of their duties (with the

---

[4] Regulation 402 adds "internal or external person, organization or entity" to the definition.

[5] Regulation 352/2009 has been in force since 1 July 2012. However, this Regulation has applied since 19 July 2010:

   (a) to all significant technical changes in the vehicles, which are defined in Art. 2 of Directive 2008/57/EC;

   (b) to all significant changes in structural subsystems, when required by Art. 15 paragraph.1 Directive 2008/57/EC or TSI.

   Regulation 402/2013 has been applied since 21 May 2015.

exception of the competent administrative authorities in the country where they perform those activities), in accordance with this Regulation.

Regulation 402/2013 sets much higher requirements. It requires the accreditation status of the assessment body or its recognition. According to this regulation:

1. An assessment body must meet all the requirements of ISO/IEC 17020: 2012 standard [8] and its subsequent amendments. In conducting control work specified in this standard, the assessment body is guided by professional judgment. The assessment body must satisfy both the general criteria for competence and independence contained in this standard, as well as the following detailed criteria for competence:
   (a) competence in the area of risk management: knowledge and experience of the standard techniques of safety analysis and relevant standards;
   (b) all the necessary competences to assess the rail system components that are affected by the change;
   (c) competence in the proper use of safety and quality management systems or in the audit of management systems.
2. Similarly to the Art. 28 Directive 2008/57/EC on the notification of notified bodies, the assessment body must be accredited or recognized for the individual areas of competences associated with the railway system, or its components, for which the essential safety requirements apply, including the area of competence for the operation and maintenance of the railway system.
3. The assessment body must be accredited or recognized for the purpose of assessing the overall consistency of risk management and safe integration of whole system under assessment with the entire railway system. This includes assessment body's competence in the field of control:
   (a) the organization, i.e. mechanisms necessary to ensure a coordinated approach to ensure the safety of the system by a common understanding and application of risk control measures for subsystems;
   (b) methodology, i.e. the assessment methods and resources used by different stakeholders to support safety at the level of the subsystem and system; and
   (c) technical aspects necessary to assess the relevance and completeness of the risk assessment and the level of safety in relation to the system as a whole.
4. The assessment body may be accredited or recognized in relation to one area, several or all of the areas of competence specified in paragraphs 2 and 3.

Both groups of the criteria presented above apply to processes having the nature of inspection aimed at checking whether the process of risk evaluation and assessment has been conducted correctly in the railway company and checking whether the change is appropriate and whether it will manage to maintain the level of safety as before the change. It is necessary to check whether the conducted risk evaluation meets the requirements of this Regulation and whether the principles of risk acceptance have been applied properly [12]. This process should be professional.

5 The Application of the Accreditation Procedure in the Process of Selecting Bodies Assessing the Adequacy of the Risk Management Process

As it has already been mentioned, bodies assessing the adequacy of the risk management process must be accredited for compliance with ISO/IEC 17020: 2012 standard. According to the definition of **"assessment body"**, it is an independent and competent internal or external person, organization or entity that conduct research to assess, based on the evidence, the ability of the system to meet safety requirements which apply to it. This type of an assessment body has a nature of the inspection body. There are three types of inspection bodies:

Type A - legally and functionally autonomous entities, conducting inspections only as a third party.

Type B - bodies which are functionally part of a larger organization (parent), conducting inspections solely for the larger organization.

Type C - bodies that are a branch or department of a larger organization. They can provide services to external organizations, but they are not bodies acting as an independent third party.

In Poland, bodies of types A and B are likely to be more common. They will have to fulfil in particular requirements for the impartiality of their activity. According to the ISO/IEC 17020: 2012 standard, inspection bodies should be responsible for the impartiality of their inspection activity and should not allow commercial, financial and other pressures to undermine their impartiality. In addition to this requirement, they will have to fulfil a number of requirements of a technical and organizational nature. These bodies should be accredited on the basis of the accreditation programme defined by an accreditation body. In the case of type B inspection bodies, these entities can conduct an independent assessment through their own structures and own specialists. The problem, however, is in the process of ensuring independence, which will be difficult, particularly in small companies. Therefore, external bodies need to be established, which will ensure independence and professionalism in the evaluation process. These external bodies should meet the above requirements. In Polish conditions, the accreditation process for compliance with ISO/IEC 17020: 2012 standard is conducted by the Polish Centre for Accreditation. This process is time consuming and costly. As the experience in other processes show, for example the accreditation process necessary to conduct compliance assessment conducted by the notified bodies, preparing this institution for the process will require a reasonable period of time. This process will certainly lead to new problems which will require effective and efficient solutions. The tasks of assessment bodies will end with preparing the relevant report. To illustrate the wide range of activities taken by this body, the examples of the contents of this report have been shown below.

The contents of the Report prepared by the assessment body

1. The name of the assessment body and its characteristics.
2. The name of the applicant.
3. The plan of an independent assessment

4. The development of an independent assessment
5. The scope of independent assessment
6. The description of the method/methods and procedures for independent assessment, which were applied with specifying guidelines in relation to the agreed methods and procedures
7. The identification of equipment used for measurement and testing
8. The use of sampling methods
9. The place of the independent evaluation
10. Environmental conditions when applied
11. The results of the various stages of evaluation
12. The main principles of risk management
13. The description of the risk assessment process
14. The identification of risks
15. Using the code of conduct in risk assessment
16. Using the reference system in risk assessment
17. The use and evaluation of explicit risk
18. Management of risks – a risk management process
19. The evidence resulting from applying the risk management process
20. Final conclusions of an independent assessment - recommendations including all cases of non-conformity with the provisions of Regulation 402/2013 and orders of an assessment body.
21. Conclusions
22. Reference documents related to the assessment
23. Annexes

Note: In each report, it is stated that the report of the independent assessment must be reproduced only in its entirety (partial reproduction is prohibited) and a statement that the inspection results relate only to the work ordered or the object (s) or the parties that were inspected; the inspection report of an independent assessment includes the sign or seal of the instructor.

The current problems in the functioning of independent assessment bodies, the adequacy of the risk management process:

1. An inspection body dealing with the assessment of the adequacy of the risk management process is specific compared to the existing, PCA accredited inspection bodies, for example the inspections of goods quantity and quality, inspections of manufacturing processes, services inspection, surveillance inspections, health inspections, veterinary inspections, environmental inspections, verifications of environmental technologies, inspections for the approval and release. The scope of inspections of these body refers to the issue of safety management.
2. Certainly, there will be a problem with proving the independence and impartiality of the expert bodies operating on the market, consisting of a small group of experts having professional competence to conduct assessments in respect of railway traffic safety.
3. Currently, irregularities can be observed related to diminishing the significance of changes in order to avoid the need to perform complex procedures in accordance

with Regulation 402/2013 by infrastructure managers, railway undertakings and entities responsible for the maintenance of freight wagons.

4. Applicants will have to be more responsible when qualifying technical, organizational and operational changes.
5. The key and unresolved problem is to determine the price of liability insurance and its value.
6. Shaping the market will be a challenge especially in the context of the need to document the inspection body's expertise in relation to the scope of accreditation.

6 The Use of Assumptions Independent Assessment of the Risk Management Process in Other Modes of Transport

In addition to rail transport also in other modes of transport you can observe the phenomenon of increased concentration on risk management processes. This is particularly important in the aviation and maritime transport. Although it is difficult to find a similar solutions in the conduct independent assessments of the risk management process it seems reasonable to apply the similar solutions in other modes of transport. Independent bodies assessment of the adequacy of the valuation and risk assessment can also be used in road, air and sea transport. However, for this to happen it would be appropriate to look at this process in a holistic manner where risk management system can be a universal way to eliminate hazards. The approach to this process should be standardized. Standards should be changed only in the context of the specificities of the functioning of various modes of transport. Hazard identification should be very similar, and the differences should result only from specific technical conditions. Activities of the specialized units dealing with supervision of risk management processes by transport operators in their respective fields can increase the professionalization of services in terms of quality and safety criteria. Therefore, we recommend to use the similar approach in other areas of transport because it can improve the level of services in range of quality and safety.

7 Conclusion

The process of risk evaluation and assessment in the context of significant changes is difficult. It is also difficult to identify significant changes. Knowledge of the subject that railway undertakings, infrastructure managers, entities in charge of maintenance, manufacturers and other entities obliged to apply these requirements have is growing. Entering the market by new bodies assessing the adequacy of the risk management process will introduce a new area to improve safety management systems in rail transport. Currently, it is difficult for rail transport companies to move among complicated legal, technical and organizational procedures resulting from the requirements on safety management systems. In other modes, there are also needs for risk management. The use of an approach based on an independent assessment of the risk management processes can be successfully applied to other modes of transport.

References

1. Damodaran, A.: Ryzyko strategiczne, Podstawy zarządzania ryzykiem. Wydawnictwa Akademickie i Profesjonalne, Warszawa (2009). Akademia Leona Koźmińskiego
2. Directive 2004/49/EC of the European Parliament and of the Council of 29 April 2004 on safety on the Community's railways and amending Council Directive 95/18/EC on the licensing of railway undertakings and Directive 2001/14/EC on the allocation of railway infrastructure capacity and the levying of charges for the use of railway infrastructure and safety certification (Directive on rail safety)
3. Directive of the European Parliament and Council Directive 2008/110/EC of 16 December 2008 amending Directive 2004/49/EC on safety on the Community's railways (Directive on rail safety)
4. Directive of the European Parliament and Council Directive 2008/57/EC of 17 June 2008 on the interoperability of the rail system within the Community (Recast)
5. Jabłoński, A., Jabłoński, M.: Implementation and managing of innovation in the conditions of legal and economic constraints on the based of rail transport. In: Mikulski, J. (ed.) TST 2012. CCIS, vol. 329, pp. 423–432. Springer, Heidelberg (2012)
6. Jabłoński, A., Jabłoński, M.: Transfer of technology in the field of rail transport through cluster initiatives management. In: Mikulski, J. (ed.) TST 2013. CCIS, vol. 395, pp. 58–66. Springer, Heidelberg (2013)
7. Koursi, E.M.E., Mitra, S., Bearfield, G.: Harmonising safety management systems in the european railway sector. Saf. Sci. Monit. **11**(2), 1–14 (2007)
8. PN-EN ISO/IEC 17020: 2012, Conformity assessment - General criteria for the operation of various types of bodies performing inspection
9. BS - IEC 300-3-9, reliability management, the guide of uses, risk analysis in technical systems
10. Guide for the application of Commission Regulation on the adoption of a common safety method in risk evaluation and assessment referred to in Art. 6 paragraph 3 point A of the Directive on the railway safety, Reference no in ERA: ERA/GUI/01-2008/SAF
11. Examples of risk assessment and any supporting tools to the Regulation on common safety methods (CSM) Reference no in ERA: ERA/GUI/02-2008/SAF
12. Commission Regulation (EC) No 352/2009 of 24 April 2009 on the adoption of a common safety method on risk evaluation and assessment
13. Commission Regulation (EU) No 1158/2010 of 9 December 2010 on a common safety method for assessing conformity with requirements for obtaining railway safety certificates
14. Regulation Commission (EU) No 1169/2010 of 10 December 2010 on a common safety method for assessing conformity with the requirements for obtaining a railway safety authorization
15. Commission Regulation (EU) No 445/2011 of 10 May 2011 on the system of certification of entities in charge of maintenance for freight wagons and amending Regulation (EC) No 653/2007
16. Regulation of the Minister of Transport of 19 March 2007 on the safety management system in rail transport
17. Commission Implementing Regulation (EU) No 402/2013 of 30 April 2013 on a common safety method on risk evaluation and assessment and repealing Regulation (EC) No 352/2009

Pricing Policy After the Implementation of Electronic Ticketing Technology in Public Urban Transport: An Exploratory Study in Poland

Anna Urbanek[✉]

University of Economics in Katowice, 1 Maja 50, 40-287 Katowice, Poland
anna.urbanek@ue.katowice.pl

Abstract. Systems used for selling paper tickets for the use of public urban transport services have specific limitations, not only those concerning collection of data on demand, but mainly regarding the possibilities of differentiating prices and developing fare systems. The type of fare used depends not only on social expectations and income policy, but also on the technical possibilities of differentiating fares. Thus, worldwide as well as in Poland, automated fare technologies in public urban transport that are ever more widely implemented, are most often based on electronic cards. The aim of the paper is to compare e-ticketing systems implemented in the largest Polish conurbations, to deal with payments for the use of public urban transport, as well as to present directions of changes in the pricing policy.

Keywords: Pricing policy · Electronic tickets · e-ticketing systems · Public urban transport · Smart cards · Price differentiation

1 Introduction

Development of efficient fare policy is a very complex and has many dimensions, as it requires taking into account not only economic factors, but also social ones. Prices are a key factor for competitiveness of public urban transport services, as well as for sustainable development of towns, as properly conducted public transport pricing policy can improve modal shift and sustainable urban mobility. Contemporary automated fare technologies create a chance to use the potential resulting from new possibilities of price differentiation, and to develop such a functionality of electronic tickets (e-tickets), which will constitute added value for the passenger.

The research conducted extends the knowledge concerning pricing policy in urban public transport, particularly in the aspect of various possibilities created by modern technologies of electronic tickets. The paper makes an in-depth analysis of e-ticketing systems implemented in five biggest conurbations in Poland. The results of exploratory study create an avenue for further research, particularly in the area of international comparisons.

© Springer International Publishing Switzerland 2015
J. Mikulski (Ed.): TST 2015, CCIS 531, pp. 322–332, 2015.
DOI: 10.1007/978-3-319-24577-5_32

2 Urban Public Transport Fare Policy

Prices of public urban transport services perform various functions, also the expectations and preferences differ: of institutions that decide the prices, those who use public urban transport, and those who manage public urban transport. Prices of public urban transport are subject to substantial regulations, as they are subsidized from budgets of public entities [1]. In the process of price development, also the social factor is of particular importance, namely being accustomed to the scope of services provided, which often is the case, and which reduces the possibilities of fare change. It is expected that prices of urban public transport tickets shall provide appropriate income, yet at the same time shall be an incentive for using public transport services. Of importance here is the re-distribution of funds among various social groups, which is manifested by the substantial percentage of people who are authorized to use public transport free of charge or for a reduced fare [2].

Broadly speaking, economic results are expected from public urban transport services, which may be grouped into three categories [3]:

- impacts on the transport system itself, assessed in terms of transport service performance (accessibility, modal split, congestion, efficiency),
- impacts on environment and health (air quality, noise levels etc. for which transport is responsible)
- impacts on the economy and society, which can be estimated through the assessment of income distribution effects, equity and welfare effects of pricing policies.

Transport fares are constructed, in practice, by means of specific price differentiation tools, referred to as differentials. Two types of differentials are distinguished: vertical and horizontal ones. Vertical differentials reflect the distance and route along which transport services are provided. Horizontal differentiation of prices occurs when the price differs depending on who/what is transported and organization of the transport process (e.g. modes of transport, route, speed, time of day). In public urban transport, three types of fares are used most frequently [4]:

- flat fare, also referred to as uniform fare (no vertical differentiation of ticket prices, e.g. single tickets),
- section-based fare (prices differentiated depending upon the number of sections travelled), which has two variants: distance-based and time-based systems,
- zonal based system (prices depend upon the number and type of zones, for which the ticket is valid, sometimes additionally the criterion of validity in time is introduced, which leads to the zone-and-time fare.

Contemporary fare systems in public urban transport are characterized by being substantially differentiated, which takes into account both the type of the area being served, its population, as well as specific transport needs. It results from research conducted in Europe, that zonal-based fares dominate in public urban transport [4]. Zone boundaries are delineated in various ways, they may be the administrative borders of towns, town districts, or arbitrarily determined – having in mind the perspective of public urban transport. The advantages of zone based systems include making the fare dependent (to a certain degree) on the distance travelled, having also a fairly simple fare, in which it is easy for the passenger to calculate the fare [2].

The type of fare used depends, on the one hand, on the expectations, on the other hand on the technical feasibility of application a particular differentiation of fares, provision of efficient ticket distribution systems, keeping the ticket sales system within the assumed cost limits, securing ticket availability and easy use of the fare systems [5].

Tickets can have paper or electronic form. Ticket distribution systems based on paper tickets have numerous limitations, concerning mainly the possibility of price differentiation and collection of data concerning demand, along with high maintenance costs [6]. Thus, automated fare technologies have been ever more widely used worldwide, they are expected first of all to enable more efficient price management in public urban transport [7].

3   E-ticketing Systems for Urban Public Transport

Electronic fare collection systems are the main element of intelligent transport systems (ITS) and ever more often used tool for price management in urban transport, and a basis for integrated ticketing [8]. The automated fare systems presently implemented enable, among other things, automatic selection of the best fare for the passenger, differentiation of prices depending on the time of day, line, mode of transport, or various reduced fares passengers are entitled to. In public transport, three types of e-ticketing systems are in use worldwide at present [8, 9]:

- magnetic stripe cards,
- mobile ticketing,
- contactless smart cards.

First electronic tickets appeared with the development of the technology of cards with a magnetic stripe London in 1964 [10]. It is a relatively simple and cheap technology, but magnetic stripe cards and tickets require a physical swipe and, unfortunately, do not allow for collection of data concerning demand, the cards can be easily read and copied and are not re-programmable [5]. At present, this technology is considered obsolete and it is slowly going out of use.

In case of mobile ticketing, the mobile phone, smart phone, tablet or personal digital assistant (PDA) is used as an electronic version of a ticket. Such a ticket may be purchased at any place. The role of mobile phones and the Internet in everyday life has been increasing continuously, it is predicted that their use in public transport ticketing will continue to increase. There are three different possibilities for mobile ticketing [8]:

- premium SMS based transactional payments – the user pays fare with the next phone bill or pays the fare using funds available on prepaid telephone card,
- optical character recognition (OCR) – the user receives a special code for example QR code that contains all needed information,
- Near Field Communication (NFC) - a process that is very similar to OCR technology, yet in case of NFC the information is stored in the NFC memory of the phone.

In case of contactless smart cards technology passengers use plastic cards, which are provided with chips, storing the most important information. This type of cards requires only holding it near the electronic reader, which can read it from a distance up to about 10 cm, with which the card gets connected by high-frequency waves similar to Radio Frequency Identification (RFID) [11]. Presently, it is the most popular technology of electronic ticketing in the public urban transport. First smart cards began to be used on a large scale in the 1980s. Nowadays they are in common use in banking, health care, government and transportation. The microprocessors presently used in contactless smart cards are produced on the basis of standards of EMV technology (the acronym for Euro pay, MasterCard, and Visa) [8, 11]. It provides huge possibilities as regards processing of information and management of transactions, which is of much importance in case of dynamic settling of costs and travel time in urban public transport.

Each of those technologies creates specific possibilities concerning vertical and horizontal differentiation of prices, using additional functionalities that make up added value for the passenger, as well as other possibilities for data collection from the market, e.g. concerning demand. In Table 1 we have compared the three technologies of e-ticketing for urban public transport, from the point of view of selected functionalities for price differentiation and other passenger conveniences.

The "best fare" policy consists of limiting the total amount that the passenger may pay in a defined time. For example, the singles fares paid in one day shall not exceed the price of a day ticket. Distance-based fares and real-time origin fares and destination

Table 1. Selected functionalities for pricing, available in three e-ticketing technologies [7]

Potential Applications	Magnetic stripe	Smart Card	Open Payment System/NFC
Discounts by passenger class (senior, student)	X	X	X
Daily, monthly passes	X	X	X
Seamless intermodal transfer*	X	X	X
Distance-based fares	X	X	X
Time-of-day based fares**		X	X
Real-time origin and destination data		X	X
"Best fare" policy		X	X
Use of fare card as debit/credit card		X	
Use of fare media for retail purchases, parking, tolls, bike sharing		X	X
Passenger top up cards, check past transactions online		X	X
Personalized marketing	Limited***	X	X

*Passenger can transfer between different modes of transport without acquiring a ticket or other proof of payment.
**It could be accomplished with a magnetic stripe system, but it would preclude other functions.
***It is limited to passengers who pay by automated debit, for example when setting up automatic payments for yearly passes.

data collection, in all three technologies analysed require the passenger to swipe or tap (very often called "tag") at the entry and egress or only at egress [7].

Section-based fare, distance-based fare, and time-based fare are examples of fares in which, thanks to modern e-ticketing technologies, one deals with dynamic settlement of the costs and time of travel, sometimes referred to as the "Pay as you go" fare, which requires identification of getting on and off the vehicle. Three technologies of identification of boarding and leasing the vehicle are distinguished [8]:

- Check-in/Check-out (also called CICO, Tap-In/Tap-Out or Touch-In/Touch-Out): it requires the passenger to physically register the entrance to the vehicle and leaving it, by placing a smart card or mobile phone in front of a reader. The system then calculates the fare due and debits the passenger account with it [12].
- Be-in/Be-out: it does not require the passenger to register her/his presence in the vehicle, as the system automatically detects the presence of smart cards (or other fare media) in the vehicle. The system automatically calculates the fare which is most advantageous for the passenger. Passengers pay afterwards for example on a monthly basis [12].
- Walk-in/Walk-out: it functions much like Be-in/Be-out, the difference being only in the fact that passenger's presence in the vehicle is detected when s/he enter the door of the vehicle [13].

What is interesting, the research conducted indicates that a very frequent phenomenon worldwide is the parallel application of various technologies of e-ticketing in urban public transport, not only in one region, but also in one town/city, often parallel to the use of paper tickets [14].

4   Urban e-ticketing for Public Transport in the Largest Conurbations in Poland

E-ticketing systems for urban public transport are ever more often implemented in Polish cities and towns. Most of the big conurbations in Poland either already implemented such systems, or are in process of implementing them. It results from the research conducted that almost all e-ticketing systems for urban public transport in Poland are based on the contactless smart cards technology and mobile ticketing. They differ in functionalities, first of all as regards the possibilities to differentiate prices, to collect data on demand, and the scope of services available with the card. Moreover, which is worth stressing, in most Polish cities the e-ticketing systems function in parallel to the paper tickets distribution systems. Rare are the cases where organizers of urban public transport decide to completely give up paper tickets. In Poland this happened only in Rybnik. Table 2 provides a comparison of selected e-ticketing systems for urban public transport, implemented or being implemented in the biggest Polish conurbations.

At present, one of the biggest systems based on contactless smart cards, and undergoing implementation, is the project of Silesian Card of Public Services (ŚKUP).

Table 2. Comparison between e-ticketing systems for urban public transport in the largest conurbations in Poland [own study]

Item	Poznan Electronic Card for Agglomeration (PEKA)	Warsaw City Card (WKM)	Urban Card Wroclaw	Cracow City Card (KKM)	Silesian Card of Public Services (SKUP)
Started	2014	2001	2010	2005	2015 (planned)
Technology	MIFARE	MIFARE	MIFARE Plus	MIFARE	MIFARE DESFire
Scope of city-related services	public transport, parking, libraries, electronic signature, prepaid payment card (micropayments up to 50 PLN without pin code)	public transport, parking	public transport, parking, culture-related services, sports and recreation services, prepaid payment card (micro-payments up to 50 PLN without pin code)	public transport, parking, prepaid payment card (micro-payments up to 50 PLN without pin code)	public transport, parking, payments in municipalities, libraries, culture-related services, sports and recreation services, electronic signature
Dynamic settling of costs "Pay as you go"	Yes distance-based fare, fare calculated for each stop	No	No	No	Yes (all types of fare: time-based fare, zonal-based fare, time-based fare)
"Best fare" policy	Yes	No	No	No	No
Single-journey tickets available on smart card	Yes T-purse (funds converted into points, passenger pays using points)	No Single journey tickets cannot be encoded on the card	No Single journey tickets cannot be encoded on the card	No Single journey tickets cannot be encoded on the card	Yes ePurse (electronic money)

(Continued)

Table 2. (*Continued*)

Item	Poznan Electronic Card for Agglomeration (PEKA)	Warsaw City Card (WKM)	Urban Card Wroclaw	Cracow City Card (KKM)	Silesian Card of Public Services (ŚKUP)
Multi-journey tickets and season tickets available on smart card	Time- and zonal-based fare (3 zones) or season tickets for a definite number of stops. Season tickets can be valid for any number of days (minimum 14 days).	Time-based fare, season tickets for a long period of time only, in fixe fare, with strictly defined validity (30 or 90 days, or yearly tickets)	Time-based fare and differentia-tion because of type of line, with strictly defined validity (e.g. 7 or 90 days)	Time-based fare, differentia-tion due to number and type of lines, validity expressed in months (1 to 12 months)	Time and zonal-based fare, differentiation due to presence or absence of limit as to the number of trips
Journey registration requirement	In case of "Pay as you go" Check in required, check Out – cost of trip settlement	No	No	No	Check in obligatory in each case (all types of tickets and all types of fare), Check Out – cost of trip settlement in "Pay as you go".

(*Continued*)

Table 2. (*Continued*)

Item	Poznan Electronic Card for Agglomeration (PEKA)	Warsaw City Card (WKM)	Urban Card Wroclaw	Cracow City Card (KKM)	Silesian Card of Public Services (SKUP)
Possibility to pay for another person with a single card	Yes	No	No	No	Yes
Mobile ticketing	Yes (single-journey tickets)	Yes (time-based, season tickets, e.g. valid for 20 min, and weekend passes)	Yes (single-journey tickets and time-based, season tickets, e.g. valid for 30 min or 72 h)	Yes (single-journey tickets and time-based, season tickets, e.g. valid for 20 min and for 7 days)	Yes (time-based and zonal-based, single journey tickets)

It is a project implemented by the Municipal Transport Union of the Upper Silesian Industrial District (KZK GOP) – the biggest public urban transport organizer in Poland and one of the biggest in Europe. KZK GOP currently comprises 28 municipalities from the central part of the Province of Silesia [15]. ŚKUP card will be a carrier of electronic money, which will enable paying not only for public transport, but also for culture-related services, sports and recreation services, library services, and parking. Thanks to the electronic purse (ePurse), dynamic settlement of trip costs will be possible, in the "Pay as you go" system, in various fare systems [16].

The "Pay as you go" functionality is also available in case of the Poznan Electronic Card for Agglomeration (PEKA) [17]. In this case, however, passengers do not use ePurse, as the funds are converted into points, which are used for paying fares for each section travelled, measured by the number of stops. In both cases analysed, maximum fare for a given router is accrued when entering the vehicle, upon leasing the vehicle and Checking out it is corrected to the amount due for the section actually travelled.

The requirement to register trips in the Check in – Check out system is particularly important from the perspective of managing the transport offer, as it allows to identify passenger flows, identify revenues from tickets, and – in case of integrated tickets – to make settlements between various parties. In the ŚKUP system, as opposed to analysed systems (see [18–20]), the requirement for trip registration will also be in place for all types of multi-journey and season tickets.

5   Conclusion

E-ticketing systems constitute an important IT tool assisting pricing policy and optimization of transport offer. Those systems create substantial possibilities for price differentiation, defining rebates, or management of promotions, while a more efficient fare policy is an important instrument for enhancing competitiveness and attractiveness of public urban transport. Automated fare technology allows for dynamic settlement of trip costs, on the basis of various fare systems and application of "best fare policy", which is of much advantage for the passenger. Smart cards are more and more often used also for paying for other municipal services, which will in future allow to conduct integrated municipal policy.

However, having seen the implementations made in Poland so far, it can be stated that not always the possibilities provided by smart cards technology are fully utilized. The above concerns in particular price differentiation and possibilities of obtaining information about demand. Also the passenger's choice is limited, as regards the possibilities of defining the validity of season/multiple journey tickets, as in a decisive majority of cases electronic tickets are but a copy of paper ones. One can risk making a statement that a barrier for more efficient pricing policy is not technology any more, but legal or organizational constraints, or economic factors.

References

1. Fearnley, N.: Efficient pricing of urban public transport with budget constraints. In: 9th Conference on Competition and Ownership in Land Transport, Lisbon (2005). http://www.thredbo-conference-series.org/downloads/thredbo9_papers/thredbo9-workshopC-Fearnley.pdf. Accessed 20 February 2015
2. Urbanek, A.: Directions of broadening the range of tariff systems functionalities in urban transport. Arch. Transp. Syst. Telematics 7(4), 50–54 (2014)
3. Ricci, A.: Urban transport pricing. Discussion Paper. Instituto di Studi pero l'Integrazione di Sistemi. UNECE Workshop on Sustainable and Healthy Urban Transport Planning, Nicosia, pp. 3–5 (2003). http://www.thepep.org/en/workplan/urban/documents/ISIS.pdf. Accessed 13 February 2015
4. Tomanek, R. (ed.): Ceny transportu miejskiego w Europie. Prace Naukowe Akademii Ekonomicznej, Katowice (2007)
5. Bąk, M., Borkowski, P.: Integrated ticketing in passenger transport as a chance to improve interconnectivity. In: 12th WCTR, Lisbon, pp. 4–6 (2010)
6. Ampélas, A.: Automatic fare collection. In: Proceedings of 2001 IEEE Intelligent Transportation Systems, Oakland, pp. 1164–1166 (2001)
7. Perrotta, A.: Fare collection and fare policy. In: Transit Leadership Summit. Research Papers, pp. 1–8, Singapore (2013), http://library.rpa.org/pdf/TLS-2013-Research-Paper-Fares.pdf. Accessed 5 February 2015
8. Integrated urban e-ticketing for public transport and touristic sites. Science and Technology Options Assessment. European Parliamentary Research Service, Brussels (2014). http://www.europarl.europa.eu/RegData/etudes/etudes/join/2014/513551/IPOL-JOIN_ET%282014%29513551_EN.pdf. Accessed 5 February 2015
9. Kos-Łabędowicz, J.: Integrated E-ticketing system – possibilities of introduction in EU. In: Mikulski, J. (ed.) TST 2014. CCIS, vol. 471, pp. 376–385. Springer, Heidelberg (2014)
10. Turner, P., Smith, B.: Integrated electronic ticketing – field of dreams? Eighth World Congress on Intelligent Transport Systems, Sydney, Australia, 4 October 2001
11. Pelletier, M.-P., Trépanier, M., Morency, C.: Smart card data use in public transit: A literature review. Transp. Res. Part C: Emerg. Technol. 19(4), 557–568 (2011)
12. Integrated mobility with eTicketing. The intermodal and interoperable eTicketing platform for consistent, end-to-end mobility chains in cities. Siemens AG (2012). http://w3.siemens.com/topics/global/en/events/hannover-messe/metropolitan-solutions/Documents/eTicketing_EN.pdf. Accessed 5 February 2015
13. Be-in-be-out payment systems for public transport - final report. Contract No. PPRO 4/12/37, GWT-TUD GmbH, London (2009). http://webarchive.nationalarchives.gov.uk/20091203214536, http://www.dft.gov.uk/pgr/scienceresearch/orresearch/paymentsystems.pdf. Accessed 5 February 2015
14. Mezghani, M.: Study on electronic ticketing in public transport. Final Report, European Metropolitan Transport Authorities (2008). http://www.emta.com/IMG/pdf/EMTA-Ticketing.pdf. Accessed 5 February 2015
15. Dydkowski, G.: Effectiveness of the urban services electronic payment systems on the example of silesian card of public services. Arch. Transp. Syst. Telematics 7(4), 3–8 (2014)
16. Silesian Card of Urban Services (ŚKUP). http://www.kartaskup.pl. Accessed 5 February 2015
17. Poznan Electronic Card for Agglomeration (PEKA).https://www.peka.poznan.pl/web/portal. Accessed 5 February 2015
18. Warsaw City Card. http://www.ztm.waw.pl/?c=557. Accessed 5 February 2015

19. Cracow City Card. http://www.kkm.krakow.pl/. Accessed 5 February 2015
20. UrbanCard Wroclaw. http://www.urbancard.pl. Accessed 5 February 2015
21. Karoń, G., Mikulski, J.: Problems of ITS architecture development and ITS implementation in upper-silesian conurbation in Poland. In: Mikulski, J. (ed.) TST 2012. CCIS, vol. 329, pp. 183–198. Springer, Heidelberg (2012)

Navigational Information Exchange and Negotiation System

Zbigniew Pietrzykowski[1][✉] and Jacek Skorupski[2]

[1] Faculty of Navigation, Maritime University of Szczecin,
Wały Chrobrego 1-2, 70-500 Szczecin, Poland
z.pietrzykowski@am.szczecin.pl
[2] Faculty of Transport, Warsaw University of Technology,
Koszykowa 75, 00-662 Warsaw, Poland
jsk@wt.pw.edu.pl

Abstract. The article addresses issues of the automation of communication processes in maritime and air transport, in particular in sea and airspace navigation. The communication process refers to transmitting information between the sender and the receiver, which comprises information exchange as well as negotiations resulting from divergent objectives of the process participants. The authors, presenting the current state and concepts of communication automation, indicate similarities and differences. The concept of a joint automated maritime and air communication platform is considered.

Keywords: Communication · Maritime navigation · Air navigation

1 Introduction

The development of individual modes of transport, including means of transport and necessary infrastructure on the one hand and information technologies on the other hand, opens new ways to improve the operation of all transport modes. The links between these modes become increasingly stronger within a complex transport chain. The need for a comprehensive approach to transport services offered is more and more emphasized. This refers to the transport development strategy as well as specific organizational and technological solutions. Examples already exist: sustainable development strategy in various modes of transport, logistics regional and global systems, or intelligent transport systems (road, maritime and others).

Efficient and safe execution of a transportation task requires access to traffic information, where information exchange between participants of one or more transport processes is essential. Efficiency refers to the organization of transport processes (loading, carriage, discharge), safety refers to adequate control of a transport vehicle. The concept of navigation, formerly used for sea-going vessels and aircraft, has been increasingly used in reference to movement control of vehicles on land. Navigation is understood as a safe conduct of a vehicle (sea-going vessel or aircraft etc.) from a starting point to an end point. Solutions in automatic exchange of navigational information, i.e. information used

J. Mikulski (Ed.): TST 2015, CCIS 531, pp. 333–342, 2015.
DOI: 10.1007/978-3-319-24577-5_33

to assure safe navigation, mainly cover one specific mode of transport (e-navigation – sea transport, SWIM concept (System Wide Information Management) in the air transport, ERMTS – rail transport, intelligent transport systems – road transport). Concepts covering all modes of transport have been recently addressed, e.g. e-transport (EU). These broadly use telematic equipment and systems.

At the same time more attention is paid, apart from typical presentation or exchange of information, to communication issues such as selective acquisition of information and negotiations, by analogy to similar processes involving humans. Development of such methods will permit to improve communication processes by their automation and reduction of human errors - one of the most common causes of accidents. This paper discusses communications issues in maritime and air transport that can be extended to other modes of transport.

2   Transport Development Trends

The demand for various kinds of transport services, except for periodical downward fluctuations, is constantly rising. Potential benefits from the execution of transport tasks lead to actions aimed at broadening the range of transport services offered by carriers. Maintaining a firm position on the market requires actions for assuring safe and efficient transport. This is achieved by enhancing the safety and reliability of transport vehicles, infrastructure and by reduction of human errors and their consequences on the one hand, and cost optimization on the other hand. Growing social awareness enforces pro-ecological actions, such as the reduction of environment pollution. Limiting human errors is mainly achieved by supporting transport operators in gathering, processing, integration and presentation of information needed in taking decisions and by supporting decisions to be made through a generation of specific, justifiable solutions. To this end, various methods of risk analysis, assessment and management have been increasingly employed. At the same time more and more interest is taken in designs and practical implementations of unmanned remotely controlled and autonomous vehicles. In practice, such solutions have already been implemented in sea and air transport.

2.1   Maritime Transport

In maritime shipping, apart from traditional forms navigation performed by cargo, passenger, fishing vessels and leisure boats, offshore services have been gaining importance due to the exploration, transport and processing of mineral resources (crude oil, natural gas, concretions) and growing offshore wind power generation (wind farms). For economical reasons, the number of operating sea-going ships is constantly on the rise. Their number changes due to ongoing trends on the shipping market. Besides, we can observe the growth of specialized ship fleets, i.e. tankers, container vessels, ro-ro and heavy lift ships. Another specific group of ships deserving attention is high speed craft.

A rapid development of technologies on the one hand and attempts to reduce or eliminate health and life threats lead to a broader application of unmanned vehicles, remotely controlled or autonomous, employed in the military and civil areas. While the former depend on humans, the control by man on autonomous vessels as a rule is minimal. In both types of vehicles, prior to decisions and resultant actions, information on the system and its environment has to be acquired, processed and utilized.

2.2 Air Transport

Air transport has enjoyed a constant increase of traffic for many years. For instance, the number of passengers grew from nearly 1.8 billion in 2003 to over 2.9 billion in 2012. The largest rise took place along Asiatic connections (Near and Far East), slightly less increase was noted in South America. To handle such a huge traffic, the global fleet of airplanes is also being expanded by carriers. At present about 25 thousand mainly jet airplanes are operated throughout the world. However, the growing number of aircraft is not proportional to higher demand. Meeting that demand is possible by increasing the efficiency of the fleet – reducing turn-around time at the airports and increasing the so called load factor. To achieve these goals, low-cost carriers, who have mastered these solutions best, use aggressive business strategies.

The proper and effective exchange of information and advanced telematic solutions play an essential role in each of the mentioned areas. Passenger trade increase leads to intensification of air traffic (particularly on selected routes), which in turn results in more complex tasks of the organization, coordination and supervision of air traffic (traffic-specific tasks). The air traffic controller has to continuously and reliably exchange information with an ever-growing number of aircraft as well as other air traffic related services [7]. Naturally, appropriate management of air traffic flows is based on the collection of a multitude of data on aircraft positions, movement plans, movement characteristics etc. Increasingly important are also unmanned aerial vehicles, which are to play a number of roles - both civilian and military. Work is also ongoing on the possibility of remotely take control of the aircraft in case of an emergency or sabotage.

The problem of current supervision over the transport process is strictly connected with service processes at the airports. Fast and timely completion of ground services is a key element of carrier business plans, and is equally important for services responsible for air traffic management. Therefore, these services have to acquire, process and quickly exchange information on all delays, route changes, airplane changes, meteorological conditions etc. Co-operation of entities engaged in the transport process is being enhanced within the so called Collaborative Decision Making scheme. The proper organization of communication processes is the key to its effectiveness.

3 Communication Processes

Communication is a complex process that encompasses various aspects: transmission of information, message perception and interaction of process participants in, e.g. negotiations.

Essentially, communication is a process of conveying information between a sender and a receiver using a specific channel and means of communication. Its context and feedback are important features of communication. Communication can be executed by various means and using different carriers (transmission medium). Although this diversity increases the safety (redundancy, alternative communications devices), it may lead to difficulties in the perception of the message, and consequently, wrong interactions between the communicating parties.

Both maritime and air transport communications involve electronic form of information exchange, including electronic data interchange (EDI), and voice communication. The latter has lost its major role in maritime transport, particularly in standard situation communication. In many cases, however, it is an essential supplement to the EDI. In air transport, verbal communication between the controller and the pilot continues to be the basic tool of communication for the assurance of safety of traffic participants. However, as telematic technologies get more advanced, electronic data interchange becomes more important, particularly in onboard systems of conflict detection and resolution.

3.1 Communication Processes in Maritime Navigation

Effective communication is particularly important in situations that threaten the safety of people, vehicle, cargo and/or environment. The GMDSS (Global Maritime Distress and Safety System) has rules and procedures of priority communications:

- distress communication (collisions, rescue of life and property),
- urgency communication (person overboard etc.),
- safety communications (navigation and storm warnings, etc.).

Apart from the three priority modes of communication, the GMDSS features routine communication mode, enabling ships to report their presence in traffic separation schemes or in mandatory reporting systems. Routine communication, unlike priority messages, is not strictly defined in the GMDSS in terms of procedures or circumstances in which ships must or should exchange information, due to lack of appropriate legal regulations.

Bearing the above in mind, the authors of [15], while developing principles of automatic communication in maritime shipping, have proposed and adopted for consideration four areas of communication that exactly correspond to the four mentioned modes of communication: distress, urgency, safety and routine.

3.2 Communication Processes in Air Navigation

Air transport information exchange runs at different levels. Besides, there are many technical solutions used in aviation systems [8].

At the phase of flight preparation, the Aeronautical Fixed Telecommunication Network is mainly used. Messages sent within the network include flight plans, meteorological information and alerting. Flight plan messages convey information on planned departure, departure changes or flight cancellations to all air traffic control sectors involved.

At the flight execution phase, three areas of communication process can be identified. One is information exchange intended to define the traffic situation in the air. The major information sources include surveillance radars, ADS-B system (Automatic Dependent Surveillance-Broadcast) and weather radars, that after synthesis and data filtration permit to locate an aircraft in the airspace and display the information to air traffic controllers. Another area of communication is information exchange and transfer of responsibility for flight safety between air traffic control sectors. Recent years have witnessed a rapid development of the on-line data interchange (OLDI) network, which replaced former telephone communications [20]. Finally, there is voice ground-air communication during the flight, for the exchange of traffic information and clearances granted by air traffic control (ATC).

Besides, special communication relating to safety takes place in the flight phase. Thanks to the TCAS (Traffic Collision Avoidance System), this communication is conducted between two aircraft located in vicinity of each other, providing data such as position and vertical speed of the aircraft involved. In a close quarters situation the TCAS takes over the function of conflict resolution by working out and transmitting instructions for conflict solving to aircrews involved in a TCAS event.

4 Automation of Communication Processes

Information interchange may be performed in the form of information presentation or by selective information transmission. At present, the automation of communication processes in marine and air navigation basically refers to a typical interchange of data acquired from navigational equipment and systems installed on seagoing ships, in the aircraft and land-based centers. Information interchange is faster and easier thanks to progressing standardization of the scope and format of data (navigational, operational, other), which enables the electronic data interchange, thus making it possible to automatically process and visualize information. This also increases the amount of available information. More information entails the necessity to integrate and select data.

4.1 Automation of Communication in Maritime Transport

One of the proposed solutions in maritime information interchange and presentation is the concept of a single window, an element of e-navigation strategy developed at the forum of the International Maritime Organization (IMO). The concept is based on an increasingly broader range of standardization of information format and the standardization and automation of information interchange processes. Other concepts underway are the Motorways of the Sea and CISE (Common Information Sharing Environment).

The concept of Motorways of the Sea [4] aims at the improvement of transport processes in short-sea shipping and intermodal transport. In this approach the Motorway of the Sea includes the infrastructure and organization in two ports of EU member states. According to the relevant guidelines, it should comprise electronic systems of management of passenger and cargo transport logistics, safety systems and simplified administration and customs procedures making real-time information available to all interested and authorized parties engaged in maritime transport.

The CISE concept [5] aims at the creation of legal and technical conditions for the exchange of information on activities involving maritime surveillance between competent organs of EU and EEC states. The scope covers law enforcement, border control, transport, control of sea pollution, fisheries, customs. CISE consists in combining the existing maritime surveillance systems and networks, not a creation of a new system.

The automation of communication processes also covers issues of selective information acquisition, interpretation, assessment of current or predicted situation, identification of intentions of traffic participant etc. This requires the development of sub-ontology for communication. Previously proposed standards for messages [2] enable the execution of communication processes in the form of a dialogue – similarly to a dialogue conducted by humans. The standardization and strict interpretation of navigational information is of major importance in this context. Several standards for information exchange are being developed.

4.2   Automation of Communication in Air Transport

In recent years air transport has noted a trend to integrate and standardize methods of access and use of information needed by all users engaged in flight execution: carriers (airlines), air traffic controllers, airport managers etc. This trend has been manifested in work on the SWIM concept (System Wide Information Management) [19]. Its full implementation is expected to lead to the integration of constant and dynamically changing aeronautical data on individual flight plans executed in the airspace, airports, meteorological information, air traffic flow or surveillance data [17].

Due to high speed of flying aircraft, the speed of transmission and processing has to be high as well. Hence most of these processes have predetermined protocols and algorithms. Many elements of communication occur on the basis of previously made agreements. This is the case when the responsibility is handed over between air traffic control sectors, which usually takes place in the time and place previously fixed by agreements. Such arrangement facilitates possible automation of the process. On the other hand, it reduces a possibility of flexible response to untypical or emergency situations. For such events it is necessary to develop principles and procedures of negotiations acceptable by all interested parties.

The ground-ground communication has automatic procedures relatively easier to introduce. It seems that in terms of automatic procedures the air-ground communication (controller-pilot), so far performed as traditional radio communication, is much more difficult. This is due to different scope of responsibility: pilot is responsible for the safety of his own aircraft, while the controller is responsible for traffic safety, which means he has to separate an aircraft in time and space from other aircraft or dangerous areas. Implementation of automatic solutions will be rather evolutionary: first by additional support and increased range of available information, then by partly parallel processes, till all actions are taken over by automatic systems. Their development will be preceded by efforts to solve problems similar to those faced by maritime navigation [1].

TCAS is an example of automatic information exchange system in an emergency situation. A brief exchange of information on the position and vertical speed takes place between the onboard systems concerned, then a resolution for a conflict situation is automatically determined. The algorithm used, however, is very simple, corresponding to the core of the problem – find a way to avoid a midair collision. The system, however, can be substantially expanded to operate over a longer time interval. This will allow for more comprehensive negotiations to resolve a conflict [1].

5 Joint Platform for Sea and Air Navigational Communication

The automation of communication processes, apart from simple information exchange, comprises selective information acquisition, its interpretation, assessment of a current or predicted situation, identification of traffic participant intentions, and quite often – negotiations and compromises between parties concerned. Navigators need to establish communications because they are obliged to conduct their ships safely by any available means. These include VHF radiotelephone communications with an average range of not more than 100 km. The exchange of information between navigators of sea-going vessel or aircraft has a form of verbal dialog, consisting of questions, requests, or statements. However, in marine practice VHF communication is often negligent, incorrect or deliberately omitted. The lack of effective communication may be due to:

- language barrier (watch keeper has difficulties in expressing messages in English, or in proper interpretation),
- human traits of character or behavior, such as carelessness, fear, shyness and others,
- technical causes, e.g. equipment failures, reception disturbances, etc.

This is essential in negotiation processes, when decisions and/or actions are being agreed on. The automation of such processes is much more difficult. Another reason justifying the process automation is possible reduction of time needed to complete arrangements or negotiations.

As already stated, an air traffic controller, an outside agent for traffic participants, decides in air navigation who will occupy a conflict point on the route. There are concepts, however, suggesting that separation between aircraft should be a responsibility of the crews of aircraft concerned [18]. If this happens, the situation will resemble that in maritime navigation. As pilots' workload is considerably high, implementation of this concept will have to involve support of automatic systems. As present solutions do not allow for pilot-pilot negotiations on possible flight routes or collision-free passing, possible introduction of the concept of self-separation will definitely be executed by an automatic system.

The above remarks refer to sea and air modes of transport considered separately, as well as jointly, especially if co-operation is required, like in joint search and rescue operations.

5.1 Assumptions

We wish to expand the concept of automatic maritime communication, presented in a dialog [13–15], similarly to verbal exchanges of human operators. To make the information exchange process automatic, we need to define the ontology of navigational information, messages sent and formats of recording, a necessary step when it comes to transmitting an intention, question or request (demand).

Navigational information ontology is understood as a meta-linguistic term describing the structure and form of navigational information, taking into account information types and scopes. The work [9] presents an example classification, definition of set structures and their interrelations. The mentioned meta-language should also conform with the adopted standards addressing selected areas of navigational information.

The remarks above also refer to the way messages will be formulated and exchanged in ship/aircraft to ship/aircraft and ship/aircraft-to-shore/ground communications. One way of solving the problem is the use of appropriately constructed ontology of navigational information and a sub-ontology for communication (dialog), where an emphasis would be put on terms connected with information exchange and negotiation processes.

Research on these issues in maritime communications has been done at the Maritime University of Szczecin [15]. The ontology was created, edited and expanded with the use of Protége software [2], extended by an authored plug for automatic generation of ontology in the XML-Schema format. The ontology itself was developed in compliance with standards used in communication at sea [10], with assistance from navigating officers, and is systematically broadened.

An essential element of the proposed concept of a platform for automatic sea and air navigational communication will be negotiations as a process of interpersonal communication, in which parties of partly divergent interests attempt to reach an agreement satisfactory for both parties. In this connection, a specific negotiation strategy (co-operation or competition) will have to be defined and executed.

To analyze and interpret contents of dialogs in the automation of selective information acquisition and negotiation processes we need inference methods. They are built on a knowledge base containing a set or sets of implications enabling interpretation of premises and formulation of conclusions. The methods should comprise two levels of inference: effective selective acquisition of information (identification of needed information and its source, automatic analysis and interpretation of information), and execution of negotiation processes (development of negotiation strategies, development of the ontology permitting to comprehend correctly the intentions of both parties).

5.2 Concept Development

Work is in progress on the verification and extension of the navigational information ontology and communication sub-ontology in maritime transport to incorporate elements characteristic of air transport. Despite existing differences, an integrated approach is possible. At the same time, communications-specific regulations and procedures are being examined. The outcome will allow to standardize communication and negotiation strategies, and ascertain individual schemes in disjoint areas. The existing differences mainly refer to the scope and legal framework for individual solutions, also the responsibility for assuring the safety of traffic participants.

While the incorporation of the regulations in force and procedures on a joint platform is feasible in a relatively short time, difficulties lie in areas lacking legal norms for both maritime and air navigation. Such requirements and standards are needed for:

- decision support systems for manned ships/aircraft,
- decision support systems for unmanned autonomous ships/aircraft,
- requirements for and principles of communication for unmanned ships/aircraft, particularly for autonomous ones; these should include:
  - requirements and principles of electronic data interchange for unmanned, particularly autonomous ships/aircraft,
  - requirements and principles of negotiations for unmanned, particularly for autonomous ships/aircraft.

Work is continued on these issues by various research centers and research-industrial consortia throughout the world. Associated projects have a national range [3, 6, 11, 16] or international (EU: [12, 19]).

Legal regulations binding regionally are easier to introduce than international regulations and standards that will certainly take longer to enter into force. Autonomous unmanned objects are a fact, and stakeholders are aware that effective arrangements and solutions have to be worked out. The approach we propose may considerably facilitate the preparation process.

6 Conclusion

This paper deals with issues of navigational information interchange and negotiations between sea and air traffic participants. Increased throughput, advancements in navigation and surveillance methods, and efforts to enhance the safety of transport enforce gradual implementation of continually improved automatic methods and techniques in the organization and control of marine or air traffic. In this context, navigational information interchange and automated negotiations in situations of potential conflict pose a challenge for support system designers. This work proposes a concept of a joint communication platform for maritime and air navigation, and presents assumptions and directions of further work.

References

1. Bone, R.S., Long, K.M.: Flight Crew and Air Traffic Controller Interactions when Conducting Interval Management Utilizing Voice and Controller Pilot Data Link Communications, MITRE Technical Report 130300, Center for Advanced Aviation System Development
2. Banaś, P.: Using the Protégé environment for building ontology for automated communication system at sea. Sci. Pap. Marit. Univ. Szczecin **30**, 12–17 (2012)
3. Dopping-Hepenstal, L.: Autonomy in the Air, International Navigational Conference 2015, Manchester (2015)
4. EC Communication, Communication from the Commission providing guidance on State aid complementary to Community funding for the launching of the motorways of the sea (2008/ C 317/08) (2008)
5. EC Communication 538 final, A common information sharing environment for the EU maritime domain (2009)

6. Fanshawe, J.: The Development of a UK Regulatory Framework for Marine Autonomous Systems Drawing on Recent Practical Operational Experience and MAS Stakeholder Community Consensus, International Navigational Conference 2015, Manchester (2015)
7. ICAO 2001. Aeronautical Telecommunications, Annex 10 to the Convention on International Civil Aviation, Ed. 6
8. Kocot, B.: Systemy komunikacyjne na potrzeby zarządzania ogólnym ruchem lotniczym w polskiej przestrzeni powietrznej. Część II - kierunki rozwoju, Przegląd Telekomunikacyjny 5, 14–22 (2013)
9. Kopacz, Z., Morgaś, W., Urbański, J.: Information of Maritime Navigation. Its Kinds, Compon. Use, Eur. J. Navig. 2(3), 53–60 (2004)
10. IMO, Standard Marine Communication Phrases (English-Polish edition), Maritime University of Szczecin, Szczecin (2005)
11. IMO, Sub-Committee on Safety of Navigation, NAV 59/INF.2, Development of an e-Navigation Strategy Implementation Plan, Report on research project in the field of e-navigation, Submitted by Poland
12. Motorways & Electronic Navigation by Intelligence at Sea MONALISA. http://www.monalisaproject.eu
13. Pietrzykowski, Z., et al.: Exchange and interpretation of messages in ships communication and cooperation system. In: Mikulski, J. (ed.), Advanced in Transport Systems Telematics. Publisher Jacek Skalmierski Computer Studio, Katowice 2006, pp. 313–320 (2006)
14. Pietrzykowski, Z., et al.: Automation of message interchange process in maritime transport, monograph international recent issues about ECDIS, e-Navigation and safety at sea. In: Weintrit, A. (ed.) Advances in Marine Navigation and Safety of Sea Transportation. CRC Press/Balkema, pp. 119–124 (2011)
15. Pietrzykowski, Z., et al.: Information exchange automation in maritime transport. Int. J. Mar. Navig. Saf. Sea Transp. 8(2), 189–193 (2014)
16. Pietrzykowski, Z., Borkowski, P., Wołejsza, P.: Marine integrated navigational decision support system. In: Mikulski, J. (ed.) TST 2012. CCIS, vol. 329, pp. 284–292. Springer, Heidelberg (2012)
17. Scarlatti, D.: Identification of Technology and Services Options, Programme SWIM-SUIT, Doc. E366-02-05692-NOTE (2008)
18. Shortle, J., Zhang, Y.: Safety comparison of centralized and distributed aircraft separation assurance concepts. IEEE Trans. Reliab. 63, 1–11 (2014)
19. SESAR. WP 14 - SWIM Technical Architecture, DoW v.4 (2008)
20. Siergiejczyk, M.: Współczesne systemy wymiany danych w ruchu lotniczym - modele i metody: Skorupski J. (red.): Współczesne problemy inżynierii ruchu lotniczego - modele i metody, pp. 103–124. Oficyna Wydawnicza Politechniki Warszawskiej, Warszawa (2014)

Electric Taxis in Berlin – Analysis of the Feasibility of a Large-Scale Transition

Joschka Bischoff[1]([⊠]) and Michal Maciejewski[1,2]

[1] Department of Transport Systems Planning and Transport Telematics,
Technische Universität Berlin, Berlin, Germany
{bischoff,maciejewski}@vsp.tu-berlin.de
[2] Division of Transport Systems, Poznan University of Technology,
Poznań, Poland
michal.maciejewski@put.poznan.pl

Abstract. Battery operated electric vehicles (BEVs) offer the opportunity of running a zero-emission car fleet. However, due to their current range constraints, electric vehicle operations are mainly attractive for inner-city transport, such as the taxi business. This paper is bringing together facts and assumptions about Berlin's taxi transport and the current conditions of BEVs in Germany to provide the scope of electrification. Firstly, the necessary amount of fast chargers is determined taking general constraints of Berlin's taxi business into account. For charging, especially busy days during cold winter days will be critical. Furthermore, a pricing scheme for fast charger usage is introduced. Based on this, operating operation costs of a hybrid electric vehicle and a battery electric vehicle are compared. The authors conclude that BEV operation will only pay off if the vehicle's battery life can be warranted over a long span or costs of electric energy in Germany drops.

Keywords: Berlin · BEV · Electric taxis · Fast charging infrastructure · Electric cars

1 Introduction

Battery electric vehicles (BEVs) are on the top list of currently discussed topics concerning private transport. Research in BEVs is driven both privately and by the public with huge investments. At the same time, however, the general public looks rather sceptical at electric cars. Especially, the short range is a restraint that prevents people from switching to BEVs. Therefore, it seems a plausible idea to evaluate BEVs in those fields of usage where the vehicle range is not of major importance. Inner city taxi services are one of them. Each single task is usually short so that the vehicle range does not prevent taxis from fulfilling single requests. On the other hand, the taxi overall daily mileage is comparably high, so that they would have to be re-charged at some time of the day. Moreover, the use of BEV as taxis has the potential to reduce inner city greenhouse gas emissions, especially since conventional taxis have relatively high share in these emissions. At the same time, taxis may be seen as a lighthouse project for BEV usage in general: Taxi passengers will gain the opportunity to try out an electric

J. Mikulski (Ed.): TST 2015, CCIS 531, pp. 343–351, 2015.
DOI: 10.1007/978-3-319-24577-5_34

car on the passenger seat and some may get convinced to buy one at a later stage if they are satisfied with the quality of the electric taxi service.

This study aims to provide an overview about possible impacts of using BEV for Berlin's taxi business on a large scale. To provide a high quality service, there are several issues that have to be addressed prior to the introduction of electric taxis. Among them is the question of where and when taxi drivers should recharge their vehicles' batteries and how many chargers are needed to warrant a smooth service. With the Berlin taxi business being highly competitive, it is also of major importance to determine the impact of BEV usage the taxis' operating cost.

2   Related Work and Current Real-World Appliance

The usage of BEVs in taxi fleets has rapidly increased over the last years. In Europe, the biggest fleet has been announced to operate in Amsterdam using 167 Tesla Model S [12]. Worldwide, Shenzhen has the largest fleet with roughly 1000 operative vehicles [13]. Electric taxis may now also be found in regions with colder climate conditions, such as several cities in Estonia [14]. Several authors see taxi operators as potential buyers of BEV [8].

For New York City, a large-scale feasibility study comes to the conclusion that BEV operations for one third of the city's yellow-taxi taxi fleet would require at least 300 fast chargers and cost 20 million $ annually that could only partly be recovered by user costs [11]. The study also comes to the conclusion that one fast charging outlet is required per 13 taxis.

The authors have evaluated possibilities of electric taxis in smaller cities [3] using a microscopic simulation approach [7, 10]. It could be shown that electric taxi operation works well under ordinary demand conditions, yet conventional powered taxi fleets are capable to serve sudden peaks in taxi demand better.

3   General Context

Using BEV as taxis leads to some constraints that come both from the taxi business as such, as well as from the current state-of-the-art technology.

Currently, some 8000 taxi vehicles are licensed to operate in Berlin. These are operated by around 18000 taxi drivers [5]. Taxi fares are regulated by the city authority and mainly depend on distance rather than time. During a typical 8-hour shift, a taxi drives between 100 and 120 km in total and yields between 100 to 120 € of metered fares. A recent study by the authors shows that under normal conditions taxis are idle (either standing at ranks or cruising) around 50 percent of their online time [4]. However, during trade fairs and similar events, yields and driving distances for part of the fleet may be twice as high, as it was the case during a railway strike in October 2014 [9].

In contrast to other cities, there is no standard type of vehicle operating in Berlin. Both vehicles from the upper and lower end of the car market may be found. Diesel is still the preferred fuel for taxis, but both hybrid-gasoline as well as natural gas powered cars may be found. Especially the usage of natural gas was subsidized in the past.

The amount of available BEV models on the market which are suitable for taxi usage has increased substantially. Volkswagen (e-Golf), Renault (Kangoo Z.E.), Nissan (Leaf), Mercedes-Benz (B-Klasse Electric Drive), Ford (Focus Electric) and Tesla (Model S), all offer potential candidates for taxicabs in different price ranges. With the exception of the Model S, all vehicles come with a nominal battery capacity of 20 to 28 kWh, of which around 80 % are usable at moderate temperatures and only around 70 % at -20°C.

There are also several case studies for designated electric taxi vehicles. Some of them focus rather on comfort, high battery capacities and ultra-fast charging [2], while others are rather proposing more light-weight concepts [1].

Calculations in this paper are based on the Nissan Leaf, mainly because it is the most popular BEV on the European market. Moreover, it has been on the market long enough so that detailed consumption statistics exist. An energy consumption of 11 kWh/100 km at city conditions was measured [6] as a realistic value for a Leaf *without* any auxiliary power consumers such as lights, radio or climate control. In every day operations, a value of 15 kWh/100 km at an outside temperature of 15°C is more realistic [15]. Auxiliary devices, heating and cooling further increase consumption, typically between 1 and 3 kW, depending on the weather conditions [16].

4   Energy Consumption and Battery Charging

To evaluate the effects of satisfying all short-haul taxi demand in Berlin using BEVs, the whole currently operative fleet is considered. Long-distance taxi trips are generally not part of this paper, mainly because they are very rare (e.g. 20 + km long trips account for about 1 % of all trips [5]; moreover, trips 50 + km long follow different taxation rules and do not count as a form of public transport. Several scenarios taking into account different outside conditions in terms of demand for taxi trips and the weather have been developed. Table 1 provides an overview about the mileage and drive times assumed [5, 10].

Table 1. Assumptions about average daily mileage per vehicle during ordinary and busy days [own study]

	Standard demand	Increased demand
Work time [h]	16	16
Busy mileage [km]	150	225
Idle mileage [km]	75	75
Overall mileage [km]	225	300
Average speed [km/h]	30	30
Drive time [h]	7.5	10
Idle time [h]	8.5	6

In the default scenario, all cars are able to charge at a rate of 50 kW under standard conditions (the rate of the currently available fast charging standards CHAdeMO and CCS), vehicles are operating 16 h a day, split into two 8-hour shifts, and their average driving speed is 30 km/h.

It is assumed that taxis start their first shift fully charged and end the second one discharged, so additional (slow) charging may take place during off-shift time. The detailed energy consumption under different scenarios is provided in Table 2.

4.1   Standard Conditions

With standard climate conditions (i.e. neither air conditioning nor heating in constant use) and a typical demand for taxi trips (225 km of travel distance a day, of which 70 km are without any customers on board) roughly 42 kWh of electric energy per vehicle will be consumed, of which at least 26 kWh need to be supplied by fast chargers during the day. This would require about 30 min of charging, separated at least into two cycles. Considering the moderate Berlin climate conditions, this scenario represents around half of the year.

4.2   Hot and Very Hot Summer Conditions

During hotter summer days, constant usage of air conditioning while driving will increase the overall energy usage to 57 kWh per vehicle and day. Thus, almost 50 min of charging will be required per car (divided into at least three sessions). If taxi drivers keep on using air conditioning also when standing, energy consumption climbs to 70 kWh and fast charging time to over 1 h. The car would therefore most likely need to charge four times during a day. However, climate conditions in Berlin usually do not require such behaviour.

4.3   Cold and Very Cold Winter Conditions

Wintertime operations are somewhat more extreme. Battery charging is highly temperature dependent and the lower the temperature, the longer the charging process takes. Charging power may drop to 25 kW and below [2]. At the same time, vehicle heating increases battery usage. Heating vehicles only during drive time will raise the average daily energy consumption to 64 kWh. If charging can now only take place at 25 kW, each vehicle would likely need to charge for almost two hours during work shifts. Should drivers require vehicle heating also during breaks, energy consumption will rise even further (106 kWh per vehicle), which requires a sizeable charging infrastructure.

4.3.1   Busy Days

Extreme winter days with constant heating combined with a city-wide high taxi demand (resulting in an average driving distance of 300 km per vehicle) would require roughly 117 kWh of energy per vehicle. However, even then, wait time is lower than the required charge time of more than 4 h.

This means that vehicles have technically enough time to charge, given the charging infrastructure is well developed. The occurrence of such days is somewhat predictable in advance, so drivers may plan their charging behaviour accordingly.

4.3.2 Alternative Heating

Most wintertime charging problems could be solved by using a fossil heating unit. In this case, vehicle operations would only be carbon neutral if bio-fuels are used. With less roughly half a litre of fuel per hour [17], emissions would still be negligible. Each vehicle's electric energy consumption would lower to 42 kWh (as in the standard scenario), of which 26 kWh would need to be charged during the day. At low temperatures, this would lower the average charging time per vehicle to 1:05 h. Under increased demand, when energy consumption rises to 53 kWh, daily charge time would still be just under two hours. Such charging times are manageable. The use of alternative heating sources can definitely reduce the size of the charging infrastructure needed.

5 Charging Infrastructure

5.1 Size

As described in the previous section, an electric taxi fleet will require a city-wide fast charging infrastructure. At the time of writing, Berlin-wide there are less than ten fast chargers available to the public. This number will certainly increase over the next years, but is not likely to be sufficient any time soon to satisfy the charging demand for a whole taxi fleet. Therefore a dedicated fast charging network exclusively for taxis might be desirable. Chargers could be positioned at taxi ranks, allowing taxis to use idle time for charging. A practical consequence is that a pre-booking of charging slots is easily possible. Also the whole charging infrastructure would need to be financed by taxi usage.

Accurate estimation of the optimal size of the charging infrastructure is a challenging task. As the overall electric taxi dispatching process is highly stochastic in terms of both time and space, it requires carrying out simulation in order to take into account the mutual relationships between taxi demand, taxi supply and charger availability. Such detailed analysis is, however, beyond the scope of this paper and is the subject of ongoing research.

It is assumed that there are 720 chargers available exclusively for taxis, which gives one charger per 10 vehicles. The chargers are allocated to taxi ranks proportionally to the ranks' occupancy. As in Sect. 4, the analysis is carried out for a single day and for each of the defined scenarios (e.g. summer, winter, etc.). Table 2 presents the average utilisation of chargers. Since taxi demand is much higher in the morning and in the afternoon than during the rest of the day, an utilisation below 100 % does not mean that

Table 2. Energy consumption, charger usage, charging infrastructure and costs [own study]

Scenario	Standard	Summer	Hot Summer	Winter	Cold winter	Cold winter	Cold winter	Cold winter
Busy day	–	–	–	–	–	+	–	+
Fossil heating	–	–	–	–	–	–	+	+
Driving								
Drivetrain [kWh]	33.75	33.75	33.75	33.75	33.75	45.00	33.75	45.00
Auxiliary [kWh]	8.00	8.00	8.00	8.00	8.00	8.00	8.00	8.00
Heating [h]	–	–	–	7.50	16.00	16.00	–	–
Heating [kWh]	–	–	–	15.00	48.00	48.00	–	–
Cooling [h]	–	7.50	14.00	–	–	–	–	–
Cooling [kWh]	–	7.50	14.00	–	–	–	–	–
Total [kWh]	41.75	56.75	69.75	64.25	105.75	117.00	41.75	53.00
Charging								
Speed [kW]	50.00	50.00	50.00	25.00	25.00	25.00	25.00	25.00
Vehicle charging time [h:mm]	0:32	0:49	1:05	1:56	3:36	4:02	1:02	1:29
Chargers								
Daily charging time per charger [h:mm]	10:45	8:09	5:09	19:18	35:54*	40:24*	10:18	14:48
Utilisation ratio [%]	44.8	34.0	21.5	80.4	149.6*	168.3*	42.9	61.7
Dispensed energy per charger [kWh/day]	537.5	407.5	257.5	482.5	–	–	257.5	370.0
Charging costs Infrastructure per kWh [€]	0.03	0.04	0.07	0.04	–	–	0.07	0.05
per min [€]	0.03	0.04	0.06	0.02	–	–	0.03	0.02
Electricity per kWh [€]	0.20 (all scenarios)							
User costs per kWh [€]	0.23	0.24	0.27	0.24	–	–	0.27	0.25
per min [€]	0.19	0.20	0.22	0.10	–	–	0.11	0.10

* Infeasible charging time

there will not be taxis waiting in queues for charging. Also the spatial variability of taxi demand over time may lead to temporal shortages of available chargers at certain taxi ranks. Therefore, the utilisation level of 80 % (the winter scenario) may not prevent such queues.

According to Table 2, one may speculate that with 720 fast chargers (the ratio of 10 vehicles per charger) dispatching of electric taxis is feasible all over the year except for winter. In order to make the electric fleet operational also during that period, either the vehicles should be equipped with external heaters or the number of chargers be doubled or even tripled.

5.2 Costs

At current prices, the costs for a combined CHAdeMO/CCS fast charger are roughly priced at 18500€ per unit (including the set-up). Assuming a 5-year deprecation and the annual maintenance cost of 2500€, the daily cost of a fast charger equals 17€. With the ratio of 10 taxis per charger and the use of external heating, the consumption-based infrastructure charge (cf. Table 2, lower part) is predicted to be between 0.03 and 0.07 $\frac{€}{kWh}$, depending on the consumption scenario. Taking into account the energy price of 0.20 $\frac{€}{kWh}$, the cost of charging oscillate between 0.23 and 0.27 $\frac{€}{kWh}$.

From the infrastructure provider's point of view, it is preferable to charge users on a time base in order to grant a high throughput of customers at the chargers. This would provide an incentive for drivers not to charge longer than efficient (fast chargers slow down once 80 % SOC is reached). Moreover, the risk of weather or vehicle-dependent slower charging process would lie on the customers' side. In this case, the rate should be 0.10 $\frac{€}{min}$ in winter (given two times slower charging) and around 0.20 $\frac{€}{min}$ during the rest of the year (fast charging).

It should be noted that the calculation above is based on the infrastructure and maintenance costs of a single charger. Hence scale effects are not included but would most likely lead to lower costs.

6 Operating Cost Comparison

From an operator's point of view, the decision whether to use a BEV fleet or to continue to use a conventional fleet is mostly an economic one. As mentioned in Sect. 3, there are several BEVs available in the same pricing range as similar hybrid electric vehicles (HEV), such as the Toyota Prius.

Considering the lower price segment of cars, possible BEV taxi operators will most likely see HEV as an alternative in fleet planning. Table 3 provides an overview of annual costs for both car types. An average electric taxi with an annual mileage of 75000 km will consume approximately 20 MWh. Based on the energy price of 0.20 $\frac{€}{kWh}$, and the annual cost of a single charger (including depreciation) of 6200€, the annual cost of energy per vehicle totals to 4620€.

With the average consumption of a Toyota Prius in inner-city traffic being roughly 5.5 $\frac{l}{100\ km}$ and fuel prices of around 1.55 $\frac{€}{l}$, the example above with an annual mileage of 75000 km accumulates to 6390€ of fuel costs per year. Thus the energy-wise monetary saving of a BEV is around 28 %.

Table 3. Annual operating cost comparison of BEV and HEV [own study]

	BEV	HEV
Annual mileage [km]	75,000	
Energy cost [€]	4,620	6390
Battery cost [€]	2,500	
Engine maintenance [€]	150	1,000
Overall operating costs [€]	7,270	7,390

However, BEV manufacturers generally do not grant a warranty for the car's battery for more than 150000 km [18]. It is therefore likely that the battery needs a replacement every second year.

Since Nissan offers a battery replacement for a Leaf battery for roughly 5000€ [19], the annual cost of a battery is 2500€. A longer warranty time or a fleet wide battery replacement agreement could bridge this gap. On the other hand, the BEV will require substantially less engine-related maintenance. The exact savings in this field are hard to predict, as they are highly vehicle- and owner-dependent. For New York City the saving was estimated at more than 3000$ a year [12].

For a HEV taxi, engine-related costs of roughly 1000€ a year need to be covered [20]. For a BEV, this sums up only to roughly 150€ [21]. The remaining operational costs should be roughly comparable for both BEV and HEV, as are procurement costs of the vehicle itself.

7   Conclusion

A transition of Berlin taxi vehicles to an all-BEV-fleet using currently available infrastructure and vehicles will take considerable effort in organisational and financial terms. To warrant a smooth service, about one 50-kW fast charger per 10 taxis would need to be installed in the city. Refinancing them by usage should be based on the time spent at a charger rather than the energy consumed. Winter operations will result in a peak in energy consumption and charger usage. It seems advisable to invest in fossil-based heating units rather than heating vehicles using battery power.

From the taxi operator's point of view, given the state-of-the art technology, using BEVs as taxis will only pay off if some kind of agreement concerning the battery life is in place, or the energy price would drop significantly; otherwise the service will need to be subsidised.

Acknowledgement.   The authors would like to thank the Einstein foundation for co-funding this paper.

References

1. Adaptive City Mobility: Project CITY eTAXI, 2014, see. http://www.adaptive-city-mobility. de/. Accessed from 25 February 2015
2. Andersson, D., Carlsson, D.: Measurements of ABB's prototype fast charging station for electric vehicles. Master's thesis, University of Technology Gothenburg (2012)
3. Bender, S., Pannirsilvam, V., Khoo, R.: Concept of an electric taxi for tropical megacities. In: 3rd Conference on Future Automotive Technology (CoFAT 2014) (2014)
4. Bischoff, J., Maciejewski, M.: Agent-based simulation of electric taxicab fleets. Transp. Res. Procedia **4**, 191–198 (2014)
5. Bischoff, J., Maciejewski, M., Sohr, A.: Analysis of Berlin's taxi services by exploring GPS traces. Accepted for MT-ITS (2015)

6. BZP - Deutscher Taxi- und Mietwagenverband e.V.: Zahlen über den Taxi- und Mietwagenverkehr 2013/2014, Berlin (2014)
7. Faria, R., et al.: A sustainability assessment of electric vehicles as a personal mobility system. Energy Convers. Manage. J. **61**, 19–30 (2012)
8. Horni, A., Nagel, K., Axhausen, K.W. (eds.): The Multi-Agent Transport Simulation MATSim, forthcoming (2015)
9. Lieven, T., et al.: Who will buy electric cars? An Empirical Study Ger., Transp. Res. Part D: Transp. Environ. **16**(3), 236–243 (2011)
10. Maciejewski, M., Bischoff, J.: Large-scale microscopic simulation of taxi services, submitted to ANT2015
11. Michal, M.: Dynamic transport services. In: Horni, et al. 8 p. forthcoming
12. http://cleantechnica.com/2014/10/21/amsterdam-airport-enlists-167-tesla-taxis/. Accessed from 25 February 2015
13. http://www.tdm-beijing.org/files/news/Factsheet_GoodPracticeChina_ElectricTaxi_20130409.pdf. Accessed from 25 February 2015
14. http://www.elektritakso.ee/. Accessed from 25 February 2015
15. http://www.spritmonitor.de/de/uebersicht/33-Nissan/1296-Leaf.html?powerunit=2. Accessed from 25 February 2015
16. http://www.fleetcarma.com/electric-vehicle-heating-chevrolet-volt-nissan-leaf/. Accessed from 25 February 2015
17. http://www.gizmag.com/bio-ethanol-powered-heater-volvo-c30/18250/. Accessed from 25 February 2015
18. http://www.nissan.de/DE/de/vehicle/electric-vehicles/leaf/prices-and-equipment/services-warranty.html. Accessed from 25 February 2015
19. https://transportevolved.com/2014/12/07/nissan-announces-leaf-battery-replacement-program-europe-cheaper-youd-think/. Accessed from 25 February 2015
20. http://www.taxiforum.de/forum/viewtopic.php?t=8332. Accessed from 25 February 2015
21. http://www.goingelectric.de/forum/nissan-leaf-allgemeines/noetige-wartung-pflege-nissan-leaf-ausserhalb-garantie-t1600.html. Accessed from 25 February 2015

Development of Electronic Payments in Poland Using the Example of Local and Regional Collective Transport

Barbara Kos[(✉)]

University of Economics, 1 Maja 50, 40-287 Katowice, Poland
barbara.kos@ue.katowice.pl

Abstract. The development of information technologies and data transmission, as well as their increasing availability resulted in ever more frequent implementation of fare collection systems that use electronic cards and carriers of information about having paid the fare or being authorized to ride, on another basis. Over the last several years, many solutions with the use of electronic tickets have been implemented in Poland. Their common feature most often is that the card – ticket is dedicated only to services related to collective urban transport; there have been few solutions which extend the functionality of the card – ticket by adding the possibility of paying for other municipal services, or paying fares in regional transport. The solutions that implement payments with the use of electronic cards belong to the general strategy of dissemination of non-cash transactions, in this case in the public sector. The paper presents issues related to the development of non cash transactions and settlements, and – in the background – the scope as well as institutional and organizational solutions, which meant are to provide openness and interoperability of the implemented systems that allow card payments for public services.

Keywords: Public services · Card payments · Electronic cards

1   Introduction

For dozens of years – in urban and regional collective transport - paper tickets have been the carrier informing about having paid the fare; validated - depending on the solution - when sold or upon entering the vehicle. Despite the many advantages of such a solution, it also has its drawbacks. One can list here the difficulty in managing prices – restricted possibilities of differentiating prices and lack of possibilities of changing them quickly. What is more, ticket punching systems, in case of paper tickets, do not identify the type and nominal value of the validated ticket, thus it is impossible to obtain data and carry out the required settlements, e.g. for the purpose of public financing of transport, or concerning integrated/common tickets [1].

The development of information technologies and data transmission, as well as their increasing availability resulted in ever more frequent implementation of fare collection systems that use electronic cards and carriers of information about having paid the fare or being authorized to ride, or on another basis. Those systems have numerous applications in collective transport – also in transport with national or international range [2].

© Springer International Publishing Switzerland 2015
J. Mikulski (Ed.): TST 2015, CCIS 531, pp. 352–361, 2015.
DOI: 10.1007/978-3-319-24577-5_35

Over the last several years, many solutions with the use of electronic tickets were implemented in Poland. Their common feature is, most frequently, the fact that the card-ticket is dedicated only to collective urban transport services; few are the solutions which extend the functionality of the card-ticket, by adding the possibility of paying for other municipal services, or fares in regional transport [3]. The services of local/municipal as well as regional collective transport are mass-type services, thus the implementation of payment systems becomes an important element of the development of e-administration in Poland [4].

2 Non-cash Transactions in Relations with Private and Public Sector in Poland

In most general terms it may be stated that Poland is still a country with significant share of cash transactions. This is supported, among other things, by the share of cash in M1 monetary aggregate. Despite the fact that this share is regularly reduced, it remains higher than the average for EU member states or the Euro zone (Table 1). Table 2 presents the share of cash transactions in the M1 aggregate in selected European countries – it can be seen that there are countries, in which this share is significantly lower. From the point of view of economy, including the banking sector, a significant level of cash transactions is not advantageous, as it generates substantial costs. They are generated in various places, thus – case of central banks, the costs related to cash include, among others [5][1]: cost of production, sorting, distribution, and destruction of notes and coins, cost of infrastructure for handling cash (vaults, sorting facilities, etc.), cost of audits.

Table 1. Share of cash in M1 in the years 2001–2012 (in %) [own study based on [9]]

Year	Poland (%)	European Union (%)	Euro zone (%)
2001	32.3	17.1	10.5
2002	30.9	19.5	12.5
2003	30.3	19.4	14.6
2004	28.9	19.3	15.9
2005	25.9	17.5	15.3
2006	24.9	17.1	15.8
2007	23.0	18.0	16.4
2008	26.0	19.7	17.9
2009	23.1	18.5	16.9
2010	20.6	18.1	17.0
2011	21.8	19.2	17.6
2012	21.1	18.6	17.0

Source: Own study, based on: ECB Statistical Data Warehouse, http://sdw.ecb.europa.eu, quoted after [9].

---

[1] That strategy has never been finally accepted by the Council of Ministers. As a result, the document prepared was [6].

Table 2. Share of cash transactions in M1 in 2012 (in %) in selected European countries [own study based on [9]]

Country	Cash in M1 in 2012 (%)	Average for Euro zone (%)	Average for European Union (%)
Bulgaria	36.93	16.95	18.55
Romania	35.36		
Hungary	35		
Lithuania	28.77		
Latvia	22.39		
Poland	21.14		
Czech Republic	16.65		
Denmark	6.41		
Sweden	5.2		
UK	4.86		

What is more, the costs and risks related to cash transactions also affect businesses – costs related to the physical movement of cash, delivery of cash to the bank or to the entities concerned, security (many actions are manual – restricted possibility of reducing labour consumption, e.g. checking at every stage whether cash in notes and coins is genuine), as well as individuals (the risk connected with obtaining forged notes or that the cash gets stolen) [7, 8]. All this should make the state interested in disseminating non-cash payments. So far, however, a substantial share in wide spreading non-cash payments belongs to entities that are not in the public sector [9]. The development of card payments is due to the fact that such payments are convenient, as well as that the business model of that solution is good, and in that model all participants are interested. Also the development of information technologies and data transmission, including wireless transmission, is of importance, as well as the decreasing costs of infrastructure related to card payments. As result, the number of cards used for payments increases significantly (Table 3).

Table 3. Number of cards used for payments that were in use in Poland (in million pcs) in selected years from the period: 1993 – 2013 [own study based on [10]]

Year	Years elapsed from previous period	Number of debit and credit cards in Poland (in millions)	Increase in comparison with previous period (in millions)	1993 = 100 (%)	Previous period = 100 (%)
1993	–	0.042	–	100	–
1999	6	8.29	8.248	19738	19738
2005	6	20.37	12.08	48500	246
2009	4	33.21	12.48	79071	63
2013	4	34.66	1.45	82524	104

Analyzing payments and cash flows, various directions and entities between which funds flow are indicated. Individuals – consumers are listed, as well as public institutions and businesses (Consumer - Government – Business) [9]. Confining further considerations to payments between individuals and public institutions, it needs to be said that – despite significant increase of the number of bank accounts and debit/credit cards in circulation, cash still remains a frequent form of payments in institutions [9]. This is due to various reasons, among them one can list the fact that tax or another financial commitment must constitute – in the Mount stipulated – income in the budget of the entity, which is not enabled when card payments are accepted in the existing card payment settlement model, this refers in particular to payments with credit cards.

However, various activities are undertaken in order to disseminate card payments in public institutions. One of them concerns changing the settlement principle, that is crediting the income account with the entire amount paid by the one paying via card, and treating payment of remuneration to settlement agents at expenditures. Another solution is adding the transaction fee to the amount due, which - in turn - is not positively assessed by payers. Another solution is the introduction of city cards, that enable making payments for various public services, which is part of the general tendency to widespread non-cash transactions. With the provision of a wide range of functions that such a card can perform, it will be possible to enable individuals as well as businesses making payments in public entities. Providing the card with a wide range of functionalities is connected with a multitude of titles and types of payments to be made to public institutions [11].

3   The Range of Electronic Payment Systems Being Implemented

Preparing the implementation of a payment system with the use of electronic cards, one has to decide whether the system will be a closed one, limited only to payment for collective transport services, often organized by one entity, or whether it is planned to implement an open system, which - besides collective transport – also comprises payments for other public services (e.g. parking, recreation and sports services, library services [12]), as well as other payments (various types of taxes or charges paid in offices). A more simple and thus much more often implemented (at east at the first stage) solution is to limit the card functionalities to payments for local collective transport services [3]. This is also substantiated by the fact that the revenues from local collective transport services in a given area are at least one order of magnitude bigger than the revenues from other services – e.g. parking, admission fees to swimming pools, museums, theatres, etc. [3]. Thus, the system, despite its limited range, allows to cover with electronic payments a substantial part of payments for public services.

A more complicated, mainly from the organizational and legal point of view, is the solution in which the payment collection system, which uses electronic cards, is to comprise all payments made for the benefit of local self-government. This is even more complicated in a situation where the card is the authorize payments in different legal entities, e.g. in different towns/cities, for various entities that organize collective transport. Such a situation arises nowadays not only in big conurbations. Commuting to work or school every day does not necessarily happen within the administrative borders of one town/city, hence the usefulness of the card by which payments are made increases in a situation where it is not limited to the city area or one service only. As a result, when striving to extend the card's functions, it is assumed it can be used for payment of public tributes, fees, and charges for other public services. As a result, most often the basic functions of the card include:

- making payments for collective transport,
- making payments for parking,
- making payments in commune offices,
- making payments in commune centers (sports and recreation centers, libraries, museums),
- introduction of applications with electronic signature.

A precondition for wide use of the card, thus also for reduction of unit costs of its implementation, is the maximum extension of its functionalities. However, one should pay attention to the fact that the public sector may not carry out tasks which are beyond its legally determined catalogue of own tasks, which should be executed by non-public entities and regulated by market processes. In practice it entails limiting the card functionalities to payments for services or public tributes – no payments outsider the public sector can be made by means of such cards. It means that those cards are complementary to debit cards offered by banks, and fill the gap that opened as regards non-cash payments in public entities.

One should also pay attention to the fact that electronic cards that enable payment for services rendered by various public entities, including those providing collective transport services, become a significant tool serving the tariff integration in transport. Of importance here is the easy registration of data concerning services that are used, in particular the data on travels exist in the check-in check-out systems, which means that cards are read upon entering and leaving the vehicle. In Poland, over the last twenty years, many projects have been implemented, as regards integration of transport – including tariff integration – some of which are characterized by durability and continue to function; yet a part of them did not stand the test of time. Dissolution of contracts and discontinuance of common ticket formula – and a subsequent barrier for integration – resulted from not being convinced that the settlements are correct, which concerns in particular the division of income from tickets valid on lines operated by various organizers/service providers [13]. Provision of possibilities to use cards in various institutions results in the obligation of the payment systems' compliance with the requirements of the acts of law: on electronic payment instruments [14] and on payment services [15].

The implementation of payment collection system based on electronic cards, which takes place in case of IT systems implementation [16] is an undertaking connected with substantial expenditures, both during the investment period and during system maintenance. That is why of particular importance is to use the possibilities and benefits which can be obtained as a result of implementation of the solution. In most general terms, the following benefits based on electronic cards are expected [17]:

- savings on expenditures for transport services, due to more efficient management of the transport offer,
- reduction of costs connected with printing paper tickets and preparation of stamps for season tickets,
- reduction of expenditures connected with vehicle occupancy surveys, because data for analyses can be obtained straight from the system,
- increase of income from sales of tickets, due to better price management.

Irrespective of the benefits obtained by the parties involved, internal benefits are expected, among others in the following forms [17]:

- benefits related to the reduction of amounts paid in cash, and replacing them with non-cash payments,
- tools for optimizing the transport offer – benefits for the environment due to provision of existing quality of services, while the operation work is reduced,
- obtaining data in electronic form, which simplifies data procession and use for ongoing management of services.

In this context, consequence is indispensable in the course of implementation of a payment system utilizing electronic cards, in such a way as to implement not only the functions related to the payment system itself, but also those which allow to manage a substantial database containing data obtained as a result of such a way of fare collection. It is of importance, as in practice – unfortunately – in many implementations the functions that are complementary to the basic ones get reduced, which significantly limits the possibilities of achieving the assumed effects, after the system is implemented.

4   Agreements Assuring Openness and Interoperability of Card

A significant feature of systems, in which many entities participate, is the provision of interoperability – the possibility of relatively easy operation, with acceptable costs of adding new users, or extending the scope of services for the existing users. In case of collective transport systems it is important to enable the collection of fares by means of cards, for collective transport services provided by various organizers, not only of urban transport but also of regional railway transport of passengers, in the long run of national-wide long distance transport as well. Interoperability is provided by multidirectional activities, of course the initial ones are those undertaken during designing, description of requirements, or assumption of standards of the IT system itself. Interoperability is promoted by application of standards that already exist in electronic payments: in data processing, data transmission, and the card itself. However, the openness and interoperability of a payment collection system utilizing electronic cards requires organizational and institutional solutions, besides IT ones. At present, the common way to regulate co-operation between parties is to conclude appropriate contracts – in this case one should prepare an entire set of contracts, which will stipulate the responsibilities of parties and settlement system.

The starting point is the moment when designing of the project begins, usually one of the parties – more often than not the one which has suitable resources which enable management of the designing and later the execution of the entire project – becomes its leader. Jointly with others, that entity prepares and subsequently concludes the contract on execution of the joint project. The contract determines the framework of the entire project, principles of financing it during the investment period and its operations. The infrastructure of the project is usually divided into common/shared and individual one – partners participate (in a accordance with specified key) in financing of a joint infrastructure, which serves all project participants (e.g. servers that process data, devices for data transmission) and independently finance individual infrastructure (e.g. devices installed on board the vehicles of specific providers). From the point of view of the system's openness it is advantageous – as early as that – to authorize the leader to conclude contracts (with clearly defined principles) with other parties, as regards joining the given undertaking. Settlements may pose a certain problem, as the leader may over-estimate her/his input to the undertaking, while partners participating in the project are not always convinced as regards balanced relations with the leader – it is difficult to achieve balance between entities that differ, e.g. in terms of size, financial means, the volume of services provided. That is why – irrespective of legal regulations – the solution chosen may be entrusting the financial settlements to an independent authorized institution, which meets the requirements stipulated in the act of law on electronic payment instruments and payment services. The implementation of an open payments system also requires the participation of other entities, which entails conclusion of several contracts, in which the following will participate, in various configurations:

– organizer of collective urban transport (e.g. project leader),
– other organizers of collective transport, service providers, and legal public entities that provide services, for which payments via cards will be possible,
– bank or another financial institution performing the function of card issuer, issuer of electronic money, and city card billing agent,
– in case payments with such cards as VISA or MasterCard are allowed, the entity being the billing agent for those pay cards.

The provision of correct functioning of the system of payments and settlements between participant requires at least the existence of a contract between the collective urban transport organizer (project leader) and a bank or financial institution having suitable powers, in which the following will be stipulated:

– rights and responsibilities of parties, concerning settlement of payment transactions within the system, and principles that regulate settlements between participants, carried out by the bank,
– rules governing issuing city cards by the bank, and their delivery to the distribution network, issuing of electronic money by the bank, encoding season or subscription tickets on the city card; moreover a solution can be introduced in which the bank or financial institution runs service points, in which the above actions and transactions are performed.

Moreover, the organizer of collective urban transport (project leader) must conclude a contract with other public entities, which provide services, for the use of which payment can be made using city cards; a contract in which the conditions and rules common for participants of the undertaking will be defined. It is necessary to provide a suitable network for card distribution, charging cards with electronic money, encoding and sales of various services, e.g. season tickets; thus the organizer of collective urban transport should conclude contracts with entities that will carry out those activities. The latter entities most often function as commercial ones and belong to the private sector. In order to become independent of such entities, it is advantageous to conclude contracts with a few of them, so as to avoid monopolization of those activities by one entity, which can later try to dictate conditions. In addition, the parties which will provide the possibility of charging the city card with electronic money, have to conclude a contract with the bank, as issuer of electronic money. Such a contract will define the rules and conditions concerning the performance of actions connected with charging city cards with electronic money, acceptance of currency in return for the issued electronic money, as well as settlement of electronic money.

Organizers of collective transport, providers of transport services, or other legal public entities will become entities accepting payments with city card, in the system of collecting payments for services rendered by them. In connection with that, it will be necessary for them to conclude agreements with the bank, as billing agent, by the virtue of which the bank will enable them to accept non-cash payments made by means of electronic money. What is more, the entities accepting payments for services by means of pay cards must concluded an agreement with the entity performing the function of billing agent for pay cards (e.g. VISA, Mastercard). In case of launching the charging via Internet of city card, it will be necessary to additionally conclude a contract with the entity that performs the function of billing agent for transfers made via Internet. Those contracts will contain specification of procedures required (including safety procedures), as well as rights and responsibilities of parties in connection with conclusion of payment transactions.

It is clear on the basis of what has been said above, that the implementation of a city card, by means of which it will be possible to make payments for various public services, provided by different public entities, requires a whole system of contracts, in which rights, responsibilities, and risks should be divided, payment systems should be defined, as well as rules governing the flow of funds. Those contracts are concluded between parties that function in various sectors of public finances and banking, which vary as to their principles of operation. On top of that all there are IT solutions, which assist the actions defined in the concluded contracts.

For an entity from the sector of public finances, as such are the entities implementing electronic payments in the public sector, it is a challenge - standards, division of risks, the manner of performing settlements, determined by entities in the payment service sector are standards for private entities, and it is difficult to adjust them to those that are binding in the public sector. Another barrier is the fact that public sector does not generate significant flow of funds in payments by cards, and for various reasons - e.g. time consuming procedures – is quite a difficult sector, thus it is difficult to achieve a satisfying equilibrium in the contracts that are concluded. The implementation of such a system requires extensive knowledge, experience, but also conviction that the direction assumed is right, which in practice allows to make compromises and develop solutions in the difficult reality created by the public procurement law, principles governing functioning of entities in the public finance sector, as well as expectations and principles according to which IT and banking sector entities functioning on the market.

5 Conclusion

Dissemination of non-cash transactions gives numerous advantages, which are nation-wide, as well as which affect specific sectors or entities. The steadily developing infra-structure for non-cash transactions, together with a well-functioning system of cards issued by banks, make payment for products and services provided by private sector universal. In comparison with that, the public sector does not look too good: often the possibilities of using cards to pay for services or public tributes are limited. This gap is to be filled by payment systems using electronic cards, which enable making payments for selected services, e.g. in collective transport, or for various services provided by different public entities. Such solutions are not easy, though, as the require – besides developing the entire IT infrastructure – the co-operation of many actors, including the introduction of the entire set of contracts which are, in general, connected with issuing of city cards and servicing payments made using them. Thus, the city card project being implemented – besides the issues and problems arising in the course of implementation of a large IT system – is additionally complicated by the necessity of developing proce-dures required for electronic money instruments, and the provision of complementarity for co-operation with banks and entities that are billing agents. However, in the long run such solutions should bring numerous advantages. Using IT tools and solutions, it is possible to differentiate prices better, to manage services, to improve their quality, as well as to implement solutions that simplify the use of services for passengers. What is more, electronic cards are a useful tool for transport integration. Also the facilitation connected with the use of cards as electronic tickets is of importance.

References

1. Dydkowski, G.: Selling mass transport services using mobile telephone systems. In: Transport Systems Telematics, 4th International Conference, "Transport", Katowice-Ustroń (2004)
2. Kos, B., Urbanek, A.: Areas of using telematic tools in the high speed rail integration process in europe. In: Mikulski, J. (ed.) TST 2014. CCIS, vol. 471, pp. 341–349. Springer, Heidelberg (2014)
3. Krukowski, P.: Warszawska Karta Miejska na tle innych systemów karty miejskiej i biletu elektronicznego w Polsce. In: Prezentacja, Biuro Drogownictwa i Komunikacji Urzędu m. st. Warszawy. Warszawa (2008)
4. Kos, B.: Rozwój e-administracji w lokalnym i regionalnym transporcie zbiorowym na przykładzie Śląskiej Karty Usług Publicznych. In: Europejska przestrzeń komunikacji elektronicznej. Zeszyty Naukowe Uniwersytetu Szczecińskiego Nr 763, Ekonomiczne Problemy Usług Nr 105, pp. 117–130. Szczecin (2013)
5. Strategia rozwoju obrotu bezgotówkowego w Polsce na lata 2009 – 2013 (projekt). Narodowy Bank Polski, Związek Banków Polskich – Koalicja na rzecz Obrotu Bezgotówkowego i Mikropłatności, pp. 44–45. Warszawa (2009). www.nbp.pl. Accessed from January 16, 2015

6. Program rozwoju obrotu bezgotówkowego w Polsce na lata 2014 – 2020, Część 1. Dokument strategiczny, Część 2. Plan operacyjny na lata 2014 – 2016, Część 3. Rekomendacje dla Rządu, Koalicja na rzecz Obrotu Bezgotówkowego i Mikropłatności. Warszawa (2013)

7. Pietraszkiewicz, K.: Koalicja na rzecz obrotu bezgotówkowego i mikropłatności. Warszawa (2008)

8. Wolski, A.: Obrót bezgotówkowy - jako podstawa reformy systemu płatniczego w Unii Europejskiej. Prezentacje, Warszawa. Witryna Internetowa Związku Banków Polskich (2008). www.zbp.pl. Accessed from 16 January 2015

9. Diagnoza stanu rozwoju obrotu bezgotówkowego w Polsce. Narodowy Bank Polski, Departament Systemu Płatniczego. Warszawa (2013). www.nbp.pl. Accessed from 16 January 2015

10. Liczba wyemitowanych kart płatniczych na przestrzeni kolejnych kwartałów od 1998 r., website of Narodowy Bank Polski

11. Art. 5 of the Act of Law of August 27, 2009, on public finances (Official Journal of Law - Dz. U. - of 2009, Nr 157, items 1240 and 1241, with subsequent changes)

12. Kos-Łabędowicz, J.: Integrated E-ticketing system – possibilities of introduction in EU. In: Mikulski, J. (ed.) TST 2014. CCIS, vol. 471, pp. 376–385. Springer, Heidelberg (2014)

13. Dydkowski, G.: Integracja transportu miejskiego. In: Prace Naukowe Akademii Ekonomicznej im. K. Adamieckiego w Katowicach. Katowice (2009)

14. Polish Act of law of September 12, 2002 on electronic payment instruments (Official Journal of Law - Dz. U. - of 2012, item 1232 – Obwieszczenie Marszałka Sejmu Rzeczypospolitej Polskiej z dnia 13 września 2012 w sprawie ogłoszenia jednolitego tekstu ustawy o elektronicznych instrumentach płatniczych)

15. Polish Act of law of August 19, 2011 o usługach płatniczych (Dz. U. of 2011, Nr 100, item. 1175 and. Dz. U. of 2014, item. 873, 1916)

16. Dydkowski, G.: Effectiveness of the urban services electronic payment systems on the example of Silesian card of public services. In: Archives of Transport System Telematics, vol. 7, Issue 4, November 2014

17. Dydkowski, G.: Koszty i korzyści wynikające z wprowadzania elektronicznych systemów pobierania opłat za usługi miejskie. In: Niedzielski, P., Tomanek, R. (eds), Innowacje w Transporcie. Organizacja i Zarządzanie. Zeszyt Naukowy nr 602. Problemy Transportu i Logistyki nr 12, Szczecin (2010)

Dependencies Between Development of Information and Communications Technologies and Transport

Joanna Kos-Łabędowicz[✉]

University of Economics, 1 Maja 50, 40-287 Katowice, Poland
joanna.kos@ue.katowice.pl

Abstract. Transport and communication heavily influence the economic environment and shape conditions in which all economic entities operate. Such situation is a consequence of different, yet complementary roles those two components fulfil. Historically, both those systems – transport and communication – were inseparable. Wide application of technological solutions based on electricity allowed for removal of this dependency; since then, transport and communication technologies can be considered separate. This development is important from economic and business point of view – it makes access to geographically distant new markets easier; moreover, better communication technology improves the control the enterprises hold over their environment, resulting in potential increase of revenue. The goal of this paper is to analyse existing dependencies between ICT and transport, along with an attempt to indicate future trends.

Keywords: ICT · Transport · Transport demand

1 Introduction

Transport and communication heavily influence the economic environment and shape conditions in which all economic entities operate. Such situation is a consequence of different, yet complementary roles those two components fulfil – transportation systems make movement of resources, goods, and people possible, while communication systems allow the information of any kind – including those relevant to transportation processes – to be transmitted.

Historically, both those systems – transport and communication – were inseparable. Until electricity was discovered and its use popularised in XIX century, information transfer was limited in both time and distance by the means of transportation. Wide application of technological solutions based on electricity allowed for removal of this dependency; since then, transport and communication technologies can be considered separate. This development is important from economic and business point of view – it makes access to geographically distant new markets easier; moreover, better communication technology improves the control the enterprises hold over their environment, giving them better judgement of chances and threats, resulting in potential increase of revenue. The goal of this paper is to analyse existing dependencies between information and communication technologies and transport, along with an attempt to indicate future trends.

© Springer International Publishing Switzerland 2015
J. Mikulski (Ed.): TST 2015, CCIS 531, pp. 362–370, 2015.
DOI: 10.1007/978-3-319-24577-5_36

2   Development of ICT and Transport Technologies

Modern information technologies have taken the current form due to convergence of two, initially independent technologies – communication technologies that enabled information exchange possible, and computer technologies that were created for the purpose of processing information.

Nowadays, both areas of technology relay mainly on digital solutions, contrary to their analogue origins. Digitalization makes computer processing possible, simplifies manipulation, storage and near-immediate transmission to virtually any location in the world. Dynamic development and expansion of the Internet, along with mobile communication and noticeable evolution of electronic mass media are the reasons for numerous global changes that occur on every level: from individuals, thorough households, local communities, countries and, clearly, enterprises, especially international corporations.

Transport and communication hold the greatest influence on the shape of the economic environment and creation of conditions that surround all economic subjects. The main reason for this situation is the nature of those technologies: they fulfil different, yet complementary roles: transport system enables movement of resources, goods, and people, while communication systems enable information transfers in form of instructions, documents, images, etc. [1].

Historically, those two systems were one – this was the case for most of human history. Before discovery and application of electricity in 19th century, information transmission speed and distance on which it could be delivered was limited by the coverage of available transport systems. Widespread application of electricity-based solutions allowed for separation of transportation and communication systems. From economical and business point of view, this development was critical due to great simplification of access to geographically distant markets, along with increase of control the company could exercise over its own environment, resulting in better judgment regarding opportunities and risks. That in turn, results in potential increase in revenue.

In recent decades, distance has been steadily becoming less relevant. Transport costs are becoming less important factor in imported goods cost as well. This trend, often called "shrinking of the world" is a consequence of growth of two kinds of transport: air- and container-based.

Commercial air transport influenced activities of companies in two major ways. In the first place, it made fast movement of people possible, facilitating face-to-face meetings in previously impossible places and times. Greatest influence of commercial air transport can be noticed in operations of transnational corporations – direct control and coordination of geographically distributed operations became far easier – it is reasonable to claim that development of air transport that happened in 20th century '50 was a turning point for transnational corporations' development [2]. Ability to transport certain goods via air vessels was another important factor that changed business conditions.

Another important transport innovation was the introduction of the container, designed for mass transportation. Application of containers in both sea and land transport simplified the transition between means of transportation (e.g. goods were transported via rail to the seaport, where they were loaded on an ocean-going ship).

Unfortunately, fast increase in size of container ships marginalised small ports that are incapable of servicing 300-meter ships; it also resulted in creation of bottlenecks and delays in larger ships that were equipped with sufficient infrastructure [3].

It must be also mentioned, that not all regions of the world benefit equally from access to development of transport technologies. Transport system development is usually focused in areas of greatest economic significance, which in consequence promise greatest returns from the investments. In result, large urban agglomerations and developed economies become even closer, while non-urbanised areas and areas devoid of industry remain unconnected and become increasingly distant in relation to main transport nodes.

Communication technologies and communication systems have experienced a dynamic growth over last 20–30 years as well. In case of communication infrastructure, the greatest factor contributing to the development was invention of two new communication mediums – satellite and optical fibre.

First communication satellites were launched in mid-sixties of 20th century; they quickly revolutionised global communication system. Currently, satellites are used for both data transmission and voice communication. Due to lack of connection between transmission cost and distance in their case, satellite technologies are used mainly in areas of low population density – which are areas of low investment return for other communication technologies (for instance, optical fibre). Biggest flaw of satellite technology in comparison to wire-based communication is lower durability of the satellite itself and limited amount of useful space in orbit in which the communication satellite could be located [4].

First optical fibres were designed in USA in the beginning of '70. Optical fibre based communication system allows for fast data transmission, provides significant bandwidth, and – most importantly – transmitted signal retains its strength. Progression made in optic fibre based technology increased those parameters even more, resulting in increase of data throughput and transmission speed. Fibre optic infrastructure is continuously developing and expanding, mainly because growing demand for Internet access.

Nowadays, Internet largely replaced traditional communication channels. Major part of communication between businesses, both internal and external, takes place over the Internet [5]. Similar change in communication was caused by development of mobile communication. Such changes were rarely predictable – first radio-based mobile phones that appeared in '70 s were bulky, heavy, unwieldy, expensive, and unpopular – very few people chose to use them [6]. Today, few people can even imagine day-to-day life without a mobile phone. Data collected at end of 2014 show that there are about 7.4 billion mobile phones in use worldwide. In comparison to 2013 usage, it is about 497 million new mobile devices that became active in 2014 [7].

Similar to transport technology access, there are severe discrepancies in access to Internet and general communication technologies. Most backbone networks exist in North America and Europe; this causes the differences in access between developed and developing countries to continuously increase. A way to bridge the gap lies in deployment of mobile and wireless (radio and satellite) means of communication and Internet access [8].

Further part of this paper will present some of the most common applications of ICT in transport, both from the point of view of private users, as well as companies and public administration.

3   ICT Influence on Transport Demand

Internet is perceived as an efficient tool that makes trade exchange simpler and more efficient. Application of the Internet, along with information and communication technologies associated with it provides numerous advantages: reduction of communication cost, shortening the time required to deliver products and services to the market, transmission of needed information in digital form, decrease in cost of transport and distribution, and extension of cooperation and integration between trade and business partners. Internet becomes a global trade platform; its development causes new, more efficient ways of information exchange, along with new ways of goods and services exchange. For example, large companies implement supply chain and storage management systems based on information and communication technologies. Additionally, companies use the Internet as tool for learning the opinions of consumers, way to communicate with media, channel to transmit information required by public administration, tool to manage and track packages, and channel to transfer and manage finances with better efficiency [9].

Application of Internet in company activities both influences and is influence by other market participants (both other companies and customers). The greater the acceptance level of Internet as a channel of communication, the more companies chose to use it in order to remain competitive. Implementation of Internet use and ICTs by the given area dominant company will cause other companies to follow and adapt those solution themselves [10].

ICT use by people and companies influences demand for transport services noticeably. Demand for transport services may either be reduced (or eliminated altogether) or it may become larger [11]. Tables 1 and 2 present influence of ICT application on transport service demands by – respectively – people and companies [12].

Application of Internet and ICT allows for virtually instant communication, in turn creating a truly global market and new array of services, negates trade barriers such as distance, borders, and technological standards. This changes the very nature of many goods: for instance, music industry offers not only physical audiovisual records, but paid downloads as well. Internet was a reason for changes that occurred in many services (sales, telecommunication, information delivery), to the point where some traditional forms are completely gone, replaced by demand of new forms of service. This often influences transportation.

Increasing ICT and Internet application in the role of transaction and delivery channels reduced market entry costs, increasing the competition. At the same time, companies' tendency to separate and outsource parts of their functionalities allowed for development of companies that provide the outsources functionalities while operating in other, less developed countries. Such outsourcing is usually concerning back-office services: data analysis and processing, accounting, health care, and insurance [13].

Table 1. Influence of ICT use by individuals on demand for transport services

Type of ICT use	Impact on transport demand (persons)
E-services	Lowers demand for routine transaction in service stations, public offices, etc.
	May increase transport traffic to locations offering high-quality services
Last minute offers	New demand caused by lower prices
Social networks	Reduces need for routine meetings
	May create new demand for travelling due to making new acquaintances
E-working	May reduce the need to commute to work
	May cause substitution of work-related travels by personal-motivated travels
E-office	May reduce number of business travels
	Increases the tendency to work while travelling, resulting in potential new transport requirements
E-meeting	May reduce the need to travel for routine meetings and situations
	Does not replace the need to meet in person to discuss critical matters – but may provide additional channel

Table 2. Influence of ICT use by companies on demand for transport services

Type of ICT use	Impact on transport demand (freight)
E-business (b2c)	Reduction of demand for delivery of non-material goods – may serve as and additional channel
	Packages reorganisation in order to reduce demand for transportation – in cases when time plays significant role, deliveries become small and frequent; in cases when efficiency is more important than time, deliveries become larger and rare
	Acquisition of new markets and customers, necessity of delivery for greater distances (air transport)
	New channel for services
E-business (b2b)	Access to greater range of products (global market) may cause distance increases along with reduction of delivery sizes
	Reorganisation of value creation chains may influence the transport via increase or decrease of demand
	New channel for services
R&D platforms	Reduces the need for R&D personnel to travel – may become an additional channel
Resource management	Better goods and raw material stock management may decrease deliveries frequency
	Introduction of just-in-time systems may increase deliveries frequency along with reduction of delivery size

Development and support for software is often outsourced as well, and commonly happens via remote access, reducing the need of software provider's employees to travel [14].

4 Applications of ICT in Transport

ICT are increasingly used by transport companies in order to increase efficiency of storage and transportation of goods, services, and associated information. Systems used for those purposes are divided in intrafirm and interfirm information systems. Intrafirm systems serve the purpose of integration of functionalities in the company, along with improvement of cooperation inside the company. Examples of such system would be for instance fleet management system or an intranet. Interfirm systems facilitate communication with various economic subjects outside the company. An example of such external systems would be package tracking system that allows following location of the package and its estimated delivery time, along with viewing security precautions applied. What is more important, such systems are increasingly used by public administration institutions that provide public transportation, for example in form of integrated e-ticket systems [15], systems that provide detailed information for passengers (enabling them to make informed decision regarding the route and means of transportation), and monitoring systems that provide security [16].

There are numerous ways in which ICT may influence transportation of both passengers and goods via various means of transportation. Listing and describing them, even shortly, is beyond the scope limitations of this paper. In order to demonstrate the scale of possibilities, Table 3 contains examples of ICT applications and their influence on road transport in following three areas: excessive driving reduction, congestion relief and fatality reduction [17].

Popularisation of mobile devices and specialised applications has great influence on road-based transport, due to both advantages available to companies providing transport services and changes in demand for such changes.

A good example of using advantages provided by ICT in acquiring new clients can be Hailo application [18] – it allows a taxi to be ordered to a location: taxi request is sent to taxi drivers in the area; they may take the course and pick up the passenger. Examples of demand-changing ICT are Internet services that facilitate carpooling [19]. Carpooling is essentially "renting" a seat in the car for a given trip; contrary to car rentals, passenger does not have to rent an entire car. Such solution reduces the number of cars in traffic and reduces travel cost due to sharing them between several passengers. An example could be a polish service named Bla Bla Car [20]. Additionally, carpooling makes multi-passenger cars lanes (a solution used in some countries) accessible. Of course, there is another factor to consider: carpooling is advantageous to drivers and passengers, but reduces demand for rented cars, thus reducing car rentals revenue.

Table 3. ICT application in transport aiming at improving road transportation conditions

Application	Aim	Implementation
Excessive driving reduction		
Signalization	Less time is spent with engine running while the car is not moving	Widespread
Navigation system (in-vehicle)	Shorter travel time, easier path finding, shorter travel distance	Widespread in transport companies, increasingly common in personal vehicles
Congestion relief		
Video Surveillance and Response	Monitoring of traffic and general situation on the road, sending assistance if needed	Common in places with high traffic
Variable Message Signs (VMS)	Transmits road condition information	Increasingly common in critical locations
Advanced Drivers' Assistance (ADAS) (in-vehicle)	Supports the driver on the longer distances in order to reduce variation in speed and reduce periods of inactivity	Limited
Dedicated Short Range Communication	Adjusts speed, provides information that reduce waiting time	Limited
Fatality reduction		
Accident Sensors (in-vehicle)	Shortens time to assistance arrival in case of traffic accident	Limited
Extended Viewing Systems	Warns about vehicles behind the car, blind spots and obstacles not visible at night	Limited
Speed Advisory/Control	Advices (or forces) reducing vehicle's speed	Increasingly common
Advanced Drivers' Assistance (ADAS) (in-vehicle)	Controls car's positioning and adjusts speed	Limited
Automated guided vehicles	Maintains stable (with constant speed and distance relative to other vehicles) position in traffic	Non-existent

5   Conclusion

Changes that occur in transportation business because of growing ICT application in both transportation service providers as well as other market participants influence both commercial transports and personal travels. The changes influence flow of information connected to transport as well. Wide application of devices responsible for security, information flow, navigation, safety, and monitoring changes accessibility may lead to further decentralisation of metropolitan activities.

Intelligent transport systems (ITS) [21] and initiatives that aim to improve city transport (for instance, projects that are part of CIVITAS: DYN@MO [22] or 2MOVE2 [23]) increasingly influence city transport and public passenger transportation. Advantages that come from applying ICT in transport leave no doubt to future trends: their use will increase, further improving efficiency and safety of the transports. Progress in development of ICT allows for speculations regarding future uses and improvements, such as creating aids for aging and disabled drivers, creation of intelligent cars, completely automated cars, and automated roads.

It is difficult to predict how increased ICT use will influence demand presented by markets. Increasing use of Internet as communication channel may lead to reduction of demand for travel for routine tasks (replaced by Internet-based communication with public administration and banks), but may in turn create need to visit unknown locations or people met via social networks. Application of ICT influences business travels as well – teleconferences and remote work replace visits in the office and face-to-face meetings, reducing number of travels. Companies as whole change as well – access to new markets and reorganisation of supply chains cause the goods to travel longer distances, but may in turn reduce size of the shipments. E-commerce and additional channel for delivery of non-material products may reduce demand for transport services.

References

1. Dicken, P.: Global Shift – Mapping the Changing Contours of the World Economy. Sage, London (2011)
2. Zorska, A.: Korporacje transnarodowe – przemiany, oddziaływania, wyzwania. Polskie Wydawnictwo Ekonomiczne, Warszawa (2007)
3. Kent, J., Parker, R.: International containership carrier selection criteria: Shippers/carriers differences. Int. J. Phys. Distrib. Logist. Manag. 29(6), 399–401 (1999). http://dx.doi.org/10.1108/09600039910283613. Accessed 10 January 2015
4. Ryzenko, J., Badurska, A., Kobierzycka, A.: Raport I fazy Projektu Forsight – Kierunki rozwoju systemów satelitarnych: łączność satelitarna. Polskie Biuro do spraw Przestrzeni Kosmicznej (2007). http://www.kosmos.gov.pl/download/komunikacja.pdf. Accessed 10 January 2015
5. Keefer, A., Baiget, T.: How it all began: a brief history of the Internet. VINE 31(3), 90–95 (2001). http://dx.doi.org/10.1108/03055720010804221. Accessed 10 January 2015
6. Brookes, T.: A brief history of mobile phones. http://www.makeuseof.com/tag/history-mobile-phones/. Accessed 10 January 2015
7. Cisco Visual Networking Index: Global Mobile Data Traffic Forecast Update, 2014–2019, http://www.cisco.com/c/en/us/solutions/collateral/service-provider/visual-networking-index-vni/white_paper_c11-520862.html. Accessed 10 January 2015
8. Gani, A., Clemes, M.: Information and communications technology: a non-income influence on economic well being. IJSE 33(9), 651–653 (2006). http://dx.doi.org/10.1108/03068290610683431. Accessed 10 January 2015

9. Secrets of Electronic Commerce: A Guide for Small and Medium Exporters, 2nd edn. International Trade Centre, Geneva (2009)
10. Nguyen, T., Barrett, N.: The adoption of the internet by export firms in transitional markets. APJML **18**(1), 29–42 (2006). http://dx.doi.org/10.1108/13555850610641073. Accessed 14 January 2015
11. Hubers, C., Lynos, G.: Assessing future travel demand: a need to account for non-transport technologies? Foresight **15**(3), 211–227 (2011). http://dx.doi.org/10.1108/fs-10-2011-0043. Accessed 14 January 2015
12. Black, W.R., van Geenhuizen, M., Cerit, A.: ICT innovation and sustainability of the transport sector. EJTIR **6**(1), 39–60 (2006)
13. Saez, S., Goswani, A.: uncovering developing countries' performance in trade in services. In: Economic Premise, No. 39 (2010), Poverty Reduction and Economic Management Network (PREM), World Bank. http://siteresources.worldbank.org/INTPREMNET/Resources/EP39.pdf. Accessed 14 January 2015
14. Lehmann, A., Tamirisa, N., Wieczorek, J.: International trade in services: implications for IMF. In: IMF Policy Discussion Paper, vol. 6 (2003). http://www.imf.org/external/pubs/ft/pdp/2003/pdp06.pdf. Accessed 14 January 2015
15. Kos-Łabędowicz, Joanna: Integrated e-ticketing system – possibilities of introduction in EU. In: Mikulski, Jerzy (ed.) TST 2014. CCIS, vol. 471, pp. 376–385. Springer, Heidelberg (2014)
16. Saatçioğlu, Ö., Deveci, D., Cerit, A.: Logistics and transportation information systems in Turkey, e-government perspectives. Transform. Gov. People Process Policy **3**(2), 144–162 (2009). http://dx.doi.org/10.1108/17506160910960540. Accessed 19 January 2015
17. van Geenhuizen, M.: ICT applications on the road to sustainable urban transport. Eur. Transp. **41**, 47–61 (2009). http://www.openstarts.units.it/dspace/bitstream/10077/6059/1/vanGeenhuizen_ET41.pdf. Accessed 19 January 2015
18. Hailo. https://www.hailoapp.com/. Accessed 16 January 2015
19. ICT and the future of transport. Networked Soviety Lab, Ericsson (2014). http://www.ericsson.com/res/docs/2014/ict-and-the-future-of-transport.pdf. Accessed 19 January 2015
20. Bla Bla Car. http://www.blablacar.pl/. Accessed 19 January 2015
21. Intelligent transport systems. What do we want to achive? http://ec.europa.eu/transport/themes/its/index_en.htm. Accessed 19 January 2015
22. CIVITAS DYN@MO. http://www.civitas.eu/content/dynmo. Accessed 19 January 2015
23. CIVITAS 2MOVE2. http://www.civitas.eu/content/2move2. Accessed 19 January 2015

Transport Telematics Development in the New European Cohesion Policy

Kinga Okrzesik-Faruga[✉] and Robert Tomanek

University of Economics in Katowice, 1 Maja 50 street, 40-287 Katowice, Poland
{kinga.okrzesik-faruga,tomanek}@ue.katowice.pl

Abstract. The new Instruments of European Cohesion Policy for 2014–2020 in relation to Poland assume increasing the importance of IT solutions, including transport telematics systems. In particular, telematics is to be applied in balancing transport and reducing congestion. Telematic solutions are to be implemented in the following national operational programs: *The Operational Programme Infrastructure and Environment* and *The Operational Programme Development of Eastern Poland.*

Keywords: Public transport · Cohesion policy · Sustainable transport

1 Introduction

The assumptions of European Cohesion Policy for the period 2014–2020 indicate the need for change, but also the development opportunities for the European transport system. An important issue of the European Cohesion Policy (ECP) is its territorial dimension, which means the preference for integrated solutions in urban areas, especially agglomerations and functional areas. EU Common Strategic Framework (CSF) of eleven thematic objectives captures promoting sustainable transport, and several other objectives also involve problems of development and balancing transport and mobility. The main tools for the implementation of EU cohesion policy will be the Operational. Programmes (OP) adopted for 2014–2020. The intervention areas connected with transport infrastructure will be included in the OP Infrastructure and Environment and OP Eastern Poland. One of the cornerstones of the ECP are Integrated Territorial Investments (ITI) that determine sustainable transport as a key intervention direction. They do not replace other tools and operational programs. Their financing at 4.5 % may increase the integration of agglomerations, leading to metropolitisation of these areas, including transport integration.

2 Development of Transport Within the European Cohesion Policy 2014–2020

Transport and transport policy have played and will play a key role in the development of the common market and the social development of the European Union [11].

© Springer International Publishing Switzerland 2015
J. Mikulski (Ed.): TST 2015, CCIS 531, pp. 371–377, 2015.
DOI: 10.1007/978-3-319-24577-5_37

Over the years, the conditions and the direction of transport development change. Currently, the integration and sustainable development are particularly stressed. Despite the principle of subsidiarity, ever stronger emphasis frequently falls on the development of the integrated and low-carbon urban transport.

European Cohesion Policy (ECP) in the period of 2014–2020 (defined by regulations adopted on the basis of the strategy "Europe 2020", approved by the European Council 17.06.2010 [7]). Even the title of the strategy ("A strategy for smart, sustainable and inclusive growth" [1]) defines its priorities and also indicates the importance of telematic solutions. From the point of view of the development of transport, the second priority - sustainable development understood as "promoting a more resource efficient, greener and more competitive economy" - is of particular importance. The development is to take place through the implementation of [1]:

– flagship "Efficient Europe resources", where particular attention is paid to the development of intelligent, low-carbon and intermodal transport and logistics decarbonisation,
– the flagship initiative "An industrial policy for the globalization era" which declares that "transport and logistics networks" will improve the accessibility of the European industry to the EU and international markets [6].

3   The Significance of Transport System in the Financial Perspective for 2014–2020

Operational Programmes adopted in new financial perspective for 2014–2020, in particular the Operational Programme Infrastructure and Environment and Operational Programme for Eastern Poland are a response to the challenge of creating a modern transport system in Poland [11]. In fact, the national transport system faces a double challenge - to ensure efficient and productive infrastructure that would promote economic development, and at the same time serve the objectives of low-carbon economy. One of the priorities in the process of creating a modern and competitive economy, meeting the requirements of low-carbon emission, is to complete the construction of a coherent transport network in Poland, to improve the competitiveness of sustainable transport and the integration of all modes of transport [11].

Unfortunately, the national road infrastructure is still underdeveloped in relation to the intensity of production and exchange of goods and the increasing mobility of people. The problems include the lack of a coherent network of highways, a high percentage of national roads running in urban areas and insufficient length of roads compared to the scale of the existing traffic. The national road network is still characterized by a low level of territorial accessibility and a low level of road safety. It is therefore important and necessary in the perspective of 2020 to focus on the expansion of the road investment in the TEN-T, as well as improving the accessibility and relief from excessive traffic, especially transit, of the urban areas. In spite of the previous support for public transport, the overloading of urban infrastructure with individual traffic as well as the underdeveloped public transport system remain to be the major issues.

Another problem is posed by the railway network, still in poor technical condition as result of years of insufficient investment [10]. The unattractive prices, inadequate technical condition of railway infrastructure and insufficient integration with other modes of transport are the main causes of low levels of use of this transport sector (both passenger and freight). Increasing the competitiveness of the railway sector requires a significant shortening of travel time as well as improving the passenger and cargo service standards by increasing the speed and capacity of transport. Other important steps towards the proper functioning of the transport network in Poland will involve the integration of rail transport with other transport modes in multimodal transport chains and the improvement of railway safety.

Integrating transport with the use of intelligent transport systems (ITS), which will improve the efficiency and safety of transport, becomes a necessity. The use of ITS significantly contributes to the integration of the transport system as well as improving the information services, traffic optimization, management of infrastructure, transport safety and reduction of carbon emission [10].

4 The Development of Transport in Operational Programme Infrastructure and Environment (OPIE)

Operational Programme Infrastructure and Environment for 2014–2020 will be the largest source of funding for transport infrastructure [4]. The budget of the program (the so-called "Allocation") totals more than 27.4 billion Euro (or approx. 115 billion Zloty) from the European Funds. The largest funds will be allocated to transport projects, such as roads, railways, urban transport, air and sea transport. The program consists of 10 priority axes, of which up to 4 relate to transport:

Priority Axis III. Development of the TEN-T road network and multimodal transport - the allocation of 9 532.4 million, where particular attention is paid to the development and improvement of the road network infrastructure in the TEN-T, improvement of the road safety, intermodal transport, sea and inland waterways.
Priority III will be implemented through the following priorities for investment (PI):

PI 7.I - Support for multi-modal Single European Transport Area by investing in the TEN-T, specific objective "Better road connection status of the TEN-T in Poland." The anticipated outcome is a coherent network of high-speed roads, connecting all provincial capitals of the TEN-T. The financial support will have a horizontal character for the whole country;

PI 7.II development and improvement of environment-friendly and low-carbon transport systems, the specific objectives are to increase the transport capacity both in terms of competitiveness and environmental friendliness.

Priority Axis IV. Road infrastructure for cities - allocation of 2970.3 million, dedicated to improving the availability and capacity of urban road infrastructure (in the cities and routes leading out of urban centers).

The priority axis IV will support two investment priorities for thematic objective 7. Actions under Priority Axis IV are in addition to the investments envisaged under Axis III.

PI 7.A - modal Single European Transport Area by investing in the TEN-T, where the specific objective is the increased availability of urban transport in the TEN-T and eliminating the traffic congestion in the cities. The main support will be focused on the national road network investments for linking urban networks with rural TEN-T network, including improving the accessibility of the national roads and sections of expressways with cities.

Priority Axis V. Development of railway transport in Poland- allocation of over 5 million Euro, including support for the development of railways in the TEN-T network outside the urban areas. It will be implemented through investment priority 7.I, where the scope of intervention will be to strengthen the role of rail transport in an integrated transport system of the country. The intervention from the EU funds will be targeted for investment in the modernization and rehabilitation of existing rail routes.

Priority Axis VI. Development of low-carbon public transport in cities - allocation of 2 349.2 million, where the funds will be used mainly for infrastructure and rolling stock for public transport in cities and their functional areas [4].
Priority Axis VI provides for implementation of the following investment priorities:
    4.V Promoting low-carbon strategy for all types of territories, particularly in urban areas, including the promotion of sustainable multimodal urban mobility and adaptation measures to mitigate the impact of climate change, where the transport support is one of the activities under the plans prepared by local emission economy. The actions will concentrate on issues of public transport in order to improve its competitiveness, availability and promotion of sustainable urban development based on low-carbon economy plans of individual cities. As part of the OPIE for urban transport, funding priority will be given to projects resulting from the Strategy of Integrated Territorial Investment (ITI) for the 13 provincial cities with the exception of the cities in Eastern Poland, to which a separate Operational Programme is dedicated.

5   OPEP as a Tool for the Transport System Development

Eastern Poland macro-region consists of five provinces: lubelskie, podkarpackie, podlaskie, świętokrzyskie and warmińsko-mazurskie [5]. Four of the above five regions, i.e. lubelskie, podkarpackie, podlaskie, and warmińsko-mazurskie are situated on the eastern border of the European Union. The peripheral character of Eastern Poland has not only a geographical dimension (measured by the distance from the developed centres of EU) but also a socio-economic one. The level of economic development of these areas is among the lowest in the European Union. The spatial availability of Eastern Poland is characterized by low values of accessibility indicators, both in multimodal scenario, as well as in road variant only.

    The relatively low transport accessibility of Eastern Poland is related to its peripheral location (relative to the national and European development centers), and is the result of poor development of transport infrastructure linking the macro-region (especially the main urban centers) with the major national centers [2]. Another problem is the density of the road network in Eastern Poland, which is lower than the national average.

Similarly, the rail network is characterized by low intensity of passenger rail transport as a result of lower density of the rail network and the poor state of infrastructure. This results in reduced standard of rail services connecting the sub-areas to the main urban centers of Eastern Poland and, in the external dimension, the rail links connecting the regional capitals with major cities in the country. The poor state of the railway infrastructure not only adversely affects the passenger transport, but also the potential for the development of rail freight [3].

The specificity of the socio-economic situation indicates that Eastern Poland is an area of particular interest to regional policy that requires undertaking additional initiatives towards accelerating the economic growth in order to draw level with the more developed regions, which is confirmed by all key national strategic documents concerning policy development, i.e. the Long-term National Development Strategy (LNDS), Medium-Term National Development Strategy (MNDS), the National Strategy for Regional Development and the National Spatial Development Concept (NSDC).

The intervention of PO Eastern Poland in transport infrastructure falls in line with the implementation of the Europe 2020 priority, which is the sustainable growth - promoting a more resource efficient, greener and more competitive economy, including the flagship initiative Resource-efficient Europe. Allocation of financial resources throughout the OP Eastern Poland is 2 billion Eur [5].

The program consists of four Priority Axes (PA), in which the transport issues are included in the PA II and III.

Priority II scope of intervention covers the thematic objectives 4 and 7, the investment priorities:

PI 4e - promoting low-carbon strategies for all types of territories, particularly for urban areas, including the promotion of sustainable multimodal urban mobility and adaptation measures to mitigate the impact of climate change.

The priority will be implemented through specific objective: Increased use of public transport in provincial cities and their functional areas. The main objective of the PI 4e is the support of the metropolitan functions of five cities of Eastern Poland, i.e. Kielce, Białystok, Rzeszów, Olsztyn and Lublin, constituting the trans-regional catalysts of the development processes. The projects within this priority will involve the creation of new or expansion of existing integrated, sustainable public transport networks. The tasks will include:

– construction/reconstruction of the transport networks (trolleybus, bus, tram) and the purchase of low-emission rolling stock;
– construction/reconstruction of infrastructure for public transport (intermodal change stations);
– upgrade/implementation of the existing telematics systems.

Support will be possible only through the mandatory inclusion of the investment in ITI and drawing up plans for low-carbon economy, which in its scope also includes the issue of mobility.

PI 7b - enhancing regional mobility through connecting secondary and tertiary nodes of the TEN-T infrastructure, including multimodal nodes.

PI 7b priority will be implemented through specific objective: Increased availability of provincial cities and their functional areas in the field of road infrastructure. Expected results are focused on increasing the level of efficiency and availability of transport systems of the provincial cities and their functional areas or areas covered by the ITI. The support within this priority will contribute significantly to the improvement and to creating conditions for further development of the five provincial cities. Investments are planned for national and regional road networks to improve the connection of provincial towns with the national road network, including the TEN-T.

Priority III. SUPER-REGIONAL Railway Infrastructure.
Contains thematic objective 7, which includes investment priority:

7d Development and rehabilitation of comprehensive, high quality and interoperable railway systems and to promote noise reduction. The specific objective of the PI 7d is *increased accessibility of Eastern Poland in the area of railway infrastructure*. It involves implementation of projects on existing railway lines, Constituting the Eastern Railway Network. Improving the technical parameters, use of modern technologies and solutions for the infrastructure elements will help to increase the speed of the train service and significantly enhance the availability of rail transport within the macro-region [9]. These actions are included in the assumptions of the EU Strategy for the Baltic Sea Region, whose primary aim is to increase the efficiency of transport links, increasing the efficiency of these systems, and as a result to reduce the impact on the environment. The implementation of activities under POPW is designed to constitute an additional element of support for investments under OPIE 2014–2020 [5].

6   Conclusion

The new tools of the European Cohesion Policy Operational Programmes which are the Operational Programs and ITI have lead to the implementation of this policy in the sub-regional dimension. The founding perspective of 2014–2020 is increasingly based on the principle of subsidiarity [10]. The Operational Programmes provide the regions with the opportunity of deciding on 80 % of the funds allocation. The quest for sustainable development falls in line with the efforts towards creating an integrated city and national public transport. This objective will be based increasingly on the implementation of telematic solutions, in particular on the improvement of infrastructure and the availability of a dynamic transport information and, above all, traffic control systems.

References

1. Europe 2020. A strategy for smart, sustanaible and inclusive growth, COM (2010) 2020, Brussels, 3 March 2010
2. Komornicki, T., Śleszyński, P., Rosik, P., Pomianowski, W.: Dostępność przestrzenna jako przesłanka kształtowania polskiej polityki transportowej, Biuletyn KPZK, nr 241. Komitet Przestrzennego Zagospodarowania Kraju PAN, Warszawa (2010)

3. Kukliński, A.: Problem Polski Wschodniej. Doświadczenia i perspektywy [w:] Błaszczuk, D.J., Stefański, M. (red.): Strategiczna problematyka polski Wschodniej. Lublin: Wyższa Szkoła Ekonomii i Innowacji w Lublinie (2010)
4. Program Operacyjny Infrastruktura i Środowisko 2014–2020. Ministerstwo Infrastruktury i Rozwoju, Warszawa, 16 December 2014. http://www.funduszeeuropejskie.gov.pl/media/ 1238/POIS_2014_2020_13022015.pdf. Accessed 20 February 2015
5. Program Operacyjny Polska Wschodnia, Ministerstwo Infrastruktury i Rozwoju. https:// www.polskawschodnia.gov.pl/media/942/POPW_akcept_KE.pdf. Accessed 20 February 2015
6. Tomanek, R.: Public transport in the new EU cohesion policy on the example of integrated territorial investments strategy. In: Sladkowski, A., Gelashvili, O., Goletiani, G. (eds.) Transport Bridge Europe-Asia, red, pp. 9–13, Tbilisi (2014)
7. Regulation (EU) No 1303/2013 of the European Parliament and of the Council of 17 December 2013 laying down common provisions on the European Regional Development Fund, the European Social Fund, the Cohesion Fund, the European Agricultural Fund for Rural Development and the European Maritime and Fisheries Fund and laying down general provisions on the European Regional Development Fund, the European Social Fund, the Cohesion Fund and the European Maritime and Fisheries Fund and repealing Council Regulation (EC) No 1083/2006
8. Rozporządzenie Wykonawcze Unii Europejskiej (UE) NR 821/2014 z dnia 28 lipca 2014 r. ustanawiające zasady stosowania rozporządzenia Parlamentu Europejskiego i Rady (UE) nr 1303/2013 w zakresie szczegółowych uregulowań dotyczących transferu wkładów z programów i zarządzania nimi, przekazywania sprawozdań z wdrażania instrumentów finansowych, charakterystyki technicznej działań informacyjnych i komunikacyjnych w odniesieniu do operacji oraz systemu rejestracji i przechowywania danych
9. Urząd Transportu Kolejowego: Funkcjonowanie rynku transportu kolejowego w 2011 r. Urząd Transportu Kolejowego, Warszawa (2012)
10. http://www.polskawschodnia.gov.pl/media/942/POPW_akcept_KE.pdf. Accessed 20 February 2015
11. USTAWA z dnia 11 lipca 2014. r o zasadach realizacji programów w zakresie polityki spójności finansowanych w perspektywie finansowej (2014–2020)
12. Zasady Działania funduszy, Ministerstwo Infrastruktury i Rozwoju, Warszawa (2014). https://www.funduszeeuropejskie.gov.pl/strony/o-funduszach/zasady/. Accessed 20 February 2015
13. Zasady realizacji Zintegrowanych Inwestycji Terytorialnych w Polsce. Ministerstwo Rozwoju Regionalnego, Warszawa, lipiec 2013. http://www.mir.gov.pl/rozwoj_regionalny/ Polityka_regionalna/rozwoj_miast/Documents IT_na_WW_26_02013.pdf. Accessed 20 February 2015

Author Index

Printed in the United States
By Bookmasters